READINGS IN
THE SOCIAL CONTROL
OF
INDUSTRY

BLAKISTON SERIES OF REPUBLISHED ARTICLES ON ECONOMICS

Volume I

Selection Committee For This Volume

EDGAR M. HOOVER, JR.

JOEL DEAN

The participation of the American Economic Association in the presentation of this series consists in the appointment of a committee to determine the subjects of the volumes and of special committees to select the articles for each volume.

READINGS IN
THE SOCIAL CONTROL
OF
INDUSTRY

Selected by a Committee of

THE AMERICAN ECONOMIC ASSOCIATION

THE BLAKISTON COMPANY

Philadelphia . . . Toronto

1949

PRINTED IN THE UNITED STATES OF AMERICA
BY LEVERING-RIEBEL CO., CAMDEN, N. J.

PREFACE

The present series grew out of informal conversations among members of the American Economic Association regarding the desirability of having in convenient form articles of permanent interest which tended to lose their full usefulness by being widely scattered through old issues of the various journals. The Executive Committee of the Association approved a specific suggestion of The Blakiston Company in December 1940 and entered into an agreement with the company that the latter would publish at least one volume annually for an initial term of five years. The subjects of the volumes are to be selected by a committee of the American Economic Association and the articles for each volume are to be chosen by special committees of the Association.

The articles in this first volume in the series were selected by a committee of which Professor Edgar M. Hoover, Jr., was chairman. The selection of articles for a second volume, on the theory of business cycles, is now being prepared by a committee under the chairmanship of Professor Gottfried von Haberler.

The process of selection of articles for the volumes in the series will probably always encounter much difficulty in arriving at a suitable focus of interest and purpose as a guide to inclusion and exclusion. The necessary delimitation of the subject of each volume will invariably have the result that many articles of great merit deserving to be included will have to be excluded. In the case of the present volume, it was decided to follow the principle of confining attention to the more general problems of public policy toward industrial organization and control, and to exclude the special fields associated with the term "public utility." As the selection developed it became increasingly apparent that it would be desirable to have a companion volume dealing with the subject of industrial price and production policies. The choice of articles for the present volume has accordingly been limited in the light of the expectation of publishing such a companion volume early in the series.

A further difficulty lay in deciding to what class of readers this and future volumes should be addressed. On this point the ultimate emphasis came to be placed upon pedagogical usefulness in connection with courses for advanced students, although it is believed that the contents of the volume will be of wide interest to economists in general. Suggestions for the subjects and contents of future volumes will be appreciated. They can be addressed to Professor James Washington Bell, Secretary, American Economic Association, Evanston, Illinois.

PAUL T. HOMAN.

WASHINGTON, D. C.
April 15, 1942.

CONTENTS

1

CAN THE ANTITRUST LAWS PRESERVE COMPETITION?*

By Corwin D. Edwards†

In recent years it has become fashionable in academic and, to a lesser extent, in business circles to assume that the competitive system is on its way out. With some persons this opinion springs from wishful thinking based upon their allegiance to alternative types of organization ranging all the way from unsupervised private cartelization of industry to a collectivist economy. Others come reluctantly to the belief that competition is passing and regard the decline of competition as the source of problems and dangers which they would gladly avoid. This paper is not intended to discuss the issues between these groups. It is addressed to the belief both have in common, that whether we like it or not, competition is doomed. It is an attempt to assess the chances that the dominant American sentiment for continuance of the competitive system can be made effective.

But even of this problem I shall discuss only a part. Preserving competition by law depends not only upon the effectiveness of the antitrust laws in implementing the antitrust policy but upon the scope and direction given to a variety of other policies by the laws which implement them. The policies toward exploitation of the public domain, tax and

* *The American Economic Review*, Volume XXX, Number 1, March 1940, Part 2, Supplement, Pages 164–179. Reprinted by the courtesy of the American Economic Association and the author.

† Department of Justice.

inheritance policies, the nature of the supervision of corporate finance and of investment banking, the character of the patent system, the breadth of the area which is deliberately removed from the competitive field in order to be publicly regulated: these and many other matters of law, federal and state, must help determine the further importance of competition in America. It is conceivable that the antitrust laws might preserve competition wherever they are given a chance to operate but that the policies expressed in other statutes might progressively reduce the competitive area until competition became a vestigial matter like the vermiform appendix. Conversely, the antitrust laws might fail in much of their task and yet other public policies might go far to shorten the lives of monopolistic aggregates of capital and to set up new genera-tions of small competitively-minded independents. My sub-ject is limited to the antitrust laws and time does not permit stretching it. Hence I can discuss only the extent to which these laws can preserve competition within the area which the community may regard as their proper field of operation.

Doubt of the efficacy of the American policy toward monop-olies and unreasonable restraints of trade has been due chiefly to the industrial history of the last fifty years. Doubtless economists have been predisposed to believe that competition was collapsing because the neoclassical theory of competition, which had once been regarded as a sufficient tool of economic analysis, was obviously doing so. But events around them supported the belief. In most industries corporate units grew in size and declined in number until industrial giants like those which caused alarm in 1901 came to seem commonplace.

Size means concentrated financial strength. One per cent of the manufacturing corporations have been estimated to have 63 per cent of the total wealth of all such corporations. In 1935 the two hundred largest manufacturing corporations produced more than $17\frac{1}{4}$ billion dollars' worth of goods, nearly 38 per cent of the total value of manufacturing production.

Size means also a series of oligopolistic markets.   The largest four producers produce more than half of the total product in 3 industries of major size, 6 industries of medium size, and 28 industries of small size.   The largest eight producers make more than one half of the output in 6 large industries, 13 medium sized industries, and 117 small industries.   Since these concentration figures are based upon the census classification of industries, each so-called "industry" includes various products which may be made by different concerns.   Hence the concentration in the control of products sufficiently alike to compete against each other in the market must obviously be higher than these figures indicate.   Moreover, many commodities which are not sold in national markets must be more highly controlled in quasi-autonomous regions than in the country as a whole.   Although we cannot state in quantitative terms either the concentration by regions or the concentration by individual commodities, it is clear that the figures, if available, would further strengthen the view that oligopoly has become prevalent.

With the growth of big business have come price policies similar to those which economists have traditionally called monopolistic.   The price leadership of large concerns may establish a unity of action the effect of which is scarcely distinguishable from the effect of a collusive agreement.   Where there are several large concerns, each may be convinced that price cutting will invoke retaliation and that the result will be lower profits for all; and consequently their individual price policies may establish rigid prices at a high level.   For convenience I shall refer to this situation as group monopoly.   In maintaining such price policies members of an industry may set up systems of pricing in accord with a formula similar to the well-known basing-point systems; or they may develop a cost accounting orthodoxy coupled with a habit of basing policies upon costs.   Such trade practices, once established, may function as smoothly as the cruder forms of old-fashioned price conspiracy. A series of such developments in various markets has contributed to uniformity and rigidity of prices and periodical idleness of productive resources, indistinguishable from the results of more formal collusion; and yet these ways of pricing have appeared to be inherent in the nature of things in a sense in which crude collusion is not.

Along with this development of monopolistic structure and monopolistic price policy has come a tendency to legalize practices which have been contrary to the antitrust laws. I do not refer to the removal of specific industries from the competitive field, but to broad grants of permission to do what was once forbidden. The most conspicuous of such grants in recent years was under NRA, which authorized the setting aside of the antitrust laws in order to permit industrial groups to operate under codes of so-called "fair" competition which in fact were intended to restrict and regulate competitive practices and even to substitute group control of prices and output for competition. Under other statutes, systems of price fixing and production control over agricultural commodities were authorized. Though such legislation was avowedly intended to meet an emergency, and the NRA portion of it was quickly terminated, the setting aside of competition by law has continued, largely through the state governments. Nearly all of our states have made it possible to abolish by private contract price competition among distributors of identified products. Nearly a third of our states have adopted requirements limiting the freedom of distributors to reduce prices below some figure which is taken more or less arbitrarily to represent cost. Other statutes, less general, have conveyed even more sweeping powers. The California agricultural marketing act, for example, permits the state director of agriculture, with the assent of 65 per cent of the producers and 65 per cent of the handlers, by volume, to limit the quantity of any agricultural commodity processed, to allot the amounts which may be purchased by distributors, to apportion the quantities which each processor may process, to establish reserve pools of the commodity, and to apportion the proceeds of the sale of such pools.

Thus the doubts about the future of the antitrust laws have been based upon an increasing size of the business unit, carried so far as to give many concerns a quasi-monopoly position; upon the development of price policies, many of whose effects are like those of collusive pricing; and upon legislative tendencies to sanction price and production controls. Some have drawn the conclusion that the principle of monopoly has won in the market in spite of public efforts to destroy it, and that the victory is in process of being recognized at law. Since all victorious economic systems create their own philosophies of history and of justification, it is not surprising that many who take this view think that the monopolistic trend is inherent in modern technology and modern wide markets and that it is justified as a means toward technological efficiency.

I do not believe these theories of inevitability nor of beneficence. During most of the development just sketched the antitrust laws did not fail but went by default. As the present assistant attorney general, Thurman Arnold, has pointed out, the great trust-busting campaign of Theodore Roosevelt was conducted with 7 lawyers and 4 stenographers. In 1933 the Antitrust Division had a professional staff of only 26. When Mr. Arnold took office in March, 1938, this staff numbered 59. Even today, there are in the Antitrust Division only 190 lawyers and 17 experts. During most of the Antitrust Division's history, one or two major cases have been more than sufficient to absorb the entire time of the personnel, and today it would be easy to use the whole staff in the prosecution of restraints upon housing alone. Indeed, 27 per cent of it is being so used. The simple fact has been that until recently no broad effort could be made to enforce the law for lack of people to do the work. Even now the staff is less than a fourth of that found necessary to administer the securities acts and about one seventh of that which administers the Inter-state Commerce Act.

This fact, more than any other, accounts for the past lack of vigorous enforcement, which in turn tended to bring the law itself into disrespect.   Charles Stevenson, head of an industrial engineering firm in New York City, now under indictment for violation of the Sherman Act, expressed the point of view which necessarily arose under such circumstances in the fol-lowing words:

Practically, under the Harding, Coolidge, and Hoover Administrations industry enjoyed, to all intents and purposes, a moratorium from the Sherman Act, and, through the more or less effective trade associations which were developed in most of our industries, competition was, to a very considerable extent, controlled. The Department of Justice acted with great restraint and intelligence and only enforced the Sherman Act against those industries who violated the laws in a flagrant and unreasonable manner.[1]

A further consequence of the limitations of staff was the fact that until recently the Division could not proceed toward clearly conceived economic objectives.   Cases were neces-sarily sporadic and isolated—an average of only about eight or nine a year, including all duplications, during the life of the antitrust laws.   It was impossible to bring a considerable number of cases simultaneously, and hence impossible to envisage the monopoly problems of a major industry as a whole and deal with them in a co-ordinated fashion.   Since a single court proceeding cannot be broader than the group of conspirators against whom it is directed, the inability to bring numerous cases necessarily resulted in attacks upon isolated groups, without regard to the industrial setting in which they found themselves.   Such administrative action was not likely to keep the public keenly aware of the constructive possibilities

---

[1] Charles A. Stevenson, *Price Control and Allotment of Business* (address before the Annual Convention of the National Association of Cost Accountants, Cleveland, Ohio, June 26, 1934).

of the antitrust laws. Rather, it provoked in thoughtful people feelings of futility. Thus it fostered a political environment in which the demands of pressure groups, particularly those representing small and precarious business, for special legislation in their behalf might be granted without serious thought about the effect of such laws upon competition.

This procedure of sporadic prosecution may be contrasted with the present procedure of the Antitrust Division's building campaign. Convinced that the removal of a single restraint upon building at a single point will do nothing appreciable to lower building costs and will have no appreciable economic effect upon the operation of the industry, the Division has investigated and is now prosecuting simultaneously restraints which run all the way from the manufacturers of the various building materials, through the distributors and the various types of contracting organization, to labor in various trades on the construction site. To give these proceedings nation-wide effect, grand juries are now sitting in eleven cities and some form of investigation is under way in a still larger number of other cities. So broad a program provides an opportunity for a simultaneous breaking up of restraints throughout the industry, and consequently an opportunity for housing costs to come down and for vigorous competition to become a dominant influence in the construction of houses. The breadth of the program, indispensable for its economic effect, has meant likewise a favorable reception from the building industry itself such as would never have accompanied helter-skelter prosecutions. Many organizations in the building industry have declared their hearty support for the program, and only two have been openly hostile. Indeed, individuals and groups who knew that they were themselves in danger of prosecution have repeatedly offered cooperation and urged the Department to proceed, because they believed that their personal risks were worth taking if the broad industrial result could be achieved.

A third weakness in the law's attack upon monopoly has been at least partly due to this same lack of enough people to prosecute vigorously. There are a number of important blind spots in the law, areas of industrial action whose legal status has not been authoritatively determined. It has been only natural that a limited staff, unable to handle the cases brought to it, has given preference to the clear-cut violations concerning which the attitude of the courts is known. The absence of prosecutions in other cases has given business a sort of squatter's tenure of the ground, and has resulted in widespread adoption of the questionable but unlitigated methods of achieving market control.

One of these blind spots is the use of del credere agents to establish control over a market. Manufacturers anxious to control the prices of potential competitors or of distributors sometimes make agreements with such concerns by which they hope to secure most of the benefits of transferring risk to the purchaser and yet retain the legal right to control the prices at which the purchaser resells. Many of the problems involved have never been raised in prosecution. Hence, it is impossible to say to what extent agencies may be legally used to induce rival manufacturers not to compete, nor to what extent modified systems of agency will be treated as subterfuges designed to accomplish unlawful control over resale.

Again, many issues along the boundary between the patent laws and the antitrust laws have never been brought to trial. Patents are being used to allocate markets to particular enterprises, to set up systems of production control, to control the terms of sale of products, to erect an elaborate control of the price of a finished product upon a basis of some small patented detail of the product, and to develop contracts which have the effect of extending controls like those just mentioned, not for seventeen years, but for two, three, and four times that period. A federal grand jury has been called in New York to consider many of these problems with a view to prosecutions designed prevent the abuse and undue extension of patent privileges.

Perhaps the most important of the blind spots is the legal status of mergers.   In the Clayton Act the Congress forbade the acquisition of stock in a competing corporation where the effect might be to lessen competition between the two companies involved.   In a series of court cases this provision has been interpreted in such a way that the prohibition of the Clayton Act prevents substantially nothing except what was already forbidden as an attempt to monopolize by the Sherman Act.   Meanwhile, partly to evade the Clayton Act, the importance of stock acquisition in uniting competing enterprises has been greatly diminished and mergers by acquisition of the assets of competing concerns have become the outstanding methods of eliminating competitors.   Nevertheless, there has not yet been a clear-cut judicial test of the question whether a contract to acquire the assets of a competitor may be interpreted as a contract in restraint of trade.   And yet the answer to this question must determine whether we have in the present law any means of preventing the continued reduction of the number of competitors and the continued growth of the scale of big business by a process of buying up rival plants.

This sketch of the history of industrial development and of antitrust law enforcement seems to me to emphasize two conclusions.   The first is that if we seriously want to enforce the antitrust laws there is no reason why the record of the last fifty years should in itself make us doubt our ability to do so. Until a sustained attempt with an adequate personnel has continued long enough to clarify the law and to demonstrate its impact upon the economic environment, opinions on this matter must be based upon analysis rather than experience. The second conclusion is that the politico-economic temper of the American people must be appraised as the first step in predicting the success of the antitrust laws.   Unless one assumes that the public wants the antitrust laws enforced and wants it vigorously enough that the agencies doing the job will be supported with men and money, one might as well grant that the effort will fail. I shall not attempt to turn this discussion toward political prognosis, but I shall assume as the necessary condition of any further relevant discussion that the recent tendency to enlarge the staff of the Antitrust Division will continue far enough to give us a reasonably adequate personnel. In support of this view there is evidence that the recent growth of the Antitrust Division has been the direct result of the support won by its vigorous enforcement policy. This support has been most conspicuous in the case of the housing program, which represents thus far the high tide of planned and co-ordinated action under the antitrust laws.

Granted the resources to make a sustained and serious effort, can the antitrust laws preserve competition? It is necessary at this point to be precise about what is to be preserved. We have not and probably never had perfect market competition of the kind described by the classical economists, and the preservation of such a state of things is not a practical administrative objective. The competition we seek to preserve must necessarily be in some respects imperfect or monopolistic. In their reaction from the highly artificial antithesis between pure competition and pure monopoly, economic theorists have recently been emphasizing the fact that elements of competition and monopoly appear in all markets; and in their enthusiasm for this limited truth they have provided not much theoretical basis for distinguishing differences in degree. Nevertheless, businessmen who trade in markets and government people who must cope with market behavior habitually use the antithesis of competition and monopoly to express distinctions which they regard as important. They do not have in mind differences in the location of points on hypothetical demand and cost curves under conditions of perfect knowledge. They are concerned with differences in the behavior of those with whom they deal and differences in the opportunities which this behavior presents to those who must cope with it.

By competition I mean merely the conditions that buyers and sellers call competitive. For simplicity, I shall speak of conditions only on the supply side of the market. A competitive market is one in which there are alternative sources of supply. Without such available alternatives, buyers may refuse to buy lest they become dependent upon the ture vagaries of one management's price and production policy, as the automobile companies refused to buy aluminum from the Aluminum Corporation. Competition implies also that there are alternatives available in the market in business policies, whether toward price, production, or the kinds of goods and services which are furnished. Those options of policy afford, of course, the most important reason why the buyer wants more than one seller in the market. By shifting his purchases to the concern which offers the most attractive prices and the best goods the buyer can exert pressure. In markets where all producers are united in a common price policy there is no way of exerting pressure on price. In markets in which they are all united in a common policy toward the terms of sale or toward the characteristics of their products, effective option by the buyer is likewise destroyed so far as these aspects of market transactions are concerned. Hence there may be a sharp distinction between the buyers' influence in two markets, each of which depends for its supply of goods upon the same number of companies of about the same size.

In some markets in which one or two small concerns diverge from the typical pattern of policy, they may do so on sufferance because their dominant rivals have no need to fear their expansion. These cases afford no real alternative of policy for most buyers and thus present only an illusory showing of competition. Alternatives of policy must be either numerous or available from sellers with capacity to survive and grow, if they are to provide competition.

A third characteristic of competitive markets is flexibility of business policies toward prices and other important terms of the market bargain. Reconsideration of price policy in the light of changing conditions, not the least of which is the changing price policy of rivals, provides a basis for experiment and a means for recognizing the impact of the economic environment.

A fourth characteristic of competition is freedom of entry into an industry. The potential competition of new concerns encourages moderate and flexible policies by those already in the market and affords a second line of defense for the buyer if he is not protected by the alternatives already available. It prevents established concerns from stopping progress in order to protect their vested interests. Though the scale of enterprise is so large that in many industries considerable funds and investment banking support are requisites for a new concern, there is an appreciable distinction between industries like cotton textiles, in which new enterprises may rapidly change the whole geographical face of the industry, and industries like the manufacture of aluminum ingot, in which for over thirty years no would-be competitor has been able to get started.

I am concerned here with these basic characteristics of competition rather than the effects which are supposed to flow from competition. The political and business community has long believed that competition in this sense has results somewhat similar to those attributed by classical economists to competition in the classical sense. They have believed that in competitive markets there is a safeguard against exploitative bargains; that the check upon high prices which competition affords promotes a fuller use of existing productive facilities; that free entry into an industry encourages a type of industrial expansion which is likely to establish a better balance in the use of resources than would otherwise exist. The degree to which these beliefs are justified lies outside my present subject. It involves the question whether many short-comings of the current economic structure are due to too much competition or too much private industrial control. It involves also a consideration of what alternatives to competition are practicable, and how far such alternatives may be relied upon to establish fair play, full use of resources, and balance in the industrial structure. It is not my task today to argue the relative merits of competition and other forms of directing activity to social use. It is sufficient to point out that nobody wants uncontrolled monopoly power to be in private hands and that the techniques of public control thus far available in democracies are suited to deal with exceptions to the policy of competition, but not to provide general public control of production and prices.

Enforcement of the antitrust laws requires the preservation of alternatives in business policy and the preservation of freedom of entry into markets. The key statutes available to accomplish these ends are the Sherman Act, the Clayton Act, and the Federal Trade Commission Act. The Clayton Act prohibits specific types of behavior: price discrimination which injures competition, tying contracts which prevent customers from buying other lines of goods from rival sellers, the acquisition of stock in competing corporations when the effect is to lessen competition, and interlocking directorates in competing corporations any of which has an owner's equity of a million dollars or over. The Sherman Act forbids, in general terms, monopolies, attempts to monopolize, and combinations in restraint of trade. The Federal Trade Commission Act forbids unfair methods of competition and unfair acts and practices. Except for the limited provisions of the Clayton Act, the policy of preserving competition is expressed in broad phrases which describe the results of business action rather than the action itself. The prosecuting agency and the courts are left free to determine in each case whether a line of business conduct falls within the prohibitions of the acts.

Such statutes are flexible. They are broad enough to cover new types of business behavior and to take account of the changing economic significance of old practices. On the other hand, since their exact meaning must be developed case by case, this meaning depends upon the insight of the prosecuting agencies and of the courts. Judicial interpretations may extend or limit the content of the statutes in ways which laymen find it hard to understand. Prosecutions which do not dig into the economic facts may give the courts no adequate information upon which to determine the reasonableness of business conduct.

Sometimes these characteristics of the law are urged as grounds for belief that it is unworkable. It is quite true that the judicial process is in some ways unsuitable to the working out of broad economic policies. The fabric of the economic commonwealth does not break neatly into pieces at state lines, nor does it divide readily into separate domains of intrastate and interstate commerce. In handling so broad a problem as the collapse of the construction industries, it is apparently necessary to spend much time and attention upon questions of whether federal jurisdiction over each part of the industry can be established by showing that specific building materials have moved across state lines. Again, a structure of market control often arises by a series of overlapping understandings, whereas in judicial proceedings the boundaries of a single prosecution may be no wider than the boundaries of a single conspiracy. Thus if three companies have agreed to restrain trade and each of them has separately agreed with various other concerns to extend the effects of that restraint, it may be necessary to bring four or more separate proceedings, in no one of which the full pattern may be admissible in evidence. Even in the presentation of evidence relevant to a single conspiracy, the rules of evidence which were developed for personal crimes and torts are misfits as means to bring out the facts of an industrial market. Judicial evidence is that which individuals have done, seen, heard, felt, smelt, and tasted. There are few techniques for bringing before the court broad situations of which no single person has direct firsthand experience.   In the prosecution of the aluminum case, for example, the Department of Justice wished to present two pages of import statistics.   Under the rulings of the court, which may have been somewhat overscrupulous, it became necessary to present in evidence every statute since 1890 under which the government had collected such statistics, every administrative regulation pursuant to each statute under which the collections had been made, and the original books of record, year by year, which contained the relevant figures.   About a week of continuous testimony was necessary to verify a two-page table of aluminum imports.   Had it not been possible to demonstrate the authoritative character of these figures, they probably would have been rejected as evidence.   By a strange quirk of judicial reasoning, however, a person who had made a considerable study of statistics not admissible as evidence might have been qualified as an expert witness and might have testified as to his opinion, even though it was derived from sources which the court would have rejected as improper.

The judicial process is likewise an awkward means of providing such incidental administrative safeguards as may be needed in the enforcement of economic policies.   Proceedings under the antitrust laws often result in equity decrees which prescribe limits for a future course of business conduct or which require the reorganization of business enterprises to terminate a monopoly.   In such cases surveillance may be necessary to determine whether the provisions of the decree are being adequately carried out.   Since courts are not administrative bodies, the facilities which they have available for such supervision are few and awkward, and in consequence the follow-up of decrees in equity has usually been inadequate.

Finally, the lack of an effective civil penalty in the present laws has enhanced the problems of enforcement.   The only choices open to the enforcement agencies are either criminal indictment or else proceedings in equity or by Federal Trade Commission order which, if successful, will involve no punishment for past conduct but only a requirement as to the future. Since equity cases are not punitive, they afford no deterrent. The only way to make lawbreaking hazardous is to indict. In a criminal case, however, the defendant has the benefit of many safeguards with which the law has surrounded criminal actions. The most obvious of these is the requirement that the prosecution establish its case beyond a reasonable doubt, whereas in ordinary civil proceedings a case may be established by the preponderance of evidence, even though the proof is not overwhelming. To prove a far-flung business conspiracy beyond any reasonable doubt is more difficult than to supply such proof of a personal crime. Moreover, juries are unwilling to convict nice people, and the ordinary defendant in an antitrust suit is well dressed, soft spoken, and obviously not, in an ordinary sense, one of the criminal class. The consequence is that the law is both too severe and too lenient. The punishment sought frequently fails to fit the crime, and sensing this fact, the juries sometimes refuse to punish at all. Amendment of the law to provide strong civil penalties as an alternative to criminal action would make punishment more sure and at the same time permit it to be less severe in suitable cases.

Though such procedural shortcomings often handicap the effort to use the antitrust laws for economic ends, the gap between legal process and economic fact creates less difficulty under the antitrust laws than under statutes designed to regulate monopolistic enterprises. The elaborate legal futilities of the utility rate cases have provoked formal comment by a member of the Supreme Court itself. The problems of adapting to broad public purposes a legal structure which grew up chiefly to settle private disputes and punish individual crimes are common to any industrial policy except complete laissez faire. Better legal procedures would improve the working of the antitrust laws, but the need for them would be even more pressing if the laws were abandoned.

Moreover, though the laws need to be a more effective instrument, the administration of the present laws need not, for that reason, fail. Most governmental instrumentalities have obvious defects and function with no more than partial efficiency. As in the case of traffic control, many individual violators may go unpunished, and yet the broad effect of the system may be sufficient to safeguard the flow of traffic. The basic question is whether antitrust procedures can catch enough of the anti-competitive tendencies in modern business to halt or reverse the trend.

One sort of monopolistic tendency of business is easy to deal with. This is the old-fashioned kind of collusion which, before I joined the staff of an enforcement agency, I thought had gone out of date with the turn of the century. Instead, it is still one of the very prevalent elements of business policy. As in the days of Adam Smith, groups of businessmen get together to fix prices; and they seek to conceal what they are doing by the secrecy of their proceedings. To cope with such efforts is a mere matter of personnel, for there is scarcely a collusive agreement of any size or duration which does not leave unmistakable traces. If there are many persons in the conspiracy, one of them is almost sure to develop a grievance and turn state's evidence. If the plan is complicated, it is almost certain to leave written records. If no letters or memoranda are written, there is evidence that meetings were held and evidence of the identity of action which followed the meetings. If files have been stripped, stray carbons and references to the missing documents in other documents make it possible to trace what happened. Once proved, a collusive agreement is relatively easy to terminate by law, since it operates through a system of joint action which may be stopped.

To prevent collusion is important not only because of its prevalence but because collusion which results in fixing prices is usually the least defensible kind of anti-competitive policy.

When monopoly arises by a growth in size, it usually involves a change in the managerial methods of the concern. There may sometimes be gain in efficiency; there is often gain in industrial stability. In such cases a preference for competition is a choice of a balance of good where something may be said on each side of the issue. In collusive price fixing, however, the conspiring concerns are engaged in a crude attempt to get more income without appreciable change in productive methods and with no guarantee of a stable future. Indeed, among the most violent and disastrous of business fluctuations are those which occur when a collusive agreement drives prices too high and the consequent production of an enlarged supply shatters the agreement and drives prices too low.

A much more difficult problem is presented by the unity of price policy which results from price leadership or from group monopoly. In price leadership a large concern so over-shadows its rivals that they find it safest and most profitable to surrender independent business judgment and to copy the price policies of the dominant concern. The head of one such small company was asked in a TNEC hearing what would happen if he chose to disregard the prices of his large competitor. He replied, in effect, that he hoped he might never have occasion to find out. When the pressure upon the small concern is a matter of overt threats and of business policies expressly designed to destroy the enterprise, there is a clear basis for action under the antitrust laws. When, however, the small concern's choice is merely between sheltering itself under the umbrella or taking the risks of market competition against a stronger enterprise, the various degrees of price leadership are hard to distinguish and hard to make the basis of an antitrust charge.

Similarly, the uniformity of prices sometimes developed by a few large concerns may be difficult to proceed against. With two sulphur producers in the United States, each can readily see that its own price policy will affect that of the other. The individual business judgment of either concern that the best thing to do is to maintain a high price in the hope that the other will do likewise may result in large profits and in prices that remain unchanged for a decade. Nevertheless, the process by which this result is reached may be indistinguishable from any other exercise of private discretion in determining a concern's prices.

The ability to catch collusion is the ability to prevent a great deal of such quasi-monopolistic pricing. A modern price structure involves such complicated differences of trade and quantity discounts, geographical price differences, differentials in price between related products, adjustments for long-term contracts, and the like, that the maintenance of identical prices becomes a matter of great technical difficulty. Even during the formal price fixing which some industries enjoyed under NRA, there were frequent variations in the prices because of differences in the application of the price formulas. In some industries standing committees were necessary to interpret the rules. To simplify the technique of price fixing, sellers often find collusion upon the terms of sale indispensable to the maintenance of uniform prices, even though the basic prices can be kept in line by some loose form of price leadership or of individual self-restraint.

When collusion about terms of sale is not present in these two classes of cases, a successful prosecution would require either that the government prove that a tacit conspiracy existed among those involved or that the government establish a new principle, as yet untested in the courts, that there may be monopoly as the joint effect of the separate action of members of a group as well as monopoly in a single enterprise. If the government chose to try by prosecution to alter the policies of those concerned, it would have to insist directly that in making their individual prices they should give different weight to various strategic considerations than they now individually give. If such a program did not seem feasible, the only other remedy would be to seek dissolution of the large concerns involved in order that, with companies smaller and more numerous, the market might provide less opportunity for such tacitly concerted price fixing. The development of price rigidities apparently based upon size or price leadership has been so great in recent years that the effort to remedy the condition by breaking up going concerns probably would amount to an effort to reshape by law a considerable part of the industrial structure of the United States. Half a century of neglect is difficult to overcome retroactively.

There is another and less dramatic way in which the problems of group monopoly and price leadership might be dealt with more slowly but with more likelihood of success. Fortunately we do not appear to have come to the end of the dynamic development of technology, the rise in the standard of living, and the expansion of our total market. Industries which were strategically important twenty years ago have been superseded by the development of substitutes. Regional markets have been expanded by the improvement of transportation. By further developments of this kind it is probable that many of our highly concentrated industries will be exposed to new competition. If we can take steps to limit the future growth of large enterprises, to preserve competition in the new industries, and to prevent expansion of the power of our present large enterprises, we may be able to reduce the problems of price leadership and group monopoly to manageable proportions. Such a policy involves peculiar care to protect the opportunities for new enterprises to enter the market as well as care to keep them from being swallowed up by the old concerns.

Moreover, something can be done to prevent the growth of tacit collusion in fields in which the small number of concerns have not yet found it possible to work together. In most cases in which a few concerns dominate the market, a diversity in their policies expresses an important difference in their strategic opportunities. One may be manufacturing many lines, and another only a single line; one may be distributing through small independent concerns, and another through mass distributors; one may be operating nationally, whereas another may be intensively cultivating a regional market. In so far as further development wipes out such difficulties the obstacles to group monopoly will disappear. Thus it becomes peculiarly important to preserve an open field for the competition of different kinds of distributive outlet, not only because the distributive trades need competition but because such diversities protect competition in manufacturing.

The problems presented by price leadership and group monopoly suggest the need for special emphasis upon the problems presented by growth in the size of the business unit. Economists have long pointed out the anomaly in preventing the union of competing productive facilities by agreement while permitting it by merger. As early as 1914 the Congress dealt with an aspect of this matter in passing Section 7 of the Clayton Act; but if that statute was intended to check the union of competitors it failed in its purpose by leaving the door wide open for purchase of the assets rather than the stock of the rival concern. Though adequate figures are not available, I believe that more of the growth of large American corporations during the last thirty years has come through the acquisition of competitors than through the construction of new plant and equipment. Instances of merger piled upon merger are found throughout our industries. Already the trend has contributed much to the problems of tacit collusion. Left alone for another quarter of a century, it may well give us substantial monopoly in many of our major industries.

An illustration of the trend is to be found in copper production. The best available figures of the output of the three largest copper companies indicate that in the last ten years they have increased their control from a little more than 40 per cent of the total American production to a little more than 80 per cent.   Most of this increase has come by absorption of other companies.

There is a widespread belief, carefully cultivated by those directly interested, that the growth of business enterprise involves a growth in efficiency.   There may be some question in the development of any enterprise large enough to have appreciable bargaining strength whether its prospects of profit furnish any clue to efficiency in an engineering or social sense.   Nevertheless, when concerns expand from profits or when they raise money in the open market for expansion, there is at least a presumption that the desirability of greater size has been measured by some pecuniary standard of comparison against other possible uses of the funds.   In the case of mergers of going concerns, there can be no such presumption.   The alternative is for the companies to compete or merge.   So far as productive economies go, there is little reason to think that the union of two established plants will often make possible so close a dovetailing of processes or such a nice adjustment of facilities to markets as to lower costs of production.   Economies in distribution might be expected to appear more frequently, but in the distribution field there is no clear evidence that the distributive activities of large enterprises capable of supporting their own distributive machinery are more economical in the social sense than specialized distribution through middlemen. On the other hand, the bargaining advantages of a merger are usually obvious.   In the absence of specific facts such as are typically unavailable, there is no reason why we should set aside the public interest in preserving competition and in limiting individual bargaining strength for the problematical economies to be gained by reducing the number of competitors.

With the Clayton Act inadequate to prevent the union of competing concerns, recourse must be had either to new legislation or to the Sherman Act.   The Federal Trade Commission has repeatedly recommended that Section 7 of the

Clayton Act be altered to provide specific authority over the acquisition of a competitor's assets.   Failing this solution, it may be possible to proceed under the Sherman Act.   In a few cases the acquisition of a competitor may be interpreted as an attempt to monopolize trade either throughout the nation or in some particular section of the market.   More generally, however, successful prosecution of mergers will require a type of case which has not yet been decided in the courts.   It will be necessary to establish the view that a contract to acquire a competitor is a contract in restraint of trade. If this principle is established, the case by case procedure involved in all prosecutions of restraint of trade will become applicable to mergers and will permit the usual distinction between reasonable and unreasonable restraints according to the facts of each particular case.

A solution of the problem of size is the heart of the question whether competition can be preserved by the antitrust laws. Without competitors there can be no competition; and with the present trend of corporate growth the disappearance of most competitors in many industries can be foreseen.   Expansion for efficiency's sake probably is a self-limiting process; but expansion by fusion obviously is not.   If this trend can be halted or reversed, the other problems involved in the enforcement of the antitrust laws will amount to no more than the ordinary problems of making an administrative agency effective.   If, however, the scale of business is to continue to grow not only by expansion but by unchecked merger, it will be necessary to accept oligopolistic price policies as typical and to fight the battles against complete monopoly only as last-ditch struggles in a war already lost.   Such a prospect would require the community to consider adopting types of industrial control which operate directly upon the policies of corporations, in recognition of the fact that a giant concern with powers not limited by its rivals in the market is a quasi-public enterprise.   Such a development would involve, not the making of exceptions to the antitrust laws, but the preservation of the areas of competition as exceptions to the general economic policy. I do not relish that prospect, for it would require a vast machinery of control over the detail of industrial decisions; and in my judgment governmental control is one of our social resources which should be carefully economized.

2

MONOPOLY IN LAW AND ECONOMICS*

By Edward S. Mason†

I

The term monopoly as used in the law is not a tool of analysis but a standard of evaluation. Not all trusts are held monopolistic but only "bad" trusts; not all restraints of trade are to be condemned but only "unreasonable" restraints. The law of monopoly has therefore been directed toward a development of public policy with respect to certain business practices. This policy has required, first, a distinction between the situations and practices which are to be approved as in the public interest and those which are to be disapproved, second, a classification of these situations as *either* competitive and consequently in the public interest *or* monopolistic and, if unregulated, contrary to the public interest, and, third, the devising and application of tests capable of demarcating the approved from the disapproved practices. But the devising of tests to distinguish monopoly from competition cannot be completely separated from the formulation of the concepts. It may be shown, on the contrary, that the difficulties of formulating tests of monopoly have definitely shaped the legal conception of monopoly.

* *The Yale Law Journal*, Volume 47, Number 1, November 1937, Pages 34–49. Reprinted by the courtesy of the Yale Law Journal Company, Inc. and the author.

† Professor of Economics, Harvard College. The author wishes to acknowledge his indebtedness to the A. W. Shaw Fund and to the Harvard University Committee on Research in the Social Sciences for assistance in financing a larger study on monopoly problems of which this is a part.

25

Economics, on the other hand, has not quite decided whether its task is one of description and analysis or of evaluation and prescription, or both.   With respect to the monopoly problem it is not altogether clear whether the work of economists should be oriented toward the formulation of public policy or toward the analysis of market situations.   The trend, however, is definitely towards the latter.   The further economics goes in this direction, the greater becomes the difference between legal and economic conceptions of the monopoly problem.   Lawyers and economists are therefore rapidly ceasing to talk the same language.

Twenty years ago this was not the case.   In 1915 there appeared in the JOURNAL an article on the Trust Problem which quoted the opinions of eminent economists on the significance of a contemporary "trust" decision.[1]   The point the author was trying to make, flattering indeed to the study of economics, was "that in cases of this character no decision can be legally sound that is not fundamentally correct from an economic point of view."[2]   The question posed to the economists was the import in terms of monopoly of the production by the International Harvester Company of 65–85% of the national output of certain types of harvesting machinery.[3]   While the answers may or may not have been helpful in the formulation of legal opinion, it is a point of peculiar interest that the economists conceived the problem in much the same way as the courts.   It was not monopoly as an analytical concept but monopoly injurious to the public interest which colored their thinking.   The economists' emphasis on free entry into the industry as characteristic of competition and restriction of entry as the *differentia specifica* of monopoly was in complete harmony with the judicial predilection.   Monopoly

---

[1] Friedman, *The Trust Problem in the Light of Some Recent Decisions* (1915) 24 YALE L. J. 488.

[2] *Id.* at 493.

[3] *Id.* at 502, 503.

was thought of as the antithesis of free competition, unregulated monopoly was always and necessarily a public evil, the nature of monopoly was to be found mainly in restrictions on trade, and its remedy was, in the Wilsonian phrase, "a fair field with no favor."

Since that time, particularly in recent years, economic thinking on the subject of monopoly has taken a radically different trend. Much more attention has been given to the shaping of the concept of monopoly as a tool of economic analysis rather than as a standard of evaluation in the judgment of public policy. Some of the consequences of this trend have been the focussing of attention on the problems of the individual firm rather than those of the industry, a recognition of monopoly elements in the practices of almost every firm, a recognition of the impossibility of using the fact of monopoly as a test of public policy, and a growing awareness of the necessity of making distinctions between market situations all of which have monopoly elements. The trend has led to a split between the approach to the monopoly problem in the law and economics which requires bridging by interpretative work of a high order. The following pages are not concerned primarily with this task but rather with an economist's impression of the divergence between the present legal and economic concepts of monopoly.

II

The elements out of which both law and economics have built their ideas of monopoly are restriction of trade and control of the market. These elements are of course not independent. Restrictions of trade of various sorts are familiar devices for securing control of the market; control of the market may be used, as in predatory competition, to restrict trade and competition. Nevertheless, restraints of trade can exist without anything that the courts would be willing to call control of the market. And, control of the market, in the economic sense, can exist independently of any practice which the law would call a restraint of trade.

It is also important at this point to understand the content of several other basic concepts. The antithesis of the legal conception of monopoly is *free* competition, understood to be a situation in which the freedom of any individual or firm to engage in legitimate economic activity is not restrained by the state, by agreements between competitors or by the predatory practices of a rival. But free competition thus understood is quite compatible with the presence of monopoly elements in the *economic* sense of the word monopoly. For the antithesis of the economic conception of monopoly is not *free* but *pure* competition, understood to be a situation in which no seller or buyer has any control over the price of his product. Restriction of competition is the legal content of monopoly; control of the market is its economic substance. And these realities are by no means equivalent.

An illustration of the application of these concepts is presented by the facts of the Cream of Wheat case.[1] The Cream of Wheat Company bought purified middlings, a high-grade by-product of wheat, and, "without submitting them to any process or treatment, without adding anything to them, it puts up the middlings which it selects in packages and offers its selection to the trade under the name of 'Cream of Wheat'."[2] The court was unable to see either control of the market or restriction of trade in this practice. "The business of the defendant is not a monopoly, or even a quasi-monopoly. Really it is selling purified wheat middlings and its whole business covers only about 1 per cent. of that product. It makes its own selection of what by-products of the middling process it will put up, and sells what it puts up under marks which tell the purchaser that these middlings are its own selec-

---

[1] Great Atlantic and Pacific Tea Company v. Cream of Wheat Company, 227 Fed. 46 (1915).

[2] *Id.* at 47.

tion. It is open to Brown, Jones and Robinson to make their selections out of the other 99% of purified middlings and put them up and sell them; possibly one or more of them may prove to be better selectors than the defendant, or may persuade the public that they are."[1]

An economist, on the other hand, would be inclined to say that the product sold is not wheat middlings but Cream of Wheat, and that the Cream of Wheat Company exercises some monopolistic control of the market unless, and this is unlikely, the number and quantity of substitute products is such as to render the price independent of the quantity sold. He would add that it does not follow that the market control incident to such a monopoly position is contrary to public policy. Furthermore he would consider monopoly of the production of Cream of Wheat as perfectly compatible with competition on the part of actual or potential producers of substitute products.

The economists' emphasis is on control of the supply or price of a product. And "product" is defined in terms of consumer choice, for if consumers find that the goods sold by two competing dealers are different, they are different for purposes of market analysis regardless of what the scales or calipers say. Some control of the market exists whenever a seller can, by increasing or diminishing his sales, affect the price at which his product is sold. Since, outside the sphere of agricultural and a few other products, almost every seller is in this position, it is easy to see that if monopoly is identified with control of the market, monopolistic elements are practically omnipresent. This is the logical conclusion, it is submitted, where the emphasis is laid upon control of the market and the monopoly concept is considered as a tool of analysis only, unrelated to public policy. But if monopoly is considered to be a standard of evaluation useful in the administration of public policy then other considerations must be involved.

---

[1] *Id.* at 48.

It is so used in the law. Although the history of the term's legal usage is filled with references to control of the market as evidence of monopoly, various factors, principally the difficulties of devising tests of the reasonableness of price and output controls, have focussed the attention of courts on another element, restriction of trade, as the decisive consideration. The development of this idea may be seen in the sources of the present law of monopoly and competition, which are, according to Jervey and Deák, to be found in "(A) the Statute against Monopolies and *D'Arcy v. Allein;* (B) the old English statutes against forestalling and engrossing; (C) the judicial adaptation of the ancient law on restraint of trade to the combination acting as a unit of controlled parts; and (D) the law of conspiracy as applied to the illegal end of suppression of competition, with particular reference to labor conspiracies insofar as they were seen as restraints on the market."[1]

It is clear from the Statute of Monopolies[2] and from contemporary definitions that monopoly meant *exclusion* of other producers or sellers by a dispensation from the sovereign granting *sole* rights to some person or persons.[3] Although *D'Arcy v. Allein*[4] declared the "inseparable incidents" of monopoly to be (1) the raising of the price of the product, (2) the deterioration of its quality, and (3) the "impoverishment of divers artificers and others" because of exclusion from their accustomed trades, a monopoly was considered to exist

---

[1] HUGER W. JERVEY AND FRANCIS DEAK, THE CASE OF MONOPOLY V. COMPETITION, (Mimeo., 1934).

[2] 21 Jac. I, c. 3. (1623).

[3] Coke defined monopoly in this way: "An institution, or allowance by the king, by his grant, commission, or otherwise, to any person or persons, bodies politique or corporate, of, or for the sole buying, selling, making, working, or using, of anything, whereby any person, or persons, bodies politique or corporate, are sought to be restrained of any freedom or liberty that they had before, or hindered in their lawful trade." 3 INSTITUTES No. 181.

[4] 11 Co. 84*b*, 74 Eng. Reprint 1131 (1602).

whether or not these "incidents" followed.   It was not incumbent upon the courts to show that prices had actually been raised or quality of the product deteriorated in order to be able to hold that a monopoly existed contrary to the common law.[1] Monopoly meant exclusion from a certain trade by legal dispensation and no examination of control of the market was necessary to establish this fact.

The injuries inflicted by forestalling, regrating and engrossing were in the main conditioned and limited by an early and now obsolete system of distributing and marketing goods, principally foodstuffs.   Laws were found necessary to prohibit the spreading of false reports as to the state of the market (regrating), to prohibit the purchase of victuals on the way to market for purposes of resale (forestalling), and to prohibit the cornering of the available supply of an article (engrossing).[2] It is true that engrossing in particular was an act undertaken to secure what an economist would call control of the market. But in the absence of a combination, of attempts to exclude competitors, or of other overt acts, it was difficult for the courts to find evidence of control of the market.   There is no obvious answer to the question of how large a share of the available supply of an article an individual must purchase before he is guilty of engrossing.   If, on the other hand, the engrossing were accomplished by a combination, particularly if the combination attempted to exclude competitors, the problem appeared to be more simple.[3]   Conspiracy frequently accom-

---

[1] As a matter of fact it is quite possible that a monopoly dispensation would not give to its holder control of the market in the sense of ability to raise price or to lower the quality of the product.   Whether it did or not would depend, in economic jargon, on the elasticity of demand for that product, and this in turn would be influenced by a number of factors including the existence of effective substitutes.

[2] See Jones, *Historical Development of The Law of Business Competition* (1926) 35 YALE L. J. 905, at 907 *et seq.*

[3] "To gain a monopoly on a local market a common, organized action,

panied engrossing in the early cases and was rarely absent in the later ones.   In no engrossing case that has come before Anglo-Saxon courts in the last hundred and fifty years, so far as I am aware, has a court undertaken to discover the existence of engrossing by examining the control of the engrosser over the price.   What cases there are, and they have been few, have been complicated by the presence of combinations or conspiracies to restrain trade.   The courts have found monopoly because of conspiracy and the exclusion of others from the market rather than control of the market.   It is doubtful whether the act of engrossing itself, in the absence of a conspiracy to exclude competitors, would carry any monopoly connotation in the law.   Consequently it seems doubtful whether the ancient law respecting engrossing, forestalling and regrating has made much of a contribution to present legal concepts of monopoly.

In a somewhat different status in this respect is the law on restraint of trade.   The question of restraints originally came before the courts in cases involving the sale of a business in which, as an incident to the sale, the seller contracted not to compete with the buyer.   Until sometime in the 17th century the courts uniformly held such contracts unenforceable, the basis of the rule being "that public policy demands from every man the free exercise of his trade in the public interest."[1] Did public policy demand the free exercise of trade because

---

in other words a cartel of the most powerful competitors, often became a necessity.   The fact that competitors acted in agreement when engrossing the market is expressed in the English anti-monopolistic legislation by the significant term *conspiracy*.   This word was first used in this connection in the Statute of 1353 [a Forestalling Statute, of 27 Edw. III], and reappears continually in the anti-monopolistic statutes.   From here it passes over to the American anti-trust legislation, being thus a continuation of the old monopoly prohibitions."   PICTROWSKI, CARTELS AND TRUSTS (1933) 148, quoted in JERVEY AND DEAK, *op. cit. supra*, note 7.

[1] Cooke, *Legal Rule and Economic Function* (1936) 46 ECON. J. 21.

in the absence of such free exercise there would be a control of
the market?

Restrictive covenants, if enforceable, certainly may lead to
control of a local market, but control of the market is not
dependent on the existence of such contracts. Doctors,
lawyers, or tradesmen dealing in a particular type of article
may be, and frequently were in the period in which restrictive
covenants were unenforceable, the sole practitioners of their
profession or trade in a given locality possessing a control of
the local market. Yet this fact does not appear to have led to
legislative or judicial concern. It appears more consistent
with the early decisions to say that restrictive covenants were
feared because one who contracted himself out of a livelihood
might become a public charge.

The development in the 17th and 18th century of the doctrine of "reasonable restraints," as applied to restrictive
covenants in connection with the sale of a business, does not
seem to have involved any closer consideration of the monopoly problem. Although it is sometimes said,[1] or implied, that
the reasonableness which concerned the courts in such contracts was understood not only in relation to the interests of the
contracting parties but also to the public interest in prevention
of control of the market, it is difficult to substantiate this view
by an appeal to the decisions.[2] The application of the doctrine of reasonableness to the interests of the contracting
parties is clear. The interest of the buyer was a property
interest, that the value of the purchased business not be
lessened by competition from the seller in the immediate
vicinity, while that of the seller was not only a property interest, since he obtained through the sale the full value of the
"good will" of the business, but also an interest in safeguarding
the possibility of continuing somewhere and at some time his

---

[1] See, *e. g.*, Pope, *The Legal Aspects of Monopoly* (1907) 20 HARV. L. REV.
167; Cooke, *op. cit. supra*, note 14.

[2] Mitchel v. Reynolds, 1 P. Wms. 181 (1711).

trade or profession.   The language of the courts indicates that
the public interest was considered affected when the public
was deprived by such a contract of a source of supply without
justification, *i. e.*, when such a deprivation was unnecessary to
the protection of the private interests involved in the contract.
This protection of the public interest was levelled primarily
not against monopolistic control of the market but against the
loss to the common weal of the services of a productive agent.
There is no evidence that the courts examined the data relevant to the question whether such a contract might lead to
control of the market.   If any monopoly consideration was
involved, it was monopoly in the sense of restriction of competition, not of control of the market.

If the test of reasonableness referred to the extent of competition or control of the market which would result from the
restrictive contract, might we not have expected the courts to
compare the market situation in the locality affected by the
contract with the market situations in other localities?   If
the restrictive covenant reduced the number of possible competitors by one, this might have a very different effect on control of the market in a locality in which competitors were
many from its effect in a locality in which only one remained.
There is not much evidence, however, that the courts considered the easily available facts relative to extent of market
control, and the cause seems to be that the "reasonableness"
with which they were concerned in cases involving restrictive
covenants was rarely, if ever, related to the monopoly problem.

The gradual relaxation of the law on restrictive covenants
is easily understood with reference to the interests of the contracting parties and requires no examination of the changes in
the scope of market control.   With the increase in economic
opportunities incident to increasing division of labor the
means of gaining a livelihood open to a seller of a business
expanded, and the restrictions imposed on his activities by
these covenants became less serious.   On the other hand, with

the growth of transportation facilities the area within which the competition of the seller might lessen the value of what he has sold had increased. For both these reasons the scope permitted restraints of trade of this sort has been enlarged.[1] Moreover, whether or not the establishment of a competing enterprise in a given locality was likely to affect the value of the business sold, and whether or not a limitation in trading in a given locality was likely to deprive a man of the means of earning his livelihood and the public of the fruit of his activity were questions to which common experience might be said to provide a tolerably satisfactory answer. The question whether the elimination of one unit of competition would result in control of the market, however, could hardly be answered without an examination of the number of competitors left in the restricted area and of the behavior of prices. To such an examination the courts were hesitant to proceed.

The application of the rule of reason to contracts between competitors designed solely to limit competition among themselves stands on different ground. It is frequently said that, as distinguished from restrictive covenants connected with the sale of a business, the interests of the contracting parties are here not at issue since such contracts will not be entered into unless there is prospect of gain to all from the limitation.[2] While this may or may not be true, if the rule of reason is to be applied to such cases, it must be applied on different grounds, or it must be a different rule than that used in the older cases of restraint of trade. For in this type of contract the public interest in the monopoly problem is paramount, and the question of the private interests of the individual contractors is only secondary.

The disposition of American courts has been, at least until very recently, to hold all contracts for division of territory,

---

[1] Handler, *Restraint of Trade*, (1934) 13 ENCYC. Soc. SCIENCES 339.
[2] Pope, *op. cit. supra*, note 15; Cooke, *op. cit. supra*, note 14.

pooling, fixing of prices, common marketing control of supply, or which restrict the freedom of the contractors to compete
in other ways, unenforceable and, since the Sherman Act,
illegal. The opinions of the court in these cases constantly
refer to monopoly in the sense of control of the market, but
little examination of evidence pertinent to the question of
market control is ever undertaken. The test of monopoly,
or attempt of monopoly, is here restriction of competition.
American courts have in this class of cases been willing to
accept the contract itself as evidence of restriction and, consequently, of an attempt to monopolize, without inquiring
further into the question of how great a control of the market is
secured to the contracting parties.[1] The rule of reason enunciated with much fanfare by Chief Justice White purporting to
provide a standard of judgment dividing those contractual
restrictions which are in the public interest from those which
are not has had, at least until the *Appalachian Coal* case[2] in
1933, a much narrower application than might have been
expected.

The British courts, confronted with the same problem of
applying a rule of reason to contracts between competitors
designed to limit competition, have returned a somewhat
different answer. They have tended to accept every contract
designed to limit competition among the contracting competitors as reasonable in the absence of intention or actual

---

[1] In another class of cases, however, dealing principally with trade association activities, the Courts have drawn a distinction between limitation of
competition and a regulation by business agreement of competitive methods.
Nowhere is this distinction better expressed than by Justice Brandeis in
Board of Trade of the City of Chicago *et al*. v. United States, 246 U. S. 231,
at p. 239. "Every agreement concerning trade, every regulation of trade,
restrains. To bind, to restrain, is of the very essence. The true test of
legality is whether the restraint imposed is such as merely regulates and
perhaps thereby promotes competition or whether it is such as may suppress
or even destroy competition."

[2] Appalachian Coals, Inc. v. United States, 288 U. S. 344 (1933).

attempt to injure or destroy a competitor.[1] On the other hand, the trend of American opinion has been to regard all such contracts as unreasonable restraints of trade. In neither case has the rule of reason been given any intelligible content in terms of control of the market despite the frequency with which this phrase has graced judicial utterances.

Cases involving a union between competitors accomplished by amalgamation or fusion or merger have in this country most frequently involved the application of the rule of reason, and it is in these cases that the characteristic legal conception of monopoly is most evident. An amalgamation of competing firms may, and ordinarily does, take place for reasons other than to secure control of the price of the articles produced or sold by these firms. The courts could not, therefore, plausibly assume, as they did in the case of contracts to limit competition, that all amalgamations were *prima facie* evidence of an attempt to monopolize.

Since under the Sherman Act both the contract and the combination as an attempt to monopolize or restrain trade were illegal, some way had to be found of making the law on combinations equivalent to the law on contracts limiting competition. If monopoly had meant to the courts control of the market, some such equivalence might well have been

---

[1] See the dictum of Lord Parker in the *Adelaide* case: " . . . it is clear that the onus of showing that any contract is calculated to produce a monopoly or enhance prices to an unreasonable extent will be on the party alleging it, and that if once the court is satisfied that the restraint is reasonable as between the parties the onus will be no light one." Attorney-General of Australia v. Adelaide Steamship Co., 1913 A. C. 781, 796. Such a contract *may* produce an "unreasonable" control of the market but the British courts have rarely found one. A contract which restricts competition by the destruction of a competitor's market is a different matter. Here there is an overt act, an obvious restraint of trade, partaking of the nature of conspiracy, that does not compel the courts to examine the behavior of prices and outputs which are the most obvious sources of information concerning control of the market.

found, although the problem would have been, and is, difficult. Yet the sources of evidence of control of the market are
known: the behavior of prices and outputs, the relation of
prices and costs, profits before and after the combination,
share of the market controlled, the existence of business practices such as price discrimination, price stabilization and many
others. The evidences of a control of the market established
by combination would be found in the same sort of data as
in control established by contract, and a rule of reason which
set up as its standard control of the market would have yielded
approximately the same results in both types of cases.

By monopoly, however, the courts did not mean control of
the market but restriction of competition. While a contract
between competitors designed to limit competition carries the
evidence on its face of an attempt to monopolize, a merger
between competitors does not, so that the courts had perforce
to enquire, (1) into the intentions of the merging interests, and
(2) into such acts of the merger as might indicate restriction
of outside competition. If the intention behind a merger were
control of the market it is unlikely that it would be communi-
cated to the courts, and since the only evidences capable of
indicating intention to control the market were ignored we
may conclude that the courts found the presence of monopoly
in other ways. If the manifestation of the intention to limit
the competition of outsiders took the form of overt acts such
as local price discrimination, espionage, or securing of railway
rebates, the courts could find evidence of restrictions directly
relevant to their conception of monopoly. As a matter of fact
it is clear that this was the direction taken in the judicial
application of the rule of reason. The size of the combination
or its share of the total output of a product became important
only when accompanied by predatory practices affecting the
freedom of others to compete. In the words of one commen-
tator it had become clear by 1918 "that the Sherman Act had
evolved from an anti-trust act into an act relating to the legal

control of competitive methods."[1] Since monopoly meant restriction of competition rather than control of the market, this evolution was only logical.

The decision in the Standard Oil-Vacuum merger in 1931, it is true, gave somewhat more consideration to the problem of market control than has been usual in merger cases.[2] The court took into account (1) the merged concerns' share of sales of their various products in the *local* market, (2) the state of intercompany competition in the New England market, the number and size of companies, the area of their operations, and recent changes in the market position of the various companies, and (3) potential competition. Despite the advance, the dicta of Judge Kimbrough Stone in this case cannot be said to indicate a clear conception of monopoly in terms of market control. "Competition," he declares,

"is the antithesis of monopoly. In a sense, any elimination of competition is a movement in the general direction of monopoly. But competition is, in its very essence, a contest for trade, and any progress or victory in such contest must lessen competition. . . . It is only when this lessening is with an unlawful purpose or by unlawful means, or when it proceeds to the point where it is or is threatening to become a menace to the public, that it is declared unlawful. . . . The point of danger is reached when monopoly is threatened."

We might now expect some indication of tests which the court will apply to determine when monopoly is threatened. But the opinion continues, "This threat of monopoly exists, irrespective of intent, whenever competition is lessened to the danger point." In other words monopoly is threatened when "competition is lessened to the danger point." Competition

---

[1] McLaughlin, *Legal Control of Competitive Methods* (1936) 21 Iowa L. Rev. 280.

[2] United States v. Standard Oil Co. of N. J., 47 F. (2d) 288 (C. C. A. 2d, 1931). For another realistic analysis of a market situation, see International Shoe Co. v. Federal Trade Commission, 29 F. (2d) 518 (C. C. A. 2d, 1931).

is lessened to the danger point when "monopoly is threatened."[1]
Judge Stone in subsequent remarks appears to be able to get no
farther forward with this idea and finally falls back on a dictum
of Justice Holmes that "a combination in unreasonable
restraint of trade imports an attempt to override normal
market conditions."[2] Since nothing is more "normal" than
monopolistic market conditions, this too does not get us very far.

This summary review of the law of monopoly must lead to
the conclusion that whatever are considered to be the evils
resulting from monopoly—enhancement of price, deterioration of product, or the like—a monopolistic situation, or an
attempt to monopolize, is evidenced to the courts primarily,
if not exclusively, by a limitation of the freedom to compete.
The original meaning of monopoly, an exclusion of others
from the market by a sovereign dispensation in favor of one
seller, has continued to mean exclusion, in the broad sense of
restriction of competition.   Although "undue" or "unreasonable" control of the market is constantly inserted in judicial
decisions as the meaning of monopoly, the data capable of
indicating this control are almost universally ignored by the
courts.   In this country there has been a growing tendency in
the law to declare every contract between competitors which
restricts competition unenforceable and, since the Sherman
Act, illegal, whatever the extent of the control made possible
by the contract.[3]   In the case of mergers the monopoly or

---

[1] United States v. Standard Oil Co. of N. J., 47 F. (2d) 288, at 297
(C. C. A. 2d, 1931).

[2] American Column Co., v. United States, 257 U. S. 377 (1921).

[3] There is no evidence that the courts in interpreting the Sherman Act and
later anti-trust legislation in the light of common law concepts of monopoly
and restraint of trade were violating legislative intention or substituting
their understanding of the monopoly problem for that of the Congress.
On the contrary there is every reason to believe that the principal acts
which the Sherman Act sought to prevent were the predatory practices of
combinations which in many cases already enjoyed a commanding control
of the market.   The particular practices which received special legislative

attempt to monopolize is discovered primarily in predatory practices designed to hamper the competition of outsiders and not in control of the market.

III

It has been noted above that the elements on which the idea of monopoly has been built both in law and in economics have been control of the market and restriction of competition. If in their development of the law of monopoly the courts have tended to give mere lip service to the former and to identify monopoly with restriction of competition, the principal reasons are probably the following:

(1) The courts have been faced with the necessity of devising and applying to particular situations a standard of evaluation relevant to a vague concept known as the public interest. The injury to numerous private interests, and consequently to the public interest, from predatory attacks on established business enterprises, or from other attempts to restrict competition, was much more direct than that which might possibly be inflicted on buyers or sellers by a control of the market exercised independently of any attempts to restrict competition.

(2) The formulation of a standard of monopoly or monopolizing contrary to the public interest required the selection of tests capable of distinguishing competitive from monopoly situations. If monopoly were conceived as control of the market, the tests must necessarily be related to the behavior of prices, outputs and other variables indicative of control, an

---

attention were railway rebating, local price-discrimination and price maintenance. The sponsors of the Act announced on many occasions that it was not designed to prevent combinations either of labor or capital, and in answer to the specific question whether an enterprise would be considered a monopoly if, because of superior skill, it alone received all the orders for a particular article, Senator Hoar replied, "The word 'monopoly' is a merely technical term which has a clear and legal significance, and it is this: it is the sole engrossing to a man's self *by means which prevent other men from engaging in fair competition with him.*" 21 CONG. REC. 3152 (1890).

exceedingly difficult problem. If, on the other hand, monopoly is identified with restriction of competition, the devising of tests is comparatively simple.

(3) There is reason to believe that in an earlier period control of the market was much more dependent upon restriction of entry and other types of restriction of competition through predatory practices and harassing tactics than at present. The law of monopoly, though directed against restrictions of competition, may once have had more relevance to control of the market than it at present possesses.

(4) Before the Sherman Act monopoly actions were brought, with but few exceptions, before the courts on the suit of private interests. These interests were more likely to be directly affected adversely by predatory practices or attempts at exclusion from the market than by control of prices.

Although these considerations may help to explain the almost complete preoccupation of the courts with restrictions on freedom of competition, it must be recognized that our modern law embraces an antiquated and inadequate conception of the monopoly problem. Attention and criticism has therefore centered around the following aspects of our public policy with respect to monopoly and competition: the tendency of the courts to find illegal every contract limiting competition among the contracting competitors regardless of the effect or probable effect of such a contract on control of the market; the tendency to judge the legality of a combination or merger primarily on the basis of its competitive practices without examination of the extent of its control of the market; the absence of a developed public policy with respect to unfair practices, in particular the unwillingness of the courts to extend the concept of unfair competition beyond injury to a competitor and to take account of the nature of the injury to the public.

The weakness of our public policy is not the result of judicial interpretation but of the inadequacy of legislation. It can only be corrected by legislation which will re-define the monopoly and trade practice problem and provide tests by means of which market situations and business practices considered to be favorable to the public interest can be separated from those that are not. Since Congress has wrestled with this problem, off and on, for fifty years without conspicuous success, it does not appear likely that a ready-made solution can be found close at hand. Certainly economics has none to provide. Nevertheless, the economic approach, which is in some ways very different from the legal, can be utilized in the shaping of a more satisfactory public policy.

For its own purposes economics has found control of the market a much more useful approach to the concept of monopoly than restriction of competition. Some control of the market may be said to exist whenever the share of the sales or purchases made by any one seller or purchaser (or group of sellers or purchasers acting by means of an agreement) is sufficiently large to influence the price of the article sold. In a market from which control is completely absent every seller and buyer, acting independently, could increase or decrease his purchases or sales without appreciable effect on the price. Such markets, which may be said to be purely competitive in the sense of being completely devoid of any element of control over price, are comparatively rare. In most markets some sellers or buyers (or both) exercise some degree of control. Of course such control is perfectly compatible with the existence of some degree of competition. A seller with complete control of the market would be able to determine his price without regard for the actions of other sellers or the prices of other products; in other words, he would have no competition. No seller or buyer has such control. All markets, practically speaking, exhibit a fusion of monopoly and competitive elements.

It follows that, if monopoly is identified with control of the market, (a) it is impossible to separate markets into those that are competitive and those that are monopolistic; (b) a public policy which attempted to eliminate all positions of monopoly would confront a problem of impossible scope and complexity. It is, furthermore, by no means clear that the preservation of all the competitive elements and the suppression of all the monopolistic elements would be in the public interest, however conceived. Consequently, the existence of some control of the market is not likely to be in itself a good indication of the necessity or wisdom of applying preventative measures.

Having identified monopoly with control of the market, economics has proceeded further to an examination of certain typical monopoly situations. But the most that can be said of the results of monopoly investigations in economics is that they cast doubts on a number of traditional legal attitudes on the question of monopoly and restraint of trade, and that they emphasize a number of relevant considerations usually neglected by the interpreters of public policy. The significance of the existence of a relatively small number of buyers or sellers is a case in point. If the number of sellers (or buyers) is small enough to induce each seller, before changing his own selling policy, to take account of the probable effect of this change upon the policies of his rivals, the results of joint action by agreement, which might well be illegal, may be accomplished without collusion of any sort. It is quite obvious from the behaviour of cigarette prices that the manufacturers of cigarettes are in something like this situation. No one can change his prices without an overwhelming probability that his rivals will immediately follow suit, and one result is that price changes are very infrequent. To produce many of the consequences of joint action no one seller has to have a preponderant share of the total output; if the number of sellers is relatively small, their individual share of the total output is of secondary importance.

Nor is control of the market to be inferred merely from the number of existing competitors. Potential competition must be considered. Indeed the dicta of many trust cases might be interpreted as indicating a judicial opinion that in the absence of legal restraints or of overt predatory acts against potential competitors, free entry to the market precludes any element of control. Free entry in this legal sense, however, is compatible under certain circumstances with a considerable degree of market control. The capital resources necessary to establish a new firm in an effective competitive position may be so large as to eliminate potential competition as a practical consideration. The fact that no new motor car company has been established in the last decade or that no new brand of cigarettes has been able since the war to capture a sizeable share of the market cannot be taken to indicate that no control of the market exists.

The legal significance attached to trade marks and trade names provides another example of the divergence between legal and economic conceptions of monopoly. Economics, primarily concerned with the fact of market control, has emphasized the control of price made possible by the exploitation of a mark or name. Extensive advertising expenditures may successfully differentiate in the minds of buyers the product of a given seller from those of his rivals. The more successful this differentiation the greater the control of the market it is possible for the seller to achieve, and, consequently, the more entrenched his monopoly position. But since there is no restriction of competition in the legal sense, the law, primarily concerned in trade mark and trade name cases with protection of intangible property interests, can see no element of monopoly. On the other hand, economic opinion does not proceed from the fact that there is a monopolistic significance in the use of a mark or name to the conclusion that this institution or practice is necessarily contrary to the public interest.[1]

---

[1] See Handler, *Unfair Competition* (1936) 21 IOWA L. REV. 175, 185. For

It is fully consistent with the legal conception of the monopoly problem that the courts should enquire into the actual or probable results of agreements to restrain competition. But to do so would be to give up the traditional tests of monopolizing and to grapple with the problem of what is an unreasonable control of the market. The *Appalachian Coals* case[1] may indicate a tentative first step in this direction and somewhere between this and the *Sugar Institute* cases[2] is to be found the indistinct dividing line between certain types of restrictions which are and are not at present considered to be in the public interest. The ways in which competition may be restrained or "regulated," however, are many, and if the courts are now willing to delve into the problems of market control they will have to rely more and more on economic analysis of the different types of control situations. The significance of market controls established through various kinds of open price quoting, basing-point and zone price systems, agreements as to price terms and the like, are not apparent without a study of data hitherto considered by the courts to be irrelevant to the monopoly problem.

On the other hand, if economics is to be put itself in a position to contribute to the formulation of public policy, it must conceive the monopoly problem in a more extensive way than is at present customary. It is not enough to find evidence of the existence of market controls, nor is it sufficient to conduct purely analytical and descriptive studies of various types of control situations. While this is important, the formulation

---

the views of an economist on these matters, see CHAMBERLIN, MONOPOLISTIC COMPETITION (1933) Appendix E.

[1] Appalachian Coals, Inc. v. United States, 288 U. S. 344 (1933).

[2] United States v. Sugar Institute, 297 U. S. 553 (1936), *aff'g.*, 15 F. Supp. 817 (S. D. N. Y. 1934). For a thorough discussion of the problems, both legal and economic, raised by these cases, see Fly, *Observations on the Anti-Trust Laws, Economic Theory and the Sugar Institute Decisions* (1936) 45 YALE L. J. 1339, 46 *id.* 228.

of public policy requires a distinction between situations and practices which are in the public interest and those that are not. And this requirement imposes the necessity of elaborating tests which can be applied by administrative bodies and by the courts. It is easy enough to present evidence of monopoly situations, which, to economics, is merely the absence of pure competition. The existence of price discrimination, of price rigidity, advertising expenditures, price leadership and other practices are sufficient to indicate the presence of monopoly elements. But these practices are hardly sufficient evidence of the presence or possibility of market controls adverse to the public interest. A further study of different types of industrial markets and business practices and of their effects on prices, outputs, investment and employment designed to indicate means of distinguishing between socially desirable and undesirable situations and practices may or may not be fruitful. It is, in any case, the only way in which economics can contribute directly to the shaping of public policy. A simultaneous movement by legal and economic thinking away from entrenched positions might be conducive to progress on this front.

3

BUSINESS AND THE LAW*

A Comedy in Three Acts

By Myron W. Watkins†

Scene: On the right half of the stage is a dense Jungle, with a treacherous morass every few feet, huge boulders in between, and tangled vines overhead which shut out the light quite effectually. It is a dismal scene. On the left side, separated from the Jungle only by the distinct boundary of a flood of light which envelops this half of the stage, is a smooth grassy plain, which might be mistaken for an elysian field were it not identified by a posted warning to trespassers as a Well-Ordered Economic System. At the back of this side of the stage, upon a little eminence, sits an august body on a Bench. He bears a close resemblance to God and is invariably addressed or listened to in awesome reverence, but he goes by the name of Justi. At opposite ends of a low table (Regulated Equilibrium), which is of short length in the First Act but is extended in each of the succeeding acts, sit two abstractions, Producer and Consumer, in full view and under the steady scrutiny of Justi. They appear to be happily wed. As the curtain rises for the First Act, however, it is evident that no children share their board. A meal is being served. The menu discloses Maximum Product to be the *pièce de résistance*, with a sauce of

* *The Journal of Political Economy*, Volume XLII, Number 2, April 1934, Pages 178–201. Reprinted by the courtesy of the University of Chicago Press and the author.
† New York University.

Minimum Cost. Numerous ghostly figures flit about in a rarefied atmosphere busily occupied in catering to every desire, fulfilling every wish, of the serene couple seated at the table. These wraiths move with such celerity that it is not easy to identify all of them, or always to distinguish them, but the following are seen frequently: Free Competition, Private Property, Principle of Supply and Demand, and the Market. They are observed closely by Justi, whose practiced eye appears to be able to follow their deft movements even when the spectator finds difficulty in keeping them in focus.

The dishes are not actually prepared by these ethereal servants but are stealthily "found" at the edge of the Jungle, and are then discreetly "dressed up" before being served. The consequence is that they are not invariably what they seem, and every now and then when the lid is taken off a pot Consumer raises her eyes, wrinkles her nose, tightly puckers her lips, and leaves the table in a high dudgeon. But such as they are, the dishes are provided by a rather bold not to say brutal, crafty not to say covetous, rugged not to say rapacious, and yet withal singularly hard-headed and beady-eyed, race inhabiting the Jungle. These savages (on account of their pronounced tendency toward cannibalism one cannot conscientiously soften that designation) are known as Businesses. Though there appears to be no sharp line of demarcation, two fairly distinct species of this genus may be seen prowling about in the Jungle: the giants and the pigmies. As they play quite diverse rôles in the drama, it is well to bear in mind this peculiar composition of the tribe.

Synopsis

ACT I

The dialogue of Producer and Consumer reveals that the inhabitants of the Jungle are their offspring, directly or indirectly, some of them being of the second or even third generation removed.   They have left home at an early age, however, and now pay little, if any, attention to their simple-minded parents.   The latter are becoming vexed at this studied indifference and persistent neglect and they finally decide to send one of the guards who have been standing very rigid and immobile in the background to fetch the oldest boy home. The guard selected for this job is named State Law.   He sallies forth into the Jungle and presently returns dragging a reluctant pigmy who goes by the name of Elevator Business.   He protests vehemently against being deprived of his "liberty" and against having to "break bread" with his mother and father—especially the former.   He appeals to Justi to free him from the clutches of this "tyrant," the State Law officer, who, he alleges, is only masquerading as Due Process.   The latter alone has power to come into his preserve in the Jungle, he claims, and adds that in any event he is not the oldest boy, or even one of the old boys.   Justi, dozing, does not seem to hear the boy or at least to take his loud complaints seriously.   Brusquely he tells Elevator Business he must mind his parents and do whatever State Law directs in carrying out their commands.[1]   As for his not being the oldest boy, that makes no difference; he is one of the same breed, isn't he?

Producer and Consumer seem to enjoy having "one of the boys" back home again.   They soon learn, however, that he has developed a voracious appetite.   Despite their kind-heartedness in offering him generous portions, he yearns for the wild haunts of the Jungle and presently when they are more than occupied with some of their other recalcitrant offspring, this diminutive Business slips out through an underground passage and makes his way back to the Jungle. State Law still keeps an eye on him but seldom molests him.[2]

---

[1] *Munn.* v. *Illinois*, 94 U.S. 113 (1876).

[2] *Budd* v. *New York*, 143 U.S. 517 (1892); *Brass* v. *Stoesser*, 153 U.S. 391 (1894).

Meanwhile Producer and Consumer decide they must have their oldest boy back so they instruct State Law to go out and fetch Common Carrier Business, wherever he may be found.[1] This proves more of a task than State Law at first realized, for Common Carrier Business had changed greatly since State Law had watched him as a baby playing at his father's knee. He has grown into one of the largest of the giant Businesses and has adopted the nickname of Railroad Business, which he had early acquired in the Jungle from his ruthlessness in driving through to whatever he wanted. Eventually State Law has to ask for the assistance of another one of the guards, named Federal Law,[2] before he can get the old boy out of the Jungle and over into the region of Well-Ordered Economic System. There, still fighting, squirming, and kicking, Railroad Business raises an horrendous cry of oppression. State Law has no authority, he maintains, to compel him to come in and sit meekly down with his parents and live on the thin fare habitually served by Free Competition or the still thinner fare which Producer and Consumer are directing State Law to substitute for it. But the Voice on the Bench, less curtly than in addressing his little brother, nevertheless positively tells him, too, to mind his parents and to do what State Law directs.[3] The Voice does not this time so firmly repudiate the suggestion that State Law and Due Process (a mysterious x of uncertain sex) may not be the same person. The former is accepted as the *alter ego* of the latter, however, for the purpose in hand.

So Railroad Business is compelled to take his place at the table, and his parents are in consequence separated quite a distance on account of his giant stature and great girth. He,

---

[1] E.g., *Laws of Wisconsin*, 1874, c. 273. Act of March 11, 1874. Other statutes, similar in scope and purport, are referred to in the Granger Cases, 94 U.S. 155, 164, 179, 180, 181 (1876).

[2] Act of Feb. 4, 1887; 24 Stat. 379, c. 104; U.S.A., Title 49, c. 1.

[3] Granger Cases, *op. cit.; Ruggles* v. *Illinois*, 108 U.S. 526 (1883); Railroad Commission Cases, 116 U.S. 307 (1886).

too, proves to have developed a remarkable appetite, and he does not relish the strict diet which State Law at the behest of his parents forces upon him. The parents soon become convinced that State Law has too many other duties to enforce effectively the diet regimen upon such a sly and greedy boy as Railroad Business so they determine to appoint a governess for him. A slender and seductive girl called State Commission is selected for this job. Her duty is supposed to be to remain constantly on watch to see that Railroad Business does not help himself to a larger portion of the Maximum Product than Principle of Supply and Demand would sanction. Her ward continually wheedles her and rumors are heard that once or twice, perhaps, their relations may not have been strictly proper. Still Railroad Business hungers for a richer fare.

Five years later (represented by five minutes in the play, to save time!) he turns and appeals once more in a loud voice to Justi, sitting on his bench dreaming dreams of perfect bliss in his enlightened realm. Awakened with a rude shock from his revery, Justi inquires what all the rumpus is about. He is informed by the blustering Railroad Business that State Law and State Commission are "starving him to death" and trying to rape his spiritual bride, the impeccable Private Property. His own parents evidently connive in these evil designs, and hence he and his bride will shortly be quite undone unless Justi, the Omnipotent, comes to the rescue. Justi agrees to take the case under advisement and consider what may be done in the premises. He fears disorderly and mischievous forces may be afoot and is determined to have none of them prowling about in his Well-Ordered Economic System—whatever may happen, perhaps, occasionally, in exceptional cases, according to hearsay at least, out in the Jungle.

Presently, therefore, Justi announces an extraordinary discovery and a firm stand. Speaking in most solemn and oracular tones, he reveals these facts: (1) that Free Competition has "fallen down on its job" in serving Railroad Business at the table of Regulated Equilibrium, though Justi hopes and supposes that it is still faithful to its sacred trust in distributing favors out in the Jungle, (2) that neither the irate parents nor the stern State Law nor the fair State Commission can be relied upon to see that Railroad Business gets a decent living, (3) that State Law has been ogling the chaste Private Property whom Railroad Business claims as his bride, and (4) that this mysterious person, Due Process, has finally been located but her skin is so fair and her constitution is so delicate that Justi deems it unsafe for her to be at large in the company of such rude fellows as the legislative guards, much less in the company of such "slender reeds" as the administrative commissions.[1] Justi will keep her in his own custody, it is announced (with a straight face, not a trace of a smirk), and consult her upon what ought to be done whenever the legislative guards get to "raising a row" and especially when they start disciplining this poor giant Business, who seems to be set upon so heartlessly by all those who might be expected to treat him with due consideration. Justi expresses his grief and chagrin, of course, at the discovery that all this is necessary, but reaffirms his determination at all costs to protect Railroad Business from starvation and Private Property from outrage.

Under this new dispensation, Railroad Business gradually reconciles himself to the loss of his Jungle "freedom." His fare, indeed, is much more plentiful, as well as being undoubtedly more wholesome, than what he had been able to forage out in the Jungle. Of course, at the request of State Law or

---

[1] *C.M. & St. P. Ry.* v. *Minn.*, 134 U.S. 418 (1890); *Reagan* v. *Farmers' L. & T. Co.*, 154 U.S. 362 (1894); *Smyth* v. *Ames*, 169 U.S. 466 (1898). See, Max Lerner, "The Supreme Court and American Capitalism," *Yale Law Journal*, XLII (March, 1933), 668, for an interpretation of the significance of the judicial expansion of the scope of constitutional restrictions embodied in the "due process" clause. Cf., also, the pregnant "ifs" in the concluding paragraphs of Justice Brandeis' dissent in the New State Ice case, 285 U.S. 262 (1932).

Federal Commission or one or another of these meddlesome guards, he is always having to put on gloves or shine his shoes or something of that sort, but whenever any of the orders becomes too onerous, and especially whenever they try cutting down on his rations, he "shows them a thing or two" by appealing to Justi. The latter evinces his good-will by adopting the elastic rule that whatever Railroad Business "reasonably" requires (but not, of course, what he thinks he requires) to keep him strong and fit, that shall he have.[1] Consequently, already a giant, he grows and grows and grows. To speak truly, he gets fat and rather sluggish. Until one fine day an impudent pigmy slips slyly out of the Jungle and grabs some cake right out of Railroad Business's hands and makes off with it. And this he does again, and again.[2] The name of this pigmy is Motor Transport Business. But all of this is getting ahead of the story—or rather synopsis.

Meanwhile, Producer and Consumer, still undisillusioned about the advantages of having "their boys" boarding at home again, command State Law or Federal Law to fetch in others. Despite vehement protests upon being compelled to give up their wild life in the Jungle, Water Supply Business,[3] Stock Yards Business,[4] Gas Business,[5] Street Railway Business,[6] Elec-

---

[1] Ex parte Young, 209 U.S. 123 (1908); Minnesota Rate Cases, 230 U.S. 352 (1913); U. Pacific Ry. v. N. Dakota, 236 U.S. 585 (1915); New England Divisions Case, 261 U.S. 184 (1923); Banton v. Belt Line Ry., 268 U.S. 413 (1925); O'Fallon Ry. v. U.S., 279 U.S. 461 (1929).

[2] Motor Bus and Motor Truck Operation, Docket No. 18300, 140 I.C.C. 685 (1928); Co-ordination of Motor Transportation, Docket No. 23400, 182 I.C.C. 263 (1932).

[3] Spring Valley Water Works v. Schottler, 110 U.S. 347 (1884); San Diego Land Co. v. National City, 174 U.S. 739 (1899); Knoxville v. Water Co., 212 U.S. 1 (1909).

[4] Cotting v. Kansas City Stock Yards, 183 U.S. 79 (1901); Stafford v. Wallace, 258 U.S. 495 (1922).

[5] Willcox v. Gas Co., 212 U.S. 19 (1909). Also, State v. Columbus Gas Co., 34 Ohio St. 572 (1879); Des Moines Gas Co. v. Des Moines, 238 U.S. 153 (1915).

[6] Galveston Elec. Co. v. Galveston, 258 U.S. 388 (1922). Also, State

tricity Business,[1] Telephone Business,[2] Ferry Business,[3] Insurance Business,[4] Banking Business,[5] Pipe Line Business,[6] Taxicab Business,[7] to mention no others, are collared by stern State Law and seated at the parental table. There each reaches at once for a sizable portion of the Maximum Product, and the unfortunate parents begin to think that they will do well if given an opportunity to "lick the platter" after each meal.

But before the process of bringing the wandering sons into the Well-Ordered Economic System has proceeded quite to this stage Justi, consulting Due Process, decides to limit the traffic. Listening to the cries of Packing Business,[8] Coal Business,[9] Gasoline Business,[10] Brokerage Business,[11] and Ice Business,[12] he orders State Law to release these boys and let them return to the Jungle. The explanation given is that it is an "unreasonable and arbitrary" interference with the private rights of these Businesses, contrary to the injunction of Due

---

v. *Spokane Ry. Co.*, 19 Wash. 518 (1898); *Detroit* v. *Street Railway*, 184 U.S. 368 (1902).

[1] *Jones* v. *North Ga. Elec. Co.*, 125 Ga. 618 (1906); *Union Dry Goods Co.* v. *Georgia P. Serv. Co.*, 248 U.S. 372 (1919).

[2] *C. & P. Telephone Co.* v. *Manning*, 186 U.S. 238 (1902). Also, *State* v. *Bell Telephone Co.*, 36 Ohio St. 296 (1880); *Home Telephone Co.* v. *Los Angeles*, 211 U.S. 265 (1908).

[3] *The Nassau*, 188 Fed. 46 (1911). Writ of certiorari denied. *City of N.Y.* v. *U.S.*, 223 U.S. 722 (1911). *Nearhoff* v. *Washington*, 134 Wash. 677 (1925).

[4] *German-Alliance Insurance Co.* v. *Kansas*, 233 U.S. 389 (1914); *O'Gorman* v. *Hartford Fire Ins. Co.*, 282 U.S. 251 (1931).

[5] *Noble State Bank* v. *Haskell*, 219 U.S. 104 (1911).

[6] Pipe Line Cases, 234 U.S. 548 (1914).

[7] *Terminal Taxicab Co.* v. *D. of C.*, 241 U.S. 252 (1916).

[8] *Wolff Packing Co.* v. *Kansas*, 262 U.S. 522 (1923).

[9] *Dorchy* v. *Kansas*, 264 U.S. 286 (1924).

[10] *Williams* v. *Standard Oil Co.*, 278 U.S. 235 (1929).

[11] *Tyson* v. *Banton*, 273 U.S. 418 (1927); *Ribnik* v. *McBride* 277 U.S. 350 (1928).

[12] *New State Ice Co.* v. *Liebmann*, 285 U.S. 262 (1932).

Process, for their parents to reclaim them. "But," plead the parents, "they are our offspring, precisely as much and by the same token as all these other boys whom you have allowed to be brought in and seated at the table of Regulated Equilibrium. It looks to us as though Due Process were the 'arbitrary' creature. Who is that little hussy to tell us what we may or may not do with our own children?" Justi, playing safe, ignores the insult to his concubine and with pontifical solemnity and a straight face tells the parents that these Businesses which cannot be compelled to come into Well-Ordered Economic System are "not affected with a public interest."[1] Producer and Consumer puzzle over this for a time. They observe that some of the boys released were giants and some pigmies, as also of both species were the boys brought under discipline. Some in each group were fat, moreover, and some lean; some lusty, thick-framed, hairy, and of dark complexion, others with opposite features. There seems to them to be no rhyme or "reason" in the discrimination; but as Justi has said there is one and as they are becoming weaker and weaker from undernourishment, they keep silent.

It is the boys "affected with a public interest" who raise a clamor. They are continually appealing to State Commission for larger and larger slices of Maximum Product. Their appetites seem to have no bounds. If State Commission does not provide them with bigger "helpings," they run to Justi. If Justi thinks it might make them sick, he may deny them what they seek.[2] For example, pie is not good for them.[3] Presently, however, Justi consents to let them have the filling,

---

[1] See Walton H. Hamilton, "Affectation with a Public Interest," *Yale Law Journal*, XXXIX (1930), 1089.

[2] *Railway & Power Co.* v. *Georgia*, 262 U.S. 625 (1923); *Public Service Co.* v. *St. Cloud*, 265 U.S. 352 (1924); *United Fuel Gas Co.* v. *R.R. Commiss.*, 278 U.S. 300 (1929); *Wabash Electric Co.* v. *Young*, 287 U.S. 488 (1933).

[3] *Knoxville* v. *Water Co.*, 212 U.S. 1 (1909); *Willcox* v. *Consolidated Gas Co.*, 212 U.S. 19 (1909).

but not the crust.[1]   And so it goes.   Justi usually orders larger
"portions" or richer fare to be served them, if they demand it.[2]
State Law may then order State Commission to comply.
State Commission, not having received any specifications of
just how much "more" will be "reasonable," issues new orders
upon its own judgment. The boys then challenge these
orders as inadequate, and so new orders from Justi are invoked.
It becomes quite bewildering.   Indeed, the confusion of
orders reaches such a pass that as the First Act closes Producer
is heard to remark to Consumer in a chuckling undertone.
"This is a Well-*Ordered* Economic System, all right." And
Consumer, smiling faintly, replies, "Quite true! Our WOES!"

Act II

The "principles" having been definitely established (1) that
Producer and Consumer may order such only of their own
children brought home to Regulated Equilibrium in Well-
Ordered Economic System as Justi sitting in judgment upon
the "reasonableness" of their decisions chooses to sanction, and
(2) that the disciplinary and dietary measures adopted by
Producer and Consumer for the restored offspring and the
directions pursuant thereto given by the governesses, Federal
Commission and State Commission, are likewise contingent

---

[1] *Gas Co.* v. *Des Moines*, 238 U.S. 153 (1915); *McCardle* v. *Indianapolis
Water Co.*, 272 U.S. 400 (1926).
[2] *Gas Co.* v. *Cedar Rapids*, 223 U.S. 655 (1912); *Denver* v. *Union Water Co.*,
246 U.S. 178 (1918); *Gas & Elec. Co.* v. *Lincoln*, 250 U.S. 256 (1919); *Con-
solidated Gas Co.* v. *Newton*, 258 U.S. 165 (1922); *Electric Co.* v. *Galveston*, 258
U.S. 388 (1922); *Houston* v. *S. W. Bell Telephone Co.*, 259 U.S. 318 (1922);
San Antonio v. *Public Service Co.*, 255 U.S. 547 (1921); *Bluefield Water Wks.* v.
West Virginia, 262 U.S. 679 (1923); *Brush Electric Co.* v. *Galveston*, 262 U.S.
443 (1923); *S. W. Bell Telephone Co.* v. *Missouri*, 262 U.S. 276 (1923);
Utilities Co. v. *Ohio*, 267 U.S. 359 (1925); *Gas and Electric Co.* v. *San Francisco*,
265 U.S. 403 (1924); *McCardle* v. *Indianapolis Water Co.* 272 U.S. 400 (1926);
Patterson v. *Mobile Gas Co.*, 271 U.S. 131 (1926); *United Railways* v. *West*,
280 U.S. 234 (1930); *Smith* v. *Ill. Bell Telephone Co.*, 282 U.S. 133 (1930).

upon the approval of their "reasonableness" by Justi—all this having been firmly settled, Justi now begins to realize that he has assumed a sizable responsibility. Moreover, Producer and Consumer reflecting upon their impotence, under these circumstances, to maintain parental authority and to secure, even, a decent living from the Maximum Product provided, after the "boys" have taken their share, resolve to limit their demands (which are in reality now requests for Justi's permission) for the restoration of their children to those for whom they have an especial affection or who show themselves even more perverse, perfidious, and predatory than the ordinary run of inhabitants of the Jungle—thus jeopardizing all the others. Furthermore, they determine to erect a ban against the unsolicited infiltration of the motley aggregation of Businesses left out in the Jungle, who now observing the easy regimen and abundant fare of the Businesses "affected with a public interest," who have taken Private Property for their spiritual bride and invoked the benign protection of Justi, are plainly to be seen casting envious regards upon their more fortunate brothers.

Accordingly, Producer and Consumer order Federal Law and State Law to "post the premises." This is done by the erection of numerous warning notices, called Anti-Trust Statutes, all along the border between the Jungle and Well-Ordered Economic System.[1] Despite the penalties declared for trespassing, however, the Big Business species of the Jungle population pay slight attention to the posting. One of the first to disregard the warnings is a giant, called Sugar Business. He invades the Well-Ordered Economic System without any stealth whatever, nonchalantly draws up his chair at the table

---

[1] Act of July 2, 1890; 26 U.S. Statutes at Large 209.   15 U.S. Code Sections 1–7.   For summary of state anti-trust legislation, see Joseph E. Davies, *Trust Laws and Unfair Competition* (U.S. Department of Commerce, Bureau of Corporations, 1916), chap. iv; also, note: "A Collection and Survey of State Anti-Trust Laws," *Columbia Law Review*, XXXII (February, 1932), 347.

of Regulated Equilibrium, and prepares to carve himself a nice portion of Maximum Product without any ministration from the Commission governesses of any kind. Producer and Consumer, astonished at this impudence, order one of the guards, called Attorney General, to eject the intruder. This Attorney General attempts to do, but Sugar Business strenuously resists and, having observed the successful tactics of his big brothers already seated at the table, he appeals in a loud wail to Justi. Sugar Business claims that he, too, has taken Private Property for his spiritual bride and therefore is now exempt from the prohibitions of the Anti-Trust Statutes. This sounds reasonable to Justi so he orders Attorney General to release Sugar Business,[1] who forthwith resumes his place at the table.

Thereupon, a great throng of giants from the Jungle troop over the boundary and seat themselves with loud huzzas and a quite uncivil jostling and boasting at the table, where they proceed to the feast.[2] There is no one even to challenge them. Producer and Consumer are indignant but as Consumer expresses it, with a gesture of resignation, "What can one do?" Producer replies, glancing furtively toward the Bench, "Indeed! What *can't* one do—if one is Justi? Or one of these greedy brats!" But, as for protesting, they are too fully occupied in the vain endeavor to get a small scrap of Maximum Product from the platter which recedes farther and farther from their reach as the table is extended to accommodate the invading horde of the Big Business boys. Hence, some time passes while the riotous feasting of the Big Business boys goes on and Producer and Consumer grow thinner and thinner, and weaker and weaker.

Suddenly out of the left wing struts a hero with a Big Stick. He calls himself Trust Buster. He asserts it was all a mistake:

---

[1] *U.S.* v. *E. C. Knight Co.*, 156 U.S. 1 (1895).

[2] See Myron W. Watkins, *Industrial Combinations and Public Policy* (Boston, 1927), Appendix I.

these Big Business boys seating themselves at the table of Regulated Equilibrium in defiance of the posted warning against trespassers. Moreover, even if they are permitted to stay, they should be given, like their brothers "affected with a public interest," a governess to prescribe their diet, see that they do not overeat. Modestly, he offers to serve in that capacity himself, if Producer and Consumer wish. That they do, they allow—better anything than this "feast or famine" experience, with the feast all along the sides of the table and the famine at both ends. Accordingly, Trust Buster appoints Corporation Bureau to watch the Big Business boys, report what they are eating, "appropriating for reserves," etc.[1] Meanwhile, he begins a "free and easy" use of his Big Stick to induce a more submissive attitude, less unruly conduct, among the boys. First he makes ready to swing it on one of the Big Business boys, called Holding Company. This fellow is somewhat of a monstrosity with one head and two bodies. Trust Buster wrathfully denounces the presence of such a giant at the table as contrary to the posted prohibitions of the Anti-Trust Statutes. He demands accordingly that he be decapitated and his two bodies be sent back at least to the edge of the Jungle (provided they should survive the operation, which Holding Company maintains is doubtful), though not so far as to be beyond the surveillance of their governesses. Justi, not without some trepidation and hesitancy, finally orders the decapitation, on the ground that a giant with one head and two stomachs is really a menace to the Well-Ordered Economic System—not to mention to Producer and Consumer![2] The first stroke of the Big Stick accomplishes the severance of Holding Company's head. Miraculously the two bodies still live, however, and presently they are back at the table again.

---

[1] Act of February 14, 1903. 32 U.S. Stat. at large 827.
[2] *U.S.* v. *Northern Securities Co.*, 193 U.S. 197 (1904).

Next Trust Buster picks out a few Big Business boys who have been gorging themselves with least restraint and most unabashed greed, and tells them "to get to the Jungle out of here." The others he admonishes to be good; if they are not the Big Stick will be wielded upon them, too, and if they have any doubts about what amounts to "being good" these may be set at rest by consulting him. This the somewhat mollified Big Business boys do—to their advantage; they find Trust Buster less ferocious in action than in words.[1]

The first group is defiant, however. They laugh at the order to flee to the Jungle. No more of that life for them, they say; and they appeal to their protector, Justi, to humble this swash-buckling Trust Buster trying to make himself a hero in the eyes of Producer and Consumer. They remind Justi of how stalwartly he had defended Sugar Business from no less "arbitrary and unreasonable molestation in the pursuit of his private rights and lawful interests." But somehow these inspiring words do not have quite the same ring to Justi's ears now. He is much impressed with the righteous indignation and *savoir faire* of the new hero, and he observes that Producer and Consumer are all excited about the "progressive" tactics of this chivalrous St. George. After some deliberation, therefore, Justi reluctantly decides to order the removal of Oil Business, Tobacco Business, and Explosives Business to the Jungle again.[2] He will make an example of them. They have exhibited an unseemly disrespect toward their parents. They have not even observed the etiquette of the Jungle. They have been not only carnivorous but cannibalistic, in fact

---

[1] As shown, for example, in the U.S. Steel–Tennessee Coal & Iron episode. Concerning this, consult: *Report on the Steel Industry*, by U.S. Bureau of Corporations (Washington, 1911); also, H. R. Seager and C. A. Gulick, *Trust and Corporation Problems* (New York, 1929), c. xiii.

[2] *U.S.* v. *Standard Oil Co.*, 221 U.S. 1 (1911); *U.S.* v. *American Tobacco Co.*, 221 U.S. 106 (1911); *U.S.* v. *E. I. du Pont de Nemours & Co.*, 188 Fed. (one of Justi's subordinates) 127 (1911).

distressingly savage. But worst of all, they have tried to deceive Justi. They set up that Private Property was their spiritual bride, whereas, he has discovered, that shameless wanton, Monopoly, has been the object of their spiritual courtship, all along. For these offenses—and more—Oil Business, Tobacco Business, and Explosives Business are sent back to the Jungle. But Justi is at pains to point out that it is only for their "unreasonable" conduct in achieving a place at the table of Regulated Equilibrium and in "regulating" themselves after they got there, not the fact that they reached the table, much less the fact that they belong to the tribe of Big Business, for which he has condemned them.

The action of Justi in these cases greatly heartens Producer and Consumer, but his words occasion them profound misgivings. Contrariwise, his action greatly disturbs the Big Business boys still hanging on to their places in the charmed circle of Regulated Equilibrium, but his words are reassuring to their sensitive ears. Producer and Consumer for their part, optimistically choosing to be encouraged more by the outcome than discouraged by the dicta, forthwith decide to undertake a great engineering project. They commission a skilled technician, called Trade Commission, to drain the Jungle and raise its level. For this job they equip him with some brand new tools, called Anti-Trust Amendments.[1] In this manner they think to make the Jungle more habitable, and indeed entertain grandiose hopes of making the place so salubrious that it may scarcely be differentiated from Well-Ordered Economic System itself. Thereupon, they are persuaded, some of the Big Business boys, whose recent influx has made the table of Regulated Equilibrium so crowded and separated Producer and Consumer so far they can scarcely recognize each other, may voluntarily decide to return to the

---

[1] Act of October 15, 1914, 38 Stat. at Large 730; 15 U.S. Code, sects. 12–27. Act of September 26, 1914, 38 Stat. at Large 717; 15 U.S. Code, sects. 41–51.

Jungle. This will "relieve the pressure" all around, they observe.

The Big Business boys, on the other hand, for their part decide to "sit pretty," as the saying goes, and wait to see what turns up. Things happen fairly swiftly, as expected, but alas not, at first, very decisively. Trust Buster follows Trust Buster, but there develops no great exodus of the Big Business boys from their places at the festival board. Some are ordered to go but are permitted to cut off their little toes and to send them off instead.[1] Some "consent" to go, but most of these remain, for one reason or another.[2] Some are permitted to remain.[3] Finally, Justi ends the uncertainty of the status of all these Big Business boys by giving positive assurance to Steel Business, the biggest of the lot, and Shoe Machinery

[1] *U.S.* v. *Reading Co.*, 226 U.S. 324 (1912); cf. however, for subsequent litigation, *ibid.*, 253 U.S. 26 (1920); *U.S.* v. *Great Lakes Towing Co.*, 208 Fed. 733 (1913), 217 Fed. 656 (1914); *U.S.* v. *International Harvester Co.*, 214 Fed. 987 (1914); see also, *The Federal Anti-Trust Laws with Amendments*, List of Cases Instituted by the United States, U.S. Department of Justice, December 31, 1930, p. 117; *U.S.* v. *Corn Products Refining Co.*, 234 Fed. 964 (1916); *U.S.* v. *Eastman Kodak Co.*, 226 Fed. 62 (1915); see also, "List of Cases," *op. cit.*, p. 126.

[2] *U.S.* v. *General Electric Co.*, petition filed March 3, 1911, and decree entered October 12, 1911, in C.C., N.D. of Ohio, see "List of Cases," *op. cit.*, p. 107; *U.S.* v. *Patterson* (National Cash Register Co.), 201 Fed. 697 (1912), 222 Fed. 599 (1915); see also, *U.S.* v. *National Cash Register Co.*, "List of Cases," *op. cit.*, p. 113; *U.S.* v. *Victor Talking Machine Co.*, petition filed and decree entered May 3, 1918, in S.D. of N.Y.; see "List of Cases," *op. cit.*, p. 147; *U.S.* v. *Aluminum Co. of America*, petition filed May 16, 1912, and decree entered June 7, 1912, in D.C., W.D. of Pa.; see "List of Cases," *op. cit.*, p. 55. *U.S.* v. *Burroughs Adding Machine Co.*, petition filed and decree entered March 3, 1913, in D.C., E.D. of Mich.; see "List of Cases," *op. cit.*, p. 125; *U.S.* v. *American Coal Products Co.*, petition filed March 3, 1913, and decree entered March 4, 1913, in D.C., S.D. of N.Y.; see "List of Cases," *op. cit.*, p. 125.

[3] *U.S.* v. *Quaker Oats Co.*, 232 Fed. 499 (1916); *U.S.* v. *Keystone Watch Case Co.*, 218 Fed. 502 (1915); *U.S.* v. *American Can Co.*, 230 Fed. 859 (1916); 234 Fed. 1019 (1916).

Business, almost unique of his kind, that they may remain.[1] No Attorney General shall disturb them, he thunders. In unequivocal terms he defends them against the charge of courting Monopoly, absolves them from all guilt in "crossing the border," declares indeed that they had to do it or else sink from sight in the mire "over there," and even extols them in effusive terms for their alleged contributions to the Maximum Product, the while not even inquiring into their deductions from it. As for the charge that they are big, that their very size is a menace, particularly to Producer and Consumer being crowded farther and farther from the center of the table, Justi dismisses this with a blunt and (in tone) quite convincing: "Size is no offense." Thus is Justi's "rule of reason" confirmed. It has now become quite baldly and quite unblushingly the rule of Justi's reason.

Great pains are taken in a series of solemn pronouncements to make it plain that the "reasonableness" required of Big Business boys by Justi, as a condition of his continued toleration, protection, and good-will is not that they shall retain any of the "competitive" earmarks or traces of their youthful sojourn in the Jungle (that they will lose such traits is taken for granted), nor that they shall exhibit more than a certain sophistication and a minimum of civility (which is to say cool indifference) in their relations to their parents, but above all that they must forsake the practice of cannibalism. Once they have reached the table of Regulated Equilibrium there is no longer need for this antiquated custom, says Justi, and it should be abandoned—except perhaps occasionally, when the Big Business can show that he wants the little brothers whom he reaches over into the Jungle and grabs, not to satisfy his own appetite, but only to add to the Maximum Product! This distinction is a plain one, of course, and is especially marked from the standpoint of the little businesses. This is a great

---

[1] *U.S.* v. *U.S. Steel Corp.*, 251 U.S. 417 (1920); *U.S.* v. *United Shoe Machinery Co.*, 247 U.S. 32 (1918).

triumph for Justi, since it makes his policy—the rule of (his) reason—so crystalline clear.

In these circumstances the Big Business boys obviously have no longer much to fear either from an annoying Trust Buster or from the pestiferous little brothers over in the Jungle. The Big Business boys and they alone, thus far, have been permitted to join the giants and pigmies "affected with a public interest" at the table of Regulated Equilibrium. They are delighted with this arrangement, and duly grateful to Justi for his benign solicitude—for them. His rule of reason—tempered with his faulty eyesight, which prevents him from seeing the size of the slices they are busily engaged in carving out of the Maximum Product—is even more divine than that of the Invisible Hand of Free Competition, who still hovers over the scene but whose lineaments grow ever more ghostly and whose Hand appears now quite atrophied.

The next development is not unexpected. It is fateful, in terms of the classic drama. There is a rush of Big Business boys, now sometimes called Mergers, out of the Jungle.[1] Indeed, for about ten years (ten minutes in the play will suffice) they literally swarm into Well-Ordered Economic System and push their way forward to find advantageous places at the table of Regulated Equilibrium. Producer and Consumer are thus thrust farther and farther apart and their plates at every meal become steadily more nearly bare. They are glad now to get a few crumbs. Contemplating their pittances in contrast to the plenty on the platter of Maximum Product, and reflecting on the enthusiastic hopes with which they had welcomed the first Trust Buster, disillusionment and despair envelop them. In a weak voice, scarcely audible, says Consumer to Producer, "I wonder how our engineering project is developing. Has Trade Commission succeeded in draining the Jungle? Has he raised the plane upon which the

---

[1] See Willard L. Thorp, "The Persistence of the Merger Movement," *American Economic Review*, XXI, No. 1 (March, 1931), 77.

little businesses carry on their playful rivalry?" Dejectedly
Producer replies, "Not so you could notice it, from this distance.   He seems to content himself with putting up 'Keep
Off' signs on one slough or another and warning the boys when
they get close to the brink to run away.[1] But what of it?
That only makes a safer playground for the Business boys;
it doesn't fill our plates—so far as I can see."   Consumer:
"That's no more than I expected.   I was only wondering if
the improved playground for Business might not make a good
burying-ground for us."

ACT III

The population of the Jungle now consists predominantly, if
not exclusively, of pigmies. These little Businesses look
enviously upon their big brothers proudly strutting about in
the Well-Ordered Economic System and at meal time glut-
tonously grabbing whatever they can lay hands upon at the
table of Regulated Equilibrium.   The little fellows counsel
together and decide they will see if they, too, cannot evade the
frontier guards and join the feast.   The first strategy tried is to
form an acrobatic pyramid.   It is something of a circus stunt.
The several pigmies, called Cast Iron Pipe Business, closely
locked together form a sort of agglomerative body roughly
resembling a giant, but the manifold individual shapes of the
constituent members are not concealed.   Justi is not deceived
by this trick, however.[2] He sees at once that this is not a
genuine Big Business but only a crude imitation, properly
denominated an Auction Pool. He orders the acrobatic
pigmies to disentangle themselves and to scurry back to the
Jungle where they belong.

---

[1] "An Appraisal of the Work of the Federal Trade Commission," *Columbia
Law Review*, XXXII (1932), 272.

[2] *U.S.* v. *Addyston Pipe and Steel Co.*, 175 U.S. 211 (1899); see also, *U.S.* v.
Swift & Co., 196 U.S. 375 (1905).

The next strategy tried is to form a huddle under a large cloak, resembling the garb of the Business giants. Only one head protrudes from the collar of the cloak, and the whole group of pigmies thereby address strangers with one voice. This is a favorite ruse for some time. Successively the pigmies called Coal Business, Wooden-Ware Business, Paper Business, and Window Glass Business, to mention only a few, congregate into a compact huddle and, throwing over themselves the cloak of a Joint Selling Agency, advance as nonchalantly as may be, if a little cumbrously, towards the Well-Ordered Economic System.[1] But Justi has an eagle eye for this ruse, and in any case it is not difficult to distinguish the huddle from the giant. The former lacks the stature (financial) of the latter, even though it may wear the same kind of (corporation) cloak. With a dramatic gesture of triumphant wit, therefore, Justi pulls off the cloak from these huddles whenever they come sidling over the border and with a resounding thwack shoves the unmasked pigmies back into the bogs and thickets.

Another strategy tried is called Going Forward While Looking Backward. The procedure here is for a number of pigmies belonging to the same tribe, e.g., the Tile and Mantle Business, simultaneously to start walking backward toward the forbidden land just as though they were unaware of the direction in which they were going. At the same time they pretend to be under a withering fire from some hidden enemies in the Jungle, to which they of course respond with appropriate and not less deadly ammunition. This gives the sortie the aspect of a purely defensive maneuver, and is intended, of course, to enlist Justi's friendly sympathy, thus enabling the embattled forces to reach their objective—a secure place at the table of

---

[1] *Chesapeake and Ohio Fuel Co.* v. *U.S.*, 115 Fed. 610 (1902); (see also, *U.S.* v. *Jellico Mt. Coal Co.*, 46 Fed. 432 [1891]); *Cravens* v. *Carter-Crume Co.*, 92 Fed. 479 (1899); *U.S.* v. *General Paper Co.*, "List of Cases," *op. cit.* (1906), p. 92; *U.S.* v. *Imperial Window Glass Co.*, "List of Cases," *op. cit.* (1910), p. 104.

Regulated Equilibrium. But the pigmies trying this maneuver never get that far. Justi is particularly enraged over having the peace and order of his Economic System disturbed by these belligerent, even if prudentially and defensively belligerent, tactics. He denounces them with gusto and an uncommon heat whenever they come under his observation, as they do, nevertheless, not infrequently.[1]

A fourth strategy tried is to wait for a downpour of infringement litigation and then sally forth from the Jungle under a broad patent umbrella. The idea behind this ruse is that Justi can scarcely be hard-hearted enough to force all of the pigmies collected under the shelter of an umbrella, to which each has contributed a rib, to fold up the handy contraption and take a drenching. This is indeed a crafty trick for besides counting upon ordinary humanitarian motives in Justi's breast, which should make him reluctant to compel even a pigmy to undergo the risk of "taking his death o' cold," it enlists his well-known partiality for patentees. Why should *they*, who had been invited into the Well-Ordered Economic System by the Fathers of the Constitution, be forced back into the Jungle? In truth, this argument profoundly impresses Justi, so much so that he permits to come in under this patent umbrella device the pigmies of the Agricultural Implement Business tribe,[2] as well as some rather good-sized giants of the clan called Shoe Machinery Business,[3] not to mention a group of full-grown giants of the Oil Business breed who had previ-

---

[1] *U.S.* v. *Eastern Lumber Dealers' Ass'n.*, 234 U.S. 600 (1914); *U.S.* v. *So. Wholesale Grocers' Ass'n.*, 207 Fed. 434 (1913); *So. Hardware Jobbers' Ass'n.* v. *F.T.C.*, 290 Fed. 773 (1923); *Binderup* v. *Pathe Exchange*, 263 U.S. 291 (1923); *Wholesale Grocers' Ass'n.* v. *F.T.C.*, 18 Fed. (2d) 866 (1927); cert. denied, 275 U.S. 533 (1927); *U.S.* v. *First Nat'l Pictures*, 282 U.S. 44 (1930); *Paramount-Famous-Lasky* v. *U.S.*, 282 U.S. 30 (1930); *Story Parchment Co.* v. *Paterson Paper Co.*, 282 U.S. 555 (1931).

[2] *Bement* v. *National Harrow Co.*, 186 U.S. 70 (1902).

[3] *U.S.* v. *Winslow*, 227 U.S. 202 (1913).

ously been ejected from the Well-Ordered Economic System "for good and sufficient reason."[1] However, when two other groups of pigmies belonging respectively to the Bathtub Business tribe and the Bumper Business tribe try the same ruse, except that instead of advancing under a broad umbrella they try to get in under a diminutive parasol-like device (à la Beatrice Lillie on parade), Justi tears the make-shift patent parasol from their hands and orders them back into the Jungle.[2]

Thus no strategy for getting over the border seems to be wholly reliable for the pigmy Businesses, and they continue to counsel together upon ways and means of slipping through the frontier guard. Another maneuver devised for this purpose is to persuade one of the Big Business brothers already in the Well-Ordered System to back up to the border, or else to have one of the good-sized Businesses still in the Jungle take the lead, and then set out straight for the table with a whole throng of little Businesses hanging on to his coat-tails. This strategy is called Resale Price Maintenance, but it never succeeds in landing any of the pigmy tribes at the table, despite repeated attempts.[3] Justi is "dead-set against it," as the saying goes.

Still a sixth strategy is known as that of Innocent Pilgrims Looking Heavenward. In this maneuver a group of pigmies form themselves into a band and with devout mien and

[1] *Standard Oil Co.* v. *U.S.*, 283 U.S. 163 (1931).

[2] *Standard Sanitary Mfg. Co.* v. *U.S.*, 226 U.S. 20 (1912); *U.S.* v. *Discher*, 255 Fed. 719 (1919).

[3] *Dr. Miles Medical Co.* v. *Park & Sons*, 220 U.S. 373 (1911); *Bauer* v. *O'Donnel*, 229 U.S. 1 (1913); *Strauss* v. *Victor Talking Mach. Co.*, 243 U.S. 490 (1917); *Boston Store* v. *Graphophone Co.*, 246 U.S. 8 (1918); *U.S.* v. *A. Schrader's Son*, 252 U.S. 85 (1920); *Frey* v. *Cudahy Co.*, 256 U.S. 208 (1921); *Beech-Nut Co.* v. *Fed. Trade Commiss.* 257 U.S. 441 (1922); *Butterick Co.* v. *Fed. Trade Commiss.*, 4 Fed. (2d) 910 (1925); cert. denied, 267 U.S. 602 (1925); *Hill Bros.* v. *Fed. Trade Commiss.*, 9 Fed. (2d) 481 (1926); *Shakespeare Co.* v. *Fed. Trade Commiss.*, 50 Fed. (2d) 758 (1931); cf., however, *U.S.* v. *Colgate & Co.*, 250 U.S. 300 (1919).

measured step they set out over the border. They carry their own Canterbury Tales[1] under their arms and with eyes aloft and hands clasped behind their backs the pilgrimage is calculated to be truly an impressive spectacle. But it does not soften Justi's heart. "Pigmies are pigmies, even when they become pilgrims," Justi declares, "and so long as the Anti-Trust Statutes are posted all over the place I must do my duty." Accordingly, he orders the Hardwood Business pigmies and the Linseed Oil Business pigmies ejected when they come strolling into the System.[2] A little later, however, a group of pigmies belonging to the Cement Business tribe[3] and another of the Maple Flooring Business clan[4] try the same ruse, and this time, *mirabile dictu*, it works! Justi permits these little businesses to stay in the Well-Ordered Economic System, but only on the strict condition that they must not seat themselves at the table of Regulated Equilibrium. He wants it distinctly understood that that is no place for a motley band of pigmies, even if they be devout pilgrims.[5]

There are several other types of strategy successively employed by the pariah pigmies. One is called the Racket strategy and consists of making such a stench that, it is hoped, Justi will turn his head in disgust and the racketeers may steal over to the table. But it does not work.[6] Another is pred-

---

[1] Arthur J. Eddy, *The New Competition* (New York, 1912).

[2] *U.S.* v. *Amer. Column & Lumber Co.*, 257 U.S. 377 (1921); *U.S.* v. *American Linseed Oil Co.*, 262 U.S. 371 (1923).

[3] *Cement Manufacturers' Protective Ass'n.* v. *U.S.*, 268 U.S. 588 (1925).

[4] *Maple Flooring Manufacturers' Ass'n.* v. *U.S.*, 268 U.S. 563 (1925).

[5] See also, *Fed. Trade Commiss.* v. *Pacific Paper Trade Ass'n.*, 273 U.S. 52 (1927).

[6] *U.S.* v. *Brims*, 272 U.S. 549 (1926). Cf., *Industrial Ass'n.* v. *U.S.* 268 U.S. 64 (1925), in which interstate commerce was held not materially, or directly, affected. *Live Poultry Dealers' Ass'n.* v. *U.S.*, 298 Fed. 139 (1924); *Ibid.*, 4 Fed. (2d) 840 (1924); *U.S.* v. *Greater N.Y. Live Poultry Dealers' Ass'n.*, 30 Fed. (2d) 939 (1928); *Ibid.*, 33 Fed. (2d) 1005 (1929); *Ibid.*, 34 Fed. (2d)

icated upon Justi's benign charity toward the aged and decrepit. This does work. Justi weeps copiously and the tears so hamper his vision that he does not observe a Big Business bad boy slinking into the forbidden land behind the backs of a group of senile, old pigmies of the same Window Glass Business tribe.[1]

The cumulative frustration represented by the repeated failures of these, as they believe, adroit attempts to secure admission to the Well-Ordered Economic System, and particularly to reach the table of Regulated Equilibrium, finally leads some of the pigmies to exasperation. The little fellows of the Sanitary Pottery Business tribe, in desperation, determine to make a bold march, without any pretense, directly into the forbidden territory.[2] But Justi is neither nonplussed nor overawed. With cool dignity and great patience he explains to them that their action is not "reasonable," that therefore it violates the law, as he has more than once before told them. They retort that he has found it "reasonable" for the Big Business boys to do just what they are attempting.[3] "But that is different," says Justi, in a tone of finality, and terminates the proceedings abruptly with a solemn warning to the offenders to "return to the Jungle and be good little boys."

---

967 (1929); *Ibid.*, 47 Fed. (2d) 156 (1931); *Ibid.*, cert. denied, 51 Sup. Ct. Rep. 486 (1931); see also, *People* v. *Baff*, 166 N.Y. Supp. 136 (1917); a petition in equity against this same group was filed in D.C., S.D. of N.Y., Feb. 7, 1930. This case went to trial on November 15, 1931, and a decree adverse to the defendants (save 2) was entered on December 5, 1931 ("List of Cases," *op. cit.*, p. 217); appeal pending before U.S. Supreme Court; arguments heard April 24, 1933 (see *N.Y. Times*, April 25, 1933, p. 18, col. 6).

[1] *National Ass'n. of Window Glass Manufacturers* v. *U.S.*, 263 U.S. 403 (1923).

[2] *U.S.* v. *Trenton Potteries*, 273 U.S. 392 (1927).

[3] For an exposition of the argument along this line in behalf of the associative action of independent enterprises, see L. L. Jaffe and M. O. Tobriner, "The Legality of Price Fixing Agreements" by *Harvard Law Review*, XLV (May, 1932), 1164.

The sense of frustration weighs even more heavily on the pigmies, now, and they take common counsel on what stratagem still lies open to them. Some are strongly in favor of trying to persuade Producer and Consumer to repeal the statutes. This suggestion is laughed down. "Where have you been living all these years?" inquire the skeptics of those who advance this proposal. "Do you imagine Producer and Consumer still have something to say about what is the law? Have you never heard of Justi's 'Rule of Reason,' or of his bastard concubine Due Process?[1] Why bother about what the statutes state? If Justi finds them 'reasonable,' they are law; if he finds them 'unreasonable' they go into the discard. Our only chance is in making Justi change his mind, or reason." Someone suggests that he seems to be getting weary, and perhaps they can wear down his opposition. "We've been trying that for forty years," another pipes up, "and here we are right where we started." They all reflect on this disconsolately. Suddenly another pigmy has a bright idea. "Why not combine the best features of some of our previous stratagems?"

This suggestion appeals to a number of the pigmies and after some discussion of their past experience they finally decide to incorporate in one maneuver the least "unreasonable" features of the acrobatic stunt, the huddle with a cloak, the device of Innocent Pilgrims Looking Heavenward, and that of the Old and Decrepit Seeking a Safe Home. No sooner said than done, with these resourceful but not very sanguine little Business boys. They select the Coal Business pigmies as the ones to make the experiment, not because they have any special qualifications under the third heading, rather, despite what might appear to be serious disqualifications on that score,[2] but

---

[1] The illegitimacy of his mistress has never been acknowledged by Justi, but her questionable lineage is traced by Mr. Max Lerner, *inter alia*, in the article upon "The Supreme Court and American Capitalism," *cit. supra*.

[2] See *U.S.* v. *Jellico Mt. Coal Co.*, 46 Fed. 432 (1891); *U.S.* v. *Joint Traffic Ass'n.*, 76 Fed. 895 (1896); *Chesapeake & Ohio Fuel Co.* v. *U.S.*, 115

because they meet the requirements in respect to the adaptation of the last-mentioned maneuver exceptionally well. They are not quite senile but they are mature, and it is a matter of notoriety that they have been badly battered and buffeted of recent years by the aggressive young businesses of the Petroleum and the Electricity tribes. Presently the chosen members of the expedition are trained for their acrobatic parts, a large cloak is ready with ample folds, and a quite innocent-looking "head" has been found with soulful eyes practiced in moon-gazing and with a most mellifluous voice. The completed outfit, called Appalachian, has not a few points of similarity to the Trojan Horse. And not unlike that classic steed it proves to be the instrument of a successful ruse.

Advancing over the border slowly and cautiously, but without the slightest suggestion of stealth, it is at once challenged by one of the guards marshaled along the frontier by Attorney General. He inquires what this Jungle beast is doing in the Well-Ordered Economic System. The "head" replies that it is not a Jungle beast at all, but a new kind of Big Business coming to take its place at the table of Regulated Equilibrium. "And just consider," it adds, with a look of injured innocence, "how much I have suffered in that chaotic Jungle, where I do not belong, what an undernourished body I have beneath this fine caparison, which I have just now thrown over my emaciated skeleton as a garb more fitting to a resident in the Well-Ordered Economic System, how strong and sinewy I shall become, living at the table, how much more work I can then do, how docile and dutiful I shall be. But, above all,

---

Fed. 610 (1902); *Union Pacific Coal Co.* v. *U.S.*, 173 Fed. 737 (1909); *U.S.* v. *Lake Shore & M.S. Ry.*, 203 Fed. 295 (1912); *U.S.* v. *Aileen Coal Co.*, "List of Cases," *op. cit.*, p. 138; *U.S.* v. *Algoma Coal Co.*, "List of Cases," *op. cit.*, p. 138; *U.S.* v. *Baker-Whitely Coal Co.*, "List of Cases," *op. cit.*, p. 139. The foregoing cases relate to the bituminous branch of the coal industry. For the anthracite branch, see: Note, "Judicial History of the Anthracite Monopoly," *Yale Law Journal*, XLI (1932), 439.

kind sir, I beg you to bear in mind my devotion to Free Competition. She is, indeed, if you must know, though we had
planned to keep it a secret, my betrothed. Oh! I pray you,
sir, do not separate me from my beloved, from my spiritual
bride—the lovely Free Competition!" So speaking, the
"head" turns its glance Heavenward and, fixing its gaze
resolutely upon the wraith of its spiritual bride, permits the
guard to lead it before the Bench.

Despite these fine protestations of innocence and pietistic
devotion, Justi at first regards the disjointed behemoth with
some misgivings, bordering on skepticism.[1]   But as it prances
back and forth in front of him, in judicial horse-play, a growing
appreciation of the artfulness of the creature can be observed.
moreover, as Justi never leaves his Bench, perched on the little
eminence, he is not in position to give the thing a close examination; and in any case Justi is no David Harum. So he finally
pronounces Appalachian "reasonable,"[2] and the Coal Business pigmies inside let out a joyous whoop, in their exultation
almost forgetting that it is an essential part of the maneuver
that they speak with one voice. But quickly they remember
that this is "a business proposition," after all, and forthwith
Appalachian draws up a chair to the table of Regulated
Equilibrium and prepares to help itself to a generous portion of
the Maximum Product. Thereupon all the pigmies of the
Lumber Business, the Paper Business, the Copper Business,
the Glass Business, and, indeed, all of the inhabitants of the
Jungle except the members of an inferior breed, called dwarf
pigmies, come galloping over to the left side of the stage, using
the same ruse. The Jungle shrinks to a narrow strip and the
table is extended to accommodate all these new recruits to the
Well-Ordered Economic System and the benevolent protection of Justi. The ends of the table disappear in the wings,

---

[1] *U.S.* v. *Appalachian Coals, Inc.*, 1 Fed. Supp. 339 (1932).
[2] *Appalachian Coals, Inc.* v. *U.S.*, 288 U.S. 344 (1933).

Producer and Consumer being crowded off stage. Thence come plaintive, almost inaudible, pleadings, "If it please Your Supreme Highness, where do we come in—or get off?" Justi, not quite hearing all of the question, replies: "You may not come in! Don't you see that I am very, very busy? I have my hands full in trying to work out a division of the meager Maximum Product so as to provide a 'fair and reasonable' portion for each of these Businesses. To keep them satisfied engages all of my time, energy, and patience. So run along with you! And don't complain, for you might disturb Business. Justi's will be done!"

Curtain

4

UNFAIR COMPETITION*

By Milton Handler†

I

There is probably no term in law or economics which is more difficult to define than "unfair competition." The phrase is obviously more of an epithet than a word of art. Its legal usage embodies a conclusion rather than the means of determining the legality of business behavior. Definition by illustration merely exhibits a multiplicity of usage rather than any identity of meaning. Temporal and personal factors are also significant. What was fair yesterday may be unfair today. What is deemed unfair by one group of business men may be regarded as eminently proper by another. What is offensive to a commission may be palatable to the courts. There are other variables. Practices that are economically justifiable in one industry may be reprehensible in others. What is harmless to competitors may be harmful to consumers and *vice versa*. Business men, economists, courts, legislatures, and administrative agencies have arduously striven to chart

* *Iowa Law Review*, Volume XXI, Number 2, January 1936, Pages 175–262. Reprinted by the courtesy of the State University of Iowa and the author.

This paper is based in part upon a chapter, in the preparation of which, the writer collaborated with Dr. Leverett S. Lyon of the Brookings Institution, and which is to be included in a forthcoming book by Dr. Lyon. I wish to acknowledge my indebtedness to Dr. Lyon for his generous permission to base my treatment on this study and for the many stimulating ideas I have acquired from him.

† Associate Professor of Law, Columbia University School of Law.

the boundaries of this unruly concept, to give it some definite content without destroying the elasticity which is its chief virtue. We shall examine in this paper these varied attempts to establish and enforce a plane of competition and we shall seek to discover what, if any, are the common ideas that underlie such efforts.

II

It is important at the outset to consider the economic setting and presuppositions of the legal doctrines of unfair competition. Basic to the concept, obviously, is the existence of a free competitive system. The long struggle in English economic history for the recognition of the privilege to compete is not always kept in mind.[1] In a society resting upon status and custom, dominated by the Christian notions of a fair price, in which the primary aim of production is use rather than profit, and in which there is ample business for every one, as measured by the modest ambitions of the age, there are lacking the conflicts of interest that engender the major improprieties of business

---

[1] On the exclusive privileges of fairs and markets see 1 Lipson, An Introduction to the Economic History of England (4th ed. 1926) 196–237. On the laws relating to forestalling, regrating and engrossing see Jones, Historical Development of the Law of Business Competition (1926) 35 Yale L. J. 906–920; King v. Waddington, 1 East 143 (K. B. 1800). On the guild system see Gross, The Gild Merchant (1890); 1 Lipson, *op. cit. supra*, 238–390; Cheyney, An Introduction to the Industrial and Social History of England (rev. ed. 1920) 51–62; 1 Ashley, An Introduction to English Economic History and Theory (4th ed. 1909) 67–113; Oliphant, Cases on Trade Regulation (1923) intro., 1–33; Marshall, The Emergence of the Modern Order (1929) 104–131; Toulmin Smith, English Guilds (1870); Riley, Memorials of London and London Life in the 13th, 14th, and 15th Centuries (1868); Case of the Tailors, *etc.* of Ipswich, 11 Co. Rep. 53a (K. B. 1614). On monopoly grants from the crown, see Darcy v. Allein, 11 Co. Rep. 84b (K. B. 1614); Statute of Monopolies, 21 Jac. I, c. 3 (1623–4); Gordon, Monopolies by Patents (1897); 4 Holdsworth, History of English Law (1924) 346 *et seq.*

practice.[1] The professional solidarity of the guilds was antagonistic to business rivalries. Such overreaching as there might be was more likely to be practiced upon buyers than upon the fraternal members of one's craft. The guilds, by and large, zealously regulated quality and craftsmanship and when they evaded their responsibilities to the consumer, the state stepped in.[2] The guild regulations thus established norms of business behavior, not, as in modern times, in the guise of regulating competition, but rather in the form of a paternalistic, professional discipline.

Similarly, in the modern capitalistic state, the manner in which monopolistic enterprise is conducted may be controlled by the state, as in the case of public utilities, but such edicts are not part of the competitive etiquette, although they relate to managerial activity no less than the practices that are included in competitive regulations.[3] The institutional patterns of the

---

[1] Hamilton, The Ancient Maxim Caveat Emptor (1931) 40 Yale L. J. 1133; 1 Ashley, *op. cit. supra* note 1, at 126 *et seq.;* 2 *id.* at 391–5; Just Price, 8 Encyc. Soc. Sciences (1932) 505; Marshall, The Emergence of the Modern Order (1929) 217–231.

[2] Case of the Tailors, *etc.* of Ipswich, 11 Co. Rep. 53a (K. B. 1614). On municipal control of the guilds, see 1 Lipson, *op. cit. supra* note 1, at 266–273, 339. On the switch from municipal to national economic control, see 3 Lipson, *id.* at 207 *et seq.;* 1 Cunningham, The Growth of English Industry and Commerce (1925) 261 *et seq.;* 2 *id.* at 25–44. On the control of a specific industry, the cloth trade, see 1 Lipson, *op. cit. supra* note 1, at 406–426. Generally as to regulation of trade at this time, see Government Regulation of Industry, 7 Encyc. Soc. Sciences (1932) 122, 123.

[3] *E. g.*, Interstate Commerce Act, 24 Stat. 379 (1887), 49 U. S. C. A. § 1 (1929); Smith, Dowling & Hale, Cases on Public Utilities (1926); Robinson, Cases on Public Utilities (1926) especially biblio. xi–xxiv. Excluded from consideration are the regulation of monopoly and the various social controls of industry that do not directly relate to the competitive process. Also excluded are the doctrines of restraint of trade and monopoly that are designed to preserve the competitive system. The text is concerned with that area of business life in which competition is the major instrument of social control, in which there are no exclusive privileges, in which freedom

modern authoritarian state make incongruous the current manifestations of unfair competition. Unfair competition is thus the token of free enterprise, of ballyhoo, of market strategy, and of the profit system. The law of unfair competition must consequently be appraised in terms of the fundamental conceptions of the economy of which it is a part, and not by the precepts of some other system.

III

Though definition be difficult, some delimitation of the field is essential. As we are concerned primarily with the legal notions of unfair competition, we must exclude the definitions of theoretical economists or practical business men. If, however, we restrict our inquiry to the judicial, legislative and administrative rulings which explicitly deal with unfair competition, we shall have only an incomplete and distorted picture of the plane of competition established by law. Thus, if, in our survey of the common law doctrines of competition, we were to confine ourselves to the conduct which is injurious to competitors and actionable at their suit, we should be compelled to exclude the topic of false and misleading advertising—an omission which could hardly be defended. Decisions which deny as well as those which affirm liability must be examined. The operation of competitive enterprise is affected by multitudinous regulations designed to protect interests other than those of competitors. It matters not to the business man whether the curb on a particular sales method is imposed by the courts or administrative agencies as a prohibited competitive practice or whether the inhibition is made a statutory crime. Thus the use of lotteries as a sales promo-

---

of trade prevails and the privilege to compete is unrestricted. Competition being assumed, the issue is how and on what plane competitive enterprise may be carried on. Shall it be conducted on the level of the jungle or on some other level, and if so, what? Whether the organization of any area of economic life should be competitive lies beyond the scope of this inquiry.

tional device has long been condemned by statute,[1] but only recently has it been included in the expanding concept of unfair methods of competition which the Federal Trade Commission is developing.[2] Commercial bribery is a further illustration.[3] Similarly, standards of quality and purity may be imposed by statute and enforced criminally by the state[4] and in an action of warranty[5] by the injured purchaser. It would be difficult to conceive of a more unscrupulous competitive practice than adulteration and yet the offense will not be found among the traditional competitive torts.[6] In other words, the plane of competition is determined not only by the horizontal controversies among competitors but also by the vertical conflicts between seller and buyer and by the restraints imposed and enforced by the state.

The inclusion of the latter regulations presents a dilemma to him who desires to depict the impact between competitive enterprise and the law. Every phase of production and distribution is subject to some legal restraint. He who successfully evades his legal obligations obtains a competitive advantage over his law-abiding rivals. Differences in the burden of taxation, exemptions from or disparities in minimum wage, workmen's compensation and other labor legislation, varying restrictions upon the raising of capital, and unequal

---

[1] Pickett, Contests and Lottery Laws (1932) 45 Harv. L. Rev. 1196. Compare the enforcement of such legislation by private injunction, *infra* note 290.

[2] Fed. Trade Com. v. R. F. Keppel & Bro., Inc., 291 U. S. 304 (1934).

[3] Note (1928) 28 Col. L. Rev. 799.

[4] Legis. (1932) 32 Col. L. Rev. 720.

[5] Llewellyn, Cases and Materials on Sales (1930) c. III.

[6] The closest approach to the imposition of such liability is found in cases in which the proprietor of a valuable trademark restrains the use of his mark upon an adulterated product. Nims, Unfair Competition and Trade-Marks (1929) § 297a. In such a case he is seeking to protect the good will which his brand symbolizes, but it is a far cry from these rulings to allow any tradesman to restrain the adulteration of competitive unbranded goods.

transportation charges are but a few examples of regulations, the variations in the incidence of which may produce competitive inequalities. Were all such laws to be included in a treatise on unfair competition, we would find that the "seamless web" had enmeshed virtually the entire legal domain. As some arbitrary delimitation is called for, this paper will be confined to these regulations of courts, legislatures and administrative agencies which relate to the most vital aspect of the competitive process, *viz.*—selling methods.

IV

Unfair Competition and the Courts

The judicial doctrines of unfair competition are essentially the product of the past two centuries.[1] Before reviewing the substantive content of this corner of the law, it is desirable to consider the manner in which the courts approached the subject and the methods and techniques that were employed. The courts did not start with any preconceived notions of the standards of business ethics that might be enforced by the state. Nor was there any deliberate planning or any conscious endeavor to frame a code or index of proscribed business behavior. There were no statutes nor any official declaration of policy to guide the courts. Judicial law-making could not be preceded by any convention of business men or elaborate investigation of economic conditions. Standards of business behavior were formulated by the method of trial and error,

---

[1] For general discussion see Wyman, Competition and the Law (1902) 15 Harv. L. Rev. 427; Rogers, Unfair Competition (1919) 17 Mich. L. Rev. 490; Mitchell, Unfair Competition (1896) 10 Harv. L. Rev. 275; Haines, Efforts to Define Unfair Competition (1919) 29 Yale L. J. 1; Note (1920) 20 Col. L. Rev. 328; Developments in the Law (1933) 46 Harv. L. Rev. 1171; Note (1916) 30 Harv. L. Rev. 166; National Industrial Conference Board, Public Regulation of Competitive Practices (1929); Henderson, Federal Trade Commission (1924); Davies, Trust Laws and Unfair Competition (1915); Green, Relational Interests (1935) 30 Ill. L. Rev. 1.

without any available scientific apparatus by which errors could be detected and corrected.

The impetus to judicial intervention came from the aggrieved private suitor who felt the pinch of some species of offensive conduct. The stuff out of which the law of unfair competition could be fashioned consisted primarily of legal concepts previously utilized in analogous situations. If *A* falsely represented that his wares emanated from *B's* factory, the essential issue was whether the deceit practiced upon *B's* customers could be deemed unfair competition to *B*. Once *B's* right to sue was recognized, it was an easy step to clothe it with the vestments of property and assimilate the concepts of trespass to the protection of the good will which the mark or business name symbolized or served to create. Similarly, where *A* assaulted *B's* customers, the question was whether *B* as well as the assaulted customers had an action. *B* sued not as a vicarious avenger of the King's peace, but for the injury to his pocketbook in the loss of actual custom. Here were concrete issues with visible injury to the suitor flowing from the wrong—issues which the common law courts were accustomed to handle. Out of the myriad judicial responses to the claims of suitors was constructed the common law of unfair competition.

Judicial unfair competition is thus a branch of the law of torts. It consists of the traditional torts plus those which inflict some peculiar injury upon competitors. We need not pause to consider such familiar wrongs, as libel, slander, deceit, assault and battery and the like, which may be practiced by a business man upon his rivals. The conditions of liability are not dissimilar to those obtaining in the usual action. Couched in terms of the *prima facie* theory of torts, the sole issue for judicial determination is whether competition constitutes a justification for the intentional infliction of harm. In the case of the traditional torts, the courts have been unfavorable to the claim of competitive privilege.

The question of privilege arises in its clearest form in cases in which complaint is made regarding the normal and usual effects of competition. Thus in the early *Schoolmaster's* case of 1410,[1] suit was brought by two schoolmasters against a newcomer whose competition had brought about a drastic reduction of tuition fees. Recovery was denied on the ground that such injury was *damnum absque injuria*. While this decision was somewhat in advance of its day and did not typify the law of fifteenth century England,[2] it presaged the development of later centuries and laid down a rule which is axiomatic today.[3] It will be observed that competition, though clean and honorable, can work substantial injury upon those already in the field and the damage is no less real because the means by which it was inflicted were lawful. Where the competition is but temporary and is designed to injure others, rather than to advance the defendant's economic interests, liability has been imposed.[4] The element of malice has been stressed,[5]

---

[1] Anonymous, Y. B. 11 Hen. IV, f. 47, pl. 21 (1410).

[2] *Cf.* Anonymous, Y. B. 11 Hen. VI, f. 19, pl. 13 (1433); *id.* at f. 25, pl. 2; and references *supra* note 1, p. 77.

[3] Katz v. Kapper, 44 P. (2d) 1060 (Cal. App. 1935); Goldman v. Harford Road Bldg. Ass'n, 150 Md. 677, 133 Atl. 843 (1926); *cf.* Olmsted v. Maryland Casualty Co., 218 Iowa 997, 253 N. W. 804 (1934); Bell v. Aetna Oil Service, 242 Ky. 471, 475, 46 S. W. (2d) 757 (1932).

[4] Tuttle v. Buck, 107 Minn. 145, 119 N. W. 946 (1909).

[5] Tuttle v. Buck, 107 Minn. 145, 119 N. W. 946 (1909); see Beardsley v. Kilmer, 236 N. Y. 80, 140 N. E. 203 (1923); see also Ames, Tort Because of Wrongful Motive (1905) 18 Harv. L. Rev. 411; Holmes, Privilege, Malice and Intent (1904) 8 Harv. L. Rev. 1; Note (1922) 22 Col. L. Rev. 665. In Passaic Print Works v. Ely & Walker Dry Goods Co., 105 Fed. 163 (C. C. E. D. Mo. 1900), *cert. denied*, 181 U. S. 617 (1901), the court held that malicious competition in the form of sales below cost was not tortious. See also Katz v. Kapper, 44 P. (2d) 1060 (Cal. App. 1935); *cf.* Fleetway, Inc. v. Public Service Interstate Transportation Co., 72 F. (2d) 761 (C. C. A. 3d, 1934); Comment (1934) 34 Col. L. Rev. 1566; and *infra* note 209. The dissenting opinion of Sanborn, J. in the *Passaic* case is a clear exposition of the *prima facie* tort theory, and, together with the brilliant opinion of

but the employment of so slippery a concept has naturally produced much uncertainty. A more objective criterion, although similarly difficult of application, is the permanence of the competition.[1]   Where the competition is permanent, the court is apt to find the motives of the defendant mixed and hence not malicious.[2]   If temporary, without any occasion for the short-lived contest, malice is more easily inferred.[3]   So also, where the means employed are predatory.[4]   Regardless of the vagaries of the malice rule, the point to be noted is that the privilege to compete is not unqualified, even where the manner in which competition is carried on, apart from motive or purpose, is proper. Where the competitive methods themselves are wrongful, that is to say, where the injury springs from conduct which departs from the competitive norm, as in the case of the ordinary torts or the competitive torts, which are about to be reviewed, the bounds of privilege are exceeded.

To the abnormalities of competitive conduct, which constitute the subject matter of the competitive torts we now turn. We shall examine their history, the conditions of liability, the

---

Elliott, J. in *Tuttle v. Buck*, exposes the fallacy of the familiar shibboleth, so frequently encountered in the English cases, that malice cannot convert that which is inherently lawful into an unlawful act.

See also, Landis, Cases on Labor Law (1934) c. II; Note (1922) 35 Harv. L. Rev. 957; Legis. (1931) 31 Col. L. Rev. 687.

[1] Note (1926) 26 Col. L. Rev. 594, 598.

[2] Beardsley v. Kilmer, 236 N. Y. 80, 140 N. E. 203 (1923).

[3] Tuttle v. Buck, 107 Minn. 145, 119 N. W. 946 (1909).

[4] Dunshee v. Standard Oil Co., 152 Iowa 618, 132 N. W. 371 (1911) (bogus independent; following plaintiff's agents; going after plaintiff's business exclusively; creating impression in buyers that defendants' agents were working for plaintiff); Standard Oil Co. v. Doyle, 118 Ky. 662, 82 S. W. 271 (1904) (enticement of employees, boycott, false reports, procuring plaintiff's arrest, molestation of plaintiff's employees); Boggs v. Duncan & Shell Furniture Co., 163 Iowa 106, 143 N. W. 482 (1913) (misrepresentation and price cutting); Note (1914) 27 Harv. L. Rev. 374. The term "predatory" is not very felicitous and is a shorthand expression for the acts summarized in this note.

objectives of the rules and the efficacy of the sanctions fashioned by the courts. This review will also serve to define the boundaries of the plane of competition established by the common law.

Trademarks and Unfair Competition

The origin of the term "unfair competition" is found in the cases dealing with the simulation of trademarks and tradenames.[1] Implicit in such infringements is the representation that the spurious goods were produced by the owner of the mark or name imitated. By means of such deceits, the goods of the imitator are passed off for those of the originator of the mark, with a subsequent diversion of trade. To such improper imitation, the courts applied the name "unfair competition."

Unfair competition in the sense here used must be distinguished from the cognate tort of trademark infringement. A trademark consists of an arbitrary or fanciful word or symbol. A descriptive or generic term which has been associated with a particular article and has come to denote its source, thus acquiring a secondary or non-dictionary meaning, is a trade name. The legal remedy for the protection of trademarks is known as trademark infringement. "Unfair competition" is the remedy for trade names.

Jurists have quarrelled, almost from the beginnings of these actions, as to whether the basis of relief is the protection of the property interest of the owner of the mark or name, or the protection of the public from the deception practiced by the infringer. Both theories have their adherents; both are incapable of explaining all the decisions of the courts.

Two purposes are accomplished by prohibiting deceitful imitation. The expectancy of custom or good-will of the

---

[1] This section is based upon Handler and Pickett, Trademarks and Tradenames—An Analysis and Synthesis (1930) 30 Col. L. Rev. 168, 759. See also Schechter, Historical Foundations of the Law of Trademarks (1925).

owner of the mark—his property—is safeguarded, and, at the same time, confusion of the public is prevented. The tradesman is obviously more interested in the preservation of his good-will than in the protection of the public. By and large, with some notable exceptions,[1] judicial relief has depended upon the concurrence of the dual factors of a threatened diversion of trade and the probable deception of the public.

Numerous distinctions have been drawn between trademarks and tradenames. The conditions precedent to relief differ. A trademark must be affixed to the article with which it is associated; the infringement must similarly be attached to the spurious product. Neither requirement is imposed in the unfair competition action. Trademark rights can be acquired on the basis of some commercial and denominative use of the mark, regardless of the period of use. The use of a tradename, on the other hand, must have been of sufficient duration for an associative significance to have been acquired. Simulation of a tradename will be restrained only if there is a likelihood of confusion of the public. Commercial usage of the identical trademark in the same business field is taboo, regard-

---

[1] *E. g.*, the cases in which the mark is used upon either related goods or upon articles of a totally different nature, outside the field of the proprietor's exploitation. In such cases there is no diversion of trade or confusion of goods, but there may be injury to prestige and reputation, loss of distinctiveness of the mark, and a consequent dilution of its demand-creating properties. Schechter, Rational Basis of Trademark Protection (1927) 40 Harv. L. Rev. 813; Schechter, Fog and Fiction in Trademark Protection (1936) 36 Col. L. Rev. 60; Wilcox, Protection of a Trade Name in New York State (1928) 3 St. John's L. Rev. 1; Oates, Unfair Trade Practices of Non-Competitors (1931) 25 Ill. L. Rev. 643; Note (1925) 25 Col. L. Rev. 199; Note (1927) 75 U. of Pa. L. Rev. 197; Note (1925) 38 Harv. L. Rev. 370; Standard Oil Co. v. California Peach and Fig Growers, 28 F. (2d) 283 (D. Del. 1928); Yale Electric Corp. v. Robertson, 26 F. (2d) 972, 974 (C. C. A. 2d, 1928); Wall v. Rolls-Royce of America, Inc., 4 F. (2d) 333 (C. C. A. 3d, 1925); Walter v. Ashton, L. R. 2 Ch. 282 (1902); Aunt Jemima Mills Co. v. Rigney & Co., 247 Fed. 407 (C. C. A. 2d, 1917), *cert. denied*, 245 U. S. 672 (1918).

less of the element of confusion. A restraint against the infringement of a trademark prohibits any use of the mark. A decree in unfair competition merely requires the cessation of the deceit—the tradename can still be used if care is taken to avoid confusion. A trademark will be protected even against innocent infringement; a tradename, only against fraudulent simulation.

These, in short, are the theoretical differences between the actions.[1] In practice, the differences lose much of their significance. Most of the technical requirements of the law of trademarks can be avoided by framing the cause of action in unfair competition. The weakness of the unfair competition remedy lies in the form of decree which is sometimes granted. This consists of a general prohibition against deceitful competition, with a restraint against the use of the name, unless coupled with a qualification revealing the absence of business connection between the parties to the litigation. Thus, if Arthur Waterman introduces a new fountain pen upon the market, branded with his patronymic, and his product is confused with the renowned pen manufactured by the L. E. Waterman Company, he can satisfy the law's demands by juxtaposing the phrase "Not Connected with L. E. Waterman" to the Waterman brand.[2] That this form of decree

----

[1] See Handler and Pickett, *supra* note 1, p. 85. That most of the differences are but theoretical can be demonstrated by contrasting the decisions and decrees of the courts with their opinions. Thus, the scope of relief and the so-called "fraud" requirement are virtually alike in both actions. The affixation, confusion and secondary meaning rules differ, but analysis reveals that the differences are not very considerable and such as exist are frequently difficult to justify. Only the barest conclusions of our previous study of the subject are stated here. Documentation will be found in the article.

[2] *Id.* at 196. L. E. Waterman Pen Co. v. Modern Pen Co., 235 U. S. 88 (1914). See also Note (1927) 47 A. L. R. 1189; Note (1926) 26 Col. L. Rev. 870; Comment (1925) 38 Harv. L. Rev. 405; Comment (1932) 31 Mich. L. Rev. 292; Developments in the Law (1933) 46 Harv. L. Rev. 1171, 1811.

may engender more confusion than the bare use of the trade-name has often been remarked.[1] It is obvious that unless the public recalls the initials of the maker of the original pen, it may regard the imitation as the original and treat the original as the spurious article. Such limited protection tends to render worthless the remedy of unfair competition, and many, but not all, of the courts have framed their decrees so as to provide more effective relief.[2]

The sole explanation for the limited injunction given by the courts is the expression of fear that, if the infringing use were totally banned, a monopoly of the common words of the language would be vested in the first user. An attempt has been made elsewhere to show the fallacy of this notion and to demonstrate how inept is the term "monopoly" as applied to the exclusive rights acquired in a trademark.[3] It is not difficult to compromise the rival interests of the parties and afford adequate protection to the public without creating "homestead rights" in words of common speech.[4] We have urged the amalgamation of the two actions, the complete obliteration of the lines of distinction that have separated them, the abandonment of the technical requirements that never had any rational foundation and serve no useful purpose, and the

---

[1] *E. g.*, Wigmore, Justice, Commercial Morality and the Federal Supreme Court (1915) 10 Ill. L. Rev. 178.

[2] Compare the Hilton litigation, Hilton v. Hilton, 89 N. J. Eq. 149, 102 Atl. 16 (1917); 89 N. J. Eq. 182, 104 Atl. 375 (1918); 89 N. J. Eq. 417, 106 Atl. 139 (1918); 89 N. J. Eq. 472, 106 Atl. 139 (1919); 90 N. J. Eq. 564, 107 Atl. 263 (1919), with Chickering v. Chickering & Sons, 215 Fed. 490 (C. C. A. 7th, 1914); Westphal v. Westphal's World's Best Corp., 216 App. Div. 53, 215 N. Y. Supp. 4 (1926), *aff'd*, 243 N. Y. 639, 154 N. E. 638 (1926); Tierney Sons, Inc. v. Tierney Bros., Inc., 130 Misc. 428, 224 N. Y. Supp. 144 (Sup. Ct. 1927); and see authorities cited note 2, p. 87, *supra*.

[3] *Supra* note 1, p. 85.

[4] Cohen, Transcendental Nonsense and the Functional Approach (1935) 35 Col. L. Rev. 809, 817.

development of a single action for the protection of the public against the deceitful simulation of commercial brands.[1]

It cannot be denied that the current bewildering use of brands is economically wasteful, and undoubtedly tends to increase the costs of distribution. The tinselled phrase is frequently designed to camouflage shoddiness of quality. The fortunes spent on popularizing catch words and nonsense syllables could better be devoted to the improvement of product and the dissemination of detailed information regarding it, which is so essential to intelligent consumption. But intelligent consumption also requires some means of identifying today the articles that pleased or displeased yesterday. This is the primary function of the mark. The unfortunate excrescences of modern trademark usage should not blind our perception of this fact. The abuses of current merchandising methods should be subjected to a frontal assault.[2] A rear attack, such as denying all protection to advertised brands, would only make an already intolerable situation doubly so. The buyer needs some means of identification and is entitled to protection against confusion and deceit. The best administrative device by which this protection may be afforded is the action by the proprietor of the mark, who, by seeking to prevent the deceitful diversion of his custom, preserves the integrity of his identifying devices and vicariously avenges the fraud upon consumers.

This branch of the law may properly have a further objective. In a property economy, it is difficult to differentiate between the protection of physical objects and the protection

---

[1] This position has been sharply criticized on the ground that it blithely acquiesces in the creation of a new species of property rights and blandly assumes that anything created by effort and expenditure is *per se* entitled to legal protection without regard to the effects of such protection on the public. Cohen, *loc. cit. supra* note 4, p. 88.

[2] Compare, Handler, False and Misleading Advertising (1929) 39 Yale L. J. 22 and pp. 192–193, 230, *infra*.

of a trade expectancy called "good will." It is not easy to perceive how the interests of consumers are furthered by immunizing the deliberate appropriation of an advertising device created by another.[1] Exclusive rights in such devices can be sustained to the extent that they do not unduly handicap the newcomer in the field. His commercial needs should be the true measure of the limited property interests granted the originator of the mark or name by the courts. The mere fact that the exploitation of the mark costs money or has exchangeable value is not controlling. New competition must not be throttled, but the latecomer should be compelled to rely upon his own ingenuity, rather than misrepresentation and misappropriation, for the creation of his market. This much, at least, is demanded by the most elementary notions of honesty.

The changes in this branch of the law, it is submitted, should be directed toward simplification, abandonment of technical and unnecessary requirements, and the perfection of the technique of injunctive relief. Private litigation appears to be the most effective and, by and large, the only necessary sanction.[2] Most of the reforms could be accomplished without new legislation.

The concept of unfair competition has not been confined to the infringement of tradenames. It has been extended to the imitation of labels, packages, color, dress, form and appearance of articles. Passing off, however, is the gist of the offense. It

---

[1] Frequently the plaintiff and his product are unworthy of equitable protection, but that hardly justifies the defendant's deceit. The doctrine of unclean hands could be extended so as to ban the fraud of both parties. Handler, *supra* note 2, p. 89, at 50.

[2] The Federal Trade Commission was rebuked by the Supreme Court in Fed. Trade Com. v. Klesner, 280 U. S. 19, 25 (1929) for intervening in a purely private squabble. It seems desirable for a public agency to devote its energies to competitive abuses which are less likely to be remedied by private action.

matters not what the instrument of deceit may be as long as there is such misrepresentation of origin or source as may mislead purchasers.[1]

The courts might have taken the concept of unfair competition as the basis for prohibiting every trading method that injured competitors or consumers. Some judges have gone so far as to assert that "unfair competition consists in selling goods by means which shock judicial sensibilities,"[2] but this broader meaning of the term has not been commonly accepted. For one thing, as we shall soon see, judicial sensibilities have frequently been shockproof. While the term has been loosely used in judicial decisions to connote various practices, its chief meaning has been and continues to be passing off. Other types of competitive injury have been governed by separate rules and vindicated, in the main, in different forms of action.

Appropriation of Competitors' Trade Values

An infringement of a trademark, as we have seen, involves both misrepresentation and misappropriation. The qualified injunction may in some cases be a sufficient antidote for the misrepresentation. In most cases, however, nothing short of

---

[1] This phase of unfair competition, while not as significant from a theoretical standpoint as infringement of trade names, is probably of greater practical importance. A volume could be devoted to a description of the manifold frauds that have been perpetrated by ingenious businessmen seeking to poach upon the reputation and trade of others. See Nims, *op. cit. supra* note 6, p. 80, IX, X, XIX. Here, more than in the case of tradenames, the courts must be careful lest their decrees establish limited monopolies in the common elements of trade. Yet it is so easy for the trader to endow his product with some distinctiveness that slavish imitation is generally indefensible and bespeaks a dishonest purpose. These problems call for the skillful exercise by the courts of the art of compromise. Consideration of a host of variants of the basic unfair competition pattern must be foregone for want of space. Many are treated in a forthcoming casebook on Trade Regulation which is now in mimeographed form.

[2] Margaret Steiff, Inc. v. Bing, 215 Fed. 204, 206 (S. D. N. Y. 1914).

complete cessation will prevent confusion. Such complete cessation inevitably vests a limited monopoly in the first user, but the monopoly relates merely to the commercial and denominative use of the word or symbol.[1] In this sense, "the mark is property, protected and alienable, although as with other property its outline is shown only by the law of torts, of which the right is a prophetic summary."[2]

Where a new, but unpatented, product is imitated there is a similar possibility of consumer deception. The imitation may, as we have seen, be the instrument by which substitution is accomplished. The deception can be halted by preventing the use of those non-functional and unimportant functional features which are associated with and which identify the original article.[3] It is not essential, however, to place an embargo upon the distribution of the product in order to stop the fraud. But frequently the misrepresentation implicit in the imitation is the opposite of that inherent in passing off. The defendant in such a case does not pretend that his goods emanate from the same source as the plaintiff's. Instead, he reveals his own connection with the goods but represents the plaintiff's product as originating with him. Thus the International News Service circulated Associated Press dispatches bearing its own credit line. Or an original dress style may be copied and then sold as the creation of the copier. The antidote for such misrepresentation is a suitable acknowledg-

---

[1] The scope of the monopoly is considerably broadened when its use in other fields of trade is forbidden. For the cases, see note 1, p. 86, *supra*.

[2] Holmes, J. in Beech-Nut Packing Co. v. P. Lorillard Co., 273 U. S. 629, 632 (1927).

[3] Crescent Tool Co. v. Kilborn & Bishop Co., 247 Fed. 299 (C. C. A. 2d, 1917); Enterprise Mfg. Co. v. Landers, 131 Fed. 240 (C. C. A. 2d, 1904); Globe-Wernicke Co. v. Brown & Besley, 121 Fed. 90 (C. C. A. 7th, 1902); Shredded Wheat Co. v. Humphrey Cornell Co., 250 Fed. 960 (C. C. A. 2d, 1918). *Cf.* Rushmore v. Manhattan Screw and Stamping Works, 163 Fed. 939 (C. C. A. 2d, 1908).

ment of the true authorship.[1] Here again, it is not necessary to prevent the production and distribution of the copies in order to obviate the deception. But it is such prevention which is typically sought by the creator, who complains, not of the misrepresentation, but of the appropriation of his ideas or other trade values. A property interest in the fruits of one's labor, investment, and ingenuity is thus claimed.

But property, as Mr. Justice Holmes has taught us, is the creation of law and does not arise from value, although exchangeable. "Many exchangeable values may be destroyed intentionally without compensation."[2] We need go no further for an illustration than the familiar case where a newcomer, by dint of active but fair competition, encroaches upon the established trade of enterprises already in the field and materially lessens their business opportunities.[3] Whether and to what extent property should be created and under what circumstances compensation should be required for the intentional destruction of exchangeable values raise basic questions of policy. To brand every taking a misappropriation or piracy is to beg the issue.

The right to compete means the right to imitate. Otherwise, the first tradesman who wrapped wax paper about a loaf of bread or who bottled milk would enjoy the exclusive rights to these methods of distribution. How long would these exclusive rights endure? A court cannot restrain a tradesman from copying a style, design, or the shape and appearance of an article without according a monopoly to the first user. For one to reap with impunity the fruits of another's labor may be reprehensible, but the creation of new species of property interests and new series of monopolies by the courts may be disastrous to free enterprise.

---

[1] Holmes, J. in a separate opinion in International News Service v. Associated Press, 248 U. S. 215, 246 (1918).

[2] *Ibid.*

[3] *Supra* notes 1 and 3, p. 83.

It is not to be wondered, therefore, that the courts have found the problems arising out of the appropriation of competitors' intangible trade values the most perplexing of those encountered in the law of unfair competition. The allurements of such formal analogies as the abstraction of physical property and the infringement of trademarks have been off-set by the fear of monopoly. Administrative difficulties have prevented the formulation of any compromise. How new and original should an idea or product be to warrant withdrawal from the public domain? How prolonged and how extensive should the monopoly be? Monopolies created by legislation may be restricted and regulated so as to operate, partially at least, in the public interest. Judge-made monopolies find their origin and their regulation in the law of torts and the protection of the public interest is at best unsystematic and fortuitous.[1]

By and large, the courts have accepted imitation as inherent in the competitive process and have sanctioned the copying of ideas,[2] advertising lay-outs and schemes,[3] styles,[4] designs,[5] and

---

[1] *Cf.* Brandeis, J. dissenting in International News Service v. Associated Press, 248 U. S. 215, 248, 264 (1918).

[2] Haskins v. Ryan, 71 N. J. Eq. 575, 64 Atl. 436 (1906); Universal Savings Corp. v. Morris Plan Co., 234 Fed. 382, 386 (S. D. N. Y. 1916); *cf.* Keller v. American Chain Co., 255 N. Y. 94, 174 N. E. 74 (1930); Moore v. Ford Motor Co., 43 F. (2d) 685, 687 (C. C. A. 2d, 1930); Booth v. Stutz Motor Car Co., 56 F. (2d) 962 (C. C. A. 7th, 1932); Note (1930) 14 Minn. L. Rev. 537; Note (1934) 47 Harv. L. Rev. 1419.

[3] Westminster Laundry Co. v. Hesse Envelope Co., 174 Mo. App. 238, 156 S. W. 767 (1913); Comment (1913) 27 Harv. L. Rev. 99; Armstrong Seatag Corp. v. Smith's Island Oyster Co., 254 Fed. 821 (C. C. A. 4th, 1918); Note (1932) 45 Harv. L. Rev. 542.

[4] Montegut v. Hickson, 178 App. Div. 94, 164 N. Y. Supp. 858 (1917) *semble;* Legis. (1931) 31 Col. L. Rev. 477.

[5] Cheney Bros. v. Doris Silk Corp., 35 F. (2d) 279 (1929), *cert. denied,* 281 U. S. 728 (1930); Note (1930) 14 Minn. L. Rev. 537; Comment (1930) 30 Col. L. Rev. 135; Comment (1929) 43 Harv. L. Rev. 330; Comment (1930) 16 Va. L. Rev. 617.

the physical appearance of articles of trade in the absence of passing off[1] or other fraudulent methods.[2] When passing off occurs, the law steps in merely to stop the deception but not the imitation.[3] The only authoritative decision in which copying itself was restrained was *International News Service v. Associated Press*.[4] There the International News Service was prohibited from reprinting and circulating the Associated Press dispatches without verification, independent investigation and compilation. Many commentators, relying upon the broad language of the Court, have treated the decision as enunciating a new principle of unfair competition.[5] Under the new concept, it is tortious for a competitor to reap the fruits of another's efforts and expenditures. But the courts have shown little inclination to apply the principle of the

---

[1] Keystone Type Foundry v. Portland Publishing Co., 186 Fed. 690 (C. C. A. 1st, 1911); Eisenstadt Mfg. Co. v. Fisher Co., 241 Fed. 241 (C. C. A. 1st, 1917); Rathbone, Sard Co. v. Champion Steel Range Co., 189 Fed. 26 (C. C. A. 6th, 1911); Clipper Lacer Co. v. Detroit Lacer Co., 223 Mich. 399, 194 N. W. 125 (1923).

[2] Montegut v. Hickson, 178 App. Div. 94, 164 N. Y. Supp. 858 (1917); Margolis v. National Bellas Hess Co., 139 Misc. 738, 249 N. Y. Supp. 175 (Sup. Ct. 1931).

[3] *Supra* note 3, p. 92.

[4] 248 U. S. 215 (1918, discussed in Note (1918) 18 Col. L. Rev. 257; Comment (1919) 13 Ill. L. Rev. 708; Comment (1919) 28 Yale L. J. 387; Rogers, Unfair Competition (1919) 17 Mich. L. Rev. 490; Note (1919) 32 Harv. L. Rev. 566; Note (1919) 4 Corn. L. Q. 223; Note (1919) 67 U. of Pa. L. Rev. 191; Comment (1928) 8 Boston U. L. Rev. 303. As to rights in literary property, see Comment (1922) 22 Col. L. Rev. 182; Note (1922) 35 Harv. L. Rev. 600; Note (1930) 15 Corn. L. Q. 633; Note (1918) 18 Col. L. Rev. 257; *cf.* Uproar Co. v. National Broadcasting Co., 8 F. Supp. 358 (D. Mass. 1934); Comment (1935) 83 U. of Pa. L. Rev. 385. See also, Fonotipia, Ltd. v. Bradley, 171 Fed. 951 (C. C. E. D. N. Y. 1909); Associated Press v. Station KVOS (C. C. A. 9th, 1935) reported N. Y. Times, December 17, 1935, restraining the repetition of A. P. despatches over the radio, and reversing 9 F. Supp. 279 (W. D. Wash. 1934).

[5] *E. g.* Note (1919) 32 Harv. L. Rev. 566; Rogers, Unfair Competition (1919) 17 Mich. L. Rev. 490; and authorities cited note 4 above, *supra*.

News Case to other types of copying.[1] Thus, an original design for silk fabrics may be copied with impunity.[2] In fact, virtually all the imitations allowed before this decision are still permitted today.[3] We must look to the legislature for any fundamental change of doctrine and for the shaping of the compromise which will provide some measure of protection to the fruits of originality without shackling the competitive system.[4] For myself, I am dubious whether the price to the consumer may not be too high for any compromise to operate in the public interest.

The interest in trade secrets and other confidential information bears a close kinship to the trade values just considered, but rests upon a more substantial legal foundation. It is not easy to define a trade secret or to reconcile the jarring theories of the courts regarding the nature of the interest or the basis of its protection.[5] For present purposes, it is sufficient to note

---

[1] Note (1932) 45 Harv. L. Rev. 542; Developments in the Law (1933) 46 *id.* at 1171, 1173, 1196; Note (1934) 47 *id.* at 1419; Legis. (1931) 31 Col. L. Rev. 477. See also Gotham Music Service v. D. H. Music Publishing Co., 259 N. Y. 86, 181 N. E. 57 (1932).

[2] See *supra* note 5, p. 94.

[3] See *supra* note 51. But *cf.* Hughes, C. J. in Schechter Poultry Corp. v. United States, 295 U. S. 495, 532 (1934): "It [unfair competition] has been held to apply to misappropriation as well as misrepresentation, to the selling of another's goods as one's own—to misappropriation of what equitably belongs to a competitor." *Cf.* Comment (1932) 32 Col. L. Rev. 1447.

[4] The proposed federal legislation on design copyright is analyzed and criticized in an excellent note in (1931) 31 Col. L. Rev. 477. Many N.R.A. codes sought to perfect machinery for the protection of original designs. See also Developments in the Law (1933) 46 Harv. L. Rev. 1171, 1196; and the design patent law, 32 Stat. 193 (1902), 35 U. S. C. A. § 73 (1929), and the English Patents and Designs Acts, 7 Edw. VII, c. 29 (1907); 9 & 10 Geo. V, c. 80 (1919).

[5] For a full discussion see Note (1919) 19 Col. L. Rev. 233; Note (1923) 23 Col. L. Rev. 164; Note (1928) 42 Harv. L. Rev. 254; Nims, Unfair Competition and Trade-Marks (1929) c. 11; Note (1928) 6 Texas L. Rev. 502; Comment (1928) 37 Yale L. J. 1154; Note (1930) 14 Minn. L. Rev. 546;

that a court of equity will prevent by injunction the betrayal of the secret or its disclosure, acquisition or use in breach of confidence. Only such information as is unique and outside the fund of common knowledge will be thus protected. And it is essential that the formulas, mechanisms, and processes be held secret in fact and that reasonable efforts be taken to prevent their disclosure.

The relation of trade secrets to the plane of competition is twofold. Typically, the secrets are exploited by a former employee in competition with the original possessor of the valuable information. In many cases, competitors actively induce the employees of a rival to betray their confidence and then make competitive use of the knowledge thus obtained. Apart from the acquisition of trade secrets, espionage does not appear to have been tortious at common law.

The underlying philosophy of the law of trade secrets is similar to that of the patent system. In both cases, monopoly privilege is the stimulant and reward for inventiveness. The originator may patent his device or utilize it secretly. If patented, the monopoly has but a limited duration. If kept secret, it endures until independently discovered by others. The monopoly cannot be destroyed by a betrayal of confidence. It yields however to honest discovery.

False Advertising and Misbranding

The prevalence of misrepresentation and misbranding in modern business is too well known to require any demonstration here.[1] The question to be considered at this point is

---

Whitlock, The Law as to Trade Secrets (1912) 74 Cent. L. J. 83. The cases conflict as to whether customers' lists constitute a trade secret. Compare Colonial Laundries v. Henry, 48 R. I. 332, 138 Atl. 47 (1927) with Progress Laundry Co. v. Hamilton, 208 Ky. 348, 270 S. W. 834 (1925); Note (1923) 23 A. L. R. 420; Note (1925) 34 A. L. R. 399; Note (1928) 54 A. L. R. 343.

[1] Chase & Schlink, Your Money's Worth (1927); Kallett & Schlink, 100,000,000 Guinea Pigs (1933); Phillips, Skin-Deep (1934); Schlink, Eat,

whether false advertising constitutes unfair competition at common law. In what way is an honest competitor injured by his rival's falsehoods? The clearest case of such injury occurs when the misrepresentation is employed to divert business that normally would go to the honest tradesman. Thus if *A* is known in the market as the sole producer of burglar-proof safes, *B's* false claim that his safes are burglar proof may divert trade that was destined for *A*. Similarly, a campaign of false advertising may completely discredit the product of an industry, destroy the confidence of consumers and impair a communal or trade good will. Less tangible but nevertheless real is the injury suffered by the honest dealer who finds it necessary to meet the price competition of inferior goods, glamorously misdescribed by the unscrupulous merchant. The competition of a liar is always dangerous even though the exact injury may not be susceptible of precise proof.

Notwithstanding the manifest harm caused by these deceitful practices, the courts, in the main, have denied relief to the aggrieved competitor. In the classic *Washboard* case,[1] a court composed of Taft, Lurton and Day, JJ., refused to enjoin the defendant's misbranding of zinc boards as aluminum at the

---

Drink and Be Wary (1935); Harding, Fads, Frauds and Physicians (1930); 1 Law and Contemporary Problems, No. 1—The Protection of the Consumer of Food and Drugs (1933); Bulletins of Consumers' Research.

[1] 103 Fed. 281 (C. C. A. 6th, 1900). See also Motor Improvements, Inc. v. A. C. Spark Plug Co., 5 F. Supp. 712 (E. D. Mich. 1934). Similarly, the false claim to testimonials and prizes awarded another is not actionable. Singer Mfg. Co. v. Domestic Sewing Machine Co., 49 Ga. 70 (1872); Centaur Co. v. Marshall, 92 Fed. 605, 612 (C. C. W. D. Mo. 1899), *aff'd*, 97 Fed. 785, 790 (C. C. A. 8th, 1899); Batty v. Hill, 1 Hem. & M. 264 (Ch. 1863); Tallerman v. Dowsing Radiant Heat Co., L. R. 1 Ch. 1 (1900). Legislation forbidding the appropriation of another's prizes and testimonials has been enacted in England and some states. 26 & 27 Vict., c. 119 (1863); Pa. Stat. Ann. (Purdon, 1930) § 7671; 2 Cal. Gen. Laws (Deering, 1931) Act 6758; Mass. Gen. Laws (1932) c. 266, § 90; S. D. Rev. Code (Michie, 1932) § 4257; 1 Md. Ann. Code (Bagby, 1924) art. 27, c. 182.

suit of the sole manufacturer of aluminum washboards. There was no claim of passing off. The theory of the suit was that the misbranding was apt to divert the trade of those who desired the genuine product to the consequent injury of the plaintiff. The court, however, ruled that a competitor may not sue to prevent a fraud upon the public and confined the law of unfair competition to the traditional case of passing off.

The essence of palming off, as we have seen, is the diversion of trade by means of a misrepresentation of the source of the defendant's goods. It seems peculiar that diversion accomplished by a misrepresentation of a different character should be immune from liability. The injury rather than the means of its infliction should be controlling. This was perceived by Learned Hand, J., in *Ely-Norris Safe Co. v. Mosler Safe Co.*,[1] who ruled that misbranding is actionable where it results in a loss of customers. In the absence of such proof, he asserted, no action can be maintained, either at law or in equity, since the honest dealer cannot sue as "the vicarious avenger of the defendant's customers." The Supreme Court reversed this ruling on the ground that the complaint did not sufficiently allege that the plaintiff was the sole manufacturer of the genuine product and hence there was no foundation for the alleged claim of loss of sales.[2] Under this decision, competitive misrepresentations can be restrained only where the plaintiff is the sole competitor in the field. It is to be observed that this decision goes no further than to suggest that misappropriation plus misrepresentation of a character different from that involved in passing off may in very special circumstances be actionable. There is no suggestion that misrepresentation, by itself, would be tortious to competitors. While there are several lower court decisions granting relief where there was no loss of customers,[3] the *Washboard* and the *Norris* decisions are

---

[1] 7 F. (2d) 603, 604 (C. C. A. 2d, 1925).

[2] Mosler Safe Co. v. Ely-Norris Safe Co., 273 U. S. 132 (1927).

[3] Handler, False and Misleading Advertising (1929) 39 Yale L. J. 22, 37.

the more authoritative and, in effect, hold that false advertising is not unfair competition. Whatever recession from the inhospitable ruling in the *Washboard* case may occur, there seems little likelihood that the injury to communal good will or the competitive inequalities resulting from the practice will be deemed a sufficient basis for private action. The rule of the *Norris* case, even if adopted generally, would be of limited utility in combating misbranding.

Other ways of forbidding false advertising have been devised. The buyer may sue in deceit or warranty;[1] the state may prosecute for false pretenses or for violation of the model false advertising statute;[2] the federal government may bar the use of the mails;[3] and the Federal Trade Commission may issue orders to cease and desist.[4] Non-legal agencies such as Consumers' Research, the American Medical Association and the Better Business Bureau play a significant role in the elimination of this annoying competitive abuse. The efficacy of these sanctions has been reviewed elsewhere.[5] The role of the Federal Trade Commission and the legislature in the control of competition and their contribution to the solution of the advertising problem will be discussed later. At this point it is desirable to canvass the reasons for the common law's failure to suppress this evil.

First and foremost is the faulty definition of the offense. A misrepresentation, to be actionable, must relate to matters of

---

A species of false advertising and misbranding which has been held subject to injunction is the use of a mark upon inferior or second-quality goods on the representation that they are of usual quality. Nims, *op. cit. supra* note 6, page 80, § 297.

[1] *Infra* p. 230.

[2] *Ibid.* Additional state legislation on labelling, misbranding, marks of origin, *etc.* is cited *infra* pp. 233–234.

[3] *Infra* p. 229. The false use of geographical terms is forbidden by federal act. 41 Stat. 534 (1920), 15 U. S. C. A. § 123 (1926).

[4] *Infra* at p. 241.

[5] *Supra* note 3, page 99.

fact rather than opinion. This gives full rein to the imaginative copywriter who achieves his misleading effects by the shrewd use of exaggeration, suggestion, ambiguity, innuendo and half-truth. Moreover, the friendly doctrine of "sellers' puff" has proven to be a convenient shield for the deceitful advertiser.

Secondly, the procedural requirements of scienter, reliance, materiality, privity of contract, and proof of damage have shorn the common law remedies of deceit and warranty of most of their practical effect. While the cumulative harm to consumers may be great, only in the rare case will the loss to any one purchaser warrant the institution of proceedings.

Finally, little imagination has been displayed in forging effective remedies. The traditional sanctions of criminal penalty, damages and injunction constitute but pin-pricks, where, as here, the practice is widespread and the gains of knavery are high. The competitor who is most likely to take action is not permitted, as we have seen, to bring suit. The remedy, developed by the German courts, of injunctive suits by trade associations is not available here.[1] This sanction avoids the danger of the harrassing strike suit which private competitive action invites. Compulsory retraction, publication of judgments, and the imposition of liability upon the publishing medium have never been attempted by the courts.

Not only have the courts failed to develop remedies of their own to curb misrepresentation, but they have frustrated the legislative efforts to cope with the problem. The Federal Food and Drugs,[2] the Federal Trade Commission,[3] the Mail

---

[1] Comment (1932) 32 Col. L. Rev. 379.

[2] 34 Stat. 768 (1906) amended by 37 Stat. 416 (1912), 37 Stat. 732 (1913), 41 Stat. 271 (1919), 42 Stat. 1500 (1923), 46 Stat. 1019 (1930), 21 U. S. C. A. § 1 *et seq.* (1927). See Legis. (1932) 32 Col. L. Rev. 720; Fisher, The Proposed Food and Drugs Act, 1 Law and Contemporary Problems (1933) 74.

[3] Handler, The Jurisdiction of the Federal Trade Commission Over False Advertising (1931) 31 Col. L. Rev. 527.

Fraud[1] and the Model Advertising Acts[2] have been construed with hostility and lack of sympathy. "Puffs" have been regarded with amused tolerance,[3] misleading expressions have been treated as mere matters of opinion,[4] and onerous procedural requirements, which the legislature obviously sought to eliminate, have been callously written into the law.[5]

The story of the control of false advertising by the courts indicates how well insulated are judicial sensibilities against the shock which unfair competition is sometimes said to cause.

Misrepresentation of Competitors' Goods

The competitive practices which we have previously reviewed involved the elements of misappropriation, diversion of custom and misrepresentation, singly or in combination. We turn now to a different species of practice which consists essentially of an attack upon competitors rather than a taking of their trade values or a diversion of their custom by deceitful means. The weapons employed in the attack vary. The first we consider is the attack by misrepresentation of competitors' goods. Its kinship to the previous practices lies in the element of misrepresentation. Its kinship to those that follow lies in the attack upon competitors.

Disparagement is the legal name for the familiar practice of "knocking" competitive products. Sales are induced not on the merits of the article offered but on the alleged demerits of its rivals. It is not the product before the parties which is misrepresented but that of competitors. The aim of such depreciation is, obviously, the deflection of custom. The tort stems from the law of personal defamation. Unlike defamation, it is an attack upon property or goods rather than upon

---

[1] Handler, *supra* note 3, page 99, at 28.

[2] *Id.* at 31.   See also Comment (1927) 36 Yale L. J. 1155.

[3] Ostermoor & Co. v. Fed. Trade Com., 16 F. (2d) 962 (C. C. A. 2d, 1927).

[4] United States v. Johnson, 221 U. S. 488 (1911).

[5] *Cf.* State v. Massey, 95 Wash. 1, 163 Pac. 7 (1917).

the person.   A disparagement is a derogatory criticism of the character, quality, utility or value of another's wares.[1]   The criticism of the goods may also reflect upon the reputation of the maker or dealer and hence the same statement may be both a defamation and a disparagement.[2]   The elements of the wrong are: (1) a false statement (2) which is wilfully uttered or published and (3) which causes special damage.   It differs from libel and slander in that (1) the plaintiff must prove the falsity of the utterance, (2) malice is not presumed and (3) special damages must be proved.

It is commonly asserted that malice is one of the essential ingredients of the tort, but there is little analysis in the cases of the nature of this requirement.   The malice referred to is not the fictional malice of personal defamation.   Whether it connotes the "disinterested malevolence" of which Mr. Justice Holmes speaks,[3] or some element of bad faith, or knowledge of the falsity of the assertion, or merely a conscious utterance is not clear.   Jeremiah Smith in a stimulating article drew an analogy to slander of title in which malice destroys the qualified privilege of a rival claimant but is not an essential item of proof in an action against a third person.[4]   The

------

[1] Victor Safe & Lock Co. v. Deright, 147 Fed. 211 (C. C. A. 8th, 1906); National Refining Co. v. Benzo Gas Motor Fuel Co., 20 F. (2d) 763 (C. C. A. 8th, 1927), *cert. denied*, 275 U. S. 570 (1927); Hopkins Chemical Co. v. Read Drug & Chemical Co., 124 Md. 210, 92 Atl. 478 (1914); Evans v. Harlow, 5 Q. B. 624 (1844); Fen v. Dixe, Jones W. 444 (K. B. 1640); Alcott v. Millar's Karri & Jarrah Forests, Ltd., 91 L. T. 722 (1904).

[2] Linotype Co. v. British Empire Type-Setting Machine Co., 81 L. T. 331 (1899); Larsen v. Brooklyn Daily Eagle, 165 App. Div. 4, 150 N. Y. Supp. 464 (2d Dep't, 1914), *aff'd*, 214 N. Y. 713, 108 N. E. 1098 (1915); White v. Delavan, 17 Wend. 49 (N. Y. 1837); Mowry v. Raabe, 89 Cal. 606, 27 Pac. 157 (1891); Dabold v. Chronicle Publishing Co., 107 Wis. 357, 83 N. W. 639 (1900); Braun v. Armour & Co., 254 N. Y. 514, 173 N. E. 845 (1930).

[3] American Bank & Trust Co. v. Federal Reserve Bank of Atlanta, 256 U. S. 350 (1921).

[4] Smith, Disparagement of Property (1913) 13 Col. L. Rev. 13.   See also

competitor, in the case of disparagement, unlike the claimant of title, does not require the privilege as he runs no danger of losing any property rights through estoppel. As between a competitor and a third person who criticizes an article of trade, the good faith of the latter makes a much stronger claim for immunity. Criticism is so inveterate that one might doubt the wisdom of imposing liability upon every derogatory statement uttered in the course of conversation. If any distinction is to be drawn, it would seem that it should be the opposite of that in slander of title. But it is not clear that the basis of liability should vary according to whether the critic is a competitor or third person. The decisions give no conclusive answer to this question. In favor of the malice requirement is the interest in free speech. In opposition are the vagueness of the term and the almost insuperable difficulties of proof. If there is to be any liability, the conditions of proof must be capable of satisfaction.

The chief obstacle to recovery is the difficult burden of proving special damage. It is not enough to show general loss of business,[1] except under very special circumstances.[2] The loss of specific sales can alone be recovered.[3] The complaint must allege with great particularity the customers who have refrained from patronizing the plaintiff as a result of the disparagement. If they were under contract to purchase and have repudiated their engagements, the plaintiff is relegated

---

Note (1930) 30 Col. L. Rev. 510; Odgers, Libel and Slander (6th ed. 1929) 79; Newell, Slander and Libel (4th ed. 1924) § 160.

[1] Bowman Remedy Co. v. Jensen Salsbery Laboratories, 17 F. (2d) 255 (C. C. A. 8th, 1926); Tobias v. Harland, 4 Wend. 537 (N. Y. 1830); Reporters Ass'n v. Sun Printing & Publishing Ass'n, 186 N. Y. 437, 79 N. E. 710 (1906); Tower v. Crosby, 214 App. Div. 392, 212 N. Y. Supp. 219 (4th Dep't, 1925); Shaw Cleaners and Dyers, Inc. v. Des Moines Dress Club, 215 Iowa 1130, 245 N. W. 231 (1932).

[2] Ratcliffe v. Evans, [1892] 2 Q. B. 524; cf. Odgers, op. cit. supra note 4, page 103, at 314.

[3] Cf. Alcott v. Millar's Karri & Jarrah Forests, Ltd., 91 L. T. 722 (1904).

to his action on the contract and the loss is not a provable item of damage.[1] If there is no contract, he must show that the customer would have purchased but for the disparagement. Whether this means readiness, ability, and willingness to buy is not entirely clear. To steer clear of these legal shoals, a skill is required which, unhappily, most litigants do not possess. The reported cases in which there has been recovery for disparagement are extremely rare. The discussion of disparagement occurs chiefly in cases in which the plaintiff has unsuccessfully claimed that the publication was defamatory.[2]

Equity has been even less favorably disposed to the tort. Injunctive relief is generally denied on the tenuous ground that the injunction would impair the constitutional rights of free speech and trial by jury.[3] Dean Pound has demolished these objections in a brilliant article which he concludes by saying: "In substance, the traditional doctrine put anyone's business at the mercy of any insolvent malicious defamer who has sufficient imagination to lay out a skillful campaign of extortion."[4] The present trend of the authorities, fortunately, is in the direction of extending equitable relief.[5] The con-

---

[1] Wittemann Bros. v. Wittemann Co., 88 Misc. 266, 151 N. Y. Supp. 813 (Sup. Ct. 1914), aff'd, 168 App. Div. 930, 152 N. Y. Supp. 1150 (2d Dep't, 1915); Clark v. Dollinger, 205 App. Div. 231, 233, 199 N. Y. Supp. 527 (4th Dep't, 1923); Note (1933) 33 Col. L. Rev. 90; cf. (1929) 38 Yale L. J. 400.

[2] E. g. most of the cases cited in note 1, page 103, supra.

[3] Marlin Fire Arms Co. v. Shields, 171 N. Y. 384, 64 N. E. 163 (1902); Pound, Cases on Equitable Relief Against Defamation (Chafee, 2d ed. 1930) c. 1; Long, Equitable Jurisdiction to Protect Personal Rights (1923) 33 Yale L. J. 115; Nims, op. cit. supra note 6, page 80, §§ 255 et seq.; Nims, Unfair Competition by False Statements of Disparagement (1933) 19 Corn. L. Q. 63.

[4] Pound, Equitable Relief Against Defamation (1916) 29 Harv. L. Rev. 640, 668.

[5] Allen Mfg. Co. v. Smith, 224 App. Div. 187, 229 N. Y. Supp. 692 (4th Dep't, 1928); Old Investors' & Traders' Corp. v. Jenkins, 133 Misc. 213, 232 N. Y. Supp. 245 (Sup. Ct. 1928), aff'd, 225 App. Div. 860, 233 N. Y. Supp. 845 (1st Dep't, 1929); Maytag Co. v. Meadows Mfg. Co., 35 F. (2d)

venient ambiguity of the term unfair competition has helped the courts in breaking away from the earlier view.   Thus in a recent case in New York,[1] the court recognized the binding authority of the prior cases, but granted an injunction on the ground that the defendant's disparagements were part of a campaign of "unfair competition."   This use of the term is very interesting because it presages an eventual amalgamation of all the competitive torts into one form of action with more liberal conditions of relief.   Here we have the beginning with a branch of the law of libel engrafted upon the trunk of unfair competition.

There is no reason of policy why misrepresentation of another's product should be a permissible selling method.   It is more important that the consumer be told the truth about the seller's wares than that he be immersed in a flood of lies about another's goods.   If, however, the courts desire to legalize disparagement,[2] it is preferable that this be done directly than that the abstract prohibition be frustrated by the ineffectiveness of remedy.   The rules of damage should be relaxed.   The malice requirement might well be abandoned, but if retained, it should be satisfied by proof of the knowledge of the falsity of the charge, reckless indifference to its truth or falsity, or similar evidence of bad faith.   Without the remedy of injunction, it is impossible to curb this species of falsehood. Injunctive relief, however, should be granted only in cases

---

403 (C. C. A. 7th, 1929); Gettler v. Crystal, N. Y. L. J., Oct. 10, 1929, at 1274; see Artloom Corp. v. National Better Business Bureau, Inc., 48 F. (2d) 897 (S. D. N. Y. 1931); but see Zenie v. Miskend, N. Y. L. J., Jan. 9, 1936 (App. Div., 1st Dep't).

[1] Allen Mfg. Co. v. Smith, 224 App. Div. 187, 229 N. Y. Supp. 692 (4th Dep't, 1928).   The orders of the Federal Trade Commission operate as injunctions.   For authorities, see note 1, page 164 *infra*.

[2] Thus comparative disparagements are not actionable.   White v. Mellin, [1895] A. C. 154; Hubbuck & Sons, Ltd. v. Wilkinson, [1899] 1 Q. B. 86. Compare the earlier decision of Western Counties Manure Co. v. Lawes Chemical Manure Co., L. R. 9 Ex. 218 (1874).

where the disparaging nature of the utterance is so clear that a contrary verdict by a jury would be set aside.

The common law denunciation of falsehood extends to misrepresentations of a competitor which are neither defamations nor disparagements.[1] Typical of the untruths that have been litigated is the assertion that a competitor has retired from business.[2] The action on the case for such falsehoods is governed by the same rules as disparagement.

Closely related to these torts is the liability imposed for groundless threats of patent or trademark litigation. The claim that another's patent is invalid or that it constitutes an infringement is essentially a slander upon the title of the patent.[3] Here, it is settled that the utterance must be made in bad faith.[4] The chief issue that has been litigated is the right to equitable relief. An unwarranted distinction has been drawn between the claim of infringement coupled with threats of suits against customers[5] and the charge unaccompanied by such threats.[6] Only in the former case can an injunction be

---

[1] Ratcliffe v. Evans [1892] 2 Q. B. 524, 527–528; Al Raschid v. News Syndicate Co., 265 N. Y. 1, 191 N. E. 713 (1934).

[2] Ratcliff v. Evans [1892] 2 Q. B. 524, 527–528; cf. Jarrahdale Timber Co. v. Temperley & Co., 11 L. T. R. 119 (1894); Wolkowsky v. Garfunkel, 65 Fla. 10, 60 So. 791 (1913); House of Directories v. Lane Directory Co., 182 Ky. 384, 206 S. W. 475 (1918).

[3] On slander of title, see Odgers, op. cit. supra note 3, page 103, at 68 et seq.; Newell, op. cit. supra note 3, page 103, § 614.

[4] Wren v. Weild, L. R. 4 Q. B. 730 (1869); Oil Conservation Engineering Co. v. Brooks Engineering Co., 52 F. (2d) 783 (C. C. A. 6th, 1931); cf. Flynn & Emrich Co. v. Fed. Trade Com., 52 F. (2d) 836 (C. C. A. 4th, 1931); Gibson v. Smoot Engineering Corp., 50 F. (2d) 203 (D. Del. 1931).

[5] Emack v. Kane, 34 Fed. 46 (C. C. Ill. 1888); Sun Maid Raisin Growers v. Avis, 25 F. (2d) 303 (D. Ill. 1928); cf. Dehydro v. Tretolite Co., 53 F. (2d) 273 (N. D. Okla. 1931); Nims, op. cit. supra note 6, page 80, c. 17; Pound, op. cit. supra note 3, page 105, 31n.

[6] Kidd v. Horry, 28 Fed. 773 (C. C. Pa. 1886). Boston Diatite Co. v. Florence Mfg. Co., 114 Mass. 69 (1873) is sometimes cited as in accord with

had. To broadcast such a charge to the trade is just as devastating as a direct threat of litigation. To distinguish between express and implied threats cannot be justified and recent decisions have evinced a tendency to broaden the basis of equitable relief.[1]

Molestation and Physical Interference

Physical violence as a competitive weapon has long been outlawed. A more rugged age witnessed such practices as shooting at a competitor's customers,[2] threatening them with personal injury,[3] shadowing a rival's salesmen,[4] arranging for the arrest of competitor's employees on false charges,[5] distracting customers during the process of negotiation,[6] blocking and obstructing the entrance to a rival place of business,[7] or inducing competitors' employees to commit sabotage.[8] A

Kidd v. Horry, but there were express threats in the *Diatite* case and the decision is *contra* to Emack v. Kane, 34 Fed. 46 (C. C. Ill. 1888).

[1] *Cf.* Adjusta Co. v. Alma Mfg. Co., 36 F. (2d) 105 (S. D. N. Y. 1929); United Kingdom Optical Co. v. American Optical Co., 2 F. Supp. 174 (D. Mass. 1933), *aff'd*, 68 F. (2d) 637 (C. C. A. 1st, 1934); Gardner Sign Co. v. Claude Neon Lights, 36 F. (2d) 827 (W. D. Pa. 1929). On misrepresentation of a court's decree, see Comment (1934) 48 Harv. L. Rev. 343; Comment (1934) 34 Col. L. Rev. 1370.

[2] *Cf.* Tarleton v. McGawley, Peake's N. P. 270 (K. B. 1793).

[3] Garret v. Taylor, Cro. Jac. 567 (K. B. 1621).

[4] Evenson v. Spaulding, 150 Fed. 517 (C. C. A. 9th, 1907); *cf.* Dunshee v. Standard Oil Co., 152 Iowa 618, 132 N. W. 371 (1911); State v. Dalton, 168 N. C. 204, 83 S. E. 693 (1914).

[5] Evenson v. Spaulding, 150 Fed. 517 (C. C. A. 9th, 1907).

[6] *Ibid.*

[7] *Cf.* Gilley v. Hirsh, 122 La. 966, 48 So. 422 (1909); *cf.* London N. W. Ry. v. Lancashire and Yorkshire Ry., L. R. 4 Eq. 174 (1867); *cf.* Brown-Brand Realty Co. v. Saks & Co., 126 Misc. 336, 214 N. Y. Supp. 230 (Sup. Ct. 1926), *aff'd*, 218 App. Div. 827, 218 N. Y. Supp. 706 (1st Dep't, 1926); Comment (1926) 35 Yale L. J. 1019.

[8] *Cf.* King v. Cope, 1 Strange 144 (K. B. 1719); People v. Everett, 51 Hun 19 (5th Dep't, App. Div. N. Y. 1899).

charming bit of deception, sometimes coupled with these interferences, was the arrangement of signs and placards in such a fashion as to create the impression that the entrance of one store was the main entrance of another.[1]

The assault upon the customer is a wrong to him. To hold an assault upon a third person an unfair method of competition for which damages may be procured required an extension of legal theory. Only a sterile attachment to ancient forms of action could stand in the way of such a necessary extension and the courts merit no special adulation for curbing these competitive debaucheries. The progression of liability from the assault upon customers to the other crude interferences enumerated above was inevitable.

Interference with Trade Relations by Boycott

The law of boycott is rooted in the soil of restraint of trade rather than unfair competition. The law's concern with the boycott lies more in the preservation than in the regulation of competition. Nevertheless, the topic should be included in a discussion of unfair competition for two reasons. The legal foundations of the competitive process cannot be fully understood without some consideration of the boycott. Secondly, the boycott is so potent a weapon in any temporal struggle that its possible availability to competitors must be carefully determined.

The core of the trade boycott is the refusal to deal. This may take the form of a refusal to enter into business relations with another or the severance of those already in existence. The traditional definitions of boycott include so many irrelevant and emotional elements,[2] that it is advisable, in the interests of clarity, to adopt a more neutral meaning of the term. The direct refusal to deal will be denominated a primary boycott. The inducement of third persons not to deal with

---

[1] *Cf.* Gilley v. Hirsh, 122 La. 966, 48 So. 422 (1909).

[2] See Oakes, Organized Labor and Industrial Conflicts (1927) 602–606.

another is a secondary boycott. The degree of the boycott thus depends upon the remoteness from the actual controversy of those conscripted. The boycott may occur in a dispute between those whose relationship is that of bargaining opponents, in which event it is called a boycott in the bargaining struggle. The disputants may be competitors, in which event the boycott is in the competitive struggle. Sometimes the contestants are neither competitors nor bargaining adversaries, a situation more frequent in political and religious than in trade disputes. The boycott may be carried on by an individual or by a group. It may be accomplished by agreement, by persuasion, by threats or other forms of economic pressure. The object of the boycott, the means by which it is brought about and the economic strength of the parties to the dispute are other factors to be noted.

A few illustrations should be helpful. S is a seller, B is a buyer, C is a competitor and T is a third person. The refusal of S to deal with B is a primary boycott in the bargaining struggle. The refusal to have dealings with C is a primary boycott in the competitive struggle. The inducement by S of C or T to refrain from dealing with B is a secondary boycott in the bargaining struggle. The inducement by S of B or T to refrain from dealing with C is a secondary boycott in the competitive struggle.

Save in the case of a seller with monopoly power,[1] the primary boycott by an individual is not only permitted[2] but it

---

[1] *Cf.* Eastman Kodak Co. v. Southern Photo Materials Co., 273 U. S. 359 (1927). In this case, the refusal to deal was part of a scheme to drive the plantiff out of business and hence the decision is not a square holding on the legality of a primary boycott by a monopoly. It has been held that a refusal by one with monopoly power is not actionable. Locker v. American Tobacco Co., 195 N. Y. 565, 88 N. E. 289 (1909); Whitwell v. Continental Tobacco Co., 125 Fed. 454 (C. C. A. 8th, 1903). That such a boycott should be unlawful seems beyond question.

[2] United States v. Colgate & Co., 250 U. S. 300 (1919); Great Atlantic & Pacific Tea Co. v. Cream of Wheat Co., 227 Fed. 46 (C. C. A. 2d, 1915).

has even been intimated that any statutory interference with this right would be unconstitutional.[1] In the language of the cases, one is "at liberty to refuse business relations with any person whomever, whether the refusal rests upon reason, or is the result of whim, caprice, prejudice or malice."[2] Not even the intent to accomplish an unlawful purpose will render a direct refusal to deal unlawful.[3] It is this unqualified privilege which differentiates competitive enterprise from public callings. A tradesman need not deal with his competitors.

The secondary is, obviously, the more common competitive boycott. In fact, such a boycott is inherent in competition itself. Whenever S offers merchandise to B, he is impliedly persuading B to refrain from patronizing C. Each sale made by S *pro tanto* reduces C's selling opportunities. The requirement contract[4] is a familiar instance of the exclusion of competitors that occurs under a regime of competitive selling. Suppose S, as part of the sale, exacts an express promise from B not to patronize C. Does such agreement constitute unfair competition? We shall pretermit for the moment the effects of section three of the Clayton Act[5] and consider the problem at common law. The exclusive dealing arrangement is the objective of almost every seller and makes explicit that which is to a large extent implicit in competitive selling. While this may be the sole analytical difference between the boycott and exclusive dealing arrangements, it does not follow that both must be governed by the same rules. However, in the absence

---

[1] Grenada Lumber Co. v. Mississippi, 217 U. S. 433, 440 (1910).

[2] Great Atlantic & Pacific Tea Co. v. Cream of Wheat Co., 227 Fed. 48 (C. C. A. 2d, 1915).

[3] *E. g.*, a refusal to deal with those who refuse to maintain prices is lawful, *supra* note 1, page 110, notwithstanding the illegality of price maintenance. Dr. Miles Medical Co. v. Park & Sons Co., 220 U. S. 373 (1911).

[4] Note (1921) 14 A. L. R. 1300; Note (1923) 24 A. L. R. 1352; Note (1928) 28 Col. L. Rev. 223.

[5] 38 Stat. 730 (1914), 15 U. S. C. A. § 14 (1927). See *infra* p. 222.

of statute, exclusive agreements have been generally sustained.[1]

Does it make any difference that *B* submits to threats or other pressure in refraining from dealing with *C*? In *Deon v. Kirby Lumber Co.*[2] the defendant lumber company threatened its employees with discharge if they patronized plaintiff's general merchandise store instead of the company store which it operated. In *Celli & Del Papa v. Galveston Brewing Co.*,[3] the defendant brewery threatened to cancel the monthly tenancies of a number of saloon keepers unless they discontinued the sale of plaintiff's brew. In both cases, the defendant sought to improve its competitive position by resorting to the special power it possessed over its employees and tenants. In both cases, competition was held to constitute an unqualified justification for the injury inflicted. The decisions are generally in accord.[4]

That competition should constitute a legal justification for the boycott inherent in the competitive process requires no affirmation.[5] But whether a seller should be permitted to apply extrinsic pressure, as in the cases reviewed, is quite another question. These are, to be sure, abnormal situations, but for that very reason they are of added significance in

---

[1] Whitwell v. Continental Tobacco Co., 125 Fed. 454 (C. C. A. 8th, 1903); Sullivan v. Rime, 35 S. D. 75, 150 N. W. 556 (1915); Brown v. Rounsavell, 78 Ill. 589 (1875); Peerless Pattern Co. v. Gauntlett Dry Goods Co., 171 Mich. 158, 136 N. W. 1113 (1912). But *cf.* Segal v. McCall Co., 108 Tex. 55, 184 S. W. 188 (1916); see also note (1916) 30 Haw. L. Rev. 72.

[2] 162 La. 671, 111 So. 55 (1926).

[3] 227 S. W. 941 (Comm. App. Tex. 1921).

[4] See Robinson v. Texas Pine Land Ass'n, 40 S. W. 843 (Tex. Civ. App. 1879); Lewis v. Huie-Hodge Lumber Co., 121 La. 658, 46 So. 685 (1908); Note (1928) 52 A. L. R. 1028. For legislation prohibiting the requirement by employers that their workers trade at particular stores, see Legis. (1931) 31 Col. L. Rev. 687, 693.

[5] Andrew Jergens Co. v. Woodbury, 271 Fed. 43 (D. Del. 1920); Journal of Commerce Publishing Co. v. Tribune Co., 286 Fed. 111 (C. C. A. 7th, 1922).

determining the scope of the privilege. The use of such threats places C at a serious competitive disadvantage. Such competition reminds of a duel between one using a rapier and the other a machine gun.

Similarly, it is one thing for a seller to obtain a contract which satisfies the buyer's immediate requirements, but quite another to tie up dealers for a long period and shut the channels of trade to competitors by exclusive dealing contracts. This was perceived by Congress in enacting section three of the Clayton Act.

Thus far we have been dealing with boycotts in which the outside parties conscripted are those for whose patronage S and C are competing. Suppose, however, T, who supplies both S and C with goods, or, we will assume, is a bank, an advertising agency, or a newspaper, is induced by S not to deal with C. Such a boycott is not inherent in competition. B is a party to the competitive struggle, whether he likes it or not. T is not. B can only be neutral in part. T's complete neutrality is entirely consistent with the normal operation of competition. If there is a shortage of goods, of credit, or advertising space, in a word, if S and C are in competition for relationships with T, the situation is the same as in the boycott involving B.[1] Such competition does not normally occur. To permit S to draw T into the zone of competitive warfare is to accentuate inequalities already existing. S's economic interests are furthered without any compensating social advantage. C can be driven out of business, not because he is less efficient or because his product is inferior to S's, but because of the paucity of his economic resources. Nevertheless, in the few cases that have arisen, the courts have broadly applied the principle that competition is a justification for the boycott, without pausing to examine the foundation of the rule or its

---

[1] Rosenau v. Empire Circuit Co., 131 App. Div. 429, 115 N. Y. Supp. 511 (4th Dep't, 1909).

inapplicability to such a situation.[1] It is difficult to distinguish these cases from the line of decisions holding unlawful the secondary boycott in the bargaining struggle or in a dispute which is neither competitive or bargaining in character.[2]   In the latter cases the doctrine of justification is in the chrysalis stage and authority is too meagre to permit of any definite assertion regarding its basis or scope.[3]

It can, however, be asserted, that such factors as malice,[4] wrongful means,[5] or disparity of economic power[6] do not condition the legality of the individual competitive boycott.

---

[1] Fed. Trade Com. v. Raymond Bros.-Clark Co., 263 U. S. 565 (1924); Dye v. Carmichael Produce Co., 64 Ind. App. 653, 116 N. E. 425 (1917).

[2] *Bargaining struggle:* London Guarantee & Accident Co. v. Horn, 206 Ill. 493, 69 N. E. 526 (1903); U. S. Fidelity & Guaranty Co. v. Millonas, 206 Ala. 147, 89 So. 732 (1921); cf. Straus. v. Victor Talking Machine Co., 297 Fed. 791 (C. C. A. 2d, 1924); Victor Talking Machine Co. v. Kemeny, 271 Fed. 810 (C. C. A. 3d, 1921).

No struggle: International & G. N. Ry. Co. v. Greenwood, 2 Tex. Civ. App. 76, 21 S. W. 559 (1893); Wesley v. Native Lumber Co., 97 Miss. 814, 53 So. 346 (1910); American Mercury v. Chase, 13 F. (2d) 224 (D. Mass. 1926).

[3] *Cf.* Guethler v. Altman, 26 Ind. App. 587, 60 N. E. 355 (1901); Gott v. Berea College, 156 Ky. 376, 161 S. W. 204 (1913); Sweeney v. Coote [1906] 1 Ir. Rep. 51 *aff'd*, [1907] A. C. 221; cf. Julie Baking Co., Inc. v. Graymond, 152 Misc. 846, 274 N. Y. Supp. 250 (Sup. Ct. 1934); United States v. American Livestock Commission Co., 279 U. S. 435 (1929); Comment (1933) 33 Col. L. Rev. 1439.

[4] Malice present, no liability: Guethler v. Altman, 26 Ind. App. 587, 60 N. E. 355 (1901); Sweeney v. Coote [1906] 1 Ir. Rep. 51, *aff'd*, [1907] A. C. 221; no malice but liability: American Mercury v. Chase, 13 F. (2d) 224 (D. Mass. 1926); International & G. N. Ry. Co. v. Greenwood, 2 Tex. Civ. App. 76, 21 S. W. 559 (1893); Council of Defense v. International Magazine Co., 267 Fed. 390 (C. C. A. 8th, 1920).

[5] Threats present, no liability: Guethler v. Altman, 26 Ind. App. 587, 60 N. E. 355 (1901); Gott v. Berea College, 156 Ky. 376, 161 S. W. 204 (1913); no threats, but liability: Council of Defense v. International Magazine Co., 267 Fed. 390 (C. C. A. 8th, 1920).

[6] Rosenau v. Empire Circuit Co., 131 App. Div. 429, 115 N. Y. Supp. 511 (4th Dep't, 1909).

The element of combination, however, does. What is lawful for one tradesman to do becomes unlawful when carried on by two or more in concert. While there is some conflict in the authorities, by and large, both the primary and secondary boycotts by trade groups are unlawful at common law and under the Sherman Act.[1] There appears to be a tendency in some jurisdictions, notably New York, to sustain such concerted action where the court approves of the purposes and objectives of the combine.[2]

The combination differs from the individual only in the degree of its economic power. Both the combination principle and the rule, previously adverted to, rendering unlawful a primary boycott by an individual with monopoly power[3] evince a policy to limit the boycott to struggles between economic equals. But the combination rule has been applied somewhat mechanically. No attempt is made in the cases to ascertain the combine's economic strength. A boycott by a powerful corporation, under the *ratio decidendi* of the courts, would presumably be upheld while the combined boycott of several pigmies would be denounced.[4] Although the presence

---

[1] Mines v. Scribner, 147 Fed. 927 (C. C. S. D. N. Y. 1906); Binderup v. Pathe Exchange, 263 U. S. 291 (1923); Heim Brewing Co. v. Belinder, 97 Mo. App. 64, 71 S. W. 691 (1903); Finnegan v. Butler, 112 Misc. 280, 182 N. Y. Supp. 671 (Sup. Ct. 1920); Eastern States Lumber Ass'n v. United States, 234 U. S. 600 (1914). *Contra:* Ware & DeFreville, Ltd. v. Motor Trade Ass'n, [1921] 3 K. B. 40; Mogul Steamship Co., Ltd. v. McGregor, Gow & Co., 23 Q. B. D. 598 (1889); Bohn Mfg. Co. v. Hollis, 54 Minn. 223, 55 N. W. 1119 (1893). See also Handler, The Sugar Institute Case and the Present Status of the Anti-Trust Laws (1936) 36 Col. L. Rev. 1. As to the importance of the element of combination, see Fed. Trade Com. v. Raymond Bros.-Clark Co., 263 U. S. 574 (1924).

[2] Arnold v. Burgess, 241 App. Div. 364, 272 N. Y. Supp. 534 (1st Dep't, 1934); Wolfenstein v. Fashion Originators' Guild, 244 App. Div. 656, 280 N. Y. Supp. 361 (1st Dep't, 1935).

[3] *Supra* note 1, page 110.

[4] Compare Dunlap's Cable News Co. v. Stone, 15 N. Y. Supp. 2 (1891) with Eastern States Lumber Ass'n v. United States, 234 U. S. 600 (1914);

of a combination invites the application of the conspiracy concept, nevertheless the element of numbers seems, at best, but an adventitious factor.

A complete survey of the boycott problem is not germane to the present discussion and other phrases of this interesting topic must be passed over. From the standpoint of the law of unfair competition, we find that a secondary boycott by an individual competitor is lawful while that of a combination of competitors is unlawful. It is submitted that these rules would bear revision in several respects. Where the parties are not in competition for relations with the third party who is conscripted, the boycott should be tortious. Similarly, the use of extrinsic pressure as in the *Deon* and *Celli* cases[1] should be forbidden. It obviously is not feasible, in the normal competitive boycott induced by an individual, to measure the economic strength of the contestants and to enforce a rigid rule of competitive equality. But it is not impossible to distinguish between defensive combinations seeking to remove the disparities of economic power, and aggressive combines throttling competition. I do not contend for any rigid and inflexible rule on this score, but merely that the relative economic strength of the disputants, especially in the case of combinations, merits greater consideration than has been given it by the courts.

The boycott has also been employed by trade associations to enforce programs for the regulation of competition and has been employed against non-member competitors, recreant members and purchasers. The Supreme Court, in applying the Sherman Act, has been highly unsympathetic to such trade association efforts. The enforcement of a system of commercial arbitration,[2] the implementation of credit activi-

---

Fed. Trade Com. v. Raymond Bros.-Clark Co., 263 U. S. 574 (1924). See also Locker v. American Tobacco Co., 195 N. Y. 565, 88 N. E. 289 (1909).

[1] *Supra* notes 2 and 3, page 112,

[2] Paramount Famous Lasky Corp. v. United States, 282 U. S. 30 (1930).

ties[1] and the protection of traditional marketing channels by association boycotts[2] have all been condemned as unlawful conspiracies. The objections to such boycotts are (1) the danger of abuse, (2) the likelihood that the innocent as well as the guilty will be injured, (3) the condemnation of the party boycotted without a fair trial, (4) the drastic effects of the punishment which frequently does not fit the offense. Where the party to be boycotted is given a full and fair hearing to determine his inclusion in the boycotted class, one of the most serious objections is removed, but the Supreme Court has frowned upon the boycott even under such circumstances.[3] The law of group boycott is undergoing serious reconsideration by the courts and the next decade may witness some far-reaching changes.[4]

Interference with Trade Relations by Inducing Breach of Contract

The tort of inducing breach of contract has had the most interesting history of any of the competitive wrongs. Recognized less than a century ago,[5] and then only over the vigorous dissent of one of the ablest common law judges,[6] its development has been spectacular. The roots of the tort are to be found in the common law doctrines of enticement of employ-

---

[1] United States v. First National Pictures, 282 U. S. 44 (1930).

[2] Eastern States Lumber Ass'n v. United States, 234 U. S. 600 (1914); Southern Hardware Jobbers' Ass'n v. Fed. Trade Com., 290 Fed. 773 (C. C. A. 5th, 1923).

[3] *Supra* note 2, page 116.

[4] *E. g.*, cases cited note 2, page 115, *supra;* and see Handler, *supra* note 1, page 115. Consider also the various boycotts instituted under the N. R. A. Complete documentation of the points made in the text would require a separate article and hence the citation of authority has been suggestive rather than exhaustive.

On the relationship of the torts of disparagement and boycott see Note (1930) 30 Col. L. Rev. 510.

[5] Lumley v. Gye, 2 E. & B. 216, (Q. B. 1853).

[6] Coleridge, J., *id.* at 244.

ees, which in turn owe their origin in large measure to the Statute of Labourers.[1] In *Lumley v. Gye*,[2] a new twist was given to the doctrine of enticement and the malicious inducement of the breach of a contract of personal service was held actionable. The extension consisted primarily in expanding the category of servant-employee to include an opera singer. "With the decision of Lumley v. Gye," writes Professor Sayre, "a new doctrine was born. Prior to that time no court had ever gone so far as to hold that in general the procurement of a breach of contract constitutes a tort; the only procurement cases had been confined to procuring servants away from their masters, children from their parents, or wives from their husbands, *i. e.* enticing away dependent members of another's household."[3]

The elements of the original tort were (1) the malicious and (2) active inducement (3) of the breach (4) of a contract of personal service. The rule was stated broadly as covering all contracts, but this assertion was unnecessary to the decision in *Lumley v. Gye*. The element of malice soon degenerated to mere wilfulness and was eventually abandoned.[4] The progression from contracts between master and servant to contracts of personal service, initiated in *Lumley v. Gye*, continued until every contract, regardless of its nature, was embraced by the tort.[5] Inducement of breach then gave way to preven-

---

[1] Sayre, Inducing Breach of Contract (1923) 36 Harv. L. Rev. 663. Enticement of competitor's employees constitutes another of the practices that must be included in the list of competitive wrongs forbidden at common law.

[2] *Supra* note 5, page 117.

[3] *Supra* note 1 above at 666–667.

[4] Sidney Blumenthal & Co. v. United States, 30 F. (2d) 247 (C. C. A. 2d, 1929); Note (1928) 12 Minn. L. Rev. 147.

[5] Temperton v. Russell [1893] 1 Q. B. 715; Cumberland Glass Mfg. Co. v. De Witt, 120 Md. 381, 87 Atl. 927 (1913); Landis, Cases on Labor Law (1934) 77 *et seq.;* Note (1924) 24 Col. L. Rev. 185.

tion of performance,[1] and active procurement was expanded
to include interference with contractual relations.[2] The
unruly stream soon overflowed the banks. Negligent interferences with contracts were attacked.[3] Contracts unenforceable under the statute of frauds were protected against
inducement and interference.[4] Mere expectations which had
not yet ripened into contract were brought under the protecting arm of the tort.[5] The minority jurisdictions, which had
limited liability to the cases in which the inducement was
accompanied by such wrongful means as deceit or duress, have
begun to shed this requirement.[6]

The insatiable appetite of the tort is a constant threat to the
very existence of a law of boycott. The distinction between

---

[1] Sidney Blumenthal & Co. v. United States, 30 F. (2d) 247 (C. C. A.
2d, 1929).

[2] *Cf.* McNary v. Chamberlain, 34 Conn. 384 (1867); Carpenter, Interference with Contract Relations (1928) 41 Harv. L. Rev. 728, 730, 735.

[3] Carpenter, *supra* note 4, page 118, at 737 *et seq.;* Note (1926) 40 Harv.
L. Rev. 302. Compare Cue v. Breland, 78 Miss. 864, 29 So. 850 (1901);
The Argentino, 14 App. Cas. 519 (1889); Bradford Corp. v. Webster [1920]
2 K. B. 135 with Robins Dry Dock & Repair Co. v. Flint, 275 U. S. 303
(1927); Chelsea Moving & Trucking Co. v. Ross Towboat Co., 280 Mass.
282, 182 N. E. 477 (1932). Relief against negligent interference is denied
by the weight of authority. Comment (1932) 32 Col. L. Rev. 1444.

[4] Rice v. Manley, 66 N. Y. 82 (1876); Bliss v. Holmes, 156 Okla. 40,
9 P. (2d) 718 (1932). But *cf.* Little v. Childress, 12 S. W. (2d) 648 (Tex.
Civ. App. 1928). See also Comment (1910) 10 Col. L. Rev. 678; Comment (1927) 27 Col. L. Rev. 621.

[5] Lewis v. Bloede, 202 Fed. 7 (C. C. A. 4th, 1912). *Cf.* Hitchman Coal
& Coke Co. v. Mitchell, 245 U. S. 229 (1917) (employment at will). Lewis
v. Bloede represents the minority view in this country.

[6] Compare Ashley v. Dixon, 48 N. Y. 430, 432 (1872) with Campbell v.
Gates, 236 N. Y. 457, 460, 141 N. E. 914 (1923); Exchange Bakery &
Restaurant v. Rifkin, 245 N. Y. 260, 266–267, 157 N. E. 130 (1927); Reiner
v. North American Newspaper Alliance, 259 N. Y. 250, 181 N. E. 561
(1932), discussed in Comment (1932) 32 Col. L. Rev. 1236. Compare also
Chambers & Marshall v. Baldwin, 91 Ky. 121, 15 S. W. 57 with Friedberg,
Inc. v. McClary, 173 Ky. 579, 191 S. W. 300 (1917).

boycott and interference with contract is predicated upon the existence of a contract. Prior to the making of the contract of sale between S and B, C may use every blandishment and force to obtain B's custom. The competitive struggle ends with the making of the contract. Even competitors must respect the integrity of consensual arrangements. Competition is no justification for interference with another's contracts.[1] The few cases which have applied the pattern of this tort to mere trade expectancies have projected protection into an area which had been preëmpted by the law of boycott.[2] A head-on collision is thus inevitable. It seems extremely unlikely that the inducement of purchasers not to enter into contractual arrangements with competitors will be declared unlawful.[3] Inducing breach of contract, as its title indicates, must be confined, at least in the case of competitive selling, to actual contracts. There is no middle ground possible if a competitive regime is to continue.

These broad sweeps of the brush have not done justice to the interesting ramifications of this tort. For present purposes, however, it is sufficient to note that the legal plane of competi-

---

[1] Sorenson v. Chevrolet Motor Co., 171 Minn. 260, 214 N. W. 754 (1927); Beekman v. Marsters, 195 Mass. 205, 80 N. E. 817 (1907); but *cf.* Fairbanks, Morse & Co. v. Texas Electric Service Co., 63 F. (2d) 702 (C. C. A. 5th, 1933), *cert. denied*, 290 U. S. 655 (1933). The *prima facie* theory of torts is applied to this field but the limits of the doctrine of justification are still blurred. See Carpenter, *supra* note 2, page 119, 141 and Sayre, *supra* note 1, page 118; Note (1926) 39 Harv. L. Rev. 749.

Many expectations, based upon custom and habit, are stronger and more valuable than those embodied in a contract, but for administrative reasons, the distinction must be cast in terms of the presence or absence of a contract.

[2] *Supra* note 5, page 119.

[3] Note the faulty analysis of the problem in Union Car Advertising Co. v. Collier, 263 N. Y. 386, 189 N. E. 463 (1934) where the court, while denying liability, asserted that interferences with expectancies may be wrongful when accompanied by wrongful means. The wrongful means may be independently actionable but their presence has not hitherto destroyed the privilege of inducing customers not to deal with competitors.

tion includes a prohibition against the intentional inducement of breach, interference with, or prevention of performance of a competitor's contracts. Interferences with advantageous trade relations which have not fructified into contracts are allowed. The tort is a wilful one and liability will not be predicated upon mere negligence. The sanctions for the tort are damages[1] and injunction.[2] While the public is concerned with the integrity of contracts, the wrong consists more in the invasion of a private right than in the infliction of a public injury. The private remedies are thus adequate for the vindication of private interests.[3]

Other Competitive Attacks

Before concluding this section on the common law, reference should be made to competitive attacks which are designed to drive rivals from the field. This type of competition will be discussed more fully in the section devoted to the Sherman Law. Cases involving such intensive competition are rarely encountered, but it would be a mistake to assume that the common law sanctioned the industrial warfare which is portrayed in Sherman Act litigation.[4]

Recapitulation

The ideas which are common to the competitive torts are thus extremely simple. Misrepresentation, misappropriation, diversion of trade, interference with trade relations, attacks upon competitors—these are the stuff out of which the law of unfair competition was built. The common law reached

---

[1] For the measure of liability, see Comment (1929) 29 Col. L. Rev. 679; Note (1930) 30 Col. L. Rev. 232.

[2] Note (1933) 84 A. L. R. 43, 84.

[3] On the relationship of the torts of disparagement and inducing breach of contract, see Note (1933) 33 Col. L. Rev. 90.

[4] Dunshee v. Standard Oil Co. and Standard Oil Co. v. Doyle, both *supra* note 4, pages 84; and compare cases cited in notes 2–8 on page 108 and 1 on page 109, *supra*.

only the crudest competitive excesses.   It left untouched many
abuses which it was equipped to handle.   It had reached its
maturity without developing any principle or procedure
whereby the hosts of abuses that annoyed and hampered the
honest and efficient tradesman might be eliminated.   Judicial
regulation of unfair competition has been and still is hopelessly
incomplete and superficial and there is no hope that the inade-
quacies of common law doctrines and methods can ever be
overcome by the courts, unaided by legislation.[1]   We therefore
turn to the legislature to discover what additions, if any, it
made to the control of competition.

V

Legislative Contribution to Unfair Competition

In defining unfair competition and in devising the instruments by which it may be combated, a legislature is free to
follow its creative impulses, unshackled by the procedures and
conventions which hold the courts in bondage.   It need not
bow to the tyranny of the ready-made torts and forms of
action.   Its horizons are not limited to the narrow records
prepared by private litigants.   Nor need it await the stimulus
of the aggrieved suitor.   Its attack can be comprehensive.
Elaborate investigation and study of the evil to be controlled
can precede the formulation of remedies.   The past may guide
but need not rule.   Foreign experience can be tapped; the
creative process can be inspired by the teachings of economists
rather than by the formularies of the common law pleader;
policies can be articulated and the crust of convention broken;
and law making may be animated by a definite and consistent
economic philosophy.   The peculiar problems of particular
industries can receive special treatment; flexible rules can be

---

[1] National Industrial Conference Board, Public Regulation of Competitive Practices (1929) 37–41 enumerates various reasons for the common
law's failure.

adapted to changing conditions and needs; errors can be corrected by amendment or repeal; and the luxury of generalization and synthesis can be indulged. The choice of sanctions to implement a well-defined policy is limited only by the ingenuity of the draftsman.

These are the theoretical attributes of the legislative process. Whether the legislative contribution to the law of unfair competition has measured up to its potentialities is the subject of inquiry in this section. The regulations to be found upon the state and federal statute books are so motley and unrelated that our treatment must perforce be descriptive and suggestive. An exhaustive collation and analysis of all legislation affecting business competition would swell this paper to undue proportions.

Sherman Law and Unfair Competition

Although the Sherman Act[1] does not in terms condemn unfair competition, the term has been more commonly associated with the brutal and oppressive practices of the large trusts than with the common law competitive torts which we have reviewed. Nevertheless, there is a vital distinction between the two types of practices. The primary concern of the Sherman Law is the preservation of competition and the prevention of monopoly. The common law torts assume an active but unruly competition which has to be kept within bounds. The regulation of competition results in a competitive etiquette, in standards of business conduct, in a plane of competition. The practices of the trusts were denounced because they stifled competition and tended to create monopoly. The dominant economic position of these combines made their methods peculiarly venomous.[2] The same prac-

---

[1] 26 Stat. 209 (1890) 15 U. S. C. A. § 1 (1927).

[2] National Industrial Conference Board, Public Regulation of Competitive Practices (1929) 24–28.

tices by weaker tradesmen in a competitive market might not be oppressive and hence might be suffered as the normal and usual manifestations of competition.   Hence, the prohibitions of the Sherman Act, in effect, set a plane of monopolistic conduct rather than a plane of competition.   In short, the anti-trust laws regulate monopolistic practices which endanger competition, while the law of unfair competition proper regulates practices which are repugnant to decent business morality, which are injurious to competitors and to consumers, which are economically wasteful, but which do not jeopardize, to any appreciable degree, the very existence of competition. The distinction rests upon differences of degree only, and, if over-stressed, can be more misleading than clarifying.   Both types of practice must be included in the legal plane of competition; both types of regulation reinforce each other; both are animated by a common objective, notwithstanding the differences of their intermediate ends.

Each of the common law torts, as we have seen, had a separate history and development.   The practices condemned by the Sherman Law have not received separate consideration and hence their lines of development are indistinct.   Our information regarding their legality is derived chiefly from government prosecutions against the trusts in which the practices were relied upon as proof of monopolistic purpose and intent.[1]   Thus, the Standard Oil Company engaged in local price cutting and espionage, established bogus independents, granted rebates to preferred customers and exacted rebates and preferences from railroads, all with the purpose of suppressing competition.[2]   The American Tobacco Company employed "fighting brands" for the same purpose.[3]   The International Harvester Company closed the channels of trade to competitors by tying up all the main retail outlets with

---

[1] Cf. Swift & Co. v. United States, 196 U. S. 375 (1905).

[2] See Standard Oil Co. v. United States, 221 U. S. 1, 42, 43 (1910).

[3] United States v. American Tobacco Co., 221 U. S. 106 (1911).

exclusive dealing contracts.[1] The National Cash Register Company was guilty of espionage, enticement of competitors' employees, manufacturing inferior imitations of competitors' products, threatening infringement suits in bad faith, maintaining bogus independents, inducing breach of contract, shadowing competitors' salesmen, circulating false reports of competitors' financial standing, selling competitors' products below cost, and labelling an exhibit of the machines of competitors as junk.[2] The American Can Company cut off the sources of supplies of its weaker competitors.[3]

Numerous practices have been restrained in consent decrees, including threats to compete with competitors' customers if they continued to patronize such competitors,[4] inducing breach of contract,[5] fighting brands,[6] flying squadrons,[7] disparaging business methods of competitors,[8] local price cutting,[9]

---

[1] United States v. International Harvester Co., 214 Fed. 987 (D. Minn. 1914), *appeal dismissed on motion of appellants,* 248 U. S. 587 (1918), *supplemental bill,* 274 U. S. 693 (1927).

[2] Patterson v. United States, 222 Fed. 599 (C. C. A. 6th, 1915), *cert. denied,* 238 U. S. 635 (1915); United States v. National Cash Register Co., reported in Decrees and Judgments in Federal Anti-Trust Cases (Gov't Ptg. Off. 1918) 315. *Cases cited by page reference only, hereinafter will refer to this volume.*

[3] See United States v. American Can Co., 230 Fed. 859, 874, 875 (D. Md. 1916).

For a general discussion, see National Industrial Conference Board, Public Regulation of Competitive Practices (1929) 23–37.

[4] United States v. Central-West Publishing Co., 359 (1912).

[5] *Ibid.;* United States v. Burroughs Adding Machine Co., 457 (1913); United States v. Bowser & Co., 587 (1915).

[6] United States v. American Thread Co., 449 (1914).

[7] *Ibid.* (Salesmen exclusively engaged in marketing fighting brands.)

[8] United States v. Central-West Publishing Co., 359 (1912); United States v. Bowser & Co., 587 (1915).

[9] United States v. American Thread Co., 449 (1914); United States v. Central-West Publishing Co., 359 (1912); United States v. Bowser & Co., 587 (1915).

bogus independents,[1] commercial bribery,[2] espionage,[3] compelling sale of competitors' plants by threats of intensive competition,[4] harassing litigation,[5] disclosure of intended use of raw material as a condition precedent to its sale,[6] and exclusive dealing arrangements.[7]

Obviously, neither the decrees in the litigated cases nor those entered upon consent are conclusive on the legality of the separate practices that have been curbed. One can only speculate as to the factors that condition their validity. It seems reasonably clear that, save for the more brutal practices, most of these methods violate the Sherman Act only when they are part of a scheme to stifle competition and to obtain control of an industry.

The problem of resale price maintenance has received fuller consideration than any of the other selling devices challenged under the anti-trust laws. Agreements maintaining resale prices have been condemned as a restraint of trade[8] and as an unfair method of competition under the Federal Trade Commission Act.[9] The injury, if there be any, resulting from price

---

[1] United States v. Du Pont de Nemours & Co., 195 (1911); United States v. General Electric Co., 267 (1911); United States v. Central-West Publishing Co., 359 (1912).

[2] United States v. Bowser & Co., 587 (1915).

[3] United States v. Burroughs Adding Machine Co., 457 (1913); United States v. Bowser & Co., 587 (1915).

[4] United States v. Central-West Publishing Co., 359 (1912).

[5] United States v. Bowser & Co., 587 (1915).

[6] United States v. Aluminum Co., 341 (1912).

[7] *Ibid.*

[8] Dr. Miles Medical Co. v. Park & Sons Co., 220 U. S. 373 (1911); Bauer et Cie v. O'Donnell, 229 U. S. 1 (1913); Straus v. Victor Talking Machine Co., 243 U. S. 490 (1917); Boston Store v. American Gramaphone Co., 246 U. S. 8 (1918); Bobbs-Merrill Co. v. Straus, 210 U. S. 339 (1908); *cf.* Katz Drug. Co. v. Sheaffer Pen Co., 6 F. Supp. 212 (D. Mo. 1933).

[9] Fed. Trade Com. v. Beech-Nut Packing Co., 257 U. S. 441 (1922), Oppenheim, Oberndorf & Co., Inc. v. Fed. Trade Com., 5 F. (2d) 574 (C. C. A. 4th, 1925); Moir v. Fed. Trade Com., 12 F. (2d) 22 (C. C. A. 1st,

maintenance, is suffered not by the competitors of the producer but by the retailer and the ultimate consumer. Resale price maintenance aims at preserving the capital investment in trademarks and other advertising devices. It is a method of distribution but not a competitive weapon such as the other practices previously considered. The distinction drawn by the courts between price maintenance by agreement and price maintenance by refusal to deal[1] or through bastard agency agreements[2] favor the larger seller and thus create competitive inequalities. The prohibition against price maintenance sanctions price leadership and sales below cost by retailers and thus is a vital element in the plane of competition in that stage of the marketing process. By the same token, the recent state legislation permitting price control by manufacturers and thus prohibiting loss leaders and sales below the fixed price affects most significantly conventional retail practice.[3] For these reasons, the rules governing the maintenance of prices must be included in any discussion of unfair competition, although the problem is somewhat different from other trade practices.

This is not the place to discuss the arguments for and against price maintenance.[4] It is sufficient merely to point out its

1926); Hills Bros. v. Fed. Trade Com., 9 F. (2d) 481 (C. C. A. 9th, 1926), *cert. denied*, 270 U. S. 662 (1927); J. W. Kobi Co. v. Fed. Trade Com., 23 F. (2d) 41 (C. C. A. 2d, 1927).

[1] United States v. Colgate & Co., 250 U. S. 300 (1919); Great Atlantic & Pacific Tea Co. v. Cream of Wheat Co., 227 Fed. 46 (C. C. A. 2d, 1915); *cf.* Frey and Son, Inc. v. Cudahy Packing Co., 256 U. S. 208 (1921).

[2] United States v. General Electric Co., 272 U. S. 476 (1926); *cf.* Fed. Trade Com. v. Curtis Publishing Co., 260 U. S. 568 (1923).

[3] See Legis. (1936) 36 Col. L. Rev. 293.

[4] Gleick, Price Maintenance (1917) 24 Case and Comment 195–200; Hearings before House Committee on Interstate and Foreign Commerce on H. R. 13568, 64th Cong., 1st Sess. (Apr. 20 and June 1, 1916) and 64th Cong., 2d Sess. (Jan. 5–11, 1917); Hearings before Senate Committee on Interstate and Foreign Commerce on S. 97, 72d Cong., 1st Sess. (March 1–2, 1932); Murchison, Resale Price Maintenance (1919); Seligman & Love,

bearing on the problem of unfair competition and to indicate its illegality under the Sherman Act,[1] its validity at common law in England[2] and in some states,[3] and its validation in several states by recent legislation.[4]

Another source of information regarding the application of the Sherman Act to trade practices is the private actions brought under Section 7 of this law.[5] These actions fall into three groups. The first consists of suits against monopolistic combines for charging unreasonable prices,[6] for withholding vital supplies,[7] for refusing to deal,[8] or for maintaining a

---

Price Cutting and Price Maintenance (1932); Haring, Retail Price Cutting and its Control by Manufacturers (1935); Fed. Trade Com., Resale Price Maintenance, (2 vol. 1929–1931); Clark, Principles of Marketing (1932) 512–543; Stevens, Resale Price Maintenance as Unfair Competition (1919) 19 Col. L. Rev. 265; Rogers, Predatory Price Cutting as Unfair Trade (1913) 27 Harv. L. Rev. 139; Miller, Maintenance of Uniform Resale Prices (1914) 63 U. of Pa. L. Rev. 22; Copeland, Standardized Resale Prices (1926) 4 Harv. Bus. Rev. 393; Tosdal, Price Maintenance (1918) 8 Amer. Econ. Rev. 23; Taussig, Price Maintenance (1916) 6 Amer. Econ. Rev. (Supp. No. 1) 170.

[1] *Supra* note 8, page 126.

[2] Palmolive Co., Ltd. v. Freedman, [1928] Ch. 264; Elliman Sons & Co., Ltd. v. Carrington & Son, Ltd. [1901] 2 Ch. 275.

[3] Fisher Flouring Mills Co. v. Swanson, 76 Wash. 649, 137 Pac. 144 (1913); Grogan v. Chafee, 156 Cal. 611, 105 Pac. 745 (1909); D. Ghirardelli Co. v. Hansicker, 164 Cal. 355, 128 Pac. 1041 (1912); Clark v. Frank, 17 Mo. App. 602 (1885); Garst v. Harris, 177 Mass. 72, 58 N. E. 174 (1900); Garst v. Charles, 187 Mass. 144, 72 N. E. 839 (1905); Marsich v. Eastman Kodak Co., 244 App. Div. 295, 279 N. Y. Supp. 140 (2d Dep't, 1935), *aff'd per curiam*, N. Y. L. J., Jan. 8, 1936, at 130 (Court of Appeals).

[4] *Supra* note 3, page 127.

[5] 39 Stat. 799 (1916), 15 U. S. C. A. § 77 (1927).

[6] Chattanooga Foundry & Pipe Works v. Atlanta, 203 U. S. 390 (1906); Thomsen v. Cayser, 243 U. S. 66 (1917); U. S. Tobacco Co. v. American Tobacco Co., 163 Fed. 701 (C. C. S. D. N. Y. 1908).

[7] Hood Rubber Co. v. U. S. Rubber Co., 229 Fed. 583 (D. Mass. 1916).

[8] Eastman Kodak Co. v. Southern Photo Materials Co., 273 U. S. 359 (1927).

monopoly price on raw materials while setting an unduly low price for the finished article.[1] This group has slight bearing upon the subject of unfair competition. The second group consists of acts which are injurious when practiced by the strong upon the weak and involve the suppression of competition, as for example, local price cutting,[2] fighting ships[3] and bogus independents,[4] rebates as a reward for exclusive dealing with the combine,[5] group boycotts,[6] and combination rates making it unprofitable for buyers to deal with non-members of the combine.[7] The third group is composed of practices which were unlawful at common law as well as others, of a similar character, which are not quite as restrictive of competition as those in the preceding group. In this class falls enticement of employees,[8] espionage,[9] commercial bribery,[10]

---

[1] Baush Machine Tool Co. v. Aluminum Co. of America, 72 F. (2d) 236 (C. C. A. 2d, 1934), *cert. denied*, 293 U. S. 596 (1934). On the retrial, verdict was returned for the plaintiff, but this was reversed on appeal for minor errors in the conduct of the trial. 79 F. (2d) 217 (C. C. A. 2d, 1935). Thereafter the case was settled.

[2] *Cf.* Ware-Kramer Tobacco Co. v. American Tobacco Co., 180 Fed. 160 (C. C. E. D. N. Y. 1910).

[3] *Cf.* Thomsen v. Cayser, 243 U. S. 66 (1917).

[4] Monarch Tobacco Works v. American Tobacco Co., 165 Fed. 774 (C. C. W. D. Ky. 1908).

[5] Thomsen v. Cayser, 243 U. S. 66 (1917).

[6] Montague v. Lowry, 193 U. S. 38 (1904); Ramsay v. Associated Billposters, 260 U. S. 501 (1923); Binderup v. Pathe Exchange, 263 U. S. 291 (1923); Mines v. Scribner, 147 Fed. 927 (C. C. S. D. N. Y. 1906).

[7] Indiana Farmers' Guide Publishing Co. v. The Prairie Farmer Publishing Co., 293 U. S. 268 (1934).

[8] *Cf.* Mitchell Woodbury Corp. v. Albert Pick-Barth Co., 41 F. (2d) 148 (C. C. A. 1st, 1930).

[9] Ware-Kramer Tobacco Co. v. American Tobacco Co., 180 Fed. 160 (C. C. E. D. N. Y. 1910).

[10] American Steel Co. v. American Steel Wire Co., 244 Fed. 300 (D. Mass. 1916).

sabotage,[1] disparagement,[2] circulation of false rumors,[3] harassing litigation,[4] inducing breach of contract,[5] and free deals.[6]

The practices in both the second and third groups are only actionable when part of a scheme to monopolize or to restrain trade.[7] Thus, even here, the regulation of competition is but a by-product of the enforcement of competition. While it is true that without the Sherman Act, the law of unfair competition would be impotent, nevertheless the contribution of this statute in defining unfairness and in establishing a plane of competition has not been very substantial.[8]

Clayton Act

The Clayton Act[9] singled out two practices for special treatment, price discrimination and exclusive dealing and other tying agreements. Section 2 forbids discriminations in price, not based upon differences in grade, quality, quantity or costs of transportation which substantially lessen competition or tend to create a monopoly in any line of commerce.[10] The

---

[1] *Ibid.* (Inducing competitor's employees to ship defective goods).

[2] Kellogg Co. v. National Biscuit Co., 71 F. (2d) 662 (C. C. A. 2d, 1934).

[3] Ware-Kramer Tobacco Co. v. American Tobacco Co., 180 Fed. 160 (C. C. E. D. N. Y. 1910).

[4] Kellogg Co. v. National Biscuit Co., 71 F. (2d) 662 (C. C. A. 2d, 1934).

[5] *Cf.* Ballard Oil Terminal Co. v. Mexican Petroleum Corp., 28 F. (2d) 91 (C. C. A. 2d, 1928).

[6] Ware-Kramer Tobacco Co. v. American Tobacco Co., 180 Fed. 160 (C. C. E. D. N. Y. 1910).

[7] See American Steel Co. v. American Steel Wire Co., 244 Fed. 302 (D. Mass. 1916); Kellogg Co. v. National Biscuit Co., 71 F. (2d) 665 (C. C. A. 2d, 1934).

[8] The practical difficulties of proving a violation of the Sherman Act and the maze of procedural requirements have tended to nullify the private remedy. See Note (1932) 32 Col. L. Rev. 335; Comment (1929) 38 Yale L. J. 503; Comment (1931) 45 Harv. L. Rev. 193.

[9] 38 Stat. 730 (1914), 15 U. S. C. A. § 12 (1927).

[10] 38 Stat. 730 (1914), 15 U. S. C. A. § 13 (1927).

section does not outlaw discrimination but merely that which substantially lessens competition or leads to monopoly. It does not compel a one-price sales policy. It does not forbid sales below cost in the absence of discrimination.[1] What constitutes a substantial lessening of competition is left to judicial construction. The section is addressed to two forms of price variation: (1) the local price cutting encountered in litigation under the Sherman Law by which the large trusts sought to eliminate local competitors and (2) the price discrimination which favors one set of buyers and gives them a competitive advantage over other distributors, without injuring the seller's competitors. Curiously, there is a dearth of litigation dealing with the first form of discrimination notwithstanding the concern this practice caused during the early years of the trust movement.[2] The second form was explicitly ruled unlawful by the Supreme Court in 1929.[3] It is the latter practice which presents the most difficulty today. The former tends more to protect competition than to establish a standard of trade practice. The latter, from the sellers' standpoint, moves in the direction of a restriction on the conduct of business extending beyond the preservation of com-

---

[1] *Cf.* Boss Mfg. Co. v. Payne Glove Co., 71 F. (2d) 768 (C. C. A. 8th, 1934), *cert. denied*, 293 U. S. 590 (1934); S. S. Kresge Co. v. Champion Spark Plug Co., 3 F. (2d) 415 (C. C. A. 6th, 1923). The section does not apply to discriminatory leases, and leaves the crucial term "discrimination" undefined.

[2] Porto Rican American Tobacco Co. v. American Tobacco Co., 30 F. (2d) 234 (C. C. A. 2d, 1929), *cert. denied*, 279 U. S. 858 (1929); *cf.* Sidney Morris v. National Ass'n of Stationers, 40 F. (2d) 620 (C. C. A. 7th, 1930). The unfortunate wording of the section leaves it doubtful whether it covers the elimination of the small business man by the price-cutting of its larger competitor, since the standard of legality is the substantial lessening of competition in any line of commerce. The disappearance of one company may not substantially lessen competition in the industry.

[3] Van Camp & Sons Co. v. American Can Co., 278 U. S. 245 (1929).

petition. Mr. McAllister, in a penetrating article,[1] has pointed out both the traps in this law which may ensnare the unwary suitor and the dilemma in which the ambiguous language of the section places the sales manager of a large company. Any price policy, whether based upon quantity purchases or a functional classification of buyers, involves some discrimination. If the sole purpose of the section is to prevent monopoly, then many unfair and deceitful discriminations remain untouched. Conversely, if the purpose is to prevent unfair and deceitful discriminations, why require proof of a substantial lessening of competition? Mr. McAllister ascribes most of the uncertainty prevailing in business circles regarding the scope of the section to the fact that it is the sole instrumentality by which deceptive as well as monopolistic discrimination can be checked, and he doubts the wisdom of treating the two disparate problems in one section.[2] In view of the wording of the statute, the conclusion is inescapable that the section comes into play only upon a showing that competition among either sellers or distributors has been substantially lessened, and this has been the construction placed upon it by the courts.[3] This leaves untouched a host of price practices that may be injurious to competitors or buyers without endangering competition. It is not entirely clear that Congress intended to deal with such problems, but the decisions of the Federal Trade Commission, which Mr. McAllister reviews, and the hypothetical situations which he considers,

---

[1] McAllister, Sales Policies and Price Discrimination under the Clayton Act (1932) 41 Yale L. J. 518.

[2] *Id.* at 538.

[3] Baran v. Goodyear Tire & Rubber Co., 256 Fed. 571 (S. D. N. Y. 1919); S. S. Kresge Co. v. Champion Spark Plug Co., 3 F. (2d) 415 (C. C. A. 6th, 1923); American Can Co. v. Ladoga Can Co., 44 F. (2d) 763 (C. C. A. 7th, 1930). See also Note (1924) 38 Harv. L. Rev. 103; Comment (1929) 38 Yale L. J. 804; Note (1929) 42 Harv. L. Rev. 680; Comment (1929) 14 Corn. L. Q. 330; (1931) 44 Harv. L. Rev. 807.

reveal the need for legislation which will differentiate between the two types of discrimination.

The state legislation on the subject generally follows the federal pattern.[1] The attempt of some legislatures to establish a single-price system and forbid any discrimination, regardless of its effect on competition, has failed to run the constitutional gauntlet.[2]

Section 3[3] forbids the making of a sale, contract or lease on the condition, agreement or understanding that the purchaser or lessee shall not use or deal in the goods, wares, merchandise, machinery, supplies, or other commodities of competitors of the seller or lessor, where the effect of such arrangement may be to lessen competition substantially or to create a monopoly. The statute forbids the exclusive dealing arrangements only when ancillary to a sale or lease. A naked agreement between B and S not to deal with C is thus governed by the law of boycott. Whether such a naked agreement would be sustained if followed by a sale or lease is not at all clear. The point has not yet been litigated. If permitted, the way is open to complete nullification of the statute. The section was primarily directed at the tying practice of the *Mimeograph*

---

[1] Chamberlain, Legislative Prohibitions of Unfair Practices (1924) 10 A. B. A. J. 44; Note (1926) 26 Col. L. Rev. 614. Some of these statutes deviate from the federal law in that they specifically forbid discrimination in buying [*cf*. S. D. Comp. Laws (1929) § 4366; Wis. Stat. (1933) § 133.18] as well as in selling [*cf*. S. D. Comp. Laws (1929) § 4365; Wis. Stat. (1933) § 133.17]. In addition, some of the statutes refer to discrimination in the purchase of a particular commodity or class of commodities [*cf*. Wyo. Rev. Stat. (Courtright, 1931) §§ 117–301—purchase of dairy and mineral products].

[2] Fairmont Creamery Co. v. Minnesota, 274 U. S. 1 (1927); Comment (1928) 22 Ill. L. Rev. 533. A similar Arkansas statute deals with discrimination in the sale of ice. Ark. Stat. (Castle's Supp. Ann. 1931) § 5597e. But the type of statute cited in note 1 above *supra*, has been upheld in Central Lumber Co. v. South Dakota, 226 U. S. 157 (1912).

[3] 38 Stat. 731 (1914), 15 U. S. C. A. § 14 (1927).

case.[1]   Yet the act does not forbid all tying restrictions.   Thus it is not unlawful to compel the lessee of a gasoline pump to confine the use of the pump to the storage and sale of the lessor's gasoline provided that the lessee is free to handle competing brands in other pumps.[2]   By the same token, if there are several mimeograph machines on the market, the seller may presumably compel the use of his paper and ink on his machine so long as the purchaser is free to obtain other machines and to use any kind of paper and ink in connection with such machines.   This construction clearly frustrates the purpose of the section, but its unfortunate wording opens the door to such evasion.   The application of the statute to full-line-forcing[3] and block-booking[4] still remains uncertain.

---

[1] Henry v. A. B. Dick Co., 224 U. S. 1 (1912).   Motion Picture Patents Co. v. Universal Film Mfg. Co., 243 U. S. 502 (1917) was decided after the enactment of the Clayton Act, but the court did not rest its decision upon Section 3, and directly overruled the *Dick* case.   See also, United Shoe Machinery Corp. v. United States, 258 U. S. 451 (1922).   On similar restrictions in patent licenses, see Lord v. Radio Corp. of America, 24 F. (2d) 565 (D. Del. 1928), *aff'd*, 28 F. (2d) 257 (C. C. A. 3d, 1928), *cert. denied*, 278 U. S. 648 (1928); Comment (1931) 40 Yale L. J. 954; Carbice Corp. v. American Patents Corp., 283 U. S. 27, 420 (1931); McCormack, Restrictive Patent Licences and Restraint of Trade, (1931) 31 Col. L. Rev. 743.   See generally Comment (1928) 38 Yale L. J. 246; Comment (1928) 28 Col. L. Rev. 828.

[2] Fed. Trade Com. v. Sinclair Refining Co., 261 U. S. 463 (1923).   See also Comment (1923) 23 Col. L. Rev. 598; Note (1923) 71 U. of Pa. L. Rev. 260; *cf.* Comment (1935) 35 Col. L. Rev. 127, and see Clare v. Ice Cream Cabinet Co., 11 N. J. Misc. 386, 166 Atl. 722 (Ch. 1933).

[3] Fed. Trade Com. v. Gratz, 253 U. S. 421 (1930); see also Comment (1920) 20 Col. L. Rev. 806; Note (1921) 6 Corn. L. Q. 320.   This decision involved a proceeding by the Federal Trade Commission and the complaint did not charge, although the record substantiated, that competition had been substantially lessened.

[4] Fed. Trade Com. v. Paramount Famous Lasky Corp., 57 F. (2d) 152 (C. C. A. 2d, 1932); Comment (1932) 1 Geo. Wash. L. Rev. 136.   This case also deals with the jurisdiction of the Commission and the court found that competition was not substantially lessened.

Not every exclusive arrangement is condemned. Only those arrangements which substantially lessen competition or have a monopolistic tendency are outlawed. So long as a substantial number of distributors are available to other sellers, it is difficult to show any lessening of competition. As a practical matter, the section restricts the large, dominant concerns;[1] in a highly competitive field, sellers run slight risk in making exclusive agreements with distributors.[2] Thus, the practices forbidden by this section fall in the category of restraint of trade rather than unfair competition. The purpose of Section 3 is the same as that of the Sherman Law.

In this brief and sketchy summary we have sought merely to suggest the major shortcoming of the statute. Without further demonstration, we conclude with the dogmatic assertion that these provisions of the Clayton Act are ambiguous, vague, and horrible exhibits of draftsmanship.[3]

Federal Trade Commission Act

In the Clayton Act, Congress attacked several competitive abuses by specific legislation. In the Federal Trade Commission Act[4] it returned to the generality of the Sherman Law and forbade "unfair methods of competition." More accurately,

---

[1] Standard Fashion Co. v. Magrane-Houston Co., 258 U. S. 346 (1922); Q. R. S. Music Co. v. Fed. Trade Com., 12 F. (2d) 730 (C. C. A. 7th, 1926). See also Note (1922) 36 Harv. L. Rev. 86; Oliphant, Exclusive Dealing (1923) 9 A. B. A. J. 311; cf. Chafee, Equitable Servitudes on Chattels, (1928) 41 Harv. L. Rev. 945.

[2] Pearsall Butter Co. v. Fed. Trade Com., 292 Fed. 720 (C. C. A. 7th, 1923). The restriction in an "agency" arrangement has been sustained. Fed. Trade Com. v. Curtis Publishing Co., 260 U. S. 568 (1923). See Comment (1923) 23 Col. L. Rev. 595; Comment (1923) 32 Yale L. J. 514; cf. Note (1927) 27 Col. L. Rev. 838.

[3] Cf. Henderson, Federal Trade Commission (1924) 300 et seq.

[4] 38 Stat. 717 (1914), 15 U. S. C. A. § 41 (1927). For similar legislation in Wisconsin see Lotwin, Trade Practice Work in Wisconsin (1932) 7 Wis. L. Rev. 213; Developments in the Law (1933) 46 Harv. L. Rev. 1171, 1200.

it endowed the Federal Trade Commission with power to prohibit, by the issuance of cease and desist orders, unfair competitive methods. The four words quoted constituted the sole guidance vouchsafed the Commission by Congress. The word "method," of the four, was the only new term to be used in this connection and is the alpha and omega of the Congressional contribution. In a later section we shall consider the execution of this vague mandate by the Commission.

Packers and Stockyards Act

A similar generality permeates the Packers and Stockyards Act[1] which forbids various restraints of trade[2] as well as "any unfair, unjustly discriminatory, or deceptive practice or device in commerce."[3] The statute is enforced by the Secretary of Agriculture under a procedure similar to that of the Trade Commission.[4]

Control of Imports

A combination of the various statutory prohibitions we have considered is found in a recent act forbidding unfair practices in the import trade. Unfair methods of competition in the importation of goods are forbidden where the methods tend to destroy or substantially injure an industry, which is efficiently and economically operated, or to prevent the establishment of such an industry, or to restrain and monopolize commerce in

---

[1] 42 Stat. 159 (1921), 7 U. S. C. A. § 181 (1927).

[2] 42 Stat. 161 (1921), 7 U. S. C. A. § 192 (1927). E. g., undue preferences, apportionment of supply, manipulating prices, conspiracy to apportion territory, purchases and sales.

[3] Ibid. See Stafford v. Wallace, 258 U. S. 497 (1922); Legis. (1922) 22 Col. L. Rev. 68. A recent amendment to the Act authorizes the Secretary of Agriculture to license live poultry dealers and handlers in order to curb "unfair, deceptive and fraudulent practices." Act of August 14, 1935, c. 532, 7 U. S. C. A. § 218 (1935).

[4] Id., § 193 (1927).

the United States.[1]   Buttressing this prohibition are the anti-
dumping provisions of the Tariff Act[2] and the Act of 1916[3] forbidding the importation and sale of goods at a price less than
their actual market value or wholesale price in the principal
markets of the country of their production or of other foreign
countries to which they are commonly exported, with the
intent of destroying or injuring an industry in the United
States, or of preventing the establishment of such an industry
or of restraining or monopolizing any part of trade or commerce on such articles in this country.   The meaning of all
these qualifications still remains to be determined by the
courts.   The buck-passing which characterizes these laws
makes a travesty of the legislative process.

Food and Drug Legislation

The Federal Food & Drug Act[4] forbids misbranding and
adulteration of foods and drugs.   A voluminous literature is
concerned with the tragic shortcomings of this law.[5]   We are
at the threshold of the enactment of new legislation.[6]   For

---

[1] 46 Stat. 703 (1930), 19 U. S. C. A. § 1337 (1934); *In re* Northern Pig-
ment Co., 71 F. (2d) 447 (Ct. Cust. & Pat. App. 1934); *In re* Orion Co.,
71 F. (2d) 458 (Ct. Cust. & Pat. App. 1934).   The Webb Act, 40 Stat. 517
(1918), 15 U. S. C. A. § 64 (1927) forbids unfair methods of competition in
the export trade.

[2] 42 Stat. 11 (1921), 19 U. S. C. A. § 160 (1927).

[3] 39 Stat. 798 (1916), 15 U. S. C. A. § 72 (1927).

[4] 34 Stat. 768 (1906), amended by 37 Stat. 416 (1912), 37 Stat. 732
(1913), 41 Stat. 271 (1919), 42 Stat. 1500 (1923), 46 Stat. 1019 (1930),
48 Stat. 1204 (1934), 21 U. S. C. A. §§ 1 *et seq.* (1927).

[5] See authorities cited note 1, page 97, *supra*, and especially Legis. (1932) 32
Col.L. Rev. 720; Fisher, The Proposed Food and Drugs Act: A Legal Critique,
1 Law and Contemporary Problems (1933) 74.   These references should be
consulted for an analysis and appraisal of the present law.

[6] As one of the draftsmen of the new law, I expounded its purposes in
Revision of Federal Food and Drugs Law, Oil, Paint and Drug Rep. (June
26, 1933) 17.   The original bill has since been considerably revised.   The
advertising provisions of the proposed law should be considered in connec-

present purposes it is enough to point out that, while these offenses were not actionable at common law, the federal[1] and state legislation[2] affords some measure of protection to the consumer and imposes serious restraint upon the conduct of business enterprise in these industries.[3]

---

tion with the discussion of false advertising in the text.   See Fisher, *op. cit. supra* note 5, page 137, at 97.   The provisions of the present law and the proposed changes merit extended treatment in any discussion of unfair competition but the writer must again bow to limitations of space.

[1] There is a vast body of statutes dealing with cognate problems: *e.g.*, Apple Act, 37 Stat. 250 (1912), 15 U. S. C. A. § 231 (1927), 21 U. S. C. A. § 20 (1927) (standard containers, standard grades, misbranding); Filled Milk Act, 42 Stat. 1486 (1923), 21 U. S. C. A. § 61 (1927) (shipment of certain type of adulterated milk in interstate commerce forbidden); Import Milk Act, 44 Stat. 1101 (1927), 21 U. S. C. A. § 141 (1934) (standards of quality); Oleomargarine Act, 24 Stat. 909 (1886), amended 32 Stat. 193 (1902), 40 Stat. 1008 (1918), 26 U. S. C. A. § 970 (1935) (taxing manufacturers and dealers of oleomargarine, standards of packing); Mixed Flour Law, 30 Stat. 467 (1898), 26 U. S. C. A. § 1020 (1935) (labeling and packing, taxation); Meat Inspection Law, 34 Stat. 1260 (1907), 21 U. S. C. A. § 71 (1927); Farm Products Inspection Law, 43 Stat. 844 (1925), 7 U. S. C. A. § 414 (1927) (Secretary of Agriculture may certify quality of farm products); see 1 Dunn, Food and Drug Laws (1927) 235 *et seq.*; 46 Stat. 1019 (1930), 21 U. S. C. A. § 10 (1935) (Secretary of Agriculture may set up standards of quality and fill for canned food and labeling requirements for below-standard goods); Federal Alcohol Administration Act, 49 Stat. 981 (1935), 27 U. S. C. A. § 205 (1935) (Administrator authorized to issue regulations *re* advertising, packaging, marking, branding and size and fill of container to prevent deception and to provide the consumer with adequate information as to the identity and quality of the products), Insecticides Act, 36 Stat. 335 (1910), 7 U. S. C. A. § 121 (1927); Caustic Poison Act, 44 Stat. 1406 (1927), 15 U. S. C. A. § 401 (1935).

[2] Pa. Stat. Ann. (Purdon, 1930) tit. 31, §§ 1–13; Idaho Code Ann. (1932) §§ 36–301 to 36–322; Maine Rev. Stat. (1930) c. 41, §§ 1–37; Wash. Rev. Stat. (Remington, 1932) §§ 6137–6164; 2 & 3 Dunn, Food and Drugs Laws (1927).

[3] Allied in purpose is federal legislation forbidding false designation of origin, 41 Stat. 534 (1920), 15 U. S. C. A. § 123 (1927); or requiring identification marks on firearms and prohibiting defacement or obliteration, 48 Stat. 1239 (1934), 26 U. S. C. A. § 1132g (1934).

Bituminous Coal Act

The recent Guffey Act[1] marks a departure from the normal patterns of federal legislation. In enacting a modified version of the N. R. A. Coal Code, Congress sought to prescribe a remedy for a single industry. Shattering precedent in still a further respect, Congress substituted specific prohibitions for general condemnations.

The Guffey Act forbids the following practices:[2]

1. The consignment of unordered coal, or the forwarding of coal which has not actually been sold, consigned to the producer or his agent: . . .

2. The adjustment of claims with purchasers of coal in such manner as to grant secret allowances, secret rebates, or secret concessions, or other price discrimination.

3. The prepayment of freight charges with intent to or having the effect of granting a discriminatory credit allowance.

4. The granting in any form of adjustments, allowances, discounts, credits, or refunds to purchasers or sellers of coal, for the purposes or with the effect of altering retroactively a price previously agreed upon, in such manner as to create price discrimination.

5. The predating or postdating of any invoice or contract for the purchase or sale of coal, except to conform to a bona fide agreement for the purchase or sale entered into on the predate.

6. The payment or allowance in any form or by any device of rebates, refunds, credits, or unearned discounts, or the extension to certain purchasers of services or privileges not extended to all purchasers under like terms and conditions, or under similar circumstances.

7. The attempt to purchase business, or obtain information concerning a competitor's business by concession, gifts, or bribes.

8. The intentional misrepresentation of any analysis or of analyses, or of sizes, or the intentional making, causing, or permitting to be made, or publishing, of any false, untrue, misleading, or deceptive statement by way

---

[1] 49 Stat. 991 (1935), 15 U. S. C. A. §§ 801–827 (1935). See Comment (1935) 45 Yale L. J. 293. The Federal Alcohol Administration Act, 49 Stat. 981 (1935), 27 U. S. C. A. § 205 (1935), is similarly based upon a prior N. R. A. code and forbids various unfair practices, *e.g.* exclusive outlets, "tied houses," commercial bribery and sales on consignment.

[2] *Id.* at § 807i.

of advertising, invoicing, or otherwise concerning the size, quality, character, nature, preparation, or origin of any coal bought, sold, or consigned.

9. The unauthorized use, whether in written or oral form, of trade marks, trade names, slogans, or advertising matter already adopted by a competitor, or any deceptive approximation thereof.

10. Inducing or attempting to induce, by any means or device whatsoever, a breach of contract between a competitor and his customer during the term of such contract.

11. Splitting or dividing commissions, broker's fees, or brokerage discounts, or otherwise in any manner directly or indirectly using brokerage commissions or jobbers' arrangements or sales agencies for making discounts, allowances, or rebates, or prices other than those determined under this Act, to any industrial consumer or to any retailers, or to others, whether of a like or different class.

12. Selling to, or through, any broker, jobber, commission account, or sales agency, which is in fact or in effect an agency or an instrumentality of a retailer or an industrial consumer or of an organization of retailers or industrial consumers, whereby they or any of them secure either directly or indirectly a discount, dividend, allowance, or rebates, or a price other than that determined in the manner prescribed by this chapter.

Most of the quoted provisions are designed to protect the price structure of the industry and hence must be regarded as price regulations rather than unfair trading prohibitions. The list also includes the familiar forms of deceit. Congress and the coal industry presumably regarded these practices as uneconomic and wasteful. Whether they are is of course another question,[1] but it is interesting to note that this is the first instance of the inclusion of such prohibitions in federal legislation.[2] When one observes the sloppiness and ambiguity

---

[1] On the problems of the coal industry, see Hamilton & Wright, Case of Bituminous Coal (1925); Hamilton & Wright, Way of Order for Bituminous Coal (1928); 3 Encyc. Soc. Sciences (1930) 582; Sachs, Coal (Aug. 30, 1933) 76 New Republic 63; Report of the Coal Commission, 68th Cong., 2d Sess., (1925, Sen. Doc. 195).

[2] The N. R. A. code experience is discussed later.

For specific prohibition in statutes affecting particular industries see e. g. the prohibition of the use of fighting ships by water carriers, 39 Stat. 733 (1916), 46 U. S. C. A. § 812 (1928), and the prohibition of house to house

of the draftsmanship of this section, one must conclude that, unsatisfactory as general prohibitions may be, they are by far the lesser of the two evils.

Postal Laws

Despite the advent of the radio, the use of the mails is indispensable to modern advertising. Consequently the restrictions in the postal laws against fraudulent schemes,[1] obscenity[2] and lotteries[3] are properly part of the plane of competition. The mail fraud section has been chiefly applied to the more blatant frauds and has had little influence upon current advertising practice.[4] The obscenity section places some limitation upon, but does not blight, the sex appeal of advertising copy. The lotteries provision has been fairly effective and has prevented not only the advertising lottery but also contests and chain-sales.[5]

---

sales of utility holding company securities, Act. of August 26, 1935, c. 687, tit. 1, § 6, 15 U. S. C. A. § 79 f (c) (1935). To be compared are the Securities Act, 48 Stat. 74 (1933), 15 U. S. C. A. § 77a (1934), the Securities Exchange Act, 48 Stat. 881 (1934), 15 U. S. C. A. § 78a (1934), the Communications Act, 48 Stat. 1064 (1934), 47 U. S. C. A. § 151 (1934) (controlling broadcasting), and the National Labor Relations Act, P. L. No. 198, 74th Cong., 1st Sess. (1935), discussed in Legis. (1935) 35 Col. L. Rev. 1098.

[1] R. S. § 5480; 25 Stat. 873 (1889), 35 Stat. 1130 (1909), 18 U. S. C. A. § 338 (1927).

[2] R. S. § 3893; 19 Stat. 90 (1876), 25 Stat. 496 (1888), 35 Stat. 416 (1908), 35 Stat. 1129 (1909), 36 Stat. 1339 (1911), 18 U. S. C. A. § 334 (1927).

[3] R. S. § 3894; 19 Stat. 90 (1876), 26 Stat. 465 (1890), 28 Stat. 963 (1895), 35 Stat. 1129 (1909), 18 U. S. C. A. § 336 (1927).

[4] See Handler, *supra* note 1, page 100, at 28. See Harrison v. United States, 200 Fed. 662 (C. C. A. 6th, 1912).

[5] There are state statutes forbidding lotteries. For a discussion of the entire problem see Pickett, Contests and Lottery Laws (1932) 45 Harv. L. Rev. 1196; Note (1925) 39 A. L. R. 1039; Note (1927) 48 A. L. R. 1115; Note (1928) 57 A. L. R. 424; New v. Tribond Sales Corp., 19 F. (2d) 671 (App. D. C. 1927), *cert. denied*, 275 U. S. 550 (1927) (chain sales).

State Legislation

The state enactments cover a wide compass and only a few illustrations can be presented. Mention should be made of the large body of licensing laws which restrict the exercise of various crafts or trades to those possessing prescribed qualifications of competence or integrity.[1] While these laws do not relate to selling methods, they directly affect the plane of competition through their exclusion of the unqualified from the competitive arena.[2]

1. False Advertising

The failure of the common law to create the new forms of action that were necessary for the suppression of false advertising led to the enactment of a model statute in many of the states. This legislation was sponsored by "Printers' Ink" and the model act is commonly called the "Printers' Ink Act."[3] The draftsmanship is somewhat cumbersome and there is sufficient ambiguity, although less than in the other legislation reviewed, to permit a hostile court to frustrate the purposes of the law. And such hostility has not been lacking.[4] The zealousness with which the statute is enforced varies in the several states. The non-legal agencies that have been most

---

[1] N. Y. Public Health Law (1917) §§ 169, 198, 219; N. Y. Village Law (1927) § 89 subd. 52; N. Y. Real Property Law, as amended 1934, Art. 12-A; cf. N. Y. Alcoholic Beverage Control Law (1934). There are other types of licensing laws designed to compel compliance with minimum standards of safety and cleanliness, cf. N. Y. Vehicle & Traffic Law (1929) § 20; N. Y. Agric. & Markets Law (1932) § 71b; id. (1934) § 251k, and to facilitate compliance with tax laws, cf. N. Y. Tax Law (1934) § 283a.

[2] It has not been possible to assay the effectiveness of these statutes. It is clear that many are but dead-letters and that administration is rather lax.

[3] Comment (1927) 36 Yale L. J. 1155; Handler, supra note 1, page 100, at 31; Legis. (1930) 43 Harv. L. Rev. 945. See also the false testimonial laws, cited supra note 1, page 98.

[4] State v. Massey, 95 Wash. 1, 163 Pac. 7 (1917).

successful in elevating the standards of advertising practice have found the statute useful as a club, to be invoked only as a last resort, against the advertisers who refuse to mend their ways.

2. Warranty

The Uniform Sales Act has given such a fillip to the development of the law of warranty that we include the topic in our discussion of the legislative contribution, notwithstanding the high stage of development of the doctrines of warranty at common law.   Section 12 of the Uniform Statute provides:

"Any affirmation of fact or any promise by the seller relating to the goods is an express warranty if the natural tendency of such affirmation or promise is to induce the buyer to purchase the goods, and if the buyer purchases the goods relying thereon.   No affirmation of the value of the goods nor any statement purporting to be a statement of the seller's opinion only shall be construed as a warranty."

In effect, this statute outlaws misrepresentation as a selling device.   It dispenses with the *scienter* requirement which weakened the common law action of deceit.   But the exclusion of statements of opinion and value, the restriction of the statute to affirmations which relate to the goods and which naturally tend to induce purchases, and the element of reliance materially narrow the field in which this section can operate. The doctrine of privity shields the manufacturer who conveniently makes the affirmations that create custom for his dealers.[1]   The cost of litigation precludes the bringing of suit except where the article purchased possesses considerable value.   He who misrepresents his wares has little cause to fear Section 12.

Section 15 imposes liability upon the seller where the article sold is not of merchantable quality or is not fit for the particular purpose for which it was purchased, assuming, in the latter

---

[1] Williston, Sales (1924) § 244; Note (1929) 42 Harv. L. Rev. 414.

case, that the purpose was made known to the seller and that the buyer relied upon the seller's skill or judgment. An article purchased by its trade name is only warranted as to its merchantability and not as to its special fitness. These implied warranties establish minimum standards of quality in the absence of contrary stipulation in the contract. The meaning of merchantability varies with the product and with the court but, in general, it signifies fair, average quality and reasonable fitness of the article for normal usage. Liability is imposed without fault and approaches that of an insurer. As consequential damages may be recovered, the implied warranty is the most potent remedy available to the consumer.

The interesting history and the ramifications of the law of warranty are not germane to the present discussion.[1] The doctrines of warranty impose standards of truth and quality which necessarily affect the plane on which competition is conducted. Enforcement is by the buyer rather than the competitor.

3. Commercial Bribery

A commercial bribe is any valuable consideration given an employee or agent to influence his decisions and actions in the course of his employment. The term bribery is not limited to pecuniary grants. It includes expensive gifts and other favors as well as secret commissions. It is generally asserted that the gratuity is wrongful only if secretly given, but under some circumstances, the knowledge of the principal may be

---

[1] Hamilton, The Ancient Maxim Caveat Emptor (1931) 40 Yale L. J. 1133. For an extraordinary collection of cases with brilliant commentaries see Llewellyn, Cases and Materials on Sales (1930) c. III. Llewellyn's arrangement is contrapuntal. The substantive law of warranty and the procedural doctrines constitute the major themes. His collection of cases reveals the long struggle not only for the recognition of liability but also for the development of suitable remedies by which liability could be enforced.

legally immaterial.[1] "Whenever there is inducement to an employee to act contrary to the interests of his employer, or to an agent to act contrary to the interests of his principal, the transaction savors of corruption."[2]

The problem of commercial bribery has not been handled very effectively at common law. There is no authority explicitly condemning the practice as an unfair method of competition, subject to injunction at the suit of a competitor.[3] The cases deal with the validity of contracts induced by bribery and with the rights and liabilities of the delinquent purchasing agent. These sanctions can be very stringent if the bribe is discovered, but the difficulty of detection naturally impairs the force of any legal remedy. The Federal Trade Commission has attempted to stamp out both the cruder forms of bribery and the more subtle methods of "wining and dining buyers," but it has run into jurisdictional difficulties and an unwillingness on the part of the courts to stretch the meaning of unfair competition to include corrupting influences of a more refined nature.[4] Criminal statutes have been passed in several states and there has been a strong movement for the enactment of federal legislation.[5] The elevation of trade ethics by law

---

[1] Note (1928) 28 Col. L. Rev. 799, 802. The text is based in large part upon this note. See also Legis. (1932) 45 Harv. L. Rev. 1248.

[2] National Industrial Conference Board, Public Regulation of Competitive Practices (1929) 155.

[3] "The trader who seeks thus to promote his sales is engaged in an unfair method of competition, for he interposes an obstacle to the competitive opportunity of other traders which is in no way related to any economic advantage possessed by him." Id. at 155. In International News Service v. Associated Press, 248 U. S. 215 (1918), the defendants were restrained from bribing employees of newspapers to furnish Associated Press news before publication, but the Supreme Court did not discuss this aspect of the case.

[4] Note (1928) 28 Col. L. Rev. 799, 803; see also Handler, Jurisdiction of Federal Trade Commission over False Advertising (1931) 31 Col. L. Rev. 527, 556.

[5] Note (1928) 28 Col. L. Rev. 799, 801.

can only be partially effective; improvement must come from within in the form of self-restraint and self-discipline. Much can undoubtedly be done by means of new legislation and by an extension of the Commission's authority, but bribery will continue as long as there are givers and takers.

4. Miscellaneous

The more important state enactments affecting competition may be classified as follows:

(a) Anti-trust laws, frequently couched in general language like the Sherman Act, but occasionally enumerating specific restraints of trade.[1] In this group also fall statutes modelled after the Clayton Act, prohibiting price discrimination[2] and exclusive dealing arrangements.[3]

(b) Trademark statutes, dealing primarily with problems of registration and providing criminal penalties for infringement.[4] Most states make it a penal offense to refill trademark containers or to deface the marks thereon.[5] In some states there are express enactments prohibiting dealers from substituting branded articles without advising the purchaser of the substitution, and from displaying marks or brands unless the branded

---

[1] For an elaborate analysis of these laws, see Legis. (1932) 32 Col. L. Rev. 347.

[2] These statutes assume various forms and deal with discrimination in purchasing, *cf*. Wis. Stat. (1933) § 133.18; in selling, *cf*. Minn. Stat. (Mason, 1927) § 10464; in buying specific commodities, *cf*. Wyo. Rev. Stat. (1931) § 117–301; in selling specific commodities, *cf*. Ark. Stat. (Castle's Supp. Ann., 1931) § 5597e.

[3] Mass. Gen. Laws (1932) c. 93, § 1.

[4] N. Y. Gen. Bus. Law (1924) § 367; Wis. Stat. (1933) §§ 132.01–132.04; Vt. Pub. Laws (1933) §§ 7821–7822. The Federal Trade Mark Act is a registry law and relates, almost exclusively, to problems of procedure, 33 Stat. 724 (1905), 15 U. S. C. A. § 81 (1927). See Handler & Pickett, *supra* note 1, page 85, at 783.

[5] N. Y. Gen. Bus. Law (1925) § 362; Ore. Code Ann. (1930) § 41–1003; Pa. Stat. Ann. (Purdon, 1930) tit. 73, § 32.

article is actually offered for sale.[1]   Such statutes are limited
to specific commodities such as soft drinks or lubricating oils.[2]

(c) Food and drugs legislation, similar to the federal law,
together with specific enactments establishing statutory standards of identity and quality for stated commodities.[3]

(d) Labelling laws, prohibiting misrepresentation,[4] requiring affirmative disclosure of ingredients,[5] place of origin,[6]
name of manufacturer[7] and similar information[8] or prescribing the form of labels that must be used on certain products.[9]
Similar in purpose are laws compelling the use of marks indicating the place of origin[10] and penalizing their defacement.[11]

---

[1] Tenn. Code (1932) § 11139; S. D. Comp. Laws (1929) §§ 7883E–
7883F.

[2] *Ibid.*

[3] *Supra* note 2, page 138; Mass. Gen. Laws (1932) c. 94, § 12 (milk and
cream); Pa. Stat. Ann. (Purdon, 1931) tit. 31, § 372 (grapes); Mich. Comp.
Laws (Mason's Supp., 1933) §§ 17115–287, 17115–288 (silver); *cf.* Waters-
Pierce Oil Co. v. Deselms, 212 U. S. 159 (1909) (illuminating oil).   See also
Atlantic Refining Co. v. Trumbull, 43 F. (2d) 154 (D. Conn. 1930) declar-
ing unconstitutional a Connecticut statute establishing standards for motor
oils.   See Hamilton, The Ancient Maxim Caveat Emptor (1931) 40 Yale
L. J. 1133.

[4] Wash. Rev. Stat. Ann. (Remington, 1932) § 2637–1; Colo. Comp. Laws
(Supp. 1932) § 3640; *cf.* Legis. (1930) 43 Harv. L. Rev. 945.

[5] Mass. Gen. Laws (1932) c. 94, § 187; Ky. Stat. (Carroll, 1930) § 2060a–
6, subd. 4.   Upholding the constitutionality of a state statute requiring
compulsory disclosure, see Corn Products Refining Co. v. Eddy, 249 U. S.
427 (1919); Fisher, *op. cit. supra* note 5, page 137, at 92; Note (1928) 57
A. L. R. 686.

[6] Ore. Code Ann. (1930) § 18–3502; see Note (1933) 83 A. L. R. 1409.

[7] Idaho Code Ann. (1932) § 22–801.

[8] Mass. Gen. Laws (1932) c. 94, § 154; Wis. Stat. (1933) § 352.075.

[9] Cal. Gen. Laws (Deering, 1931) Act 2967, § 3 (lubricating oil); Mass.
Gen. Laws (1932) c. 94, § 21 (cream); Vt. Pub. Laws (1933) § 7747 (butter
substitutes); Neb. Comp. Stat. (1929) § 71–2307 (bedding); Ind. Stat. Ann.
(Burns, 1933) § 35–1322 (skim milk products).

[10] Idaho Code Ann. (1932) § 22–801; see *supra* note 6 above.   See federal
act, *supra* note 3, page 100.

[11] N. Y. Penal Law (1934) § 435c.

(e) Prohibitory legislation, restricting or imposing heavy taxation upon the sale of such products as cigarettes[1] and oleomargarine.[2]

(f) Chain store tax laws.[3]

(g) Peddling and itinerant seller laws, prohibiting or regulating street selling or house to house canvassing.[4]

(h) Statutes prohibiting sales below cost[5] in order to injure or drive out competitors, or the granting of secret rebates for similar purposes.[6]

(i) Legislation prohibiting or regulating the use of trading stamps.[7]

(j) Regulations of weights and measures.[8]

---

[1] Tenn. Code (1932) § 11205; Vt. Pub. Laws (1933) § 8644; Gundling v. Chicago, 177 U. S. 183 (1899); Austin v. Tennessee, 179 U. S. 343 (1900); Note (1922) 20 A. L. R. 926.   The familiar liquor laws should also be mentioned.

[2] Idaho Code Ann. (1932) § 36–1001; Iowa Code (1931) § 3100–d1; Powell v. Pennsylvania, 127 U. S. 678 (1888); McCray v. United States, 195 U. S. 27 (1904); Parkinson, Cases on Legislation (1934) 359.

[3] Tax Commissioners v. Jackson, 283 U. S. 527 (1931).   But cf. Louis K. Liggett Co. v. Lee, 288 U. S. 517 (1933).   See Legis. (1931) 31 Col. L. Rev. 145; Note (1935) 44 Yale L. J. 619; Comment (1935) 45 Yale L. J. 314; note (1935) 21 Iowa L. Rev. 93.

[4] Ohio Gen. Code (Page, 1926) § 6358; Ill. Rev. Stat. (1935) c. 34, § 215; Ky. Stat. (Carroll, 1930) § 4215.   Difficulty arises under the commerce clause if the acts are applied to salesmen representing sellers in other states. Real Silk Mills v. Portland, 268 U. S. 325 (1925).

[5] S. C. Code (Michie, 1932) § 6634; Calif. Laws 1935, c. 477, § 3.

[6] Wisconsin Laws 1935, c. 52.

Reference should again be made to the lottery and gift enterprise schemes, *supra* note 5, page 141.

[7] Mass. Gen. Laws (1932) c. 271, § 30; Wis. Stat. (1933) § 134.01; Wash. Rev. Stat. Ann. (Remington, 1932) § 8359.   See Note (1931) 40 Yale L. J. 1112; Note (1923) 26 A. L. R. 686, 707.

[8] Ill. Rev. Stat. (1935) c. 147, § 1; Utah Rev. Stat. Ann. (1933) § 3–13–1; Wyo. Rev. Stat. Ann. (1931) § 123–101.   See Note (1920) 6 A. L. R. 429; Note (1934) 90 A. L. R. 1290.

(k) Fair trade acts, permitting price maintenance in order to discourage the use of loss leaders.[1]

(l) Acts prohibiting the appropriation and use of another's list of customers.[2]

(m) Restrictions upon the place[3] and method[4] of advertising, including the control of billboard advertising.[5]

(n) Proration laws[6] controlling production.

To be contrasted with these piece-meal enactments is a recent Connecticut statute regulating the retail drug industry. This act is obviously based upon the N. R. A. Retail Code and forbids inaccurate advertising, disparagement, claims "to a policy or a continuing practice of generally underselling competitors," secret rebates, commercial bribery, inaccurate billing, lotteries, use of manufacturers' salesmen or demonstrators without openly identifying them as manufacturers' agents, and sales below manufacturers' wholesale list price.[7]

---

[1] Legis. (1936) 36 Col. L. Rev. 293.

[2] Ill. Rev. Stat. (1935) c. 38 § 400; N. Y. Penal Law (1917) § 553(6).

[3] Ohio Gen. Code (Page, 1926) § 12492; Cal. Gen. Laws (Deering, 1931) Act 89, § 1; Fifth Ave. Coach Co. v. New York, 221 U. S. 467 (1911); State *ex rel.* Belt v. St. Louis, 161 Mo. 371, 61 S. W. 658 (1901). For regulations of time and place of doing business, see Note (1924) 31 A. L. R. 299, 302 (auctions).

[4] Pa. Stat. Ann. (Purdon, 1931) tit. 18, § 2322; Mass. Gen. Laws (1932) c. 266, § 90. People v. Johnson, 117 Misc. 133, 191 N. Y. Supp. 750 (Ct. Gen. Sess. 1921); Wettengel v. Denver, 20 Colo. 552, 39 Pac. 343 (1895); Note (1923) 22 A. L. R. 1484.

[5] Minn. Stat. (Mason, 1927) § 2615, subd. 3; Mass. Gen. Laws (1932) c. 93, § 30; Note (1931) 72 A. L. R. 465; Note (1932) 79 A. L. R. 551.

[6] Cal. Gen. Laws (Deering, 1931) Act 5636, § 6; Okla. Stat. (1931) § 11546; Tex. Stat. Supp. (1931) Art. 6049c, § 7; Marshall & Myers, Legal Planning of Petroleum Production (1931) 41 Yale L. J. 33; (1933) 42 *id.* 702. For sanitary regulations of premises and articles sold, see Note (1922) 18 A. L. R. 235; Note (1928) 52 A. L. R. 669.

Not included in the text are statutes similar to the N. Y. Milk Control Act regulating specific industries. N. Y. Agriculture & Markets Law (1934) Arts. 21, 21a. See Note (1934) 34 Col. L. Rev. 1336.

[7] Conn. Laws, June 17, 1935, c. 135a, 2 C. C. H. Federal Trade Regula-

An instructive note in the Harvard Law Review[1] reveals a recent tendency on the part of courts to treat a violation of a penal statute affecting the conduct of business as an unfair method of competition, enjoinable at the suit of competitors. This new doctrine has not yet won complete acceptance and has been confined to lottery, labelling and liquor laws. He who observes a law is placed at a serious competitive disadvantage by the non-compliance of competitors. The honest tradesman cannot afford to await the dilatory criminal enforcement of the statute by the state. Unless armed by the remedy of injunction, he must, to save his trade, resort to the same practice himself. The private injunction is a potent indirect sanction and should be more widely permitted.

Recapitulation

To generalize about this morass of legislation is both difficult and hazardous. Detailed investigations regarding the operation of all these special laws would be necessary before any reliable conclusions of their efficacy could be drawn. Such investigations have been made on several instances, and a few limited observations may be made. Many of the statutes are so general that their effect has been merely to shift the responsibility to the courts or administrative agencies of establishing a plane of competition. The specific enactments are sporadic, unrelated and uncoördinated. Except in one or two instances, there has been no sustained and comprehensive attack on the general problem. The legislatures have dealt with many more abuses than the courts. They have sought to facilitate as well as to regulate competition. They have condemned practices which they believed to be uneconomic as well as those which

---

tion Service, par. 60,061. See also elaborate regulation of the liquor industry with specific prohibition of certain trading practices, N. Y. Alcoholic Beverage Control Law (1934).

[1] Note (1929) 42 Harv. L. Rev. 693; see also Comment (1934) 13 Tex. L. Rev. 136 (Sunday laws); Comment (1925) 25 Col. L. Rev. 1088.

are oppressive and deceitful. Obviously no golden thread runs through these unrelated laws. Little ingenuity has been manifested in the creation and choice of sanctions. The offenses have not been well defined and the loop-holes are many. The level of draftsmanship has been deplorably low. It is doubtful whether a busy legislature can give the time and attention that these problems require. The enactment of legislation is a tedious process and laws become obsolete almost before their final passage. The road to amendment is beset by many difficulties as the experience with the food and drugs laws has proved. Without legislation, progress in regulating competition is impossible, but the legislative contribution must be supplemented by other devices for the formulation of competitive regulations. This legislative experience has widened our knowledge as to the practices which must be included in any comprehensive scheme of control, but a synthesis still remains to be perfected.

VI

THE CONTRIBUTION OF THE FEDERAL TRADE COMMISSION

With the establishment of the Federal Trade Commission in 1914,[1] a new experiment in the regulation of competition was begun. Unlike the courts, the Commission received a specific mandate from Congress, but unfortunately this mandate was too general and vague to afford any real guidance. The legislative condemnation of "unfair methods of competition"[2] could only be given content and meaning in terms of specific practices. The Commission's position, therefore, was not much of an improvement over that of the courts at common law.

Of course, the Commission had the benefit of the experience of the regulation of competition at common law and under the Sherman Act. It also had the advantage of the specific

---

[1] 38 Stat. 719 (1914), 15 U. S. C. A. § 41 (1927).

[2] 38 Stat. 719 (1914), 15 U. S. C. A. § 45 (1927).

prohibition of price discrimination and exclusive dealing arrangements in Sections 2 and 3 of the Clayton Act. Moreover, there were the debates of Congress to amplify and enlighten the statutory provision. The Commission, however, could find only divided counsel in the debates. According to Mr. Montague, the term "unfair methods of competition" was used in at least eight different senses by the sponsors of the measure. His enumeration follows:

"(a) Every act of passing off one's business or goods for another's.

"(b) All methods of competition tending to restraint of trade or monopoly which have been forbidden by the Sherman Law.

"(c) Substantially all violations of the anti-trust laws, including even wrongs arising from inter-locking directorates and allied incorporate directorships.

"(d) All unfair methods of stifling competition.

"(e) All other acts which the 'commission . . . decides . . . may lead to monopoly or restraint of trade' though not now forbidden by the Sherman Act.

"(f) All other acts affecting a competitor for which 'a remedy lies either at law or in equity.'

"(g) All other acts which either affect a competitor and are 'against public morals,' or in any way interfere with economic 'efficiency,' though heretofore quite lawful and not forbidden by the Sherman law or by any other law.

"(h) All other acts comprehended within the meaning which 'unfair competition' has today in common parlance and in literature."[1]

It will be observed that each of the separate meanings in this list requires further definition.

The proponents of the measure were not unaware of the vagueness of the language they were employing. Their purpose has been best explained by Mr. Justice Brandeis:

"Instead of undertaking to define what practices should be deemed unfair, as had been done in earlier legislation, the act left the determination to the commission. Experience with existing laws had taught that definition,

---

[1] Montague, Unfair Methods of Competition (1915) 25 Yale L. J. 20, 29–30.

being necessarily rigid, would prove embarrassing and, if rigorously applied, might involve great hardship. Methods of competition which would be unfair in one industry, under certain circumstances, might, when adopted in another industry, or even in the same industry under different circumstances, be entirely unobjectionable. Furthermore, an enumeration, however comprehensive, of existing methods of unfair competition must necessarily soon prove incomplete, as with new conditions constantly arising novel unfair methods would be devised and developed."[1]

While the congressional purpose, as stated by Senator Cummins,[2] was to permit the words "unfair competition" to "grow and broaden and mold themselves to meet circumstances as they arise," the Commission and the courts were left to flounder as to which circumstances were to be met. It is not to be wondered that as many different meanings were given the statutory phrase as there were judges construing it.[3] Some of the circuit courts of appeals adopted the same standard of legality under the new act as had prevailed under the Sherman law. What was an unlawful restraint of trade now became an unfair method of competition and, conversely, what was lawful under the anti-trust laws could not be unlawful under this Act. Other courts felt that the statutes were not coextensive. This led some to take the position that since the Commission was an administrative body, it could not assume jurisdiction of every violation of the anti-trust laws. Others, approaching the problem from another angle, held that the purpose of the statute was to reach unfair practices in their incipiency, and, hence, the Commission had the power to proceed before a technical violation of the Sherman Laws had occurred. Some courts discerned an intention on the part of

---

[1] Dissenting opinion in Fed. Trade Comm. v. Gratz, 253 U. S. 421, 429, 436–437 (1920).

[2] 51 Cong. Rec. 14003 (1914).

[3] This section is based upon a previous article of mine, Jurisdiction of Federal Trade Commission over False Advertising (1931) 31 Col. L. Rev. 527, 537–538, and the citations supporting the assertions in the text are there collected.

Congress to invest the Commission with jurisdiction over all competitive practices which were unlawful at common law, regardless of their relation to the Sherman Act.   On the other hand, it is still dubious under the cases whether the original tort of unfair competition, that is, passing off, is within the Commission's jurisdiction.   Still another group of courts upheld the authority of the Commission to "stop all those trade practices that have a capacity or tendency to injure competitors directly or through deception of purchasers, quite irrespective of whether the specific practices in question have yet been denounced in common law cases."[1]   Another view to find judicial expression was that the Commission was empowered to outlaw such fraud or deception as injured competitors or the public or lessened competition.

These views are not all mutually exclusive.   Indeed, it is not unusual to find the same circuit court of appeals favoring one theory in one case and another in a subsequent suit.

There has been a similar oscillation on the part of the Supreme Court.   In the first case that came before the court, *Federal Trade Commission v. Gratz*,[2] a static conception of unfair competition was adopted.

"The words 'unfair method of competition' are not defined by the statute, and their exact meaning is in dispute.   It is for the courts, and not the Commission, ultimately to determine, as matter of law, what they include. They are clearly inapplicable to practices never heretofore regarded as opposed to good morals because characterized by deception, bad faith, fraud, or oppression, or as against public policy, because of their dangerous tendency unduly to hinder competition or create monopoly."

This sterile definition includes (a) restraint of trade, (b) monopoly, and (c) practices which are deceptive, fraudulent or oppressive.   The first two are not properly to be regarded as

---

[1] Sears, Roebuck & Co. v. Fed. Trade Com., 258 Fed. 307, 311 (C. C. A. 7th, 1919).

[2] 253 U. S. 421 (1920).

unfair competition, as the term has been used in the present article. Since the Commission was established not only to regulate competition but to preserve and maintain it, the statute had to be given this broader meaning. Congress evidently contemplated that the Commission would devote most of its energies to the enforcement of the Sherman Act. Our concern here, however, is with the third class of acts. It is to be observed that not every deceptive or oppressive practice is within the Commission's jurisdiction, but only those which theretofore had been regarded "as opposed to good morals." By whom they must have been so regarded is not stated. But in view of the fact that the Court reserved to itself the right to say what is or is not unfair competition, the implication is that the Commission might only proceed against those practices which were previously unlawful at common law. This rigid conception left no room for growth. "New circumstances" could not be met as they arose. Only the "old circumstances," which had received attention at common law and under the Sherman Act, could be considered by the Commission.

Had this view prevailed, the Commission would have been unable to make any substantive contribution to the law of unfair competition. Happily it has not prevailed, but almost fifteen years were needed to overcome most of its mischief. In *Federal Trade Commission v. Winsted Hosiery Co.*,[1] the Commission's power to forbid false advertising and misbranding was sustained, notwithstanding that this practice, as we have seen, was neither actionable at common law nor under the Sherman Act. In *Federal Trade Commission v. Beechnut Packing Co.*,[2] the Court affirmed an order forbidding resale price

---

[1] 258 U. S. 483 (1922). On the jurisdiction of the Commission over false advertising, see Comment (1931) 40 Yale L. J. 617; Comment (1933) 31 Mich. L. Rev. 804.

[2] 257 U. S. 441 (1922).

maintenance and assimilated the concept of restraint of trade
to unfair competition.   The Court said:

> "What shall constitute unfair methods of competition denounced by the
> act is left without specific definition.   Congress deemed it better to leave
> the subject without precise definition, and to have each case determined
> upon its own facts, owing to the multifarious means by which it is sought
> to effectuate such schemes.   The commission, in the first instance, subject
> to the judicial review provided, has the determination of practices which
> come within the scope of the act."[1]

Here again, the notion that the concept of unfairness may
not be expanded was abandoned.   Nevertheless, while each
case was left to its facts, the succeeding decisions in the
Supreme Court saw the Commission consistently repulsed.[2]
The *Gratz* dictum was repeatedly quoted with approval.
Within the last two years, however, the Court has re-examined
the subject and has virtually consigned the definition in the
Gratz case to oblivion.

In *Federal Trade Commission v. R. F. Keppel & Bro., Inc.*[3] the
Court, in upholding an order forbidding the use of a modified
lottery scheme in the sale of penny candy, discussed the meaning and scope of the statute as follows:

> " . . . we cannot say that the Commission's jurisdiction extends only to
> those types of practices which happen to have been litigated before this
> Court.
>
> "Neither the language nor the history of the Act suggests that Congress
> intended to confine the forbidden methods to fixed and unyielding cate-
> gories.   The common law afforded a definition of unfair competition and,
> before the enactment of the Federal Trade Commission Act, the Sherman
> Act had laid its inhibition upon combinations to restrain or monopolize
> interstate commerce which the courts had construed to include restraints
> upon competition in interstate commerce.   It would not have been a

---

[1] *Id*. at 453.

[2] Handler, *supra* note 3, page 153, at 546–547.

[3] 291 U. S. 304 (1934).   See Comment (1934) 32 Mich. L. Rev. 1142;
Note (1934) 43 Yale L. J. 1338; Comment (1934) 82 U. of Pa. L. Rev. 664;
Comment (1934) 11 N. Y. U. L. Q. 663.

difficult feat of draftsmanship to have restricted the operation of the Trade Commission Act to those methods of competition in interstate commerce which are forbidden at common law or which are likely to grow into violations of the Sherman Act, if that had been the purpose of the legislation.

"The Act undoubtedly was aimed at all the familiar methods of law violation which prosecutions under the Sherman Act had disclosed. . . . But as this Court has pointed out it also had a broader purpose. . . . As proposed by the Senate Committee on Interstate Commerce and as introduced in the Senate, the bill which ultimately became the Federal Trade Commission Act declared 'unfair competition' to be unlawful. But it was because the meaning which the common law had given to those words was deemed too narrow that the broader and more flexible phrase 'unfair methods of competition' was substituted. Congress, in defining the powers of the Commission, thus advisedly adopted a phrase which, as this Court has said, does not 'admit of precise definition but the meaning and application of which must be arrived at by what this Court elsewhere has called "the gradual process of judicial inclusion and exclusion." ' *Federal Trade Commission v. Raladam Co.*, 283 U. S. 648. * * * *

"While this Court has declared that it is for the courts to determine what practices or methods of competition are to be deemed unfair, *Federal Trade Commission v. Gratz*, 253 U. S. 421, in passing on that question the determination of the Commission is of weight. It was created with the avowed purpose of lodging the administrative functions committed to it in 'a body specially competent to deal with them by reason of information, experience and careful study of the business and economic conditions of the industry affected,' and it was organized in such a manner, with respect to the length and expiration of the terms of office of its members, as would 'give to them an opportunity to acquire the expertness in dealing with these special questions concerning industry that comes from experience.' Report of Senate Committee on Interstate Commerce, No. 597, June 13, 1914, 63d Cong., 2d Sess., pp. 9, 11.

"It is unnecessary to attempt a comprehensive definition of the unfair methods which are banned, even if it were possible to do so. We do not intimate either that the statute does not authorize the prohibition of other and hitherto unknown methods of competition or, on the other hand, that the Commission may prohibit every unethical competitive practice regardless of its particular character or consequences. New or different practices must be considered as they arise in the light of the circumstances in which they are employed."[1]

---

[1] 291 U. S. 304, 310–314 (1934).

I have quoted at such length in order to indicate the revolutionary change of attitude of the Court. It required two decades for the view of Senator Cummins to achieve the respectability of judicial acceptance. It is now possible for the Commission to meet some "circumstances" as they arise and its determinations are conceded to have "weight." But its creative capacity is not unlimited; the censorious review of the courts still remains. A broader field of action has been opened to the Commission, the precise boundaries of which remain to be charted.[1] Nevertheless, the *Keppel* Case revitalizes the statute and affords the Commission an opportunity to make a fresh start. Despite the unwonted respect accorded the Commission, the Court refused to commit itself to any definite standard of legality and again reserved the right to have the last word on the meaning of unfair competition.

The *Gratz* case was not the only ruling which undermined the authority and prestige of the Commission. In *Federal Trade Commission v. Klesner*,[2] it was held that the courts and not the Commission were to determine whether proceedings instituted by it were in the public interest. In *Federal Trade Commission v. Raladam Co.*,[3] the Court ruled that the Commission could forbid false advertising only when the misrepresentation injured honest competitors. The Commission could not undertake to protect consumers nor could it proceed against industries in which every seller misrepresented his

---

[1] A more sympathetic attitude toward the Commission was also manifested in Fed. Trade Com. v. Algoma Lumber Co., 291 U. S. 67 (1934); Fed. Trade Com. v. Royal Milling Co., 288 U. S. 212 (1933). It is interesting to note that in Schechter Poultry Co. v. United States, 295 U. S. 495, 532 (1935), when confronted with a less palatable system of regulation, the court was willing to swallow its objections to the Commission and to speak more favorably of it. The *Keppel* and *Schechter* cases constitute a new charter of liberty for the Commission.

[2] 280 U. S. 19 (1929).

[3] 283 U. S. 643 (1931).

wares.[1] Finally, despite the explicit provision in the statute that the findings of fact of the Commission should be conclusive if supported by testimony, the scope of appellate review has been virtually as broad as in the case of appeals from the judgments of courts of equity and the findings of fact of the court have been freely substituted for those of the Commission.[2]

In our search for the meanings of unfair competition we must not limit our study to the judicial review of the Commission's orders. We must also examine the practices which the Commission has sought to ban. The most convenient summary of the Commission's activities is to be found in its annual reports. This summary constitutes the Commission's contribution to the law of unfair competition. I am setting it forth in full, despite its length, because it is so revealing of the quality as well as the scope of the Commission's work. The unfair trading practices follow:

"1. The use of false or misleading advertising, calculated to mislead and deceive the purchasing public to their damage and to the injury of competitors.

2. Misbranding of fabrics and other commodities respecting the materials or ingredients of which they are composed, their quality, purity, origin, source or qualities, properties, history or nature of manufacture, and selling them under such names and circumstances that the purchaser would be misled in these respects.

3. Bribing buyers or other employees of customers and prospective customers, without the latter's knowledge or consent, to secure or hold patronage.

4. Procuring the business or trade secrets of competitors by espionage, or bribing the employees, or by similar means.

5. Inducing employees or competitors to violate their contracts and enticing away employees of competitors in such numbers or under such

---

[1] The decision of the lower court is discussed at length in the article cited in note 3, page 153, *supra*. See also Comment (1931) 31 Col. L. Rev. 1190.

[2] *E.g.*, Fed. Trade Com. v. Curtis Publishing Co., 260 U. S. 568 (1923) and cases cited in the article, *supra* note 3, page 153; but *cf.* Fed. Trade Com. v. Artloom Corp., 69 F. (2d) 36 (C. C. A. 3d, 1934).

circumstances as to hamper or embarrass the competitors in the conduct of their business.

6. Making false and disparaging statements respecting competitors' products, their value, safety, *etc.*, and competitors' business, financial credit, *etc.*, in some cases under the guise of ostensibly disinterested and specially informed sources or through purported scientific but in fact misleading demonstrations or tests.

7. Widespread threats to the trade of suits for patent infringement arising from the sale of alleged infringing products of competitors, such threats not being made in good faith but for the purpose of intimidating the trade and hindering or stifling competition, and claiming and asserting, without justification, exclusive rights in public names of unpatented products.

8. Trade boycotts or combinations of traders to prevent certain wholesale or retail dealers or certain classes of such dealers from procuring goods at the same terms accorded to the boycotters or conspirators, or to coerce the trade policy of their competitors or of manufacturers from whom they buy.

9. Passing off goods or articles for well and favorably known products of competitors through appropriation or simulation of such competitors' trade names, labels, dress of goods, *etc.*, with the capacity and tendency unfairly to divert trade from the competitors, and/or with the effect of so doing to their prejudice and injury and that of the public.

10. Selling rebuilt, second-hand, renovated, or old products or articles made from used or second-hand materials as and for new.

11. Paying excessive prices for supplies for the purpose of buying up same and hampering or eliminating competition.

12. Using concealed subsidiaries, ostensibly independent, to secure competitive business otherwise unavailable.

13. Using merchandising schemes based on a lot or chance.

14. Cooperative schemes and prices for compelling wholesalers and retailers to maintain resale prices fixed by a manufacturer or distributor for resale of his product.

15. Combinations or agreements of competitors to enhance prices, maintain prices, bring about substantial uniformity in prices or to divide territory or business, to cut off competitors' sources of supply, or to close markets to competitors, or otherwise restrain or hinder free and fair competition.

16. Various schemes to create the impression in the mind of the prospective customer that he or she is being offered an opportunity to make a purchase under unusually favorable conditions when such is not the case, with capacity and tendency to mislead and deceive many of the purchasing

public into buying products involved in such erroneous belief, and/or with the effect so to do, to the injury and prejudice of the public and of competitors, such schemes including—

(a) Sales plans in which the seller's usual price is falsely represented as a special reduced price made available on some pretext for a limited time or to a limited class only.

(b) The use of the 'free goods' or service device to create the false impression that something is actually being thrown in without charge, when, as a matter of fact, it is fully covered by the amount exacted in the transaction taken as a whole.

(c) Use of misleading trade names calculated to create the impression that a dealer is a manufacturer or grower, importer, *etc.*, selling directly to the consumer with resultant savings.

(d) Use of pretended, exaggerated retail prices in connection with or upon the containers of commodities intended to be sold as bargains at lower figures.

17. Imitating or using standard containers customarily associated in the mind of the general purchasing public with standard weights or quantities of the product therein contained, to sell to the public such commodity in weights or quantities less than the aforementioned standards, with capacity and tendency to deceive the purchasing public into believing that they are purchasing the quantities generally associated with the standard containers involved, and/or with the effect of so doing, and with tendency to divert trade from and otherwise injure the business of competitors who do not indulge in such practices, and/or with the effect of so doing, to the injury of such competitors and to the prejudice of the public.

18. Concealing business identity in connection with the marketing of one's product, or misrepresenting the seller's relation to others; *e. g.*, claiming falsely to be the agent or employee of some other concern or failing to disclose the termination of such a relationship in soliciting customers of such concerns, *etc.*

19. Misrepresenting in various ways the advantages to the prospective customer of dealing with the seller, with the capacity and tendency to mislead and deceive many among the consuming public into dealing with the person or concern so misrepresenting, in reliance upon such supposed advantages, and to induce their purchases thereby, and/or with the effect of so doing, to the injury and prejudice of the public and of competitors, such as—

(a) Seller's alleged advantages of location or size.

(b) False claims of being the authorized distributor of some concern.

(c) Alleged endorsement of the concern or product by the Government or by nationally known business organizations.

(d) False claim by a dealer in domestic products of being an importer, or by a dealer of being a manufacturer, grower or nursery, or by a manufacturer of some product of being also the manufacturer of the raw material entering into the product.

(e) Being manufacturer's representative and outlet for surplus stock sold at a sacrifice, *etc.*

(f) Representing that the seller is a wholesale dealer, grower, producer, or manufacturer, when in fact such representation is false.

20. Use by business concerns associated as trade organizations or otherwise of methods which result, or are calculated to result, in the observance of uniform prices or practices for the products dealt in by them, with consequent restraint or elimination of competition, such as use of various kinds of so-called standard cost systems, price lists or guides, exchange of trade information, *etc.*

21. Obtaining business through undertakings not carried out and through dishonest and oppressive devices calculated to entrap and coerce the customer or prospective customer, with the result of deceiving the purchasing public and inducing purchases by many thereof, and of diverting and tending to divert trade from competitors who do not engage in such false, misleading, and fraudulent representations, all to the prejudice and injury of the public and competitors, such practices including—

(a) Securing by deceit prospective customer's signature to a contract and promissory note represented as simply an order on approval;

(b) Obtaining agents to distribute the seller's products through promising to refund the money paid by them should the product prove unsatisfactory, and through other undertakings not carried out; and

(c) Obtaining business by advertising a 'free trial' offer proposition when, as a matter of fact, only a 'money-back' opportunity is offered the prospective customer.

22. Giving products misleading names so as to give them a value to the purchasing public or to a part thereof which they would not otherwise possess, with the capacity and tendency to mislead the public into purchasing the products concerned in the erroneous beliefs thereby induced, and with the tendency to divert and/or with the effect of diverting business from and otherwise injuring and prejudicing competitors who do not engage in such practices, and to the prejudice of the public and of competitors, such as names implying falsely that—

(a) The particular products so named were made for the Government or in accordance with its specifications and of corresponding quality, or are connected with it in some way, or in some way have been passed upon, inspected, underwritten, or endorsed by it; or

(b) They are composed in whole or in part of ingredients or materials, respectively, contained only to a limited extent or not at all; or

(c) They were made in or came from some locality famous for the quality of such products; or

(d) They were made by some well and favorably known process, when, as a matter of fact, they were only made in imitation of and by a substitute for such process; or

(e) They have been inspected, passed, or approved after meeting the tests of some official organization charged with the duty of making such tests expertly, disinterestedly, or giving such approval; or

(f) They were made under conditions or circumstances considered of importance by a substantial part of the general purchasing public; or

(g) They were made in a country, place or city considered of importance in connection with the public taste, preference or prejudice.

23. Selling below cost, with the intent and effect of hindering, stifling, and suppressing competition.

24. Dealing unfairly and dishonestly with foreign purchasers and thereby discrediting American exporters generally, with the effect of bringing discredit and loss of business to all manufacturers and business concerns engaged in and/or seeking to engage in export trade, and with the capacity and tendency to do so, to the injury and prejudice of the public and of the offending concerns' export-trade competitors.

25. Coercing and enforcing uneconomic and monopolistic reciprocal dealing.

26. Entering into contracts in restraint of trade whereby foreign corporations agree not to export certain products into the United States in consideration of a domestic company's refusal to export the same commodity or sell to anyone other than those who agree not to so export the same.

27. Giving products a purported unique status or special merits or properties through pretended but in fact misleading and ill-founded demonstrations or scientific tests, or through misrepresenting the history or circumstances involved in the making of the products or associated therewith, so as to give them a value to the purchasing public or to a part thereof which they would not otherwise possess, with the capacity and tendency to mislead the public into purchasing the products concerned in the erroneous beliefs thereby engendered, to the prejudice and injury of competitors and the public, as hereinabove set forth."[1]

---

[1] Annual Report (1935) 67–71. The Commission's explanation of the list is as follows:

Without being captious, one may well question whether the Commission ought not to be able, after twenty years, to draft a summary in more precise language and to classify its rulings more logically.

This list must be contrasted with the practices sustained by the courts.[1] These follow: false advertising and misbranding, including misrepresentation as to quality and character of goods,[2] misrepresentation of business status,[3] misrepresentation

---

"The following partial list shows unfair methods of competition condemned by the Commission from time to time in its orders to cease and desist issued under Section 5 of the Federal Trade Commission Act. These do not include Clayton Act violations, which under the jurisdiction of the Commission, embrace, subject to the various provisions of the statute, price discrimination (§ 2, Clayton Act), tying and exclusive contracts or dealings (§ 3, Clayton Act), corporate-stock acquisitions (§ 7, Clayton Act), and interlocking directorates (§ 8, Clayton Act)."

[1] All the court decisions up to 1931 are tabulated in an appendix to my article in (1931) 31 Col. L. Rev. 527, 553–560 and in (1931) 31 Col. L. Rev. 1190. Only the decisions since that time will be cited in the following notes.

In addition to the secondary materials cited in this appendix see Watkins, An Appraisal of the Work of the Fed. Trade Com. (1932) 32 Col. L. Rev. 272; Malone, Meaning of the Term "Public Interest" in the F. T. C. Act (1931) 17 Va. L. Rev. 676; Ely, Work of the F. T. C. (1932) 7 Wis. L. Rev. 195; Note (1934) 32 Mich. L. Rev. 1143; (1929) 43 Harv. L. Rev. 285; Blaisdell, Federal Trade Commission (1932).

[2] Fed. Trade Com. v. Algoma Lumber Co., 291 U. S. 67 (1934); Cady Lumber Co. v. Fed. Trade Com., 68 F. (2d) 995 (C. C. A. 9th, 1934); Fed. Trade Com. v. Artloom Corp., 69 F. (2d) 36 (C. C. A. 3d, 1934); E. G. Hughes, Inc. v. Fed. Trade Com., 77 F. (2d) 886 (C. C. A. 2d, 1935); cf. Indiana Quartered Oak Co. v. Fed. Trade Com., 58 F. (2d) 182 (C. C. A. 2d, 1932) (modifying previous order in view of reversal of stand by Commission re Phillipine mahogany); James S. Kirk & Co. v. Fed. Trade Com., 59 F. (2d) 179 (C. C. A. 7th, 1932), cert. denied, 287 U. S. 663 (1932) (order restricting use of term "Castile Soap" to soaps containing olive oil set aside); Ironized Yeast Co. v. Fed. Trade Com., Report of F. T. C. (1935) 77.

[3] Fed. Trade Com. v. Royal Milling Co., 288 U. S. 212 (1933); Brown Fence & Wire Co. v. Fed. Trade Com., 64 F. (2d) 934 (C. C. A. 6th, 1933).

of origin,[1] false claim to endorsement,[2] re-issue of old films as new releases; simulation of trademarks and trade names; disparagement and malicious falsehoods; lotteries;[3] exclusive dealing arrangements and tying contracts; resale price maintenance;[4] sales below cost and sales with rebates; price discrimination; and such restraints of trade as price fixing, division of territory and trade boycotts by combinations.[5] While orders of the Commission were set aside by the lower courts, for one reason or another, in cases involving fictitious price reductions,[6] use of paid testimonials,[7] molestation, espionage, and commercial bribery, it seems reasonably clear that under the new dispensation, the Commission's jurisdiction over these practices will be sustained. Similarly, while there have been reversals of orders directed against full-line forcing[8] and exclusive dealing arrangements,[9] the Commission will probably be upheld where such practices substantially affect competition and the records of the proceedings are in

---

[1] *Cf.* Fed. Trade Com. v. Algoma Lumber Co., 291 U. S. 67 (1934); Fed. Trade Com. v. Maisel Trading Post, Inc., 77 F. (2d) 246 (C. C. A. 10th, 1935); Fed. Trade Com. v. Hall; Fed. Trade Com. v. Edwin Cigar Co., 67 F. (2d) 993 (C. C. A. 2d, 1933) (*per curiam*).

[2] *Cf.* Fed. Trade Com. v. Civil Service Training Bureau, Inc., 79 F. (2d) 113 (C. C. A. 6th, 1935).

[3] Fed. Trade Com. v. Keppel & Bro., 291 U. S. 304 (1934); Walter H. Johnson Candy Co. v. Fed. Trade Com., 78 F. (2d) 717 (C. C. A. 7th, 1935).

[4] Armand Co. v. Fed. Trade Com., 78 F. (2d) 707 (C. C. A. 2d, 1935).

[5] *Cf.* Fed. Trade Com. v. Wallace, 75 F. (2d) 733 (C. C. A. 8th, 1935).

[6] But see Consolidated Book Publishers, Inc. v. Fed. Trade Com., 53 F. (2d) 942 (C. C. A. 7th, 1931), *cert. denied*, 286 U. S. 553 (1932), affirming the Commission's order.

[7] Northam Warren Corp. v. Fed. Trade Com., 59 F. (2d) 196 (C. C. A. 2d, 1932), discussed in Comment (1933) 17 Minn. L. Rev. 681. One cannot be dogmatic in prediction, but the practice is so outrageous that wishful thinking can be pardoned. The tone of this decision is as unfortunate as the *Gratz* case.

[8] Fed. Trade Com. v. Gratz, 253 U. S. 421 (1920).

[9] Handler, *supra* note 3, page 153, at 556.

good shape.   In view of the public interest requirement, laid down in the *Klesner* case,[1] it is rather doubtful whether orders forbidding trademark and trade name simulation, except where the mark or name is inherently deceptive, will be affirmed.   The same doubt attaches to threats of patent infringement suits,[2] disparagement, and inducing breach of contract.   In view of the failure of the common law to provide effective relief against disparagement, it would be lamentable if the courts were to deny the Commission the power to forbid the practice.   The private remedies for inducing breach of contract and for threats of harassing litigation are adequate and there is no real need for intervention by the Commission. The decisions in the *Gasoline Pump* cases[3] and the recent *Block Booking* case[4] in the motion picture industry leave little room for the hope that these practices will ever be forbidden.[5]

It is not feasible at this time to consider whether each of the practices listed in the Commission's report may validly be included in its plane of competition.   The approval of the courts seems to depend upon the following factors: (1) whether the practice affects a substantially large proportion of the public to warrant proceedings by the Commission in

---

[1] 280 U. S. 19 (1929).   See Comment (1930) 43 Harv. L. Rev. 839 (deceptive trademark).

[2] Flynn & Emrich Co. v. Fed. Trade Com., 52 F. (2d) 836 (C. C. A. 4th, 1931), setting aside the order on the ground that evidence of bad faith was insufficient and that the proceeding by Commission was not in the public interest.

[3] Handler, *supra* note 3, page 153, at 556.   Compare the report of the Administrator of the Oil Code on the lease and licensing practice in this industry. (Mimeographed 1935).

[4] Fed. Trade Com. v. Paramount Famous Lasky Corp., 57 F. (2d) 152 (C. C. A. 2d, 1932).

[5] Similar hostility has been demonstrated toward § 7 of the Clayton Act. All the recent orders have been set aside.   Arrow-Hart & Hegeman Electric Co. v. Fed. Trade Com., 291 U. S. 587 (1934); Temple Anthracite Co. v. Fed. Trade Com., 51 F. (2d) 656 (C. C. A. 3d, 1931); V. Vivaudou, Inc. v. Fed. Trade Com., 94 F. (2d) 273 (C. C. A. 2d, 1931).

the public interest; (2) whether the pratice affects honest competitors; and (3) whether the practice is tainted with some deception or immorality familiar to the courts.

In the light of this analysis, it would appear that jurisdiction of this agency extends (1) to practices which restrain trade, eliminate competition, or tend to create monopoly; (2) practices which were regarded as tortious at common law and which involve some injury to the public in addition to the invasion of private right; and finally (3) practices which are inherently deceptive or immoral and which are harmful to honest competitors. Thus the Commission's list would not be approved in its entirety by the courts. The Commission has not the power to protect the interests of consumers as such, nor has it the power to forbid methods which in operation are economically wasteful, which may increase the cost of production and distribution, or which may create competitive inequalities. In the words of Mr. Justice McReynolds, the Commission "has no general authority to compel competitors to a common level, to interfere with ordinary business methods, or to prescribe arbitrary standards for those engaged in the conflict for advantage called 'competition.' "[1]

Apart from its condemnation of false advertising and commercial lotteries, the Commission has added little, or more accurately, has been permitted to add little, to the meaning of unfair competition. The courts are largely responsible for the scanty contribution. But there are other disappointing aspects of the Commission's record for which it alone is to be blamed. The very creation of the Commission betokened a congressional dissatisfaction with the procedures and techniques of the judicial system; otherwise the task of enforcement could have been delegated to the courts and the Department of Justice. Congress obviously intended the Commission to devise a speedy procedure for the prompt detection of unfair

---

[1] Fed. Trade Com. v. Sinclair Refining Co., 261 U. S. 463, 475–76 (1923).

practices and their peremptory elimination. The vindication of its policy was not to be left to the private litigant. An alert and vigilant administrative tribunal was to take action as soon as it discovered that unfair methods were being practiced.

Very few of these objectives have been attained. The Commission's procedure has proved to be cumbersome and inefficient. Litigation before the Commission has frequently been more protracted than in the courts. Numerous investigations and preliminary hearings precede the final argument before the Commission and the issuance of an order. The order is not self-executing and becomes effective only upon judicial affirmance. The Commission has devoted its energies to petty misrepresentations while major improprieties remained untouched.[1] The combination of the functions of prosecutor and judge has resulted in bureaucratic tyranny and the presentation of ill-prepared and unlawyer-like records to the courts.[2] The economic division of the Commission has been used in its investigations and economic studies and has had little influence in the shaping of the law of unfair competition.[3] The substitution by the courts of their views for those of the Commission prevented the development of the expert and specialized tribunal which Congress contemplated. A rapid turn-over of commissioners and a disappointing exercise of the appointive power by the executive contributed their share to the frustration of the congressional purpose. Since the legal staff of the Commission prosecuted every case before the Commission, the volume of business which could be handled

---

[1] Watkins, An Appraisal of the Work of the F. T. C. (1932) 32 Col. L. Rev. 272. The atrophy of the Commission's power of investigation has also contributed to its failure. See Handler, Constitutionality of Investigations by the Federal Trade Commission (1928) 28 Col. L. Rev. 708, 905.

[2] Henderson, Federal Trade Commission (1924) c. IV.

[3] Watkins, The Federal Trade Commission—A Critical Survey (1926) 40 Quarterly J. Econ. 561, 567.

was necessarily limited and only a minor fraction of competitive abuses has been attacked.

The Commission sought to avoid the deficiencies of its procedure in two ways: It encouraged the use of stipulations to settle proceedings pending before it and, in this way, increased its dispositions. While this device has resulted in a notable improvement of efficiency, experience has shown it to possess some serious shortcomings. Minor officials have used coercive tactics to compel business men to sign stipulations. Since most of the offenses are of a petty nature, it does not pay the average business man to enter into contest with the Commission, and members of the staff have taken advantage of this fact. On the other hand, the stipulation has not been of much legal significance since a violation results in no penalty other than the issuance of an order by the Commission, which in turn must be affirmed by the courts.

Trade practice conference constitutes the second method by which the Commission attempted to overcome the limitations of its procedure. Members of an industry were invited to attend a conference and to present a code of fair practice for the Commission's approval. It was hoped that by agreement of the industry a wholesome elimination of unfair practices could be effected. No extensive economic investigation preceded these conferences. Nor did the Commission develop or enunciate any affirmative standards of policy by which the proposals of industry might be measured. The regulations were prepared by industry. Those proposals which were obviously unlawful were discarded. The remainder were separated into two groups, the first consisting of practices already under legal condemnation, and the second, of "trade abuses and unethical and wasteful practices."[1] Group I rulings were to be enforced by the Commission, Group II by the industry. The Commission apparently conceived of the

---

[1] Federal Trade Commission, Trade Practice Conferences (1933) 1.

Group I rulings as mere codifications of its decisions.   Actually, however, this group included competitive practices which were unlawful at common law and which the courts had held to be beyond the Commission's power,[1] as well as prohibitions of illegal conduct not constituting unfair competition in a legal sense, such as unlawful methods of manufacture.[2]   Practices which were not unlawful at common law or under state or federal legislation such as sales on consignment,[3] and deviations from voluntary grades and standards,[4] were occasionally placed in this group.

Group II rulings covered a wide range of business conduct, including such unrelated practices as false invoicing, design piracy, repudiation of contracts, free deals, fictitious bids, use of faulty materials, deviation from industry standards, extension of credit to unqualified dealers, unwarranted returns of goods, and more than a hundred business methods that are too technical to be summarized in a few words.   This group also contained many recommended practices such as arbitration of disputes, individual installation of a system of cost accounting and adoption of standard forms of contracts.

The rules were poorly drafted and hedged about with numerous qualifications which facilitated evasion and destroyed their practical utility.   Thus the Solid Steel Window Industry Agreement provided "that the distribution among members of the industry of information covering past due credit accounts insofar as it may be lawfully done is approved."[5]   The Bituminous Coal Rulings[6] forbade sales below cost "with the

---

[1] *E. g.*, threats of patent infringement suits.   Solid Section Steel Window Industry, *id*. at 44.

[2] Fabricators of Structural Steel, *id*. at 37.

[3] Steel Office Furniture, *id*. at 27; Baby-and-Doll-Carriage Industry, *id*. at 74.

[4] Woodturning Industry, *id*. at 11–14.

[5] *Id*. at 45.

[6] Bituminous Coal Operators of the Southwest, *id*. at 39.

intent and with the effect of injuring a competitor and where the effect may be to substantially lessen competition, or tend to create a monopoly or to unreasonably restrain trade." What could such a rule mean to the tradesmen to whom it applied? The same code forbade "maliciously inducing or attempting to induce the breach of existing contracts between competitors and their customers by any false or deceptive means whatso-ever, or interfering with or obstructing the performance of any such contractual duties or services by any such means, with the purpose and effect of unduly hampering, injuring or embarrassing competitors in their business." The ineptitude of such draftsmanship is self-evident. What is the meaning of "maliciously"? What constitutes an attempt? Why limit the prohibition to cases where the inducement is accompanied by wrongful means, in opposition to the great weight of authority? When is a competitor unduly hampered? Is not every contracting party embarrassed by the inducement of breach? *Etc., etc.*

The Group I rules were no more effective than the publica-tion in annual reports of the methods of competition forbidden by the Commission. There is no basis for the naive and over-sanguine assumption that the mere formulation of a conference agreement, in and of itself, resulted in the abandonment of the forbidden practices.[1] No real machinery for detection or enforcement was devised. The Group II rules, lacking legal sanction, were as effective as the sheepskin codes of ethics of trade associations. The only basis for enforcement by indus-try was the consensual obligation of the signatories to the agreement, and there is no evidence that any serious effort was made to obtain compliance with these rules. Non-signatories, of course, were not bound. Into these Group II rulings crept restrictive arrangements suppressing competition which led to a conflict between the Department of Justice

---

[1] *Id.*, c. VIII.

and the Commission. Rules which the Commission approved were denounced by the Department of Justice and by the courts as unlawful restraints of trade.[1] Ultimately the Commission rescinded its Group II rulings and the status of these conferences remained in doubt for more than a year.[2] The attendant confusion impaired the prestige of the Commission and restricted the utility of this method of competitive regulation. Very few of the major industries availed themselves of the opportunity of self-regulation. The trade practice conferences, at best, constituted an inexpert codification of the common law and Commission rulings on unfair competition, coupled with the vague aspirations of industry regarding the elimination of annoying and irritating trade practices. The gap between the written prohibition and enforced observance was never bridged. Since the end of N. R. A., trade practice conferences have been revived, but whether a higher level of accomplishment will be attained, it is yet too early to say.

The Commission's record of achievement is not very inspiring. The causes are not difficult to discover. The failure of Congress to define its policy and purposes, the hostility of the courts, the legalistic procedure of the Commission, the low calibre of personnel, the failure of the Commission to write opinions explaining its rulings and analyzing the problems of unfair competition, the bureaucracy of its minor officialdom, the meagerness of congressional appropriations, the failure to integrate its legal and economic activities—all share responsibility. This is not to disparage the gains made in curbing false advertising, misbranding and other forms of misrepresentation. The Commission's accomplishments assume larger proportions when contrasted with the contribution of the common law. Unrestricted by the requirement of direct

---

[1] Paramount Famous Lasky Corp v. United States, 282 U. S. 30 (1934).

[2] Myers, The F. T. C. and the Anti-Trust Laws, in Handler, Symposium on Anti-Trust Laws (1932) 124.

injury to the private suitor, it has been able to proceed as the
vicarious avenger of the public. While not leaving the problem where it found it, the Commission has not carried us very
far along the road to eventual solution.

VII

The Contribution of the National Recovery Administration

The inordinate length of this paper and the maxim *de
mortuis* compel an unwonted brevity in our discussion of the
N. R. A. One of the purposes of the National Industrial
Recovery Act was "to eliminate unfair competitive practices."[1]
The codes promulgated under this statute constituted "the
standards of fair competition"[2] for the industries to which they
applied and violations of such codes were deemed "unfair
methods of competition" within the meaning of the Federal
Trade Commission Act.[3] Thus anything contained in a code
was embraced by this novel concept of fair competition. This
distorted usage made many strange bedfellows. Violations
of the wage, hour, and collective bargaining provisions of the
codes became "unfair competition." The suspension of the
anti-trust laws enabled business men to introduce into their
codes plans of industrial action that had formerly been
denounced as unreasonable restraints of trade. The inverted
logic of the statute transformed restraint of trade into fair
competition and what had previously been unlawful for business men to do now became unlawful for them to refrain from
doing. The "monopolistic practice" proviso[4] stood in the
way of the legalization of most of the practices previously
reviewed in the section on the Sherman Law,[5] but the exact

---

[1] 48 Stat. 195, 15 U. S. C. A. § 703 (1933) (Declaration of Policy).

[2] *Id.*, § 3b.

[3] *Ibid.*

[4] *Id.*, § 3a.

[5] *Supra* at p. 214.

limits of this prohibition were never determined.   The codes
also contained numerous provisions designed to rehabilitate
industry and stimulate economic recovery and non-compliance
with such programs was also regarded as unfair competition.
Finally, the codes condemned hosts of competitive practices,
and in this respect, at least in theory, were consistent with the
prior usages of unfair competition.   In practice, however,
the range of practices forbidden was almost limitless, extending
far beyond previous denunciations.

Included among the code provisions that eliminated or
"rationalized" competition were a diversity of price and
production regulations; mandatory discounts, transportation,
and credit terms; uniform cost-accounting methods; classification of customers; standard forms and terms of contracts,
commercial arbitration; control of capacity; specified classifications, descriptions and standards of industrial products;
and plans for the operation of industrial credit bureaus.

The competitive practice group included practices unlawful
at common law or under the Trade Commission Act as well as
many petty business annoyances and irritations.   A partial
list follows: misbranding and false advertising, commercial
bribery, disparagement, interference with contracts, false
invoicing, threats of litigation, espionage, imitation of trademarks and tradenames, substitution of products, price discriminations, design and style piracy, full-line forcing,
enticement of employees, repudiation of contracts, unwarranted returns, dumping, false receipts, fee splitting, false
weights and measures, giving of options, sales with repurchase
agreements, guarantees of price decline, furnishing display
cases at less than the specified charge, purchase of stolen goods,
reversal of telephone charges, shipment without order, split
shipments at a price based upon shipment of entire order at one
time, supplying goods to customers who engage in destructive
practices at prices which will enable them to continue such
practices, rebates, consignment sales, premiums, free deals,

advertising allowances, special services, trade-in allowances, delivery of goods on trial, loans to customers, missionary sales help to customers, sales below cost, *etc. etc.*[1]

This rough and inadequate summary reveals the range of trade practice problems with which N. R. A. dealt. I have not attempted any careful classification or analysis of these provisions. The codes are obviously deserving of extended treatment, but this cannot be done here. Our interest, at present, is merely in the diversity of practices included in the N. R. A. definition of unfair competition.

The code making process is too familiar to require any description. The codes, in the first instance, were drafted by industry and reflected the industrial point of view. The trade practice provisions were frequently approved by the Administration without much change as a *quid pro quo* for industry's adoption of labor standards. Industry-minded deputies were unable to transcend the limitations of their previous training and were frequently incapable of a public point of view. N. R. A. started with no consistent policy of trade regulation and not until the end of its career were any sustained efforts made to coördinate the codes and to eliminate the major inconsistencies. The ignorance of the legal and economic aspects of the trade practice problem on the part of those responsible for the formulation of policy and the approval of codes was pitiful. The criteria applied by N. R. A. in the adoption of standards of fair competition "were the criteria of compromise rather than the criteria of judicially considered public interest."[2] The clash between the various advisory boards resulted in feeble compromises rather than any clean-cut or consistent policy. The dual objectives of recovery and reform frequently got in the way of each other. The worship of speed was not conducive to careful draftsmanship and the

---

[1] These classifications are taken from the tabulation of code provisions in Lyon *et al.*, The National Recovery Administration (1935) 570–573.

[2] *Id.* at 563.

imperfections of the codes and their lack of uniformity were notorious. From a technical standpoint, the codes were a slight improvement over the abortive trade practice conference rules of the Federal Trade Commission. The draftsmanship, with some exceptions, was on the level of the Guffey Act, which, as we have seen, was derived from the Bituminous Code. It would be uncharitable to contrast these amateurish and bungling efforts with such legislation as the Uniform Sales Act. "No other agency in our history was compelled to approach the trade practice problem in such a milieu of varied counsel, conflicting purposes and atmosphere of desperation."[1] One might add that no other law in the history of the country was ever as poorly administered, and this, unfortunately, was true despite the presence of many able and brilliant persons on the roster of the Administration. The *Schechter* case[2] brought the curtain down upon a scene of unprecedented confusion, uncertainty, frustration, intrigue, and abject failure.

We are not concerned here with the causes of failure or with the validity of the economic and political postulates of this experiment in the administrative control of industry. Nor can we consider the accomplishments of the N. R. A., of which there were many. The points of value in the N. R. A. experience to the student of unfair competition are: (1) the device of defining unfair practices by administrative legislation as contrasted with the method of administrative decision employed by the Federal Trade Commission; (2) the disclosure of practices which the business world deems unfair; (3) the enlargement of knowledge regarding industrial conditions and the trade practice problems of specific industries; and (4) the pitfalls which must be avoided in the future regulation of competition.

---

[1] *Id.* at 567.

[2] Schechter Poultry Corp. v. United States, 295 U. S. 495 (1935). *Id.* at 837.

VIII

Conclusion

The definition of unfair competition by administrative legislation is incomparably superior to definition by administrative decision. The method of judicial exclusion and inclusion does not permit of a sustained, consistent, comprehensive and speedy attack upon the trade practice problem. The case by case determination takes years to cover even a narrow field; it leaves wide lacunae; false starts are difficult to correct and the erroneous decision is just as prolific as a sound ruling in begetting a progeny of subordinate rules. In a controversy between two litigants or between a Commission and a private party, the law making function is distracted by factors which are important to the contestants but irrelevant to the formulation of future policy. The fusion of law and economics, the detailed investigations and hearings, and the precise formulation of rules, all of which are so essential to a proper regulation of competition, are not feasible when law making is but a by-product of the adjustment of controversies. The combination of the two functions may have been justified when knowledge of the workings of competition was sparse and objectives ill-defined. It can no longer be justified today. It would be little short of criminal to rely upon so inefficient a method of law making when more scientific and expeditious devices are available.

The conclusions to be drawn from our survey are self-evident. The truisms can be briefly recapitulated. If competition is retained as the organic instrument of control of our economic life, it must be regulated. It can only be preserved by zealous enforcement of the laws which seek to maintain the competitive system. Even the most devout exponent of *laissez-faire* will concede the need for preservation and regulation. Controversy arises when the attempt is made, as in the N. R. A., to abandon competition. With that controversy, we are not concerned. When competition is abandoned, there will be no unfair competition to bedevil us. But we still have the competitive system and unfair competition remains a fact and not a theory. Unfair competition can not be eliminated until it is defined. Definition is only part of the task. Suitable remedies must be devised and adequate machinery for detection and enforcement created. The definitions of the common law were incomplete and its remedies ineffective. The definitions of the legislature have been diffuse and disconnected and the statutory remedies have been of varying effectiveness. The Federal Trade Commission has been hampered by its procedure, personnel, judicial review, and a curious failure to develop any philosophy of regulation. The N. R. A. is dead. The history of the control of competition has been singularly disappointing. It is distinguished only by poverty of idea and mediocrity of craftsmanship. All of these agencies, however, have brought to the surface a host of practices that are deceptive, oppressive, dishonest, tricky, uneconomic, and wasteful. Some of the practices are worthy of universal condemnation. Others have baneful effects in certain industries and under particular circumstances. We expel from consideration the efforts of the N. R. A., and the demands of business for devices to suppress competition and the expulsion, we hope, will be final. Enough is known about the practices of universal application for a uniform statute to be prepared for enactment by Congress and the states. This statute would cover the common law competitive torts, the major practices condemned by the Federal Trade Commission and the pertinent legislative and code prohibitions. Legislation affecting certain industries or dealing with complex problems that are better handled in a separate enactment would be omitted. The uniform act would cover the barest essentials of a law of unfair competition. It would not, however, freeze the present situation. Additions and modifications will always be necessary and adequate provision must be made for change and growth. It is futile to expect the legislature to revise the statute to meet changing conditions and needs. Hence we should resort to administrative legislation, at least so far as federal control of practices in interstate commerce is concerned. The administrative tribunal would have several functions. On the legislative or law making side, it would be charged with the duty of maintaining an unremitting study of the trade practice problem. It would, by rules and regulations, under a proper delegation of power and a clear definition of the standards by which it is to be guided, make additions to the general code of unfair competition. These additions would be preceded by investigation and public hearing and proposed drafts would be subject to extended criticism and study before enactment. It would also, upon proper showing, grant exemptions to particular industries from such provisions of the general law as operated harshly. Such exemptions would rarely be necessary but administration should be flexible enough to take care of the need should it arise. It would also, after thorough investigation, hearing and study, draft regulations for the facilitation, preservation, and regulation of competition for specific industries. These regulations would differ from N. R. A. codes in several vital respects. First, they would deal with the prohibition of competitive practices and not with the rehabilitation of industry or the rationalization or elimination of competition. Hence they would not be subject to the charge of regimentation. Secondly, they would be drafted by government and not by industry. Industry would be heard as in the formulation of a piece of legislation but it would not propose or command. Thirdly, the scope of the regulations would be more modest. Only practices which are demonstrably unsocial and uneconomic and which require separate industrial treatment would be thus attacked.

On the enforcement side, I should favor the conversion of the Federal Trade Commission into an administrative court with the authority, in the first instance, to issue binding injunctive orders.   Prosecution should be completely divorced from the process of adjudication.   Proceedings instituted by the government should be tried by a special division of the Department of Justice.   Trade associations and consumers' organizations should have the right to bring proceedings in their own name for violation of the uniform statute, rules and regulations and codes.   The jurisdiction of the administrative court would be limited to regulations affecting interstate commerce. Competitors and consumers, aggrieved by any violation, should be permitted to sue in the federal courts for violation of the federal enactments and in the state courts for transgression of state rules, following the usual division of authority between the two systems of courts.   To confine such suits to the new tribunal would overburden it and hence direct proceedings in the courts must be allowed.   The exact division of authority is a matter of detail.   The criminal remedy should be sparingly used, dependent upon the seriousness of the offense. Special sanctions can be devised for specific wrongs, as needed.

The task of detection must be divided among the federal and state governments, trade associations, consumers groups, individual competitors and consumers.   Such privileges as are extended to trade associations should be conditioned upon the proper assumption and discharge of the policing function.

A careful legislative and administrative definition of unfair competition, plus the net-work of judicial and administrative sanctions and public and private remedies, would go far in elevating our business standards and in facilitating competition.   It would neither prevent nor cure depressions nor bring about the millennium.   The trade practice problem, as compared with most of our economic ills, is but a modest one. The need is for sober draftsmen and not for sooth-sayers or rain makers.

5

THE ANTI-TRUST LAWS AND THE REGULATION OF PRICE COMPETITION*

By Arthur Robert Burns†

I. The Principle of the Sherman Law

Direct social control of the industrial system presents dismaying difficulties and dangers. The National Recovery Administration revealed the complexity of the economic problems that arise when conflicts of self interest are replaced by direct governmental planning. The political consequences of a high concentration of economic power in the state are less clear but no less disquieting. Efforts to meet the growing criticism of the industrial system while avoiding these difficulties and dangers[1] have taken a peculiar form in the United States. An effort has been made to preserve by law the conditions necessary for the continuance of competition. If

---

* *Law and Contemporary Problems*, Volume IV, Number 3, June 1937, pages 301–320. Reprinted by the courtesy of the publisher, the Duke University School of Law, and the author.

† B.Sc. (Econ), 1920; Ph.D., 1926, University of London. Assistant Professor of Economics, Faculty of Political Science, Columbia University. Author of *The Decline of Competition* (1936).

[1] Centralized control of monetary policy has been increasingly relied upon during the present century to provide a broad control of the industrial system without direct and detailed interference with initiative. Marriner S. Eccles, Chairman of the Federal Reserve System, has now, however, declared that the Federal Reserve System is powerless to maintain a stable economy unless other essentially non-monetary factors necessary to stability are brought into line either by private interests or the government. Statement in *N. Y. Times*, March 16, 1937, p. 9.

the prerequisites of competition could be preserved detailed controls of industrial policy would, it was hoped, be avoided. Direct appraisal of the treatment of the buyer would be unnecessary. Experience of this policy has, however, revealed the difficulty of giving specific meaning to the comfortable phrase of the economists, "assuming free competition." It has brought disillusionment because of the increasingly wide divergence of actual business conditions from the free competition of economic theory. In consequence social policy shows signs of transformation into a policy of regulating an admittedly imperfectly competitive world.

The prerequisites of competition have recently been reëxamined by economists and prove to be very difficult of attainment. There must be a perfect market in the sense that, in the absence of general changes in the conditions of demand and supply, a slight reduction in price by one firm would shift all business in the market to that firm. Buyers may have no loyalties to sellers or preferences for the product of any one of them and they must be exceedingly well informed. Sellers must be sufficiently numerous for none of them to find it profitable to take account of the effect of changes in his output upon the market price.

The Sherman Act,[1] the first federal anti-trust law, was passed in response to evidence that business was evolving away from these conditions. Market control had been obtained in some industries by the concentration of a large proportion of the business in single firms. In others, firms had become sufficiently few to get together in pools and agree upon prices. Two major explanations of these tendencies were possible. On the one hand, they might be attributed to changes in technology. Business men competing with each other in the effort to utilize the most economical methods of production had developed firms large enough to make it necessary for

---

[1] 26 Stat. 209 (1890), 15 U. S. C. §§ 1–7.

them to take account of their power over the market price. Where goods are costly to transport the markets of firms are not nationwide; even where there are many firms in the country as a whole there may be few in each local market. This explanation suggests that competition has in fact frequently proved to be self-destructive. Efforts to maintain the prerequisites of competition in these circumstances would not yield the fruits of competition which are the ultimate objective of social policy. If large firms are the most economical, any limitation, direct or indirect, upon opportunities to attain the most economical size hamper the initiative of individuals and obstruct the utilization of the most economical methods of production.

The alternative explanation of the declining numbers of firms is that they have increased in size by resort to tactics which have little relation to their economies in production. This interpretation of the events between the Civil War and 1890 suggested changes in law to prevent resort to these practices. Only the fittest would then survive and they would be numerous enough to satisfy the requirements of competition. Such appears to be the basis of the Sherman Law. It raises the question why a moral lapse should have occurred soon after the Civil War, and suggests to the enquiring mind the possibility that it may have been connected with the revolution in methods of transportation which widened markets and facilitated the utilization of large scale methods of production. Drastic methods were undoubtedly used, but they may have been due to the great economies in production methods then made available if rapid industrial concentration could be effected. The survival of large firms since that time and the rise of others suggest that they have maintained themselves either because of superior efficiency or because of continued buccaneering tactics. Either the Sherman Law has failed as a means of eliminating these tactics or the economies of large scale production have been very important. But with the latter conclusion we return to the first explanation of the decline of the competitive market.

II. PRICE COMPETITION UNDER THE SHERMAN ACT AND FEDERAL TRADE COMMISSION ACTS

A. Price Policies

The attempt by law to preserve the competitive market was expressed in a condemnation of contracts, combinations or conspiracies in restraint of interstate commerce. Monopolizing, or attempting to monopolize, or combining or conspiring to monopolize any part of interstate commerce was similarly declared illegal. By the courts "it has repeatedly been held . . . that the purpose of the statute is to maintain free competition in interstate commerce."[1] Behind the assumptions of free competition by the economists lay an assumption of the existence of private property.   Congress was faced with the problem of writing a commercial code determining the precise set of rights and duties which would constitute the kind of private property necessary to produce the results of competition.   By the vague wording of the statute it passed this problem to the courts.   In the course of their efforts to solve the problem they were presented with the question whether certain price policies were in violation of the assumption of free competition.   They have consistently refused to appraise price policies in terms of profits.   Had they not taken this position they would speedily have been involved in the regulation of prices and the problems presented by such regulation in the industries which they have decided to be affected

---

[1] American Column and Lumber Co. v. U. S., 257 U. S. 377, 400 (1921). *Cf.* "The theory of the anti-trust laws in their modern orientation is that, in the absence of adequate governmental control upon a monopolistic basis, the influence of government should be exercised to keep the markets free to all on a competitive basis."   McLaughlin, *Legal Control of Competitive Methods* (1936) IOWA L. REV. 302.

with a public interest. They have, however, sought to test price policies in terms of the intentions of the parties. An intent to drive out a rival is evidence of attempts to restrain trade or create a monopoly.[1] The basic difficulty of this policy lies in the vagueness and even inappropriateness of the criterion of intent. In times when speedy concentration of industry is induced by recognition of the economies of large scale production price cutting tactics may be drastic enough to persuade the court that it smells an evil intent. But the attainment of the economies of mass production may be the ultimate inducement to adopt such policies. Not all buccaneering tactics can be excused on this basis but the touchstone used by the court does not distinguish the vigorous pursuit of the economies of size from the vigorous pursuit of monopoly profits.

The policy of the courts tends to encourage the attainment of the economies of production by other methods than price cutting. In general they have been unwilling to interfere with mergers or to break up very large firms.[2] The smaller firms instead of being driven out tend to be bought out with consequent advantage to their owners but not necessarily to the consumer.[3] Concentration has, therefore, not been prevented

---

[1] The price wars in the tobacco industry were regarded as contributory evidence of intent to monopolize. U. S. v. American Tobacco Co., 221 U. S. 106 (1911). The intent of the Corn Products Refining Company to monopolize was inferred in part from sales below cost and the company was forbidden to resort to low price campaigns. U. S. v. Corn Products Refining Co., 234 Fed. 964 (S. D. N. Y. 1916). The Steel Corporation was held to be a "good trust" partly because it had not indulged in secret price cutting. U. S. v. U. S. Steel Corp., 251 U. S. 417 (1920). The contention that the International Harvester Company had not used its power to restrain trade was supported by the claim that it had not reduced prices below cost for the purpose of driving out competitors. U. S. v. International Harvester Co., 274 U. S. 693 (1927).

[2] Even where firms have been broken up the number in the market has frequently remained small.

[3] Cf. Burns, *The Process of Industrial Concentration* (1933) 47 Q. J. Econ. 277.

and price behavior in sharp contrast with that in the competitive market has appeared. "When the courts have been presented with evidence of such contrasts they have not regarded it as evidence of the failure of the policy of maintaining the prerequisites of competition. The Supreme Court dismissed with brusque contempt evidence that the price of steel rails had been stable for many years,[1] and in the same case it declared that "the law does not make mere size an offence."[2] Likewise it has held that price leadership "does not establish any suppression of competition or show any sinister domination."[3]

The policy of maintaining the prerequisites of competition by the control of industrial practices also provides the foundation of the Federal Trade Commission Act.[4] This act empowered the Federal Trade Commission to prevent unfair methods of competition. The Commission has also made a few, but none too successful, attempts to deal with price policies regarded as unfair. Apart from the cases concerning price discrimination which were taken under the authority of both the Clayton[5] and Federal Trade Commission Acts it has made little progress in establishing a criterion of fairness in price policies. It ordered a large distributor to cease selling sugar at a loss during the war, the sales being in combination with other sales, but it was not upheld by the court.[6] It ordered a seller to cease selling at less than the price charged by a rival on the ground that the price was not set in good

---

[1] U. S. v. U. S. Steel Corp., 251 U. S. 417 (1920).

[2] *Id.* at 451.

[3] U. S. v. International Harvester Co., 274 U. S. 693, 709 (1927).

[4] 38 STAT. 717 (1914), 15 U. S. C. §§ 41–51.

[5] 38 STAT. 730 (1914), 15 U. S. C. §§ 13–13a.

[6] F. T. C. v. Sears Roebuck & Co., 1 F. T. C. 163 (1918), 258 Fed. 307 (C. C. A. 9th, 1919). The court held that the Commission had no power to proceed against sales below cost but that misrepresentation in connection with such sales was illegal.

faith.[1]   The acceptance by the Commission in 1928 and 1929 of Trade Practice Conference rules against less than cost selling indicates pressure for such rules and the willingness of the Commission to condemn the practice.[2]

B. *Cooperative Control of Prices or Output*

Agreements between sellers concerning prices and output have generally been condemned without regard for the reasonableness of the policy pursued.   The Supreme Court has stated that it would hesitate, in the absence of express legislation, to make the difference between legal and illegal business relations "depend upon so uncertain a test as whether prices are reasonable—a determination which can be made only after a complete survey of our economic organization and a choice between rival philosophies."[3]   Nevertheless, some six years later the Court retired from this position and decided that "the mere fact that the parties to an agreement eliminate competition between themselves is not enough to condemn it."[4] The Court took into account the peculiar nature of the bituminous coal industry, its excess capacity, its difficulties in meeting the competition of oil, gas, and water power, and its "chaotic condition."   "The fact that the correction of abuses

---

[1] F. T. C. v. The Oakes Co., 3 F. T. C. 36 (1920).

[2] NAT. INDUSTRIAL CONF. BD., THE PUBLIC REGULATION OF COMPETITIVE PRACTICES (1925) 64.   In both policy and form of administration the Commission anticipated the subsequent National Recovery Administration.

[3] U. S. v. Trenton Potteries Co., 273 U. S. 392, 398 (1927).   "The power to fix prices, whether reasonably exercised or not, involves power to control the market and to fix arbitrary and unreasonable prices." *Id.* at 397. Conditions may change and a price once reasonable may be maintained and become unreasonable.   If power to fix prices depended upon the reasonableness of the prices the government, in enforcing the Sherman Law, would be compelled to shoulder the "burden of ascertaining from day to day whether it has become unreasonable through the mere variation of economic conditions." *Id.* at 398.

[4] Appalachian Coals Inc. v. U. S. 288 U. S. 344, 360 (1933).

would lead to fairer price levels does not mean that abuses should go uncorrected or that cooperative endeavor to correct them necessarily constitutes an unreasonable restraint of trade."[1] The establishment of a cooperative selling agency including a large number of the sellers in one field was held, therefore, not to be illegal. But the Court provided that the case should remain open so that evidence of any attempt by the agency to abuse its position might be brought before it. Apparently in this case the Court, interpreting the Sherman Act, has embarked upon a journey towards the control of prices, although that control is indirect and tentative.

III. RESALE PRICE MAINTENANCE

During the past decade the courts have been called upon to decide whether a seller may, without contravening the Sherman or Federal Trade Commission Acts, control the price at which his product is resold by the buyer. The very existence of the problem on a scale stimulating litigation is an indication that the prerequisites of competition have not been preserved on the selling side of the market. In fact the imperfections of competition between sellers have been tacitly accepted and policy has been framed partly in terms of the forms of business organization and partly in terms of the control of the policies of sellers in imperfect competition with each other in the hope of maintaining the prerequisites of competition at the next stage in the distributive process. Decision in terms of forms of organization has, however, enfeebled efforts by manufacturers to maintain competition at the next stage by restricting them to a variety of not entirely effective methods. At this next stage, however, there has been in process a reorganization which has threatened with expulsion small scale distributors and their suppliers. These threatened groups have recently induced legislation giving more effective power to manu-

---

[1] *Id.* at 374.

facturers of branded consumer goods to preserve the lives of small scale distributors. Thus the imperfection of competition at one stage is not only accepted but utilized with the object of maintaining the number of distributors. The control of the organization of distribution is coming, therefore, to rest partly in the hands of manufacturers.

The efforts of the courts to rest their decisions upon legal forms rather than economic consequences are indicated in a brief series of cases. Contracts providing for price maintenance are held to be contrary to the Sherman Law because they restrain trade between the buyers.[1] The same result is beyond the reach of the law if the manufacturer merely urges retailers to maintain suggested prices, announces that dealers failing to maintain these prices will be denied supplies and requests information concerning price cutters.[2] Keeping records concerning the behavior of dealers and employing systematic devices for detecting price cutting have been held to approach so nearly in effectiveness to contractual covenants eliminating price competition between dealers as to contravene the Federal Trade Commission Act.[3] But when the dealer is constituted an agent of the manufacturer, the latter is left free to control the resale price without contravening the law.[4]

The constitutionality of legislation specifically authorizing manufacturers to set minimum resale prices has recently been

---

[1] Dr. Miles Medical Co. v. Park & Sons Co., 220 U. S. 373 (1911); Bauer et Cie. v. O'Donnell, 229 U. S. 1 (1913).

[2] U. S. v. Colgate & Co., 250 U. S. 300 (1919); U. S. v. Schraders Sons, Inc., 252 U. S. 85 (1920).

[3] Beech Nut Packing Company v. F. T. C., 257 U. S. 441 (1922); Cream of Wheat Co. v. F. T. C., 14 F. (2d) 40 (C. C. A. 8th, 1926).

[4] U. S. v. General Electric Co., 272 U. S. 476 (1926). The Court seeks, however, by examination of the contracts, to ensure that a genuine agency is established. Standard Fashion Co. v. Magrane Houston Co., 258 U. S. 346 (1922); Butterick Co. v. F. T. C., 4 F. (2d) 910 (1925), cert. denied, 267 U. S. 602 (1925). Cf. BURNS, THE DECLINE OF COMPETITION (1936), 420.

affirmed by the Supreme Court.[1]   The decision rests upon the
contention that the distributors owned the commodity but
not the brand name.   They were free to sell the commodity
without identifying labels or containers at any price they
chose (not a very real alternative).   Whether price cutting in
the sale of trademarked products was injurious to the goodwill
of the producer was "fairly open to differences of opinion" but
if states decided that goodwill was thus damaged the method
of protection selected was not unconstitutional.[2]

The imperfection of competition among manufacturers rests
largely upon the use of advertising to break up the market into

---

[1] Old Dearborn Distributing Corp. v. Seagram-Distillers Corp., 57 Sup.
Ct. 139 (1936).   The state of Illinois had passed a "Fair Trade Act" providing that no contract for the sale or resale of branded goods in "fair and open
competition with commodities of the same general class produced by others"
should be illegal because it contained either of the following provisions:
(a) That the buyer would not resell except at a price stipulated by the seller;
(b) That the product should not be further resold except at a price stipulated
by the producer or first purchaser.   Such provisions in any contract were,
by the Act, deemed to imply that the commodity might be sold without
reference to the contract in three situations, *viz.*, (1) When the owner of the
commodity was closing out his stock "for the purpose of discontinuing
delivery of any such commodity" provided that the stock was offered to the
manufacturer at the original invoice price at least ten days before its sale
to the public; (2) When goods were damaged or deteriorated and the public
was so informed; (3) When they were sold by an officer acting under the
authority of any court.   The Act further prohibited wilfully and knowingly
offering for sale or selling any commodity at less than the price stipulated
"in any contract" pursuant to the above provisions of the Act *whether or not
the person so advertising or selling was a party to the contract*.   The Act did not
authorize contracts between producers, between wholesalers or between
retailers as to sale or resale prices.

[2] It was contended on behalf of the dealer that he had been deprived of
the right to dispose of his property at any price he might choose.   The
court blandly replied that, while there would have been constitutional
objection to the annexation by the state of this right to fix the price, there
was none when the right was transferred from dealer to manufacturer under
legislative sanction.

a series of submarkets.   Each of these submarkets is occupied by one manufacturer and separated from other submarkets by the preferences of buyers for one product rather than another. The absence of such advertising is, therefore, one of the pre-requisites of competition.   The sellers of unbranded goods in competition are powerless to exact the maintenance of resale prices.   The decision of the Court indicates, however, that it realizes that laws permitting resale price maintenance encour-age the building up of goodwill by advertising.   In supporting resale price maintenance state governments and the courts are, therefore, departing from the traditional policy of main-taining competition.   They are facilitating the replacement of price competition among manufacturers by competition in advertising.

The struggle between large and small scale organization of distribution has taken the form partly of price competition. The large scale distributors desire freedom to cut resale prices as they may choose.   The small scale retailers and their sup-pliers desire the maintenance of margins that will enable them to survive.   If they organize and apply pressure to manu-facturers the latter must choose between the large and the small distributors.   But the manufacturers are not impartial in this choice.   They advertise partly because they are anxious to keep in their own hands some control over the promotion of the sales of their product.   They are also fearful of the emergence of small numbers of large distributors who may overpower them.   The net outcome of this situation is, there-fore, likely to be that manufacturers will endeavor to maintain large numbers of small distributors.   By doing so they may prevent the reorganization of distribution upon what may be a more economical basis.   High cost distribution, in the form of too many too small outlets, may survive in the interests both of manufacturers and of those threatened with expulsion by the larger firms.   Manufacturers are, however, faced with the possibility that the large distributors will establish brands of their own or that they will evade resale price maintenance by combination sales or trade-ins.

The argument that increases in the size of firms are due to unfair practices has arisen in the course of the struggle between large and small distributors. Although resale price maintenance laws go far beyond the exclusion of "loss leaders" these leaders are frequently used as the main justification for the law. "Loss leaders" are condemned by manufacturers who promote their product by advertising. They are irked by the fact that the large distributors find it more profitable to reduce the resale prices of well advertised commodities especially if they have a stated price (*e.g.*, books) than to use other articles as loss leaders. Buyers can make a simple and direct comparison between the cost of the branded goods at large and small stores. Where goods vary in quality and style comparison is a task usually beyond the powers, or even the time, of the retail buyer. By using advertised products as loss leaders large distributors gain a reputation for general low prices more quickly and cheaply than by cutting all prices. Loss leaders may, therefore, be a means of deceiving the buyer into an unjustified belief that a particular store is a cheap store.

In so far as distributors recover a smaller mark-up on loss leaders than on other merchandise there may be price discrimination, although it is discrimination between groups of buyers. Whether or not it constitutes discrimination in fact depends upon the possibility of discovering the correct distribution of the cost of operating a store between dealings in different products and this is an almost impossible task.[1] Where the dealer handles the product without any mark-up or even resells at a price less than he pays discrimination is undeniable. The dealer argues that this policy is an alternative to advertising and can properly claim that, unlike almost all other forms of advertising, it results in direct gains to the

---

[1] Fast moving items like loss leaders can, of course, be handled for a smaller mark-up than slow moving ones without reduction of profit.

consumer. Moreover, in so far as his policy is deceptive, it can hardly be placed upon a lower plane than a great deal of advertising, most of which raises costs while loss leaders reduce prices. Loss leaders can also be attacked because they represent a temporary policy. Distributors are apt to turn for loss leaders from one product to another. The manufacturer claims that there is no economy in these temporary dislocations of his machinery for distribution. Smaller dealers are discouraged from handling the product during the period of price cutting and when the large distributors have turned to some other product good relations must be rebuilt and expenditure incurred for the purpose.

Thus the code of law aimed at the preservation of the prerequisites of competition is being transformed into one giving to manufacturers in imperfect competition with each other the power to control distribution during a period of reorganization. Within the past four years, legislatures in some thirty-one states have accepted this policy and are at the same time endorsing the advertising that gives the manufacturers their power to set resale prices. The Supreme Court has merely taken the view that if legislators are so disposed their actions are not unconstitutional.

IV. PRICE DISCRIMINATION

A. The Shift from the Preservation of Competition between Manufacturers to the Control of Their Prices

Local and other price discriminations were among the practices of which the early trusts were accused. They were appraised by the courts as evidence of the intent of the seller. This approach has already been discussed. In 1914, however, legislative prohibitions upon price discrimination were enacted in Section 2 of the Clayton Act,[1] which has now been replaced

---

[1] *Supra* note 5, page 186.

by the Robinson-Patman Act of 1936.[1]   In part this legislation suggests an elaboration and clarification of the Sherman
Act.   But these laws go beyond the effort to preserve the
prerequisites of competition among manufacturers.   They seek
to avoid unfair discrimination between distributors.   They
rest, therefore, like resale price maintenance laws, upon the
admitted hopelessness of maintaining anything like perfect
competition among manufacturers.   The effort to control
differentials in price to buyers of different classes rests broadly
upon an attempt to adjust the prices of manufacturers to what
they might be assumed to be if there were price competition
between the sellers.   Failure to prohibit price discrimination
between ultimate consumers suggests, however, that the old
principle lives on.[2]   It is hoped to preserve competition among
distributors and thus to avoid control of retail prices.   The
effort to maintain competition between distributors, however,
coupled with the great political pressure exerted by small
distributors and their suppliers who are fearful of elimination,
has resulted in severe modifications of the policy of controlling
price differentials by reference to those likely under perfect
price competition.   Price competition between distributors
might lead to the survival of a few large units.   When the
courts were earlier presented with this dilemma in the field
of production they chose to pursue efficiency even if it resulted
in the weakening of competitive forces in the market.   Apparently Congress has chosen the other horn of the dilemma in
dealing with the field of distribution.   The Robinson-Patman
Act contains provisions likely to handicap the development of
large distributors.   It rests, therefore, upon conflicting principles; it indicates the awkward consequences of efforts to
preserve the prerequisites of competition; it admits the
inadequacy of past efforts to preserve these prerequisites.

---

[1] 49 STAT. 1526 (1936), 15 U. S. C. §§ 13, 13a, 13b, 21a.

[2] This omission may be of little practical importance.   It is of interest
mainly as evidence of the survival of the old principle.

Discrimination has in general been prohibited under both the Clayton and Robinson-Patman Acts when the effect may be to lessen competition substantially or to tend to create a monopoly[1] in any line of interstate commerce.[2] These familiar phrases suggest an effort to continue the basic policy of the Sherman Law making clear its application to a specific practice.[3] The prohibition of discrimination where it may lessen competition or tend to create a monopoly in *any* line of commerce indicates the presence of the new principle above mentioned, namely, the control of price differentials on the selling side of the market in the hope of maintaining the prerequisites of competition at least on the buying side and, therefore, in subsequent markets on the way to the ultimate buyer. This new principle was accepted by the courts only some fifteen years after the Clayton Act was passed and then in a case affecting discrimination between fabricators and not distributors.[4]

---

[1] However, the latter act has, as will be seen, amended the Clayton Act by extending its prohibitions to cover acts the effect of which is "to injure, destroy, or prevent competition," without reference to the substantiality of the effect upon competition or the creation of monopoly. Robinson-Patman Act, § 1(a).

[2] This necessary restriction to interstate commerce is already producing a crop of difficulties in pending litigation under the latter act. It is claimed that sellers peddling goods from local branch houses are not engaged in interstate commerce. *Cf.* In Matter of Kraft Phenix Cheese Co., F. T. C. Docket 2935; In Matter of Anheuser Busch Co. F. T. C. Docket 2987. It is also claimed that differentials to retailers if they affect competition between them affect only intrastate commerce. *Cf.* In Matter of Bird & Son, Inc. and Montgomery Ward & Co., F. T. C. Docket 2937.

[3] Continuity with the Sherman Act cases is also evident in the provision in § 3 of the Robinson-Patman Act against local discrimination "for the purpose of destroying competition or eliminating a competitor in such part of the United States" and against selling goods "at unreasonably low prices for the purpose of destroying competition or eliminating a competitor." The continuity is verbal rather than one of principle, more particularly in the Robinson-Patman Act.

[4] American Can Co. v. Van Camp Packing Co., George Van Camp and Sons, 278 U. S. 245 (1929). See pp. 310–311, *infra.*

In the cases presented to the courts between 1914 and 1929 affecting the relations between manufacturers and the various classes of retailers the courts generally avoided interference with the policies of sellers and assumed that, having maintained competition between these sellers, the middlemen and the consumer had been protected. A purpose to maintain the old channels of trade was held to be illegal in 1914.[1] In the majority of subsequent cases, however, little or no emphasis has been placed upon this principle. The line between permissible and illegal discrimination has sometimes been drawn by reference to the legal forms of business organization. It was held, for instance, that a seller may refuse to sell to a cooperative of retailers at any price other than that charged to a single retailer.[2] He may, however, group together for discount purposes the stores in a chain in each locality, even though they require individual canvassing and delivery, and refuse to permit independent retailers to pool their orders for the purpose of calculating discounts.[3]

In some of these and other cases the court has refused to interfere with the price differentials of a seller on the ground that a seller is free to select his customers.[4] The Clayton and

---

[1] Eastern States Retail Lumber Dealers Ass'n v. U. S., 234 U. S. 600 (1914). The Association had arranged for the reporting and circulation of the names of wholesalers who sold direct to builders and contractors. This activity was held to be illegal partly because of the element of conspiracy and partly because of its objective.

[2] Mennen Co. v. F. T. C., 288 Fed. 774 (C. C. A. 2d, 1923), *cert. denied*, 262 U. S. 759 (1923).

[3] F. T. C. v. National Biscuit Co., 299 Fed. 733 (C. C. A. 2d, 1924), *cert. denied*, 266 U. S. 613 (1924).

[4] A producer of cereals discriminating against a chain store by refusing to sell to it at its carload rate was held not to have contravened the law. Great Atlantic and Pacific Tea Co. v. Cream of Wheat Co., 227 Fed. 46, 49 (C. C. A. 2d, 1915); F. T. C. v. National Biscuit Co., *supra* note 3 above. "Effective competition requires that merchants have freedom of action in conducting their own affairs." 299 Fed. at 740.

Robinson-Patman Acts both explicitly preserve the right if it is exercised in *bona fide* transactions and not in restraint of trade. Of course in a competitive world sellers would be free to choose their own customers but they would be unable to choose on any basis other than the price offered. Where there were differences in the cost of different kinds of business there would be a tendency to a normal rate of return[1] in each. Prices would, therefore, vary in accordance with differences in cost. The courts, presented with evidence that conditions had so changed that sellers found an opportunity to charge differentials not in accordance with the competitive pattern, replied that one of the minor prerequisites of competition must be maintained even though the major prerequisites were present only in diluted form.[2]

The effect of discrimination upon competition among buyers received serious attention from the courts[3] in 1929, when they interpreted the congressional phrase "in any line of commerce" in the conventional, and apparently obvious, sense to include competition between those engaged in subsequent processes.[4]

---

[1] Rates of profit that in the absence of changes in conditions of demand and supply would induce no change in the amount of resources in any line of activity.

[2] The right of a buyer to choose his sources of merchandise has also been upheld. Raymond Bros. Clark & Co. v. F. T. C., 263 U. S. 533 (1924). An individual wholesaler refused to buy from a seller who sold to chain stores at wholesale prices.

[3] In Mennen Co. v. F. T. C., 288 Fed. 774 (C. C. A. 2d, 1923), *cert. denied*, 262 U. S. 759, the court stated that it saw no evidence that "the public suffered injury or that competitors had reasonable ground for complaint." The court admitted that discrimination by a manufacturer might lessen competition among his customers or potential customers but decided that Congress had not intended to prohibit this kind of restriction upon competition. Its emphasis was upon the absence of any decline in competition between the manufacturer and others in the same line of business.

[4] American Can Co. v. Van Camp Packing Co., George Van Camp and Sons, 278 U. S. 245 (1929). A can manufacturer had sold cans and leased a sealing machine to one customer at 20% below published prices which

Manufacturers were then placed in a very difficult position. Pressed by large buyers for special prices they feared suits for restraining competition between the large buyers and their rivals. Where was the line between a justified and an unjustified discrimination?[1] The Robinson-Patman Act was intended in part to clarify the law on this subject. It emphasized however the application of the Act to the restriction of competition in subsequent markets by prohibiting discrimination also where it may "injure" or "destroy" competition with the person who knowingly grants or receives the discriminatory price or with the customers of either.[2] In fact it extended the application of the law. Under the terms of the Clayton Act it had been necessary to show a lessening of competition in an entire line of commerce.[3] This new clause prohibited discrimination resulting only in injury to competition.

The Clayton and Robinson-Patman laws do not prevent discrimination as such. A spark plug manufacturer who sold to an automobile manufacturer at less than cost with the object of creating a demand for replacement purposes which would be met at higher prices was held not to have contravened the

---

were apparently charged to its rivals. The Supreme Court in response to a question propounded by a Circuit Court of Appeals decided that the Clayton Act did apply to discriminations the effect of which was to substantially lessen competition or tend to create a monopoly on the buying side of the market. This reversion to the words of the Clayton Act was reiterated (American Can Co. v. Ladoga Canning Co. 44 F. (2d) 763 (C. C. A. 7th, 1930), *cert. denied*, 282 U. S. 899 (1931)) and a company discriminated against was awarded triple damages. The contention that the discrimination was made in good faith and to meet competition because the manufacturer feared that the buyer would make his own cans was rejected.

[1] These decisions also presented the problem of defining a line of business.

[2] Robinson-Patman Act, § 1(a).

[3] This requirement had proved an insuperable obstacle to prosecution in most cases.

law.[1] Presumably the automobile manufacturer and the accessory dealer are not in the same line of commerce and, therefore, the rule in the *Van Camp* case[2] would not affect this decision.   The sale of lime at one price to farmers and another to chemical manufacturers would be untouched so long as the price is uniform to all farmers and to all chemical manufacturers.   Sales of coal at one price to apartment operators and another to industrial buyers, sales of chemicals at one price to fertilizer manufacturers and others to other buyers, or of milk at one price to distributors of fluid milk and another to cheese manufacturers appear to fall in the same category. These policies do not injure competition in the restricted sense in which it is defined but they are evidence of wide departures from price competition.   Such discriminations do not occur in a competitive market.   Sellers sell at the highest price offered and are as indifferent to the use to which the product is to be put as they are to the girth measurement of buyers.   Furthermore, in so far as the broad principle of competition has been approved because of its effect upon the utilization of resources, serious departures from this utilization occur when the seller finds it possible and profitable to restrict the activities of farmers while encouraging those of chemical manufacturers.

B. *Policies of Control*

1. Differentials between the Prices of Goods of Different Quality.

In the Clayton Act differentials in prices were permitted if they were "on account of differences in the grade, quality or quantity."[3]   Whether the Act imposed any limit upon differences in price in these circumstances was never clarified.   The Robinson-Patman Act narrows the scope of prohibition upon

---

[1] S. S. Kresge Co. v. Champion Spark Plug Co., 3 F. (2d) 415 (C. C. A. 6th, 1925).

[2] *Supra* note 4, page 197.

[3] Clayton Act, § 2.

discrimination because it relates only to sales of goods "of like grade and quality."[1] The significance of this change depends upon the manner in which the courts define grade and quality. The definition is important although far from easy. If differences in brand name justify differences in price special brands may be made for each class of buyer and the manufacturer may combine the production of his own with private brands. But if, as is generally assumed, this basis of differentiation is not allowed[2] there may be a reorganization of production. The production of private brands may be concentrated in firms not selling under their own brand name. Manufacturers with brand names of their own may be compelled to seek forceful methods of increasing the sales of their own brand to make up for the loss of manufacturing business for the owners of private brand names. Large buyers may be impelled to seek purchases of the whole output of some manufacturers; no charges of discrimination can then arise.[3] These manufacturers, if they are in industries where relatively small scale production survives, may be placed in a position of complete dependence upon the single large buyer. Loss of the contract in any year would leave them without any business. Their power to protect themselves against such an eventuality depends very much upon the conditions prevailing in the industry and especially upon the existence of excess capacity.

Rejection of brands as a basis of discrimination may lead to a physical differentiation of products until their differences are sufficient for the courts to accept them as not of like grade and quality. Manufacturing costs may thus be raised. In the chemical industries it may be possible to make products offer-

---

[1] Robinson-Patman Act, § 1(a).

[2] Differences due to the cost of advertising their own brands would appear to be permissible. See p. 314, *infra*.

[3] *Cf.* Hearings before the House Committee on the Judiciary on H. R. 8442, H. R. 4995, H. R. 5062 (Amendment of Clayton Act) 74th Cong., 1st Sess. (1935), p. 19.

ing similar utility but of different physical constitution. They may sell one to large buyers and another to smaller at price differentials giving considerable benefit to the large buyers. Sellers still have the right to select their own customers in *bona fide* transactions and not in restraint of trade.

2. Differentials between Prices for Different Quantities.

Differences in the cost of selling or transportation justified differences in price under the Clayton Act if they made only "due allowance" for such differences in cost.[1] The Robinson-Patman Act includes in this type of restriction differences in cost due to differences in quantities sold.[2] It permits differentials that make only due allowance for differences in the cost of manufacture sale or delivery resulting from the differing methods or quantities[3] by which such commodities are sold or delivered. The most notable aspect of this provision is that it apparently permits a manufacturer to refuse discounts equal to differences in cost arising out of differences in quantity sold or methods of sale.[4] If, as is likely, the Act is so interpreted it cannot be defended as a means of achieving in the sale of manufactured goods the results of competition. Sellers may discriminate in favor of but not against the firms with whom dealing is more costly. Such a policy cannot be defended on the ground that the law is being modified merely to remove the unfair advantages of large firms.

This same of policy permitting discrimination against large buyers appears to be implied in the provision in the Robinson-Patman Act permitting government control of price differentials.[5] The introduction of direct control is itself notable as

---

[1] Clayton Act, § 2.

[2] Robinson-Patman Act, § 1(a).

[3] Sellers customarily classify their buyers into a few groups for the purpose of calculating discounts. Even where they are classified according to the size of orders there is some discrimination. It is doubtful, however, whether the courts will insist on separate prices for orders of each size.

[4] Hearings, *supra* note 3, page 200, p. 10.

[5] Robinson-Patman Act, § 1(a).

representing a shift toward direct control of price policy. Where the Federal Trade Commission finds that "available purchasers in greater quantities" of particular commodities or classes of commodities "are so few as to render differentials on account thereof unjustly discriminatory or promotive of monopoly[1] in any line of commerce" the Commission may "after due investigation and hearing of all interested parties, fix and establish quantity limits and revise the same as it finds necessary." But under what circumstances would differentials making "due allowance" for differences in quantity purchased be unjustly discriminatory? If the differentials do not exceed the differences in cost referred to above why interfere merely because only a few firms can qualify for them? The second ruling phrase is "promotive of monopoly." Here again the legislature was face to face with the inconvenient tendency of an individualism that encourages the survival of the fittest to destroy, by that very fact, the mechanism for the future selection of the fittest. In giving to the Commission power to fix maximum discounts under these conditions an attempt is made to limit the size of firms in the distributing industry so as to prevent the emergence of monopoly, however that may be defined. The power is given apparently in defiance of the possibility that the large firm is increasing in size because of its superior efficiency. Congress seeks to modify the dictum of the Supreme Court that "the law does not make mere size an offense"[2] by adding "except in the field of distribution." Regulation of the size of firms by way of the regulation of the prices they pay for their materials can, of course, be a far more powerful means of control in the field of

---

[1] The standard, "unjustly discriminatory or promotive of monopoly," may be held to be so lacking in precision and definiteness as to render the provision an unconstitutional delegation of legislative power if the Court continues to utilize the principle—apparently discovered in the "hot oil" case (Panama Refining Co. v. Ryan, 293 U. S. 388 (1935)).

[2] U. S. v. U. S. Steel Corp., 251 U. S. 417, 451 (1920).

distribution than in the field of manufacturing.   What size of firm will be the maximum permissible?   When the Supreme Court has sought to restore competition by partitioning large firms held to be in breach of the law it has substituted in some cases three or four firms.   Will the Commission be guided in the administration of this uncomfortable power by the precedent set by the Court, and how much protection will the consumer thereby secure?   Can sellers whose opportunities for increasing their relative volume of business are cut off by Congress be regarded as vigorously competing with each other to the benefit of the buyer?

3. Differentials due to Differences in the Cost of Selling.

The allowance of price differentials to cover differences in the cost of selling will presumably recognize advertising costs as a justification for differentials.   Neither the Congress nor the courts have taken action to curtail expenditure upon advertising although, as is explained above, such expenditures are in large part a substitute for price competition as a way of obtaining business.   They seriously interfere with competition in the market and tend to raise costs.

4. Differentials "to Meet Competition."

Discrimination in good faith and to meet competition was permitted in the Clayton Act[1] and the Robinson-Patman Act makes little change in this respect.[2]   This provision implies the possibility that discrimination may occur in defiance of the law and permits others to follow suit if some seller has started it. This attitude may be realistic but it creates difficulties.   May a seller discriminate when he honestly believes he is responding to a similar policy on the part of a rival?   Moreover the

---

[1] Clayton Act, § 2.

[2] The Act, § 1(b), provides that any seller may rebut a *prima facie* case of illegal discrimination by showing that "his lower price or the furnishing of facilities or services to any purchaser or purchasers was made in good faith to meet an equally low price of a competitor or the services or facilities furnished by a competitor."

patterns of discrimination existing on the day the law came into force can all be defended by individual sellers under this clause. So long as these price differentials are unchanged they may be beyond the reach of the law.[1] If a seller supplies superior facilities rivals may respond with a lower price.[2] It would appear to be necessary, therefore, to determine how much difference between the prices of competitors may be justified by any difference of facilities.

5. Discrimination and Changes in Price.

The Robinson-Patman Act introduces a new provision that the Act shall not prevent price changes from time to time in response to "changing conditions affecting the market for, or the marketability of, the goods concerned."[3] Sellers faced with the deterioration of goods, obsolescence of seasonal goods, or those discontinuing business may make price reductions without breach of the law. Congress was probably fearful that prices might be reduced for a short time to accept a large order and subsequently raised again. But if prices charged at different times are to be compared serious problems are likely to occur. How long a period of time is to be taken? Ultimately this question leads to the necessity of deciding what "changing conditions affecting the market" justify a price change and how large a change they justify.[4] At this point

---

[1] The Act may have the effect of permitting differentials in excess of cost differentials. If one firm can show cost differentials justifying certain discounts others may apparently grant the discounts without being able to achieve the economies on which they are based.

[2] *Cf.* Answer to Complaint, In Matter of Shefford Cheese Co., F. T. C. Docket 2936. The Company defended part of its discounts on the ground that it did not deliver at the store door while its rivals did.

[3] Robinson-Patman Act, § 1(a).

[4] *Cf.* Answer to Complaint, In Matter of Bird & Son, Inc. and Montgomery Ward & Co., F. T. C. Docket 2937. Montgomery Ward denied knowledge whether the seller's price changes had been made in good faith in response to changing conditions in the market.

apparently the policy has been transformed into one of price control.

6. Differentials in Services or Allowances.

The Robinson-Patman Act seeks to deal with some of the possible discriminations in matters other than price but having similar effects. It was alleged that large distributors had benefitted from advertising and brokerage allowances.[1] The large distributors explained that it would be uneconomical to make them purchase through brokers whose services they did not need, and whose charges would be added to their costs.[2] Such a policy would merely protect antiquated methods of distribution. Brokerage payments of this kind were, nevertheless, prohibited.[3] This clause, however, merely prevents large buyers from obtaining part of the economies of their size in the form of fictional brokerage payments. They must seek them all in the form of price differences which must meet the requirements already laid down.

Advertising allowances were defended by the large sellers as a modern method of promoting sales.[4] One large chain was reported to have received advertising allowances from one manufacturer amounting to eight million dollars in one year, of which six million dollars are said to have been spent by the buyer on advertising.[5] Allowances had also been made for window dressing although they had not necessarily been so

---

[1] Hearings, *supra* note 3, page 200, pp. 6, 69, 96, 183.

[2] *Id.* at pp. 148, 184.

[3] The Act, § 1(c), makes it illegal to grant or accept anything of value as a commission, brokerage or allowance except for services rendered in connection with the sale or purchase. Brokerage payments may not be made to intermediaries unless they are under the control of the person paying the commission.

[4] Hearings, *supra* note 3, page 200, at pp. 149, 177. See also charges of payments of advertising allowances by razor blade manufacturers contended by the Federal Trade Commission to be in violation of § 2 of the Clayton Act. *N. Y. Times*, April 21, 1936, p. 47.

[5] Hearings, *supra* note 3, page 200, at p. 61.

applied.[1] The Act does not forbid such allowances or limit
them to the cost of advertising service rendered by buyers; it
merely requires that they shall be made upon a "propor-
tionally equal" basis to all buyers.[2] It gives no indication of
the basis of calculating proportionality.[3]

C. The Effects of Control

1. Upon the Organization of Distribution.

The effect of the Robinson-Patman Act upon the struggle
between the competing types of distributor depends partly
upon the policy of the Federal Trade Commission in fixing
maximum discounts and the attitude of the courts to its policy.
Upon this subject there is little to say. So far as discounts
may be allowed up to the differences in the cost of dealing with
different types of distributors the pressures will probably be
similar to those affecting resale price maintenance and there
will be a tendency for manufacturers to favor the small

---

[1] *Id.* at p. 82. It has been stated that in 1935 department, dry goods and
specialty stores spent $212,000,000 for general publicity, of which $136,000,-
000 was spent for newspaper publicity. Manufacturers are said to have
contributed about $5,000,000 towards the cost of this publicity. *N. Y.
Times*, Aug. 16, 1936, § 3, p. 8.

[2] The Act, § 1(d), forbids payments by a seller for the benefit of a customer
as compensation for facilities or services furnished by the customer in connection with the processing, handling or sale unless such a consideration is
made available "on proportionately equal terms to all other customers
competing in the distribution of such products."

[3] Some distributors, after temporarily abandoning advertising allowances,
are reported again to have demanded them but to have required in their
purchase contracts an avowal that the manufacturer is prepared to make
similar arrangements with other purchasers similarly situated and on proportionately equal terms. While the buyer, as well as the seller, is responsible for any breach of this clause the buyer can know whether breach has
been committed only if he knows the prices charged by the sellers to all his
rivals and also the meaning of the phrase "proportionately equal." The
avowal demanded of the seller is sought as a means of defense in this difficult
situation. *N. Y. Times*, Aug. 27, 1936, p. 37. The position of advertising
allowances made in an entirely separate contract is dubious.

distributors, subject, however, to important checks already mentioned. So far as large distributors secure the full benefits of the economies of their method of distributing their discounts will depend upon the amount of the economies involved. In the first place, there will be general pressure upon manufacturers to calculate costs in order to have evidence on this subject. This pressure will reveal the arbitrariness of many conventional allocations of costs. It is not inconceivable that it will be found in some cases that the large buyers have been "carrying" the smaller, *i.e.*, that larger discounts could be given to the larger firms without contravening the law. Discounts based upon the contention that a single large order raises the rate of operation of plant more than a small order appear to have been regarded in Congress[1] as undesirable. In so far as the loss of a large order necessitates obtaining a number of small orders in order to maintain the rate of operation, and the cost of obtaining these small orders may be higher than that of obtaining the large order, differences in price would be justified by differences in the cost of selling. But, as a number of small orders can raise the rate of operation as effectively as a large one of an amount equal to the aggregate of the small orders, the manufacturing costs in the one case are the same as in the other. Neither the large nor the small orders can legitimately be singled out to bear the burden of the initial costs of running the plant at all.

Large orders for future delivery may well justify lower prices. If they permit production during "off peak" periods they may enable a plant to maintain an average rate of operation over a period of time higher than would otherwise be possible. The total amount of resources necessary to produce a given total output is less when the plant is operated regularly than when it is operated irregularly[2] yet the resulting economies fall to

---

[1] Hearings, *supra* note 3, page 200, p. 10.

[2] The Federal Trade Commission complained that the Goodyear Tire and Rubber Company had discriminated in favor of a large mail order

those able to give large orders and the large distributors may continue to obtain better prices than do smaller buyers.[1]   The social advantages of this method of organizing production are undeniable although its consequences in terms of the survival of a small number of large distributors may be disliked. Discounts based merely upon the total amount of purchases during a given period would, however, be difficult to justify. If the large buyer purchases upon a hand-to-mouth basis his

house in contravention of the Clayton Act.   The contract with the mail order house provided for a large minimum annual purchase of tires over a period of years.   These tires were sold by the mail order house under its own brand names.   Those sold to dealers were sold under the manufacturer's brand which he advertised.   Until wide publicity was given by the Federal Trade Commission, the majority of purchasers were doubtless unaware of the origin of the tires of the mail order house.   The Commission ordered the discontinuance of discrimination "by selling at net realized prices which are lower than the net realized prices at which it sells tires of comparable grade and quality to retail dealers and other customers."   Matter of Goodyear Tire and Rubber Co., F. T. C. Docket 2116 (1936).   The Commission claimed that the discrimination made more than due allowance for the cost of selling or transportation and was not made on account of differences in grade quality or quantity sold.   It emphasized that the discrimination had been kept secret from other purchasers from the manufacturer, thus suggesting doubt as to whether they represented only the economies resulting from the scale of the purchase.   Competition had been substantially restrained between the mail order houses and other distributors of tires, and the contract tended to create a monopoly in the distribution of tires.   In its order, however, it ignored differences in the cost of manufacturing or of selling as well as differences in quantity as justifying price differentials.   The Company announced the abrogation of the contract on account of the passage of the Robinson-Patman Act.   It also announced that it would appeal from the decision of the Commission concerning its operations prior to the change in law, *N. Y. Times*, July 17, 1936, p. 30.

[1] Chains often buy farther ahead than do small buyers.   Hearings, *supra* note 3, page 200, pp. 23, 24.   As large buyers buy for longer future delivery than the small the price charged on the day of the contract for immediate delivery to small buyers may be more than that for future delivery for large buyers.   Similarly the price on the day of delivery may differ between the two classes.

demands may be as spasmodic as those of small buyers and occur at the same time.

2. Effects upon the Price Policies of Manufacturers.

The policy of controlling discrimination may affect the general level of prices charged by manufacturers. The law appears to hamper if not abolish secret price cutting. A sale to one buyer at less than the "regular" price could be argued to injure the competition between rivals who paid the regular price and the buyer at the cut price. Such price cutting may not be defensible in terms of differences in the cost of manufacture or delivery. It does not necessarily favor the largest buyers. Where manufacturers are relatively few, and overhead costs an important part of total costs, there is constantly anxiety to prevent secret price cutting. Secret price cutting by one seller causes rivals to lose business and they resort to similar price cuts. The market becomes "chaotic" in the sense that there is no uniformity of prices and a price war is likely. On the other hand, a manufacturer carrying overhead costs is often tempted to obtain business by making a secret concession from his regular price. An open reduction involves a loss of revenue upon all his other business and this loss may exceed the beneficial effect of the additional business, allowance being made for the out-of-pocket costs of executing the order. But if the concession is made upon one or a few orders the gain may exceed the out-of-pocket cost of the business. There is no economy in a policy of throwing industry into price wars and little possibility of doing so. But the importance of secret price cuts lies in their tendency to operate as an entering wedge for open price reductions. In imperfectly competitive markets they indicate an imperfect foresight of sellers which supplies a downward pressure on prices. If secret price cutting is eliminated sellers act upon the assumption that any reduction in price made by them will be immediately met by all rivals. They think in terms of the total demand at each price, *i.e.*, as a monopolist, although possibly limited by the fear of new competition resulting either in a cutting of prices or a wider sharing of the market at existing prices. The sellers draw the line between a desirable and an undesirable price cut but their standards of desirability frequently depart from the general social interest. The elimination of secret price cutting, therefore, increases the imperfection of competition.

Downward pressures upon prices are also reduced by attempts to obstruct large buyers who are said to beat down the prices of manufacturers without mercy. Mercy of course found no place in the freely competitive market. How low can prices be forced? It may be said that the large order is a great temptation to the seller. Why? If it is because it saves the cost of obtaining a large number of small orders the Act does not remove the temptation. But a manufacturer may accept a low price because he has become dependent upon the large buyer; he may have allowed his selling organization to shrink and have relied upon continued orders from the large firm. Turning to small orders means incurring the initial costs of entering an alternative market. But this situation may even be encouraged under the law because a manufacturer selling his whole output to a single buyer is immune from the Act. The large buyer may obtain low prices because of the low rate at which capacity is being operated in the manufacturing industry. Any price above the out-of-pocket costs of new business yields a contribution towards overhead costs. The prospect of a large block of business promises a large aggregate contribution, although the contribution per unit of output may be low. In the absence of pressure from large buyers manufacturers in many industries where overhead costs are important have shown a preference for meeting a decline in demand by maintaining prices and allowing output to fall. The quantitative amount of the fall in output due to the maintenance of prices varies of course from industry to industry and with the period of time in view. In so far as plants not used become obsolescent, rust out, involve costs for maintenance or increased interest charges, additional costs are imposed on the industry and upon society without corresponding benefit. The large buyer may, therefore, be a means of overpowering the sellers and preventing them from pursuing this policy. At the present stage in the evolution of distribution and prior to the passage of the Robinson-Patman Act there was probably vigorous enough rivalry between distributors to ensure that the benefits of these downward pressures upon prices were passed on to ultimate purchasers. There looms in the future, however, the possibility that distributors may become so large and so few that the pressure to pass on these benefits may be seriously modified.

These problems are particularly acute in times of depression. Freedom to large distributors to press down manufacturers as far as they are able may cause the elimination of firms. Productive resources which society would have been well advised to keep in use in order to meet a later increase in general demand may be abandoned. Their abandonment necessitates the investment of new capital when the upturn of business comes, possibly stimulating the upswing of general business activity. This situation is extremely complex and the analysis necessary to provide a basis for a proper policy is not available. In the first place the pressing down of prices, if general, may restrict the depth of the downward swing in industrial activity and indirectly reduce the prospect of the elimination of firms. In the second place, the failure of firms does not always involve the abandonment of plant. It may continue in production with a lower capitalization. In the third place it is always difficult to determine the amount of investment that should be retained in an industry to meet the upturn of business. The amount and time of the upturn are always uncertain. The obstruction of the development of large distributors and the elimination of secret price cutting is likely, however, to have the general effect of strengthening manufacturers in their efforts to maintain prices, thus reducing output and possibly intensifying depression.

V. CONCLUSION

It is abundantly evident that the policy of maintaining the prerequisites of competition, either in the narrow theoretical sense or even in a somewhat broader interpretation, has failed to attain its objective. If mere unfairness in the policies of the large firms[1] is the explanation of the decline of price competition, the modifications that have been introduced into the law by the anti-trust laws have until now failed to maintain competitive markets in many industries. The more plausible explanation of the increasing imperfection of competition is that it is due to changes in the techniques of production and selling. In some of the branches of heavy industry the economies of large scale production, coupled with the fact that markets are narrower than the national boundaries are sufficient to explain the imperfections of competition.

In choosing whether to maintain the number of firms at a competitive level or to accept the economies of size and with them a decreasing number of firms, the courts have in general chosen the latter alternative. In the sale of consumers goods the other major change accounting for the size of firms lies in the development of methods of sales promotion. Neither the courts nor Congress have adequately recognized the tendency of this development to damage the market by dividing it into a series of sub-markets for specially branded products. Even when contemplating the policies of sellers powerful

---

[1] The pursuit of profit is sometimes the basis of criticism of firms, although such conduct is of the essence of capitalism. An important aspect of price policy in the steel industry has been condemned as "a network of actions by individuals and groups motivated by the desire for larger profits and acting without regard for the interests of other industries or the consuming public." Fetter, *Planning for Totalitarian Monopoly* (1937) 45 J. POL. ECON. 102.

enough to seek to maintain resale prices, and thereby restrict price competition in later markets, or to set discounts favoring one class of distributor rather than another, the courts failed to be impressed by the extent to which such sellers have been emancipated from competitive pressures.   The courts have looked back to the picture of a competitive world and refused to interfere because the seller must have power to select his customers, or even for more formal reasons.   In its recent legislation Congress appears to endorse price differentials allowing the seller to seek to recover the cost of advertising his goods.   To do otherwise would undoubtedly cause serious dislocation of business but to proceed thus is not to maintain the prerequisites of competition.   States have enacted resale price maintenance legislation which will have similar effects.

In the threefold struggle that has developed between the sellers of advertised goods, the small scale distributors and the large scale distributors, federal and state governments have been under pressure to obstruct the development of large distributors.   Those threatened with ejection from their positions in the market and in part also manufacturers seeking to maintain powerful positions by advertising, have exerted great pressure.   They have not sought to eliminate only the unfair advantages of large distributors.   Taxes against chain stores are an obstacle to one kind of large scale distribution arbitrary in amount.   Progressive taxes on gross sales also hamper large firms.   The bias against large distributors in the Robinson-Patman Act has already been mentioned. Thus, although anti-trust laws have failed to maintain the numbers of manufacturers there appears now to be an effort to restrict concentration in distribution, a process of relatively recent occurrence.   But in the process of doing so not only is the pursuit of the economies of large scale distribution hindered. Price competition between manufacturers is softened and they exercise control over the reorganization of distribution.

The type of case coming before the courts and the situations with which Congress endeavors to deal all suggest how far competition has receded in a number of markets. Efforts to rearrange the scenery so that competition could commence and continue would involve far reaching changes likely to induce drastic opposition from business and the courts and to offer the ultimate purchaser little if any benefit. In fact the control of price differentials is a step in the direction of a policy of seeking the ends of competition by social control. This policy leads on toward increasing state control. Maintaining the number of distributors beyond the economical number does not give the buyer the benefits of competition. The difficulties and dangers of control of prices are difficult to exaggerate. There may be ways of permitting a wide decentralization of economic initiative and yet securing the orientation of the economic system toward reasonably acceptable social objectives and its reasonably efficient operation. Unless such policies are speedily discovered we face the mountainous problems of price control.

6

METHODS OF DEVELOPING A PROPER CONTROL OF BIG BUSINESS*

By Edward S. Mason†

An important first step in fixing the proper setting of this problem is to focus attention on the effects of large enterprise on the structure and functioning of the economy. A traditional attitude, on the other hand, has been to interpret the so-called monopoly problem in terms of the interests of particular groups. Consumers have been said to have an interest in free competition, while producers are concerned with the maintenance of fair competition. Whatever these terms mean, the establishment or preservation of free and fair competition is not an end in itself; it must be justified principally to the extent that it promotes an efficient, full and relatively stable use of human and material resources. Recent legislation in this field, however—I have in mind particularly the Robinson-Patman and Miller-Tydings Acts—continues to pursue the problem from the point of view of particular groups. Independent distributors are to be protected against the unfair or monopolistic practices of chain stores and other mass distributors without much regard to the effect of this protection on the functioning of the economy.

As soon as the problem is presented in terms of the relation of large size to the structure and functioning of the economy, three issues stand out as fundamentally important:

* *Proceedings of the Academy of Political Science*, New York, Volume XVIII, Number 2, January 1939, pages 40–49. Reprinted by the courtesy of the Academy of Political Science, Columbia University, and the author.

† Professor of Economics, Harvard University.

First, the consequences of corporate price policies for production and employment;

Second, the effects of restraints, in the well-known legal sense, on free enterprise and free bargaining;

Third, the consequences of the so-called concentration of economic control for the social stability of the economic system.

These three issues are not strictly independent. Corporate price policies *may* involve restraints of trade. It is quite possible that basing-point practices and other types of price formulae may be and should be held to be in restraint of trade. What should be realized, however, is that monopolistic price policies are not dependent on pricing techniques of a sort which might conceivably be held in restraint of trade. They are a product of the structure of industrial markets within which the size and number of firms are of leading importance. Likewise, the existence of monopolistic price policies and of restraints of trade may influence considerably the social stability of an economy in which economic control is concentrated. Despite the fact, however, that these issues crosshatch each other, it is important that they be visualized as distinct, both for purposes of analysis and for determination of possible remedies. Public policies which are likely to prove effective in handling one aspect of the problem may not prove effective in treating another.

The traditional area of anti-trust policy has been in connection with restraints on free enterprise and free bargaining. It is important, before proceeding further, to form an idea of what are the possibilities, but especially the limitations, of this type of policy in handling the problems of large-scale enterprise already mentioned. By common admission anti-trust enforcement has been until recently half-hearted and relatively ineffective. Even so, it has accomplished much. Cartel arrangements and practices which might easily have developed in this country, had the law concerning agreements in restraint of trade not been enforced, have been substantially prevented. Predatory competitive practices of large-scale concerns, furthermore, have evidently declined in frequency and importance, a result for which the existence of the anti-trust acts is, at least in part, responsible. Undoubtedly much more can be accomplished in this traditional area. The recent increase in the staff of the anti-trust division, procedural changes which are now in progress, and the imaginative and venturesome leadership which the division enjoys promise the most effective period of administration in the history of the acts.

Nevertheless—and this is the point to be emphasized—the limitations of this type of legislation in dealing with monopoly problems are real and serious. These limitations, it is true, do not apparently impress Mr. Arnold, the Assistant Attorney General. On more than one occasion he has declared it his belief that "Our ideal is already well stated in the Sherman Law. It only requires particular application."[1] The policy of the anti-trust division under his administration would appear to be gradually, by the continual pressure of particular cases, to expand the meaning of restraint of trade in the Sherman Act until it can be made to cover among other issues price and production policies of large enterprise. In a speech in October of this year he declared that

The large organizations required today for efficient mass production have changed our conceptions of what is a reasonable restraint of trade. No one desires to break them up where they are efficient. Nevertheless, their very size gives them great control over the price structure even where that size is justified. Too often price policies of large organizations are not linked with the distribution of their productive capacity. Productive plants will be designed for ten years. Price policies will be aimed at attaining the maximum amount of the standard national purchasing power over a short period.[2] Great advertising costs, expensive and wasteful dis-

---

[1] Thurman Arnold, "Fair and Effective Use of Present Antitrust Procedure." Speech delivered April 28, 1938 before the Trade and Commerce Bar Association of New York.

[2] Mr. Arnold was here concerned with price increases for industrial products which preceded the industrial downturn of 1937. These, how-

tribution systems, will be designed to take business away from others rather than to distribute more goods by lowering prices.[1]

No one will deny that an important problem is presented here. In fact—so far as the effective functioning of the economy is concerned—it may not be too much to say that it is *the* problem of large-scale enterprise. Whether it can be effectively handled by a reshaping of the anti-trust acts, or by any conceivable reinterpretation of the meaning of restraint of trade, however, is a different matter. The price and production policies complained of, and the shift in emphasis from price competition to other types of competition economically and socially less desirable, rest fundamentally on certain technological facts which are not likely to be altered seriously by enforcement of the anti-trust acts. Among these facts are the increasing importance of durable capital and consumers' goods in the total output, an increase in the market importance of large sellers with the extension of mass production methods, a growth in the proportion of overhead to total costs in many industries, an increase in the number and importance of industries which have passed the stage of active competitive expansion. The implications of these facts are too well known to require elaboration.

One of the results is the well-established relative inflexibility of prices, during business upturns and downturns, of many industrial products accompanied by wide fluctuations in output, especially of durable goods. The extent of this inflexibility, however, is probably greatly exaggerated in conse-

---

ever, were examples of price flexibility rather than the reverse. One of the problems of price behavior is concerned with corporate price policies which are "designed for ten years." Price policies which are adapted to the "short period" may be desirable. In a price system which was really flexible we should expect to see price increases in the upturn and price decreases in the downturn.

[1] "The Enforcement of the Sherman Act." Speech delivered in St. Louis, October 1, 1938.

quence of serious limitations in the price data available for studies of inflexibility. Furthermore, recent investigations have indicated that it is not a new phenomenon.[1]   Our capitalist economy has gone through several decades of expansion with continual increase in per capita production and consumption despite the fact of price inflexibility.   This type of price behavior may not, then, be an insuperable obstacle to further progress and expansion.   Nevertheless, admitting fully these comforting objections to the inflexibility thesis, there remains a serious problem.   It may well be that a means of attaining greater flexibility would substantially promote a more stable and effective use of resources.

The inflexibilities that count are traceable directly to the price policies of large-scale enterprise.   While these price policies frequently are associated with techniques which might be reached by a reinterpretation of the Sherman Act, they rest fundamentally on technological facts of the sort already mentioned.   This does not mean that the anti-trust division should not press for such a reinterpretation or that the elimination of price control techniques is not important.   Price leadership, uniformity of price bids, the practice of rotating the lowest bidder, are examples of techniques which might quite properly be held to be sufficient evidence of restraint of trade.   Certainly the use of basing points and similar types of pricing formulae are practices which could be included in a more comprehensive meaning of restraint of trade.   When and if the use of such pricing techniques has been eliminated by effective enforcement of the anti-trust acts, will the price structure or the behavior of industrial prices be seriously affected?

---

[1] *Cf.* Humphrey, D. D., "The Nature and Meaning of Rigid Prices, 1890–1933," *Journal of Political Economy*, vol. XLV, 1937, pp. 651–666; Mason, E. S., "Price Inflexibility," *Review of Economic Statistics*, May 1938, pp. 53–64.

The answer to this question must be, in my opinion, "No." As long as the structure of industrial markets, including such factors as product durability and differentiation, number of sellers, the structure of costs and the age of the industry, remains as it is, there is overwhelming pressure on business management to pursue price stabilization policies and to divert competition away from price channels. Prosecution of the anti-trust acts may alter the structure of markets to some extent by breaking up firms and eliminating pricing techniques, but the scope of such action is distinctly limited. I should doubt, for example, whether successful prosecution of the aluminum suit followed by dissolution of the company would markedly affect the behavior of prices and production in the aluminum industry.

The moral of this is that, if corporate price and production policies are to be successfully regulated, it must be along some other line. The structure of certain markets, at least in limited areas, might be altered by the inclusion of more foreign competitors through tariff reductions. Other possibilities are present in the manipulation of government purchasing arrangements. The federal government is in the market on an increasingly important scale, and more intensive efforts on the part of such a large buyer to secure the benefit of price competition might make these benefits available to other buyers than government. In this connection it must not be forgotten that the activities of large enterprises as *buyers*, rather than sellers, are rather in the direction of price flexibility than of rigidity. If price flexibility is the *desideratum*, this end can be as effectively secured by the elimination of recent legislation as by the addition of new regulation.

It must be admitted, however, that these suggestions reveal limited possibilities. A thoroughgoing—not to say radical—treatment of the price inflexibility problem probably depends on changing and controlling the incentives which govern price and production policy. A tax on the production of inflexibly priced goods during the upturn, a bounty on condition of price reduction during the downturn would strike at the roots of the problem.   An even more drastic suggestion is associated with the application of A. A. A. techniques to the industrial problem.   A tax on the production of industrial products to be remitted on condition of fulfillment of suggested production quotas would attack the question of idle resources directly rather than through changes in price behavior.   Considerations, however, of the power and discretion which would have to be delegated to administrative agencies, together with the practical omniscience we should have to expect of such agencies, deprives these proposals of serious weight.   However useful such techniques might be to a hierarchy of commissars they seem incompatible with the principles of democratic capitalism.   The difficulties encountered by monetary policy in timing essentially similar action on a much less comprehensive scale fortify one's skepticism.

The fact of the matter seems to be that radical changes in the type of price structure and price behavior now associated with many industrial markets lie outside the scope of practicable public policy.   It should be emphasized, however, that price inflexibility is less of a deterrent to an effective use of resources in a progressive, expanding economy than if that economy is stagnant or contracting.   With the disappearance of free land and the cessation of rapid population growth the possibilities of expansion depend on holding open every door for technical change, new enterprises, new methods of production and distribution, and continued investment of capital. In a progressive economy the attempts of large enterprises to maintain their position by stabilizing prices and restricting output are doomed to be ineffective.

It is along this line that an active and imaginative enforcement of the anti-trust acts is likely to produce results, both in eliminating restraints within the scope of these acts and in laying bare other types of restraints which demand a different kind of action. A restrictive use of certain patents and the withholding of others from use entirely are examples of a different type of restraint which, if important, calls for a thoroughgoing overhauling of existing patent legislation. The present action of the anti-trust division against Chicago milk distributors has revealed the extent to which municipal sanitary regulations have been used to restrain freedom of entry into a market. These situations are best brought to light by the prosecution of particular cases. In the words of Mr. Arnold, "one function of anti-trust prosecution would be to capitalize and focus attention on economic conditions in particular industries which need adjustment."[1] Effective enforcement of the anti-trust acts is not likely to have much influence on price inflexibility but keeping the door open wide to free enterprise will definitely lessen the effect of such inflexibility on the efficient functioning of the economy.

In dealing with methods of developing a proper control of big business I have said nothing about direct governmental price control along public utility lines. Yet we are told repeatedly that the alternative to the monopolistic price policies of big business is government regulation of prices. The only method of government price control which has been extensively developed in this country is, as a matter of fact, the public utility type. To my mind the results have been extremely sad. No prices respond less readily to changes in costs, demand or general business conditions than public utility and railway rates. If we are to have direct governmental action in this field, government ownership or competition with private enterprise by public corporations offers, in my opinion, greater possibilities than the extension of public utility regulation.

Having touched, albeit inadequately, on the monopoly problem presented by corporate price policies and by restraints

---

[1] "Policies of the Anti-Trust Division." Speech delivered September 3, 1938, at Convention Banquet of Independent Bankers Association, St. Paul.

of free competition, let us turn finally to a consideration of the concentration of economic control. The existence of large-scale enterprise is only one aspect of this question. Its ramifications include such matters as corporate relations with financial institutions, interlocking directorates, and the existence of spheres of financial influence. Limiting ourselves, however, to the problems of large-scale enterprise the concentration of economic control presents, in addition to the issue of corporate price and production policies, a series of broader social questions relevant to what type of economic structure is compatible with the genius of our institutions.

Robert Jackson, former head of the anti-trust division, illuminated one aspect of this question when he said,

This concentration of business accounts in large part for the lost influence of big business, and its press, and its legal lackeys, and its business organization, in legislation and election struggles. Forty years ago big business had as its ally in every town and settlement the local merchant, local manufacturer, local banker and local utility man. Each was a leading citizen, on whom many depended for information and leadership as well as for credit and jobs. This type of man has largely gone. Why he has gone makes little difference.

In place of this strong and leading individual is a managing clerk at the chain store who cannot make a credit sale, and a local superintendent for the factory. The local bank is closed and nobody who has more authority than a bill collector represents the utility in most communities.

The small business man who used to be our most ardent capitalist and the most uncompromising of conservatives has been crushed, or merged, or consolidated, or otherwise retired.[1]

The issues raised by Mr. Jackson have to do with changing social relationships between the business group, or one element of it, and other groups making up the community; laborers, consumers, farmers, investors and others. One question involves the extent to which these relationships have actually

---

[1] Robert H. Jackson, "Should the Antitrust Laws Be Revised?" Speech delivered September 17, 1937 before the Trade and Commerce Bar Association of New York.

changed; another is concerned with the rôle of big business in producing such changes. Obviously these questions are too broad for adequate discussion here. I shall have to limit myself to two observations: (1) the extent to which the rise of big business during the last forty years is responsible for such changes as have occurred is usually grossly exaggerated; (2) changes in public policy directed toward these problems will have to be of a different sort and proceed from very different intellectual presuppositions than those underlying our traditional monopoly policies.

People who view with alarm the huge size of modern business enterprise and speculate upon its influence on traditional American democracy are apt so to speculate outside the context provided by the tremendous growth of national and business wealth. It is true that the assets of a relatively few corporations constitute a large percentage of total business assets. But so did they forty and even fifty years ago. The change has not been nearly as great as it is commonly supposed.

Furthermore, for many aspects of the problem of concentration of economic control, total assets are a poor measure of corporate size. The number of employees is a very much better measure. Recent data published by the Social Security Board indicates that the relative importance—by this measure—of large-scale enterprise in the economy is much less than asset computations would indicate.[1] The ratio of assets to employees varies greatly from industry to industry and many firms which are colossal in terms of assets are of moderate size in terms of employees. This is conspicuously true of the utility field.

The fact of concentration has a real bearing on the character of the society in which we live. But is there not a disposition on the part of the "concentration experts" to idealize the American past as one in which men were free and equal

---

[1] *Cf.* Corson, John J., *Wages and Employment Under the Old-Age Insurance Program*, Social Security Board Release, October 3, 1938.

and no group exercised more than its proportionate share of social influence?   It is my impression that this ideal departs very far from the facts.

If the problem of concentration, in so far as it is represented by large-scale enterprise, is to be attacked by public policy, then the methods applied will have to be different from those associated with our traditional anti-monopoly policy. The objective becomes not the elimination of restraints or the curbing of monopolistic price and production policies, but an attack on size as such.   The ideal envisaged is neither the maintenance of free enterprise nor a behavior of prices and production compatible with an efficient use of resources but, rather, a small enterprise economy.   The method employed might be progressive taxation of corporation income, refusal to license corporations beyond a certain size for purposes of interstate trade, or many others.   One's attitude toward this objective depends upon his evaluation of many factors which are impossible, in a limited time, to discuss.   Among the most important are the possible loss in long-run efficiency, the costs of economic dislocation involved, and the probable changes in the locus and use of economic power.   Without attempting to justify my position, I am strongly of the opinion that the advantages of such a policy are highly dubious while the costs are very real.

7

NOTES ON THE ANTI-TRUST LAW POLICY*

By Paul T. Homan†

Summary

I. Lack of focus in discussion of policy, 73.—Limiting assumptions necessary to achieve focus, 75.—II. Political assumptions stated, indicating probable continuance of general policy, 75.—III. Relative laxity of past enforcement, 78.—Changes of emphasis in discussions of policy, 81.—Continuing importance of problems emphasized in earlier discussions, 82.—IV. Possible changes in substantive law to provide more effective enforcement, 84.—V. Present deficiencies in administration, 89.—Possible improvement of administration, 90.—VI. Methods of making exceptions to anti-trust policy, 93.—Limits upon use of consent decrees, 97.—Legislative approach to exemption of particular industries, 98.—VII. Anti-trust law policy not "archaic," 100.—Does not imply government of narrow powers, 101.—Greater effectiveness possible, 101.

I

For the first time in a quarter century the anti-trust law policy is coming into the spotlight of public attention. In the meantime the policy has gone through three phases of impairment. During the World War actions under the law were largely suspended. In the decade of the nineteen twenties the laws were invoked very hesitantly during a period of corporate concentration and of increasing recourse to trade association activities of a somewhat monopolistic character. During

---

* The Quarterly Journal of Economics, Volume LIV, Number 1, November 1939, pages 73–102. Reprinted by the courtesy of the Harvard University Press and the author.

† Cornell University.

the decade of the nineteen thirties the policy was until recently further impaired by neglect, with additional positive impairment in connection with the NRA and its aftermath. Now that serious discussion is arising concerning the future of the policy, there is evidence of the utmost confusion of thought upon the tangle of issues presented. It is the purpose of this paper to allay some of that confusion and to present a set of terms within which a more orderly discussion of the issues may proceed.

The very heart of the difficulty has, I think, been the absence of any central focus in the discussion of the subject. As a *general* policy, the anti-trust law policy nominally prescribes a competitive pattern for market relations, except for specific exceptions. Since the academic study of any question of policy involves the consideration of alternatives, to question the propriety of the general policy laid down by the Sherman Act immediately involves the necessity of canvassing possible substitute principles of general applicability. The immediate consequence is that one is faced with a large number of diverse alternative, the consequences of each of which, if put into effect, become the necessary subject of analysis.

When it is suggested that the anti-trust law policy is anachronistic and incapable of effective application in the circumstances of modern technology and industrial organization, it is to the consideration of such alternatives that the mind is necessarily forced. I do not at all doubt that it is the duty of scholars to consider alternative proposals with the greatest care. But at the present point I wish merely to suggest that the questioning of the anti-trust law policy does not bring into focus any specific alternative. It diffuses the attention into all the possible patterns into which the scheme of economic relations might conceivably be reconstructed.

The lack of central focus is not to be illustrated merely from the body of preconceptions which regard the anti-trust policy as essentially archaic and inapplicable. There exists a body

of informed opinion which does not question the desirability of
the anti-trust law policy as a general policy but doubts its
applicability to all areas of industry.   One is thus introduced,
not only to the question of what industries shall be excepted,
but also to all the various suggestions which can be made as to
the forms of organization for the excepted industries and the
forms of public control to which they may be subjected.

Nor does the dispersion of discussion end there.   Even
among those who accept the anti-trust law policy as an appropriate general policy, there is little satisfaction either with the
content of the law or with the manner in which it is adminis-
ered.   One is therefore introduced to all the varied suggestions
that can be made both as to substantive content and administrative means.

There are, moreover, industries with relation to which the
anti-trust laws are meaningless, because they have no monopolistic features, but which are felt by some persons to pose a
problem in industrial organization because their markets are
"disorderly."   Since the problems of industrial organization
in detail run from curbing private monopoly at one extreme to
curbing competition at the other, with no definable area
between the extremes within which the elements of competition and monopoly are deemed to be combined in just the
correct proportions, the idea arises that there is no problem of
general policy, that the situation in each industry is a special
problem, and that special measures of public control appropriate to each situation are called for.

Finally, one arrives at the capstone of the tower of Babel.
All the different persons who have some interest in perpetuat-
ing, modifying, or abolishing the anti-trust law policy have
different conceptions, in emphasis at least, of the weaknesses or
"abuses" which characterize economic society and of the ends
toward which reforms should be directed.   They apply
different scales of value and set up different orders of priority.
The variety of preconceptions which different persons bring to

the discussion of the various possible alternatives multiplies the difficulties of achieving focus in the consideration of anti-trust law problems.

The central difficulty is, no doubt, that recent discussion has been dominated by a debate over the appropriateness of retaining the anti-trust law policy, a subject which opens the way for exploiting every economic philosophy and presents issues upon which most students have themselves been in extreme doubt. To achieve any focus upon concrete issues it is necessary to escape from this debate, and to concern one's self with the problems of policy that arise on the assumption that the anti-trust law policy either is, or is not, going to be continued. This means that discussion must proceed at every point under certain limiting assumptions. The further purpose of this article is to show how a focus can be given to the discussion of a series of inter-related problems of policy under a particular body of limiting assumptions which will be set forth in the following section.

II

In embarking upon an analysis intended to be relevant to immediate problems of policy, one must set up tests of relevancy which represent personal judgments. Such judgments of what lies within the sphere of discourse relevant to policy choices during the calculable future carry one far out of the bounds technically demarcated for economists and into the domain of public opinion. But this is, after all, the domain within which all questions of policy must be discussed. Economists may choose to ignore it—and are subject to no criticism for so doing—but insofar as they wish their analyses to be directly relevant to policy choices they cannot do so. They must adapt their work to the surrounding circumstances and climate of opinion.[1]

---

[1] I do not underestimate the hazard that one may be wrong in projecting forward his present opinion concerning future states of public opinion.

For the purposes of this paper the discussion will be limited by introducing a number of limiting assumptions.

(1) It is assumed that American opinion will not be oriented toward the conscious pursuit of a collectivist form of social organization.   One may therefore exclude the discussion of how a collectivist organization could be, or ought to be, organized.

(2) As a corollary to the preceding assumption, it is assumed that theories of social process which postulate the necessary decay of capitalist civilization are unconfirmed hypotheses incapable of demonstration.   And it is further assumed that the postulate which underlay most of the thinking upon economic planning—that the principle of scientific management carried upward through all stages of economic organization will result in an increase of productive efficiency—is equally an unconfirmed hypothesis with respect to most areas of business enterprise.[1]

(3) It is assumed that the system of private enterprise will continue to serve as the basis of the organization of industry and trade in most areas, and as a corollary that American opinion will not support any severe limitation, by public authority, upon freedom of entry into economic occupations.

It is, for example, quite conceivable that a future train of economic disaster might create a demand for public action of kinds, and to an extent, which no one would now think of forecasting.   The hazard is, however, one which must be accepted as unavoidable, along with the expectation that one's judgment will be questioned as to what ought to be included and what excluded in formulating the limiting assumptions.

[1] In making these first two assumptions, I do not wish in the least to imply any criticism of those who concern themselves with speculation upon the trend of industrial civilization, or with the ethics of capitalism, or with analysis of the problems of organization under a more collectivist system. I merely ask that hypotheses be not presented as eternal truths and that possibilities be not translated into imperatives.   And I further suggest that the terms of such discussion are relatively remote from those in which questions of American policy are likely to be formed.

(4) It is assumed that American opinion will not favor the unobstructed freedom of industries to take the form of collective monopolies (cartels), and will in general hold in disfavor the attainment of large monopolistic powers in private hands without close public supervision.

As they stand, these assumptions disclose the most basic assumption of all, namely, that there will be a substantial continuity in the American forms of industrial organization and in the development of policy with respect to its monopolistic aspects.   Given this basic assumption, one can go on to assume the continuance of the anti-trust law policy as the *general* policy.

Having arrived at that point, there is still a more than sufficient diffusion of subject-matter.   But the great advantage is that one has excluded from the terms of discussion the body of ideas which have done most to muddy it up: namely, those that suggest the necessity of finding a substitute for the general anti-trust policy.   This body of ideas has no internal unity; that is to say, the sources of the ideas are diverse and the forms of economic reorganization which they suggest are diverse. Their only bond of unity is in a common negation—that the day of "competitive capitalism" is over. This negation neglects what seems to me the most important datum of all, the body of deeply ingrained attitudes of the American public which are unlikely to be rooted out with any rapidity except under the impact of unexampled disaster.   Nor do I think that these attitudes can be condescendingly disposed of as mere "cultural lags" bound to disappear in the face of the brute necessities of modern technology.

At this point some readers will no doubt begin to think that all points worth discussing have been excluded by the limiting assumptions.   I am, however, unable to accept the putative imperatives pressed upon one by persons who think that the terms in which the anti-trust law policy can usefully be discussed are solely those of decay and abandonment.   It may, of course, happen that the mutual impact of changing objective circumstances and changing habits of thought will in the long run modify the forms of social organization in ways antipathetic to the continuance of the anti-trust law policy.   But no imaginative intellectual constructions relating to human behavior can foretell what those circumstances and attitudes may be.   In the meantime, all thinking relevant to policy in the near future must rest upon judgments of the impact between attitudes and circumstances likely to prevail in a shorter run.[1]

Since I have laid so much stress upon taking account of public opinion, it may be held that I have committed myself to limits of mere political prognosis.   But I have no intention of so limiting myself, nor do I think my earlier analysis implies such limitation.   Once the range of possible political action is defined, it is quite clear that within the range alternatives exist, and somewhat technical analysis of those alternatives is called for.   Acquaintance with such analysis is essential to those who bear the responsibility for making policy, if they are to act with reasonable intelligence.   In the space of this article it is not possible to conduct any analysis in detail, but I propose to sketch out the form in which the alternatives arise and the nature of the analyses which are relevant thereto.

If the anti-trust law policy is to be continued (not necessarily with all its present coverage), the subject-matter has to do with possible changes in the substantive law and possible changes in the administrative means.   If exceptions are to be made to the policy, it is necessary to choose the means of making the exceptions, actually to make the exceptions, to set up the forms of

---

[1] Since this article was written war has broken out in Europe.   If the United States should be drawn into the war and if the war should be long, there might well occur a sharp break in the continuity of policy.   The ultimate consequences are far out of the range of present foresight.   In this article conditions are assumed which permit the peaceful pursuit of economic welfare under prevailing American attitudes and political forms.

organization within the excepted industries, and to establish
the agencies which will supervise the operation of the excepted
industries. The various segments—substantive changes,
administrative changes, and exceptions—are taken up in
sections IV, V, and VI below. Before discussing them, it will
be well first to examine certain matters of fact and certain
changes of emphasis in the analysis of monopoly problems.

III

The simplest alternative in relation to the future content and
administration of the law would be to rest in the inertia of the
status quo.[1] If this course is followed, one knows from experience what to expect: the routine disposal of cases of "unfair
methods of competition" by the Federal Trade Commission
without effective follow-up; the selection of a few cases for
prosecution by the Department of Justice under the Sherman
Act without effective follow-up; the stagnant disuse of the
investigatory powers of the Federal Trade Commission;
the widespread and sometimes notorious violation of the
Sherman Act; the existence of varied means of evading the
Sherman Act in ways difficult to reach under the terms of
the law as judicially rendered; the absence of an effective
intelligence service for turning up cases of violation; the absence
of any body charged with the study of market structures for the
purpose of recommending means either of adapting them to
the purposes of the law or of excepting them from its provisions; the absence of financial support, and therefore of
administrative staff, commensurate with the effective performance of the enforcement duties.

---

[1] If this were an article merely in political forecasting, I should be inclined
to pick this out as the probable outcome of the current political interest in
the monopoly problem, with minor changes of law and administration.
The reasons for this opinion are rather complex, but the principal one is
that there exist no strong political groups pressing for more stringent enforcement and strong groups opposing it, both in labor and business circles.

In business circles, the pressure for the continuation of this situation is very strong, and there has come into existence a more or less reasoned argument for the protection of what may almost be called a vested interest in violations and evasions of the law. Of the situation as it existed in pre-New Deal Administrations, a promoter and supervisor of trade associations has publicly said with astonishing candor, "Practically, under the Harding, Coolidge, and Hoover Administrations industry enjoyed, to all intents and purposes, a moratorium from the Sherman Act, and, through the more or less effective trade associations which were developed in most of our industries, competition was, to a very considerable extent, controlled. The Department of Justice acted *with great restraint and intelligence* and only enforced the Sherman Act against those industries who violated the laws *in a flagrant and unreasonable manner*. Naturally, the efforts which were made to control prices during this period had to be carried on with the utmost caution, and great care had to be taken not to violate the provisions of the anti-trust acts in a flagrant way."[1]

The rules were further relaxed under the NRA in the "first New Deal," and as a carry-over from that experience together with the peculiar urge toward collective monopoly under depression conditions, there must now be supposed to exist a more extensive circumvention of the purpose of the law than has existed in a quarter century—notwithstanding recent evidence of intent to pursue enforcement more vigorously. If one may assume from recent evidence that the Administration has abandoned its early panicky conclusion that the industrial structure should be reorganized all along the line in the direction of collective monopoly, its next task must be that merely of recovering the ground which it lost by voluntary

---

[1] Address by Charles R. Stevenson, senior partner of Stevenson, Jordan and Harrison, before the annual convention of the National Association of Cost Accountants, Cleveland, Ohio, June 26, 1934. Privately printed. (My italics.)

withdrawal. From that point forward the questions to arise are the degree of energy which it will bring to bear upon more effectively carrying out the policy of the law, the more detailed definition of the objectives aimed at, and the means to be adopted thereto.

As any one with the vaguest knowledge of economic organization knows, it is not possible to make most markets conform at all closely to the pattern of perfect competition. The very common practice of postulating the "failure" of the anti-trust law policy upon the necessary divergence between competitive theory and fact is at best irrelevant and misleading, at worst disingenuous misrepresentation. The fact is that most enterprises could not arise or exist under a system of private enterprise without some infusion of what economists describe as "monopolistic" characters. Monopolistic in this sense, as applied for example to product differentiation, means no more nor less than departure from the assumed conditions of pure competition.

Beyond the minimum essential monopolistic constituents, there exist many forms and degrees of "control of the market" which cannot be described exactly as unavoidable, but which have become deeply imbedded in economic organization, either by reason of technological and marketing efficiency or of desire for exclusive market positions. With respect to these conditions the first step to be taken is the isolation of those conditions which it is deemed expedient not to disturb. The remainder, together with the more superficial and more easily eradicable monopolistic elements, represent conditions against which the force of anti-trust law policy may be more vigorously turned.[1]

---

[1] The theory of imperfect and monopolistic competition, which has aroused so much interest in academic quarters in recent years, has served to stimulate interest in problems of market structure and has aided in the development of a more adequate conceptual apparatus for analytical use. In this it has been supplemented by the more realistic and factual discussion

When the problem has been reduced to this form of statement, it is possible to establish some continuity between earlier and more recent views of the monopoly problem. It is not uncommon nowadays to hear the statement that the problem is now discussed in very different terms that those of a generation ago. This is quite true, but it does not mean that the aspects of the problem which were then deemed most important have ceased to be important. It means simply that other aspects have recently been deemed more important, or at least of more specific current interest.

The differences in the emphasis of discussion as between the earlier and later periods may, I think, be related to two primary contrasts in external circumstances. The first is that in the earlier history of the anti-trust law policy the rapid concentration of economic control was new and startling, while more recently a considerable degree of concentration has become imbedded in the accepted structure of industry. The dividing line can be put roughly at the period of the World War. The second contrast is between the circumstances of prosperity and rapid expansion, on the one hand, and of depression on the other. The dividing line here is the beginning of the depression.

---

of rigidity in the price structure. In both areas of discussion there has, however, developed a marked tendency to carry the discussion to unwarranted conclusions. In particular, there has been a tendency to use the analysis to support the thesis that the competitive principle is moribund and that the problem of policy is solely to find an appropriate alternative principle of market organization. This conclusion too easily skips over a broad intervening territory wherein all the difficult immediate questions are located. The exact decisions to be made are, on the one hand, the extent to which the competitive principle will be utilized and, on the other, the extent to which and manner in which it will be modified or dispensed with. The imperfections of the competitive pattern are part of the data upon which to base decisions, but there is no reason to pre-judge the issue by assuming that some other alternative is necessarily preferable to the effort to resist the growth of monopolistic elements.

To speak of the second of these contrasts first, the coming of the depression called into question the merits of the anti-trust law policy. In practically all markets, the members thereof were harassed by the severity of competition, providing a popular demand for measures of market control. This popular attitude provided a wide audience for all sorts of proposals involving a higher degree of monopoly in market organization. The more extreme forms of such proposals questioned the whole private enterprise principle of organization. Milder forms questioned the merits of the anti-trust law policy as barring the way to the creation of "orderly" markets. The current facts make it clear that in an unstable economic world there are problems of market structure that are not adequately cared for simply by enforcing an anti-monopolistic policy. For a time the focus of discussion was upon the question whether these problems were of a sort that could only be attacked by abandoning or greatly relaxing the whole body of anti-monopolistic rules. But even though one does not hold this opinion, there still remain the special problems of particular markets.

A second effect of the depression has been to focus technical economic analysis upon the generic problem of unused resources. The existence of unemployed workers and idle equipment in the face of the desire to work and the need for products is the central problem relevant in every sphere of economic policy, not alone in that of anti-trust law policy. It is from this angle that economists have mainly made their critical examination of the types of proposals mentioned in the preceding paragraph, and endeavored to make constructive suggestions.[1]

---

[1] It is no doubt the depression setting that has caused the monopoly problem to be discussed in recent years so largely as a problem of rigid prices. The search has been for the elements which prevent or delay readjustments within the economic system conducive to further use of resources. The failure of prices to readapt themselves readily in ways promoting this end

The recent prominence of the increased-use-of-resources approach has thrown into the background the range of topics which used to be most discussed.   Those were topics relevant in circumstances where the non-use of resources did not seriously arise.   Having become neglected, they tend to become regarded as of minor importance; but I judge that their importance carries through with unbroken continuity to the present day.   For purpose of contrast with the present day, I shall take the decade preceding the World War.   And as a point of departure I shall refer to an article by the late Professor Allyn A. Young.[1]   Writing in 1915, he succinctly stated that the policy which the Sherman Act was intended to embody was "that competition should be maintained, artificial monopoly destroyed, and its growth prevented."[2]

In stating the basis of popular belief in the anti-trust law policy, Professor Young found hostility to be directed primarily toward the great combinations, and that it was "especially directed against (1) their supposed power over prices and (2) their aggressive suppression of competition."[2]   And he went on to say that "whatever the economic advantages of monopoly *per se* may be, there will be little question of the soundness

---

has naturally and properly been regarded as an important factor in deepening and prolonging the depression.

The discussion in terms of rigid prices carries far beyond any conventional boundaries of discourse relating specifically to anti-trust law policy. Prohibitory laws can be directed only toward definable offences for which an administrable remedy is available.   But much of the rigidity in the price structure, which makes price readjustments a slow and ineffective means for accomplishing readaptations in the use of economic resources, cannot be reached by any definable offence or by any available agency.   It is increasingly recognized that most market structures in an enterprise economy are in some degree marked by monopolistic characteristics which have nothing to do with "conspiracy in restraint of trade" and cannot be eradicated by passing a law.   They are of the substance of the system.

[1] Journal of Political Economy, vol. 23 (1915).

[2] Ibid., p. 213.

of the policy which would attempt to deprive it of its power for evil in these two particulars."[1] This is a judgment as appropriate to the present moment as to a quarter-century ago.

Having raised the question of the alleged economies of great combinations, he stated the still current opinion that bigness ordinarily reaches its limits far short of unitary monopoly. Facing the stated paradox that monopoly is the desired and natural end of competition, he found it false to the operative facts of most areas of business. Following up the point of the possible economic advantages of monopoly, he added a pregnant footnote which should be written on the blackboard at every discussion of antitrust law policy:

> Most of the more weighty discussion of the economic advantages of monopoly have to do with the effect of monopoly upon the aggregate production of wealth measured in terms either of subjective satisfaction or of objective commodity units. Even from this point of view the case for monopoly is exceedingly dubious and, at best, has a validity that is restricted and conditioned in many ways. Moreover, such considerations are relatively unimportant compared with matters like the effect of monopoly upon distribution, upon the scope for individual initiative, upon economic opportunity in general, and upon a host of social and political relations. In short, it is a question less of the relative "economy" of monopoly or competition than of the kind of economic organization best calculated to give us the kind of society we want. Until our general social ideals are radically changed, it will take more than economic analysis to prove that it would be sound public policy to permit monopoly in that part of the industrial field where competition is possible.[1]

If at some points the terms of Professor Young's discussion seem a little old-fashioned, none of the issues which he raised can be regarded as superseded and none of his comments are inapt in present circumstances. And in particular in his view that the antitrust law policy must at bottom be discussed in terms of a pattern of civilization, and not on narrower grounds of economic productivity, he states an idea just recently re-awakening in the minds of large numbers of people.

---

[1] Ibid., p. 214.

To my mind, the total implications of accepting the growth of monopoly were more fully and ably discussed in a short period of years preceding 1912 than at any time before or since. The discussion went beyond the boundaries of economic analysis, beyond considerations of distributive justice, and even beyond the ingrained attitudes toward exclusive economic privilege, and came at last to the fundamental questions of the conditions necessary to the existence of a free people.

It is open to anyone to belittle the character of the liberties available to many Americans; but, given the purpose to continue the American experiment in popular government rooted in diverse liberties for the individual, it is by no means inappropriate to face the dangers of plutocratic domination of government nor the dangers of a highly regimented public control over a monopolistically organized economy. In all essential points, therefore, I judge that the topics of pre-War discussion are of as much concern as they ever were, a fact which ought not to be lost sight of merely because recent discussion has quite naturally centered on special problems brought forward by the depression.

IV

If there is to be a more vigorous effort to resist the rise of monopolistic elements in the economy, there are a great variety of ways in which the effort could be conducted. The limits of this article do not permit even a summary review of the many possibilities; but within fairly brief space the main outlines of the problems involved in such a policy may be presented. It is in the careful elaboration of such an outline that the Temporary National Economic Committee has it in its power to rescue the whole subject from the phase of vague defeatism that has tended to envelop it in recent years.

The first task is to clarify the nature of offenses against the law and to extend them by constructive amendment. The second is to set up the necessary intelligence service for discovering offences. The third is to create effective and adequate means of proceeding against them. The fourth is to create an adequate supervisory establishment to follow up and enforce disciplinary actions.[1] These may be reduced to two main topics: the substance of the law and the administration of the law.

With respect to the substance of the law there are two separable subjects. The first is the clarification of the meaning of the law as it now stands. The other is the possible substantive additions.

The alleged uncertainty as to what is now illegal has no doubt been much exaggerated, the allegation having been chiefly made and reiterated by those who have a fairly sound idea that what they want to do is illegal, and who really want, not certainty, but relaxation. Nevertheless, there no doubt does exist an area of doubt, with respect to the collective activities of trade groups, with respect to corporate combinations, and with respect to competitive practices, which might just as well be cleared up as far as possible. Since the terms of the law are general and its detailed meaning is imbedded in judicial decisions, what is therefore needed in the first instance is an exhaustive analysis of and commentary upon the cases.[2] From such a study it would be possible to catalogue all the types of offences which have been defined, all the cases of real or apparent conflict of decisions under comparable states of fact, and many of the points upon which there may be said to exist real uncertainty. Only upon the basis of

---

[1] Questions relating to exceptions from the operation of the law are postponed to section VI below.

[2] It is my understanding that such a task was undertaken in the Treasury Department under the supervision of the late General Counsel, Mr. Oliphant, as part of the work of the Temporary National Economic Committee. Whether it is being continued since his death on the scale of the original plan I do not know.

such a study would it be possible to determine intelligently what substantive additions, in either general or specific terms, could usefully be added, both in the interests of certainty for the business community and of definiteness in making the legislative intent more clear to the courts. Such a study, moreover, would assist in isolating those peripheral questions of policy which the courts cannot undertake to settle and which the Congress has not settled.

The matter of substantive additions to the law is not, however, one to which mere collation of cases would provide clear answers. The questions involved are such as require examination of many states of fact and the enunciation of new rules of policy. Of this sort, for example, is the matter of patents now under examination by the Temporary National Economic Committee. Analysis of patent cases will add light, but the situation in a variety of industries must be known to determine what might be usefully added to the law in general language and how far specific provisions are needed in particular industries.

Another question of policy presents itself as the subject of possible addition to the law, that of corporate bigness. To many persons this has appeared to be the central difficulty in the whole monopoly problem. In what is commonly called the "Brandeis philosophy," concentration of private economic power is antipathetic to the whole scheme of values which are conceived to be the peculiar virtue of American life and dangerous to the future of democratic government.[1] This philosophy went into a decline at the period of the War from which it has only partially recovered. During the decade following the war, in the dominant political circle bigness was a virtue and the captain of industry or finance was deemed worthy of the highest public esteem and honor. Under the New Deal, sentiment has been divided between a

---

[1] This was equally the view of President Wilson.

semi-collectivist acceptance of bigness and the earlier anti-concentration philosophy, with an occasional secondary deference to the views of the nineteen twenties as a political play to allay opposition by "big business." The question of attitudes toward concentrated corporate power provides the nearest thing to an acid test of political philosophies.

Bigness can, however, be discussed in an entirely different set of terms, those of market analysis. In the rôle of market leaders the large corporations can be identified as the focussing points of "control of the market," and of monopolistic price and production policies, whether by non-collusive leadership, or by their latent power to coerce competitors, or by facilitating market agreements. It is by reason of considering the influence of bigness in these respects to be non-eradicable by anti-trust law methods that many persons look for radically different methods of curbing private economic power.

Assuming the intent to curb bigness, the problem presented is one of embarrassing complexity to legislators. Proposals to limit the percentage of an industry in the hands of any corporate group have been the most common suggestion. Such a policy is feasible (with necessary exceptions), though beset by administrative complexities. And, if it were to be made generally applicable, it would involve the partition of many existing corporations or corporate groups. Moreover, concentration of control is by no means limited to industries in which there are what one thinks of as large corporations, so that to be generally applicable the law of limited percentages would have to be applied to hundreds of small industries. Necessary exceptions would have to be made of new industries in which only one or two firms might exist. And it would be necessary to define the scope of all "industries," a task of infinite complexity, as NRA experience shows.

I go into these details simply to underline the fact that, with respect to what some persons reasonably regard as the most portentous line of economic change in the past half century, policy has been permitted simply to go by default. Some charge the Supreme Court with dereliction, and it must be admitted that the Court's decisions have placed few barriers in the way of increasing corporate bigness. But it must equally be admitted that the Court's somewhat tortuous course reflected serious difficulties in applying the Sherman Act phrases to particular sets of facts. And back of the Court stood the legislature, able at any time to correct the Court with additional instructions. For nearly fifty years Congress has completely divested itself of its responsibility, and the policy of drift has permitted the structure of the American economy increasingly to embody elements which it was the purpose of the Sherman Act to hold in check. It is not at all clear that a breaking up of corporate structures would be effective enough to justify the experiment, but the nature of the issues stands out in clear relief. The failure of Congress to face them is, in its way, a making of policy—a limiting and weakening of the original policy of the anti-trust laws.

A third direction in which there lie possible changes in the substantive content of the law is the matter of the rules governing the activities of business groups, especially trade associations. It is, perhaps, possible that existing rules are on the whole sufficient to support a relatively effective enforcement of the anti-trust law policy, the weakness lying mainly on the side of administration. It is, however, mainly from trade associations that the complaint has come that the rules, as administered by the courts, are vague and uncertain, so that the careful analysis of decisions suggested above might suggest amendments to end this complaint. If, however, the amendments were designed to promote more strict enforcement, they would certainly not satisfy the complainants, who have only been concerned to make what is possibly illegal certainly legal.

The clarification of policy with respect to the status and activities of trade associations or other modes of group action is, no doubt, of at least equal importance with the matter of corporate concentration mentioned above, and is likely to be the subject of greater interest. The two matters are, in many ways, closely interrelated, since desired degrees of market control are seldom attainable on a non-collusive basis, and the existing degree of concentration greatly facilitates associative action. But in a considerable degree they are entirely separate, since associative action also flourishes in many industries that are not highly concentrated or have no outstanding corporate leaders. The boundaries between associative activities which are conducive to intelligent competitive behavior and those which support considerable monopolistic market control are very indistinct and hard to draw precisely, so that it seems improbable that the distinction can be clearly drawn in the terms of a general law. One can hardly tell, until the whole situation is more carefully canvassed, whether or not a policy of stricter enforcement of the anti-trust law policy would call for the writing of a special body of trade association law, other than administrative law which would certainly be needed. Quite possibly in some particular industries in which monopolistic practices are entrenched a considerable public initiative in shaping the working rules of market procedure could advantageously be introduced. In such special cases of individual treatment experience should aid in isolating particular markets to which the principle of competitive organization is peculiarly inapplicable.

The subject is of special interest since it is from trade associations that the greatest pressures have been exerted in the past two decades to secure substantive amendment. No one can doubt the severity of the competitive difficulties in their respective markets nor fail to sympathize with the desire of members for relief from conditions imposed by the depression. But in their demands for relief they have stated a case which, if accepted, would appear to call for a high degree of market monopoly and, correlatively, for a high degree of public supervision of associative activities, which is the last thing in the world that they want.   No one has made so good a case for the semi-collectivist wing of the New Deal as the business representatives who thronged the corridors of the NRA.

At the same time they posed a problem in alternatives to the anti-trust law policy which neither they nor the devotees of industry planning have found rational terms of resolving. The difficulty is that any plan of market organization which will approve itself to the group affected, within experience to date, is designed to be restrictive in character.   Such plans thus appear to operate in the opposite direction from the effort to induce further use of resources and appear also to increase the rigidity of prices.   They do not therefore carry the promise of remedying what are most commonly regarded as basic weaknesses in the scheme of economic relations.   It thus appears that if associative action is to be granted extensive monopolistic features, the problem of organization is driven far into the area of public regulation of business on an extensive scale.   It is against this alternative, and the problems it entails, that one has to weigh the alternative of maintenance of the anti-trust law policy.

V

The next general topic to be discussed is that of administration, still upon the assumption of a purpose to achieve relatively effective enforcement of the anti-trust law policy. Discussion of this subject encounters two serious obstacles. The first is that it may deal either with the substantive law as it stands or after constructive amendment; the second is that it may deal with the performance of the existing agencies or with agencies assumed to be created *de novo*.   To simplify the terms of discussion I propose to limit myself to the present rules of law.   I shall not, however, limit myself to the present agencies of administration.

At the beginning of the preceding section three types of administrative function were distinguished: informational services, proceedings against violators, and permanent supervision. At present all three types of function are distributed both to the Department of Justice and to the Federal Trade Commission, which have with respect to some rules separate responsibility and with respect to others joint responsibility. The areas of market organization to which their responsibility runs are not differentiated, so that both are theoretically expected to be acquainted with market behavior in all areas.

With respect to all three functions actual implementation in both agencies is entirely unrelated to the potential magnitude of their responsibilities. The investigational functions of the Federal Trade Commission, originally conceived as the very principle of its being, have become almost wholly atrophied, while the Department of Justice has no real intelligence service at all. Both agencies operate on starvation budgets, and the Department of Justice in particular can prosecute in only a few of the many potential cases of which it is aware, to say nothing of the many of which it has no knowledge in the absence of an intelligence service. Enforcement of the Sherman Act might be called "token" or "ritual" enforcement, a system of "selective justice" in which it is hoped a few "examples" will have a sufficiently deterring effect. Neither agency has any effective means of following up disciplinary actions.

Consisting of merely rudimentary agents for the performance of all three sets of functions, the administrative branch of the antitrust law policy gives evidence more of pious deploring of monopolistic tendencies than of any firm intent to hold them in check. It is perhaps through pure neglect that monopolistic developments have reached the point where many persons now doubt the continued applicability of the policy to the situation which has arisen. Given the intent to make the policy more effective, it seems that attention to administrative matters would at the outset take precedence over substantive changes in the law itself. The latter might be expected to suggest themselves in large part out of broadened administrative experience.

There are two ways in which one can approach the questions of administrative change. One is to accept the present general set-up and consider merely the means of making the Department of Justice and the Federal Trade Commission more effective agencies. Though this is definitely a second best approach, it offers extensive possibilities. A series of correlative measures would be (1) the restoration of the investigatory functions of the Commission, (2) the establishment of effective liaison between the Commission and the Department, as was originally intended, (3) greatly increased budgetary support of both agencies. The Commission would become the eyes and ears of the Department, its source of cases for prosecution, its economic consultant on matters of market organization, its agent for following up disciplinary actions, and the general overseer of trade association activities.

There is, however, inherent in the split authority between the two agencies a fundamental weakness. If one did not have to consider the existence of the existing agencies and could prescribe *de novo*, contemporary administrative experience would suggest a very different set-up. It is not wholly clear that a single agency would fulfill all requirements, but if there were more than one the division would be on functional lines. At the center there should no doubt be a single responsible enforcement agency of a type similar to the present Securities and Exchange Commission,[1] and it seems

---

[1] I do not mean to suggest that the administrative problems would be strictly comparable with those of the Securities and Exchange Commission. In the latter, as in all agencies dealing with particular industries or business groups, there exists a function of detailed supervision which could not exist for a body with the generalized oversight of business organization and prac-

highly probable that functional distinctions might better be cared for in subordinate bureaus of such a body than in wholly separate administrative entities.

Given the attainment of unity at the enforcement center, reason and experience would gradually suggest the nature of the duties of collateral bureaus. Continuity and cumulative character could be given to the informational services. It would no doubt appear necessary to institute new supervisory services, of which the most obvious are those which would be required if large corporations and trade associations, respectively, were required to have federal licenses and to conform to standards of organization and market behavior defined in their licenses. If the frequent suggestion of public representation in corporate directorates were ever to be tried, the functions of these public agents could be tied in to the same integrated administrative system.[1] A special economic bureau

---

tice which is involved in the enforcement of anti-trust laws. The Securities and Exchange Commission does, however, provide an adaptable model in many matters relating to organization, definition of powers, and procedures. It should go without saying that no excellence of formal structure can insure effective administration except in conjunction with able administrators.

[1] In some quarters one hears proposals for federal licenses or for federal representation on corporation directorates, or both, advanced as the most fundamental of reforms. I do not wish to take space here to argue the merits of these proposals, but it seems worth pointing out that they are merely mechanisms for creating a closer federal supervision over business, whether to support the anti-trust policy or some other. Neither is a contribution to the settlement of any fundamental policy question. Federal licensing or incorporation has been so much discussed as a means of limiting abuses of corporate power that the merits of the proposal are well-known. The underlying need is, of course, rendered much less by the existing powers of the Securities and Exchange Commission, but the proposal still has merit. Public directors have been proposed, for the most part, by people impressed by the problems of public relations to a system operated more on lines of "industrial self-government." The desirability of adding this instrumentality to anti-trust law enforcement machinery has hardly been discussed at all.

might be responsible for special studies of market structures, where the applicability of the anti-trust law policy was directly challenged, or where rearrangements were necessary in connection with disciplinary action, or for other purposes. It might, indeed, embody all the qualities of the much-proposed Bureau of Industrial Economics, occupying a semi-independent consultative status; and achieving some organic relation to a National Economic Council, if and when the latter were established.

I have no intention˙of developing here the details of an administrative scheme. My purpose is merely to show that there is no barrier except inertia and adverse interest to prevent a much more effective enforcement of an anti-monopolistic policy. The growth of policy directed to this end encounters strong opposition from business quarters. The urge in those quarters is toward increasingly monopolistic control of markets, either free from government supervision or attained with government aid but carrying a minimum of supervision. It is not beyond imagination that policy might orient itself strongly in that direction. In any case, the nature of the influences pressing in that direction needs to be examined with the utmost care. The drifting tactics of the last quarter century have year by year magnified the problem of coping with entrenched and almost "vested" interests in monopolistic situations; but with the potential administrative means available, added to the pervasive competitive elements still actively present in the economy, it is not too late to regard the policy of holding monopolistic tendencies in check as an available alternative.[1]

---

[1] In my opinion, the extensive analysis in recent years both of monopolistic tendencies and of competitive disorders has tended to understate the degree to which competition continues to operate as a relatively effective principle of market organization. The general analysis presented above is in no sense antipathetic to a compensatory increase in public economic functions or special attention to particular cases of severe competitive disorder.

VI

One may outline with relative clearness the ways and means of making the anti-trust laws much more effective instruments than they now are. The prospect becomes much more blurred, however, when one tries to envisage the making of appropriate exceptions to them.[1] Certain types of answers to the questions involved are to be found in the case of those industries now known as public utilities. It is proper to suppose that the category of public utility industries is not necessarily complete; and that, if needed to, it will presumably be, as in the past, by specific legislative enactment. When, however, one ponders the prospects in that direction, it seems wholly improbable that a public utility status will be found reasonably applicable, within the terms of present experience, to very many industries not already included. Exceptions,

---

[1] I leave out of account in this connection legislative measures with respect to industries to which the anti-trust laws have no relevance. Of this sort are the special measures of control relating to agriculture and bituminous coal. Of this sort, also, are measures relating to the recognized public utility monopolies. Such measures have, of course, their place in a total discussion of policy with respect to monopoly, since it becomes a matter of some interest to inquire on what grounds government should introduce and enforce total or partial monopolistic control in some markets at the same time that it is fighting it in others. Into such matters one cannot go here.

I leave out of account, also, a variety of other actual or proposed measures which lie outside the immediate subject of policy relating to industrial monopoly. One of these again has its place in a total discussion of monopoly, that of legislation relating to collective bargaining. Others are quite separate, such as wage and hour measures and social insurance measures.

In this connection, one can properly rebut the idea that the anti-trust policy must reflect a "frontier individualism" and be compatible only with a government of narrow powers. Given the desire to pursue certain social objectives, there exists a wide variety of measures of "social control" which are in no way incompatible with the maintenance of a basic anti-trust policy. One cannot accept the idea that, because the rule of competition is not sufficient as the *sole* basis of economic relations, it is somehow made unavailable as a principle of market organization.

if they are to be made, must therefore presumably involve some other status.

If exceptions are to be made, there are only two basic methods: either the setting up of some public agency or agencies with general authority to make exceptions, or specific legislative action in each particular case. These will be briefly discussed in turn.

Of the first method there exists a certain body of experience acquired under the NRA, and almost all proposals, with whatever variants, have a close relation to the purposes exemplified in NRA codes (omitting the labor sections). The underlying idea is that each market is a special case marked by its own disorders and abuses, and that special forms of organization and rules of practice, appropriate to the circumstances of each market situation, are needed. Carried to the limits of its potentialities, the carrying out of the central idea might involve, not the mere making of exceptions to the anti-trust law policy, but the substitution of another basic policy; but of course this would not be the necessary outcome under actual administration.

Proposals couched in the terms of this idea are initiated mainly, though not solely, in business quarters. The business proposals uniformly diagnose the weakness as a competitive disorder, so that the remedy is always that of contriving a less competitive market; substantially in the direction of limiting production and holding up prices. The proposed mechanism is the existence of some public agency authorized to place its imprimatur on plans of business coöperation, with possibly also some responsibility for enforcing them.

Since the end of the reckless NRA experiment in this direction, trade association attorneys have worked assiduously at creating substitutes and have circulated their proposals in a private way, but not publicly. The reason for lack of publicity is not hard to find. The authors have been unable to find any form of words in which Congress could instruct the public agency, short of full authority to permit any market organization plan which seemed to the agency right and proper.[1] The latter degree of authority would permit development toward any degree of cartelization. If such authority existed, there is no predicting to what extent industries would want strong cartel powers, nor to what extent the actual agency established would be inclined to grant them. But to delegate such powers to any agency would be a definite abdication of Congressional responsibility in favor of administrative determination of the fundamental outlines of the American economy. There are, of course, many persons who think that just this development is necessary to cope with the problems of modern industrial organization. But no one ought to accept this view without a more than superficial analysis of just what it implies in the way of the disappearance of the fundamentals of American government.

Business groups are not prepared to come before the public with proposals that would be immediately vulnerable to attack on the ground that they would create unlimited authority to introduce monopolistic market controls. It is on this rock that efforts to create an agency with power to waive anti-trust law rules have so far been broken, and there appears little prospect that the situation will change in this respect. This is one reason why many business groups prefer to let the whole issue of the anti-trust laws lie quiet, merely hoping that

---

[1] If anyone doubts this statement, let him experiment with devising a general formula which a public agency could apply to particular cases, defining the limits within which the agency could approve forms and degrees of market control deviating from the anti-trust law rules. The National Industrial Recovery Act forbade monopolies and monopolistic practices, a condition which if strictly interpreted would have made most industry groups lose all interest in code-making. In practice, the terms were so far ignored, or loosely interpreted, as to permit a high degree of compulsory cartelization in some industries.

they will be little disturbed in the practice of violations and evasions.[1]

The idea of the need for special forms of market organization adjusted to the needs of particular cases, and involving deviation from anti-trust law restrictions, is by no means limited to business groups. It is, indeed, one of the fixed ideas of many persons who look forward to a "planned economy." To them the one-at-a-time procedure is simply a transitional phase leading to a much more highly collectivized economy, public or private, than now exists, in which eventually the whole anti-trust program would be superseded. The idea need not be carried to such extremes, however, and my further discussion will be confined strictly to the problem of the methods by which particular exceptions might be made.

As in the case of business proposals, there are only the two methods, direct legislative action in each particular case and the setting up of an agency, or agencies, armed with discretionary authority. In the latter case, the difficulties are exactly of the same character as those mentioned a few paragraphs above; namely, that a general law cannot define the forms and degrees of monopolistic organization which might be permissible in application to particular cases. This difficulty is well-known to many persons who feel the need of exceptions. They also understand that the exact nature of special rules of market organization cannot be stated until the existing market structure is thoroughly understood and various alternative possibilities carefully examined. By this route they arrive at what is possibly the most widely held opinion among academic students of industrial organization, namely, that the first prerequisite is a much more intense knowledge of particular markets than now exists.

---

[1] The other reason is that, if they were to secure the privilege of authorized extension of market monopoly, the prospective public controls are, by many of them, regarded as too great a price to pay for the prospective advantages in market organization.

As a good academic person, I should be the last to dispute this need, and it seems to me amazing that in the contemporary world, where the future of the relations between government and business is the most debated of issues, the world of business should be so largely *terra incognita*. But what equally astonishes me is that in so large a number of instances the academic mind seems to have pre-judged the issue. That is to say, without knowing the markets and without having examined the available alternatives, they seem to *know* that numerous and important exceptions from the antitrust law rules will be called for. When present conditions have been explored and analyzed, and when the possible alternatives have been set forth and compared, would seem to be soon enough for the social scientist to decide whether, by his standards of reasonable choice, a given alternative was preferable to what could be done under the anti-trust laws.

When all aspects are examined, it seems clear that delegation to an administrative agency of authority to make exceptions to the anti-trust law policy is incompatible with the policy-making responsibilities of Congress. Some slight foreknowledge of the problem is presented by NRA experience, and especially in the shift of policy by which the codes approved under the first Administrator came to be antipathetic to the policies enunciated by the successor NRA Board. One is driven back, then, to the method of specific legislative exception. But before going into that, there is an intervening territory that needs to be explored briefly.

Even under the existing anti-trust laws there is considerable scope for the exercise of judicial and administrative discretion. It could hardly be said that the courts grant "exceptions," but in applying the law they give it its explicit meaning.   In such leading cases, e.g., as the United States Steel case and the Appalachian Coals case, policy-making of a very far-reaching sort was practiced by the Supreme Court in the name of judicial interpretation.   It has been suggested at an earlier point in this article that the range of such judicial discretion can be made narrower by a more explicit statement of legislative policy, but a considerable discretion residing in the Court is no doubt unavoidable.

It would, also, perhaps be straining words to say that the Department of Justice has authority to make exceptions. But something approaching it is inherent in its power to decide what cases shall be litigated. For example, for a quarter of a century the Aluminum Company of America has come as close to being a complete industrial monopoly as any in the country, and on that account the object of solicitous attention by both the Department of Justice and the Federal Trade Commission; but without any action being taken until very recently. Similarly, the urban milk markets have long exhibited features presumptively illegal. The decision not to litigate is to a considerable degree due simply to lack of funds, and could be remedied by larger appropriations. In some cases the reason is the difficulty of securing facts to prove violation; in some cases the peculiar canons of proof imposed by the courts. In still other cases, the uncertainty about there being any available remedy inhibits action. But beyond these particular causes, there exists the possibility of a mere lack of will on the part of the responsible administrative officials to go beyond a perfunctory litigation of the more obvious or notorious violations.

The present Assistant Attorney General, Mr. Arnold, has opened up the discussion of another area bordering on the field of exceptions, that of consent decrees. The primary problem is that of finding appropriate remedies where violations of the law exist. The laying of injunctions or criminal penalties does not solve the question of what positive revisions of market organization or practice will satisfy the purposes of the law without a too disruptive effect. In Mr. Arnold's mind, the problem appears to go beyond this, to a search for a means whereby, in one operation, positive action to end competitive disorders in markets can proceed hand in hand with the ending of monopolistic practices antipathetic to the spirit and purpose of the anti-trust law policy.

Since there is no body of experience upon which to base judgment, discussion of this idea has to be hypothetical. The problem is very real and difficult, but one would think the device of the consent decree a rather limited instrument for coping with it. Since such decrees have to be approved by courts, the most that could be expected would be a more extensive definition of positive forms of market organization which are legal, so that presumably the decrees could not go very far toward admitting cartel features. As related to the organization of "orderly markets," the consent decree is further limited by the fact that it can reach only those members involved in the litigation, and not all members of the market. Its terms cannot, therefore, be made applicable to the total market.

In spite of such limitations, Mr. Arnold's interest in the possibilities is relevant and perspicacious. In important anti-trust cases, the attention of officials has to run from offences to remedies, and the latter raise questions relating to the whole market, not merely to the actions of offenders. If, therefore, a more active effort is made to enforce the anti-trust law policy, there is involved a constructive attention to the reorganization of market structures, many of which now embrace long-standing monopolistic features. There is need both to prevent unnecessarily disruptive consequences and to ensure acceptable readjustments. It seems hardly probable, however, that the Department of Justice could serve as an appropriate agency for concocting revised market structures, so that the problem is thrown back into the discussion of over-all revision of the administrative methods suggested in section V above.

The problem just mentioned fits into the discussion of any scheme for making exceptions to the operation of the anti-trust laws. In such a discussion the term "exceptions" is almost too precise. The larger problem is that of dealing with the structure of particular markets in a positive way, and not in the mere negative way of legal prohibitions. In such a one-by-one treatment of markets, the actual purposes might be diverse, but falling roughly into two general categories, (1) special measures to support and supplement the prohibitory anti-trust law rules, and (2) special measures to replace conformity to the rules. Measures of the former sort might generally be initiated by an administrative body under general legislative rules defining the standards for business coöperation.

Since measures of the second sort run counter to the established general policy, it seems clear, on the basis of the analysis presented earlier in this section, that they should not be initiated except by legislative enactment for each particular case. The most persistent demand for such measures comes from groups desiring more monopolistic market controls, to be used restrictively for their own advantage, and such demands ought to be subjected to the most searching public examination. The only occasion for considering them, in terms of public policy, is under circumstances where restrictive practices are in any case deemed so serious and so inevitable as to call for a substitute to anti-trust law rules. There appears to be a disposition in many quarters to think that such instances would be numerous, but it is upon exactly this point, as noted earlier, that judgment is as yet premature. One of the branches of a properly constituted administrative body would be a bureau adequately equipped for making careful preliminary analyses of particular industries tentatively marked out for special treatment. At present, the subject is entirely in the embryonic stage of ill-informed talk.

A *prima facie* economic case for making exceptions from the anti-trust law policy arises only as plans are formulated, relating to particular markets, which promise with reasonable certainty to achieve an improved productive result in larger or more stable employment of resources. Even when the economic case is made, there remains to consider whether the collateral consequences are acceptable, as noted at a much earlier point in this article.[1] It is by no means outside the range of probability that good reason may be found for special administrative supervision in some industries where restrictive market practices are very strong; but there exists no prospect that the public interest in market organization can be protected under American conditions in the calculable future without recourse to the anti-trust law policy.[2]

---

[1] A timely illustration of the problem is provided by the building materials and construction industries. A reasonable difference of opinion exists whether the inhibitions to increased activity can best be broken down by litigation such as is now being conducted, or by some supervised organization to establish a mutual interest in reducing prices and wages, and therefore construction costs, much to the advantage of the whole industry and of the general public. The idea of stimulating the use of resources by concerted action to tap the latent demand which is ineffective at existing cost levels is a most attractive one; but, beside the elusiveness of any practicable method of arranging the coöperative cost-cutting, the question of policy raised is of the utmost seriousness. Since it is wholly improbable that the industries involved would be given *carte blanche* to enter agreements, presumably any agreements would have to be under the supervision of a public agency. It would, therefore, be necessary for each of the coöperating industries to be subject to rather close supervision, and means would have to be worked out for judging the "rightness" of the prices of particular materials, absolutely and relatively to one another. It would be equally necessary to impose a wholly unprecedented type of public supervision upon the highly monopolistic unions which operate in this field and upon groups of contractors.

[2] The discussion in the preceding section will no doubt appear to most readers to evade the really difficult questions related to the exemption of particular industries from the application of anti-trust law rules. Lack of space is the sole reason for limiting the discussion to the points raised in the text. In a subsequent paper I propose to take up the problem of defining criteria applicable in the making of exceptions and the problem of devising the means of administrative supervision.

VII

The primary purpose of this paper has now been fulfilled. That purpose was in some degree to cut through the confusion of the contemporary discussion of the anti-trust law policy, and to find some basis for focussing the discussion. We have found the primary source of confusion to be the widely held assumption that the competitive basis of American industry has "broken down" and that the anti-trust law policy is "archaic." This assumption itself gives rise to argument. But insofar as the assumption is accepted, the argument comes to concern the nature of the successor to the anti-trust law policy. This argument becomes chaotic.

Discussion of alternatives to the anti-trust law policy is interesting, and in a degree important, but it is substantially unrelated to the manner in which problems of economic control will present themselves as current issues of policy in the American scene at any foreseeable period. The useful focus for discussion is in the first instance how the anti-trust law policy can be made more definite in law and more effective in administration. The secondary useful focus is upon the immediate range of proposed exceptions, particularized in detail. Within these defined areas there are, of course, many sub-foci of discussion and room enough for serious difference of opinion. But discussion thus delimited serves some immediate purpose in crystallizing the problems of policy and directing the legislative authorities toward possible choice of means.

Having said so much, one cannot leave the subject without noting that the anti-trust law policy cannot be considered wholly in isolation. There exists, and will no doubt continue to exist, a body of economic measures which directly or indirectly affect market structures, initiated in pursuit of other objectives than that of holding in check monopolistic tendencies. Concerning the merits of these various objectives or of the actual means thereto, there is no space to enquire here. The most that can be said in a general way is that the powers of government are being extensively used to mitigate the adverse impact of economic change and instability upon various groups of persons and to initiate certain reforms in the name of "justice" and "efficiency." In this extended sphere of governmental initiative there is no evidence of a desire to make fuller correspondence to competitive conditions the *sole* principle of economic policy. In some areas, notably agriculture and labor, policy runs toward diminishing the competitive element. Elsewhere, as in the public utility industries, it runs to insistence upon monopolistic organization. In still other places it consists in the elaboration of special rules of economic behavior on grounds quite separate from considerations of monopoly or "disorderly" competition. And in the presumptively competitive areas, it elaborates rules of market behavior to set a "plane of competition" and to define the permissible basis of business coöperation. Moreover, should the possibilities of relative stagnation of economic growth continue to stand out as a spectre over the future, it would be necessary to consider ways and means of coping with the consequent structural maladjustments; and it is not impossible that the need should arise for a considerable expansion in what may be called the "public economy."

All this may be admitted. But in this setting it is wholly erroneous, and subversive to reasonable discussion, to belittle the anti-trust law policy as an obsolescent vestige of an earlier and simpler world. If the anti-trust laws implied a government of narrow powers, the gibe would be more valid. But they do not. They represent continuity of policy with respect to certain basic problems of industrial structure for which no remotely satisfactory alternative general policy is now available. They do not stand in the way of exercising ingenuity in devising unique administrative controls deemed appropriate to particular market situations. Each proposal to that end must stand examination on its own merits as a superior alternative in the particular situation.

In the meantime, the existing anti-trust laws as now administered are highly defective instruments for carrying out the policy for which they exist, that of holding in check the growth of private monopoly and the concentration of economic power. The weakness is peculiarly great on the administrative side, and grows increasingly so as the problem enlarges of coördinating the anti-trust law policy with the numerous measures of economic control which impinge upon it. The art of public administration is now sufficiently advanced to present no serious barrier to setting up administrative means capable, not only of carrying out the present laws much more effectively, but also of exercising an expanding supervision of market behavior on lines dictated by reasonable consideration of the economic facts.

When one finally gets down to these terms of discussion, there is not much difficulty in stating the precise nature of the problems or in devising improved methods of coping with them. The continued failure to do so can only be attributed to a lack of will, in legislative and administrative quarters, to make the anti-trust law policy more effectively operative where it is applicable, and to face the problems of alternative policy wherever it is deemed to be inapplicable.

8

MONOPOLISTIC COMPETITION AND PUBLIC POLICY*

By Donald H. Wallace†

I

I shall discuss some aspects of the relation between monopolistic competition and economic welfare and point out some of the problems which must be faced if we are to evolve a public policy based upon recognition of the realities of economic processes.   For several reasons I shall not attempt to outline a positive program as Mr. Simons has done.   In the first place I do not here consider either the serious political problems concerned with government control of economic activities, or other non-economic elements in the general problem.   Secondly, I restrict myself to one phase of the economic problem; that is, monopolistic competition.   Finally, I do not treat the consequences of monopolistic competition for some important aspects of economic welfare, such as the distribution of wealth and income, while I can do little more than allude to other consequences.

I have chosen the topic "monopolistic competition" rather than "imperfect competition" in order to emphasize the fact that I shall treat imperfections of a monopolistic nature.   In the actual world, elements which impair perfect attainment of that particular type of equilibrium of supply and demand

* *The American Economic Review*, Volume XXVI, Number 1, Supplement, March 1936, pages 77–87.   Reprinted by the courtesy of the American Economic Association and the author.

† Harvard University.

forces identified by the classical economists with free competition, may be monopolistic or non-monopolistic. Imperfect knowledge, specialization, and durability of equipment and labor and of "business administration" are imperfections which may exist with or without monopoly. Monopolistic elements are found in conditions which endow any seller or group of sellers with sufficient control of supply to exert an appreciable influence upon some or any of the fundamental relations of the market—the relations between investment, output, price, earnings, employment, and demand. Influence is possible (in other words, monopoly power exists) where the number of sellers in a common market is small enough, where there is an agreement wide enough in scope, or where the product of one seller is successfully differentiated from those of others. Monopoly power inheres in fewness of producers even in the absence of differentiation, and differentiation gives elements of monopoly even though a large number of firms produce articles which are closely similar. Pure competition, or the absence of any monopolistic elements whatever, obtains where the individual seller is unable to affect appreciably any of the fundamental relations of the market. For example, under pure competition a seller could not have a price policy.[1]

Professor Chamberlin and others who have developed the theory of monopolistic competition call attention to the undeniable fact that competition and monopoly are not mutually exclusive. They point out that substantial monopolistic elements exist side by side with competitive elements in many, perhaps most, markets (or industries), and maintain, of course, that the particular sorts of equilibria, both short- and long-run, which exist in such markets are determined by the interaction of monopolistic and competitive forces. The contrast between

---

[1] When buyers are few, monopoly elements exist on that side of the market. Discussion in the present paper is limited to monopolistic competition between sellers.

this view of the economic system and the traditional view is a decided one, and the two contrasting views lead, as far as purely economic considerations are concerned, to distinctly different principles of public policy toward industrial organization and business practices.

II

The traditional view of the economic system as evidenced in economic theory and the pre-War and earlier post-War trust literature was briefly as follows.[1]   There were a few "natural monopolies" where competition was held to work very badly for all concerned owing to exceptional peculiarities of technological conditions and financial structure.   These peculiar conditions were not considered to be present in consequential degree in the great majority of industries.   It was maintained that in these so-called "competitive" industries, unless one firm came to control a very large part of the total output— say 60 per cent or more—"competition" would, in the absence also of imperfections other than monopoly, actually approximate the results long supposed to ensue from the competitive process.   There would be no monopoly profits, no underinvestment, no continuous underutilization of what was considered the ideal amount of investment or of any greater amount.   Some believed that combinations controlling a very large proportion of total supply would be unable to exercise their monopoly power to any appreciable degree as long as potential competitors were free to enter.   Others maintained that dissolution of the trusts was desirable.   Nearly all favored extinction of all methods of competition which promoted the growth of trusts not based on superior efficiency.   These theories implicitly or explicitly contained a belief that in all industries except the few natural monopolies the benefits of

---

[1] I recognize with regret that the needs of brevity force me to do some violence to those theories.

competition could be obtained without sacrificing any advantages of efficiency as related to the scale of the business unit.

An implication of traditional theory is of interest in connection with questions of variety of product and competition. The long-run competitive equilibrium described a situation in which all firms were most efficiently organized and operating at their most efficient rates of output. Price was equal to average full cost at its minimum point on the U-shaped cost curve of the individual firm. The erroneous implication was that consumers might have whatever variety of product they desired without any sacrifice in productive efficiency. Again, the significance of selling costs for the allocation and utilization of economic resources went unanalyzed.

In summary, economic theory and trust literature pointed to the competitive equilibrium—which we should now call the purely competitive equilibrium—as a state in which consumers obtained both the advantages of large-scale efficiency and as much variety of product as they wished and also the full benefits of the competitive process in yielding ideal investment, best utilization of equipment, normal earnings, and hence the optimum price, in all those industries regarded as "naturally competitive."[1]

The principles of public policy proceeding from these views called for government intervention of limited scope. Natural monopolies should be regulated or owned and operated by government. If dissolution of combinations in other industries was required at all, it should be confined to those combinations, certainly a minority, which attained something approaching nearly complete control of supply. Competitive methods which did not truly measure efficiency should be eliminated; and, by implication at least, any other barriers to free entry except those inherent in differing personal quali-

---

[1] Discussion of various qualifications to this general proposition, such as that of Professor Pigou concerning industries of diminishing and increasing cost, is outside the scope of this paper.

ties or ability to obtain capital should also be removed. Since the significance of variation or differentiation of product and of selling costs was generally neglected in the explanation of competitive equilibria, no important problems of public policy with respect to these matters were envisaged.

Twenty years ago public policy concerning competition and monopoly had come in the main to accord in abstract principle with this view of economic processes. A few natural monopolies were subjected to rate regulation. Regulation of investment and earnings followed. Outside this limited sphere business was liable to the anti-trust laws. It seems to me that in so far as there was any central concept or theme in the interpretation and administration of the anti-trust laws, it was the preservation of the freedom to compete. Obviously this did not mean the preservation of what we now call pure competition, or even of anything very nearly resembling it. It meant simply that each firm was to be free to determine its own policies independent of others and that neither the entry of newcomers nor the success of existing firms should be blocked or hampered by oppressive tactics. The anti-trust laws did not, I think, make monopoly illegal. Rather, the thing condemned was monopolizing or restraint of trade, both of which seem to have meant achieving or trying to attain nearly complete monopoly in an industry by a course of combination for which no justification in greater efficiency or normal expansion could be found; or by destruction or weakening of existing competitors or blocking of potential competition by the use of bludgeoning, harassing, or obstructive tactics rather than competitive methods which measured relative efficiency in production and marketing. These laws and their interpretation represented the expression in the economic sphere of the philosophy of liberalism, the belief that the most desirable institutions, ways of life, allocation of economic resources, distribution of wealth and income, and so on, would obtain if a large measure of freedom from government interference was preserved to the individual. By 1914, public policy in abstract principle had been brought fairly well into accord with the view of economic processes presented by economists. It cannot be said, however, that effective freedom to compete was preserved in all markets. This seems to have resulted from the failure, common to both economics and public policy, to realize the significance of "power politics" in economic activity. Economic theory assumed that profits were to be made and losses avoided chiefly, if not solely, by superior efficiency. The late promise of a realistic and salutary development of the law of competitive methods held out by the 1914 legislation has for a variety of reasons turned out to be largely a boomerang. Public policy seems to have overlooked such important barriers to free entry as control of scarce resources of raw materials, lack of pure competition among investment bankers, and the impressive formidability of size and length of purse supplemented by industrial and financial affiliations.

Let us now contrast with the traditional view of the economic system and the public policy which in the abstract, at least, came to accord with it, the view presented by the theory of monopolistic competition. The policy of preserving freedom of competition in all but a few industries actually resulted in considerable freedom to business to free itself from the compulsion of the competitive market. There seems to be little doubt that monopolistic elements throughout the economy have increased since passage of the Sherman Act in 1890. When account is taken of the co-operative experience during the War and the subsequent growth of trade associations, the merger movement of the twenties, and the development of advertising and other devices for differentiation, it appears quite likely that monopoly elements have increased since 1914.

The traditional picture of the economic system is challenged by the theory of monopolistic competition in several other important respects.   Wherever monopoly elements exist, the results of monopolistic competition may diverge from the sort of equilibrium contemplated by competitive theory.   Under certain circumstances divergence is desirable; under others, undesirable.   We first consider instances of desirable divergence.   The theory of monopolistic competition emphasizes the significance of variation or differentiation of product. Successful differentiation confers some monopoly power by attracting a clientele which has some preference for the article of a particular seller.   Given differentiation, competition is likely to result in less efficient rates of output and higher prices than those described by the equilibrium of competitive theory, although earnings may not be above competitive profits.   In so far as consumers really want the variety of product which is the basic reason for this condition, the ideal competitive equilibria of traditional theory would not adequately meet their wants.   What would appear to be monopolistic exploitation according to the familiar criterion turns out to be a symptom of greater precision in the satisfaction of wants.   To the extent that advertising expenditures—which could, of course, have no *raison d'être* under pure competition—enable attainment of a larger maximum of satisfactions, the same is true of them also.   Again, in many industries efficiency might be far below the attainable maximum if the number of producers were large enough so that no one could affect the relations of the market.   Finally, it may be that the persistent creation of overcapacity in some industries composed of large numbers of small, ill-informed firms can only be prevented by a reorganization of the industry which brings an increase of monopolistic elements in the form of fewer firms or the conclusion of agreements.   Destruction of all monopoly elements would result in what would doubtless be regarded as intolerable standardization and probably in some considerable reduction of efficiency.   The problem is to preserve that degree or those sorts of monopoly power which yield desirable results and to destroy or sterilize the excess monopoly power which may, as we shall see, bring unfortunate consequences.

In so far as differentiation of product is carried beyond the degree which would really be desired by consumers if they had complete and accurate knowledge of products in the market, the national income suffers.[1] Assume that articles roughly similar in physical attributes are produced by any number of firms, each of which differentiates its product by brand, packaging, advertising slogans, and the like. The result may be underinvestment and monopoly profits in varying degree to all. But in so far as others can produce what is in essentials the same article and differentiate it to some extent, existence of monopoly profits will attract an inflow of resources; whereupon, if all producers attempt to maximize profits, the result will be overinvestment, underutilization, and no more than competitive profits to some, perhaps all. There is, of course, no more reason to expect that the extent of variation which comes into existence is automatically restricted by competition to the ideal amount, than there is to suppose that competition never permits combination to exceed a size which is just right for maximum efficiency. It is quite possible that the aggregate of monopolistic wastes in what would formerly have been called the general body of competitive industries greatly exceeds the wastes of trustified industries.

Again, when sellers of the same article are few, and when each evaluates prospective demand and supply conditions in about the same way as the others and coolly pursues the policy best calculated to maximize his profit in either the short run or the long run, the quantitative market relationship are almost certain to differ from those contemplated by competitive theory. If entry to the field is effectively barred, underinvestment and monopoly profits may result without any

---

[1] It is impossible here to go into the relations between differentiation, advertising, knowledge, and wants.

agreement.   If entry is free, there is a tendency for profits to
be brought down to normal by an influx of newcomers which
creates overinvestment.   Under such circumstances underutilization of capacity may be substantial.   If the few rivals
engage in determined price competition, however, results will
approximate the relations described by competitive theory,
unless earlier attempts to hold prices up have attracted enough
capacity to create overinvestment.

The existence of substantial monopoly elements also confers
the power to discriminate in price between markets which can
be separated.   It is probable that monopolistic discrimination
is much more widespread throughout the price structure than
economic literature would indicate.   And finally, there may
be undesirable divergence from ideal market relationships due
to monopolistic agreements, which are sufficiently familiar in
principle.

Enough has been said to indicate some of the more important possibilities under monopolistic competition of undesirable tendencies in market relations.   The extent of actual
divergence from ideal market relations depends upon degrees
of monopoly power, elasticities of demand, cost conditions,
and the way in which sellers act.   Divergence as measured by
monopoly net revenue per unit of investment, by extent of
underinvestment, or by underutilization of economic resources
may be greater in an industry comprising ten firms no one of
which controls 15 per cent of the output than in an industry
where one firm sells 75 per cent of the total volume.   Where
substantial monopolistic elements are operative, competition
does not automatically produce the ideal quantitative market
relations contemplated by the theory upon which public
policy has been based.   That theory implied a very limited
amount of government control of economic activity.   The
theory of monopolistic competition suggests that state interference, economically defensible upon either view whenever
the net addition to income is likely to be greater than the cost

of state action, may be required in a large number of markets, if maximization of national income is to be approached; and at the same time issues a warning that the use of monopoly power to add to the total income of satisfactions must be distinguished from its use to subtract.

One other exceedingly important aspect of monopolistic competition has been deferred to the end of the list because it does not slip easily into the categories used above and because it has received little theoretical analysis. I refer to the fact that existence of monopoly elements confers some measure of power to plan for the future; a firm can have an investment policy, a marketing policy, a price policy. When the enterprise which possesses the power to plan is a corporation which looks forward to continuous existence and growth, it is likely that its policies will be determined by fairly long-range rather than immediate considerations. Evidently the executives of many such enterprises believe that some appreciable stability of price contributes to long-run stability of profits or to some other desired objective. Without inquiring into the reasons for this belief or its soundness, we should note that such price rigidities must affect either the allocation or degree of utilization of economic resources. Conceivably the consequences may be good or bad, but there are cogent reasons for believing that in a majority of instances the national income is likely to suffer from such policies. It seems particularly probable that monopolistic price rigidities increase the severity of the business cycle. Even if there is no truth in the contention that serious maladjustments resulted from the failure of the prices of many manufactured commodities to decline in step with costs during the twenties, it seems most probable that price rigidities during the depression have tended to increase its severity and duration. More price flexibility might have increased output, consumption, and employment directly in the industries concerned; in any case the force of the impact upon other segments of the economy would probably have been diminished with the result of lessening the extent of bankruptcies, uncertainties, fear, desire for cash liquidity, redistribution of incomes, and shifts in demands.

III

I now turn to a brief survey of some of the problems which must be faced in order to develop a program for public policy which accords with realities.   Such facts as we have indicate that monopolistic elements are extensive.   Theory suggests that operation of some monopolistic forces may increase to some extent the consumers' satisfactions obtainable from our economic resources and that exercise of other sorts of monopoly power will reduce real incomes markedly.   Unfortunately we know none too much about either the extent of monopolistic elements or their actual results; and we do know that some undesirable consequences, such as overinvestment, may result from non-monopolistic imperfections.

First, as to the facts of monopoly power.   Much more adequate and accurate information upon the numbers and the relative importance of sellers in many different markets should be obtained.   A survey of this matter upon which I am now jointly engaged with others has disclosed above all the meagerness of available data from which satisfactory results can be secured.   This inquiry should, of course, consider foreign sources of supply and tariffs.   The nature and extent of barriers to free entry needs thorough study.   The prevalence of monopoly elements on the buyers' side also requires attention.

A second set of problems concerns the economic justification of monopoly elements.   More intensive study of the relation between size and efficiency and progressiveness is of crucial importance.   We have little more than vague knowledge about the extent to which monopoly elements would be lessened if all firms were of the minimum size necessary for maximum efficiency, although there is reason to think that the diminution would be appreciable.   The problem of distinguishing between those sorts and degrees of variation of product which better meet the wants of consumers and those which result in net subtraction is particularly difficult. Perhaps the most fruitful line of attack is in the direction of truthful advertising and the development by impartial agencies of standards of quality for all sorts of products.

A third range of questions has to do with divergence from ideal market relationships. We have noticed that when sellers are few there are different possibilities with regard to the relationships between investment, output, price, earnings, and demand. It depends upon the degree to which entry is free and the way in which sellers act. Thorough investigations of the facts in many industries of this sort are in order to discover which possibilities are more often realized. Under such circumstances is immediate advantage sacrificed to long-run stability of profits? Or do sellers act like pure competitors in their long-range programs of investment and progressive development of new adaptations of product, meanwhile pursuing monopolistic price and output policies? Monopolistic discrimination incident to basing point price structures has received considerable attention, but we need to know more about the extent of discrimination which takes the form of selling different, partially finished or finished products made from a basic product (such as a metal) at prices which after subtracting the conversion costs return different prices per unit of the basic product.

The problem of overinvestment and ruinous competition falls in this category. A large degree of monopoly is often urged as the best instrument for prevention or cure of overinvestment. In this there is some logic. When firms are few, with or without agreement, each is probably able to assess supply and demand conditions better than when sellers are much more numerous, and each has a greater incentive to do so since his policy will affect appreciably the conditions in the whole market. And once overinvestment exists it is obviously wasteful for additional resources of the same efficiency to enter the field. On the other hand a large degree of monopoly power may, unless successfully regulated, bring worse results. Prevention may be carried too far with the result of marked underinvestment. Cure may take the objectionable form of legitimizing excess capacity through enabling it to earn profits by remaining idle. Maintenance of high profits may attract additional capacity. Furthermore, as we have seen, the original development of overinvestment may be directly due to too much monopoly power. Again, in so far as overcapacity results from the introduction of more efficient equipment, it is, up to a point, a sign of health rather than disorder; for it is more economical from the standpoint of the community to have old equipment partially operated as long as it can earn something above direct costs at some rate of output than to have it all replaced with new facilities. The ideal situation would, however, give the appearance of true overinvestment to the extent that the earnings of some firms fell short of normal returns on the original cost of all equipment. Is it not likely that some part of the complaint of overcapacity during the latter part of the twenties is to be ascribed to the rapid introduction of more efficient equipment? Finally, it should be remembered that the explanation of overinvestment may often be found in uncertainties and poor knowledge, in overoptimism, in the existence of corporate surpluses to which no one seems to have any very definite claim and which may, perhaps, be reinvested on grounds other than the rational pursuit of profit. To a large extent remedies different from greater monopoly power would seem to be appropriate. The whole matter of overinvestment and rationalization requires more incisive theoretical analysis and thorough examination of the facts in a number of industries.

Finally, I wish to emphasize the importance of the relation between monopolistic policies and the business cycle. Although monetary and credit policies can exercise a salutary influence toward reducing the magnitude of fluctuations in output, incomes, and employment, it is difficult to see how they can prevent or cure the substantial residue of maladjustments incident to monopolistic forces.

IV

These are some of the more important problems which must be faced if we hope to develop a program of public policy which accords with reality. It seems altogether probable that the degree of monopoly power which is justified either by considerations of efficiency or by consumers' desires for variety differs markedly between industries, and further that the actual existing divergence from the particular organization and policies which would correspond with the ideal degree of monopoly power also varies greatly between industries. A twofold or even four- or fivefold classification of industries is hardly likely to be consistent with the facts. Evidently different types of government intervention are appropriate for different industries or markets. It is highly questionable whether the policy of general rules for large numbers of industries should be continued. I believe we should work in the direction of separate codes for separate classes of industries, in some cases for single industries—codes which in every case apply appropriate principles both of organization and of business policies. Monopoly power should everywhere be adjusted as nearly as can be to that degree which seems economically justifiable. This may mean increase in some industries and decrease in others. Monopolistic policies or practices which rather definitely seem to yield no net social advantage should be abolished and effective steps taken to prevent their reappearance. Those familiar with the none too happy results of regulation in the utility field will agree with me, I think, that a policy of getting rid of all that monopoly power which yields no net social advantage would be preferable to attempts to regulate its use.[1] In my view, for the majority of industries the problem is that of creating conditions such that monopolistic competition will be forced to bring results which approach much closer to the ideal market relationships than the actual results under the present public policy. Concretely this might mean much more serious economic surgery than ever occurred under the anti-trust laws, and codes which are more extensive and in certain respects more restrictive than those emerging from the Trade Practice Conferences of the Federal Trade Commission. It goes without saying that the codes should, in many instances at least, differ strikingly in content from those of NRA. Where it is impossible to create conditions such that monopolistic competition will function satisfactorily, government competition if carried out according to proper principles may be better than government regulation. The development of consumers' co-operation also has promising possibilities.

Formulation of any such program of public policy requires two things in particular. The development of practical criteria for economic control is imperative. This requires a social philosophy. Government control to deal with the problems here discussed must inevitably affect other elements in economic welfare such as economic security, the distribution of wealth and income, and the relative degree of economic freedom for different groups in the community, to say nothing of factors which are not strictly economic. If economists wish, in addition to describing the way economic processes work, to try to prescribe methods for increasing economic welfare, they cannot face the attendant problems devoid of a social philosophy which goes beyond economic considerations narrowly construed.

In the second place, a large amount of basic economic information about a large number of industries is manifestly

---

[1] I imply nothing here as to whether or not the extent of monopoly power in any of the utility industries exceeds that which is economically justifiable.

necessary.   We should have a grand taking of stock of the experience of many industries in the post-War period.   Investigations by individual students and research foundations into the particular problems raised here suffer from the meagerness of pertinent information.   There is need for a new edition of the Industrial Commission empowered to plan and carry through an extensive investigation and provided with legal authority to acquire the necessary information.

Before adding one more point in closing, I wish to reiterate that I say nothing about the political problems of getting a desirable economic program adopted and administered effectively and honestly.   It will, of course, be impossible to devise and administer codes in such a way that ideal results are perfectly attained.   The best practicable system of government control will still leave a large measure of responsibility with business leaders.   Hence it is of particular importance that the codes make clear to business men the guiding principles for distinguishing between economic and uneconomic conduct.   The failure to add much in this respect to older legal rules has been one of the saddest aspects of the history of the Federal Trade Commission.   If business men thoroughly understood principles for distinguishing between activities which promote economic welfare and those which act in the opposite direction, it is possible that business leaders might accomplish something in the way of developing an ethic of business concerning the use of monopoly power for the public interest.   The conservatism of most business men and their apparent lack of ideas for sane economic change may reflect to an appreciable extent simply a lack of understanding of the social consequences of economic processes.   Although substantial monopoly elements confer power over market relations, the use of which must affect the economic welfare of the community one way or the other, many business men may not understand very clearly how or why this is so, partly, perhaps, because the traditional ideas of the free market, of pure competition, have so dominated all thought about the consequences of economic activity.

It is becoming increasingly plain that the future fate of economic liberalism in this country will be determined in the fields of labor and industrial organization and business policies. Unless we are capable of discovering and successfully administering a public policy which will markedly reduce the opportunities for maladjustments due to exercise of monopoly power, and unless, also, industrial leaders who still possess monopoly power realize the implications of their positions and are willing to discharge the attendant social responsibilities of economic statesmanship, the superiority of that type of economic liberalism which we call free capitalistic enterprise and its ability to maintain itself for long in the future would seem to be open to serious doubt.

9

THE PASSING OF THE PUBLIC UTILITY CONCEPT*

By Horace M. Gray†

The term "public utility concept" is used here in a broad sense to denote that body of economic, social, and legal ideas which together constitute the institutional framework within which certain designated enterprises operate. Viewed analytically, it consists of certain economic and legal assumptions, certain social objectives sought to be attained, and certain administrative and legal procedures designed to implement these abstractions and to give them functional vitality for purposes of social control. These assumptions, objectives, and procedures will be examined critically with a view toward determining whether or not they provide a satisfactory basis for public regulation in the modern economy. No attempt will be made to trace the evolution of these ideas through the literature; rather, it will be assumed that the public utility concept, in its modern American form, is a product of the late nineteenth and early twentieth centuries, and that subsequent modification has not changed materially its essential characteristics.

During the nineteenth century, in response to the dominant belief that public interest would be best promoted by grants of

---

* *The Journal of Land & Public Utility Economics*, Volume XVI, Number 1, February 1940, pages 8–20. Reprinted by the courtesy of the University of Wisconsin and the author.

† Associate Professor of Economics and Assistant Dean of the Graduate School, University of Illinois.

special privilege to private persons and to corporations, the Federal Government, by gift, or sale for nominal sums, alienated in fee simple, and without reservation of public right, the major portion of the public domain. This basic privilege was supplemented by further federal grants in the form of patents, subsidies, banking powers, and tariffs. In the twentieth century this process has continued by means of federal grants of exclusive rights to exploit particular sectors of the public domain: hydro-electric sites (Federal Water Power Act of 1920); radio, wireless, and television channels (Federal Communications Act of 1934); public highways (Motor Carrier Act of 1935); and airways (Civil Aeronautics Act of 1938).[1] The states, following the same theory, granted corporate charters of extreme laxity; municipalities granted perpetual or long-term franchises of exclusive character. In general, the recipients of these privileges were given practically a free hand in respect to organization, finance, and price policy. They followed the historic behavior pattern of all holders of special privilege and the final result was monopoly, exploitation, and political corruption. These aggressions eventually became so apparent and so onerous that a widespread demand for legislative restraint arose, in response to which the Granger Laws, Interstate Commerce Act, Sherman Law, and the first state public utility statutes were enacted. Each sought in its own way to curb certain obvious manifestations of monopoly.

Although these laws differed in many respects—differences with which the present discussion is not concerned—they had one feature in common. They all followed the delusion that private privilege can be reconciled with public interest by the alchemy of public regulation. Consequently, none of them disturbed in the slightest degree the underlying structure of

[1] Although the licenses or certificates issued under these statutes purport to reserve to the public certain rights of recovery and control, past experience affords little basis for confidence in the effectiveness of such reservations.

special privilege; they merely reared upon it a superstructure of restraint. Monopoly capitalism, secure in its privileges, shook off the petty irritations of regulation and continued its aggressions against the public welfare. Popular opinion still adhered to the anti-monopoly, anti-corporation tradition but became increasingly confused and bewildered. Unable to detect the real source of difficulty, people were disposed to condemn existing political administrations for failure to enforce the law or to believe that additional legislation of the same character would solve the problem."[1]   It was during this period of confusion, and out of this conflict between liberal ideology and the realities of monopoly capitalism, that the public utility concept evolved. When, shortly after the turn of the century, it assumed definitive modern form in the laws of Wisconsin and New York it bore the birthmarks of the political and ideological miscegenation from which it sprang.

The Concept in the Twentieth Century

The public utility concept retained and reaffirmed the basic fallacy of the late nineteenth century—namely, that private privilege can be reconciled with public interest by means of public regulation. True to the liberal tradition, it assumed a fundamental harmony between private and public interest; this being the case, specific instances of conflict were regarded as temporary aberrations or maladjustments which in no wise vitiated the general rule. The "visible hand" of public regulation was substituted for the "invisible hand" of Adam Smith, and the continuous ministration of regulation, it was assumed, would suffice to maintain a perfect balance between private and public interest. The fact that this theory had not

---

[1] See Thurman W. Arnold, *The Folklore of Capitalism* (New Haven: Yale Univ. Press, 1937). In Chapter IX, Mr. Arnold shows how the anti-trust laws satisfied the prevailing ideology but actually encouraged combinations. The same reasoning is applicable to other efforts at public control, including public utility regulation.

worked with much success for the past generation in other sectors of the economy seems not to have disillusioned its advocates or to have lessened their faith that it could be made to work in the special field of local utilities.

But the public utility concept went far beyond nineteenth century theory. Whereas formerly it had been assumed that competition was generally beneficent and should, therefore, be preserved, it was now assumed that, in certain areas at least, competition was undesirable and should, therefore, be eradicated by state action. This new economic philosophy received general legislative sanction by the states between the years 1907 and 1920, and, more recently, by the federal Congress in respect to interstate operations in communication, electric power, motor transport, air transport, and natural gas. Thus, between 1907 and 1938, the policy of state-created, state-protected monopoly became firmly established over a significant portion of the economy and became the keystone of modern public utility regulation. Henceforth, the public utility status was to be the haven of refuge for all aspiring monopolists who found it too difficult, too costly, or too precarious to secure and maintain monopoly by private action alone. Their future prosperity would be assured if only they could induce government to grant them monopoly power and to protect them against interlopers, provided always, of course, that government did not exact too high a price for its favors in the form of restrictive regulation. If political manipulation should fail to remove this last source of danger, the Supreme Court could be relied upon to restrain any overly zealous regulatory commission.

The obvious conflict between the traditional ideology and the public utility concept was resolved by resort to rationalization. It was said that enterprises supplying gas, electricity, street transportation, water, and telephonic communication were "inherently" or "naturally" monopolistic; that they had certain "natural characteristics" which distinguished them from other enterprises and caused them to follow different laws of economic organization; that, because of this "natural" force, they tended "inevitably" to become monopolies; that all efforts to maintain competition had failed and, by the very nature of the case, were foredoomed to fail.   Thus, the fiction of "natural monopoly" was invented to explain the centripetal tendencies then observable.   Government, being powerless to resist this "natural" trend, must perforce bow to the inevitable and accept "natural" monopoly as a principle of public policy. Such a conclusion did not contradict traditional thought for these new monopolies were different; they were "natural" whereas other monopolies were, by contradistinction, "unnatural" or artificial.   Thus, by a soothing process of rationalization, men are able to oppose monopolies in general but to approve certain types of monopolies.[1]

But one rationalization led to others.   Since these monopolies were "natural" and since nature was beneficent, it followed that they were "good" monopolies.   Government, being responsible for promoting public welfare was, therefore, justified in establishing such "good" monopolies and using its power to prevent invasion by interlopers.   Moreover, those

---

[1] For a brief discussion of the contribution of economists to this rationalization see George T. Brown, *The Gas Light Company of Baltimore* (Baltimore: Johns Hopkins Press, 1936), c. VI.   See also my review of this monograph in 26 *American Economic Review* 535 (Sept., 1936) in which I pointed out that Dr. Brown had failed to give proper attention to the institutional factors that underlie such monopolies.   My conclusion on this point was: "Franchises, way-leaves, contracts, charters, patents, secret agreements, injunctions, dummy corporations, cut-throat competition, newspaper and banking influences, and political corruption are the institutional ingredients from which monopoly was forged by skillful and unscrupulous manipulators. A critical evaluation of these elements might have shed considerable doubt upon the 'naturalness' of this and similar monopolies."   For a similar view, with respect to the so-called *inevitability* of industrial monopoly, see the statement by Leon Henderson in "Investigation of Concentration of Economic Power," *Hearings* before Temporary National Economic Committee, Pt. 5, pp. 1974–5 (Washington: Government Printing Office, 1939).

who "devoted" their property to this "good" cause were
entitled to have the power of the state invoked in their behalf
to insure them a "fair return on a fair value."   A "natural"
monopoly, being a "good" monopoly, would not behave after
the fashion of "bad" monopolies.   Subject to an occasional
propensity to indulge in excessive charges and discriminations
—aberrations that would be curbed by regulation—these
monopolists would organize production efficiently, utilize
resources to the best advantage, employ the best techniques
available, maintain high standards of service, develop their
markets completely, secure capital at least cost, and in general
manage their affairs to the best interests of the public to whose
service they had "devoted" their property.   The profit
motive, although restricted, would as in competitive business,
provide the incentive for efficient performance.   The role of
the state would be entirely negative; its interference would be
confined to preventing excessive charges and discriminations.

Uses and Abuses of the Concept

It is difficult, if not impossible, to identify precisely the social
objectives of the public utility concept during this period of
confused rationalization.   Certainly many of the proponents
of public utility regulation intended it to protect consumers
against excessive charges and discriminations; all the early
state laws bear witness to this intent.   It should be remembered, however, that behind this laudable social purpose
lurked the sinister forces of private privilege and monopoly.
They desired immunity from prosecution under the anti-trust
laws, legal validation of their privileges as property rights, the
protection of the state for their monopolies, and a relatively
free hand to extend their economic power.   All these objectives they attained under the public utility status.[1]   In addi-

---

[1] Burton N. Behling, *Competition and Monopoly in Public Utility Industries*
(Urbana: Univ. of Ill. Press, 1938).   In Chapter IV, Dr. Behling shows

tion, they secured *gratis* something equally important—public acceptance and legal recognition of the economic fiction of "natural" monopoly.

Whatever relative weight may be assigned to these conflicting objectives in pre-war legislation, it seems clear that protection of consumers faded into the background during subsequent years. In the war period emphasis shifted to the problems of providing adequate service facilities, obtaining much needed capital, and adjusting rates upward to cover rising costs. After the war the utility industries entered upon a boom period during which rapid expansion was the guiding principle of both private and public policy. Private financiers and promoters were concerned with new construction, finance, consolidation, elimination of residual competition, organization of great economic empires, and speculative profits. Public regulation, in so far as the interests of consumers were concerned, practically ceased to function; the policies of commissions and courts, particularly the latter, were calculated to promote the expansionist and profit-seeking activities of private enterprise. When, after 1929, the drastic curtailment of consumer purchasing power gave rise to a widespread agitation for reduction of utility rates, commissions and courts came to the rescue of the hard pressed utilities and prevented, or minimized, rate reduction by invoking a tortured construction of the "fair return on fair value" doctrine. In extreme cases, as in railroads, rates were actually raised at a time when by every criterion of economic teaching they should have been lowered. It thus became increasingly apparent that "protection of consumers" had been superseded in large measure by "protection of property." Recently an even more menacing and anti-social use of the public utility concept has developed. In order to preserve obsolete economic organizations, it is now proposed to invoke this concept to prevent the establishment of

how the policies of commissions and courts tended to strengthen and protect monopoly without at the same time curbing its aggressions.

alternative institutions designed to serve needs not adequately provided for under existing arrangements. A number of examples may be cited to illustrate this latest stage of "institutional decadence."

The railroads have long sought to curb the development of motor transport by securing its inclusion within the restrictive confines of the public utility status. They have sponsored, and obtained, federal and state legislation designed to restrict competition by forcing motor carriers, as a condition precedent to operation, to apply for certificates of convenience and necessity;[1] the railroads, of course, have opposed the granting of such certificates. In Illinois, for example, the Commerce Commission, operating under a public utility statute, is reported to have granted 21 exclusive certificates on main

---

[1] "Regulation of Motor Carriers of Persons," *House Report* No. 783, 71st Cong., 2nd Sess., 1930. In a minority report, Congressman George Huddleston described the purpose of the proposed legislation as follows: "It [the bill] was proposed and urged by the bus operators and the rail carriers, and their affiliated interests. The main purpose of its proponents is to secure themselves against competition. This is to be accomplished through the device of the 'certificate of convenience and necessity.' The proponents of the bill admitted candidly that its main purpose was to give a monopoly, to eliminate competition. The main purpose of this bill is to create a monopoly in a situation which would otherwise be highly competitive, and then to make of the monopoly an excuse for regulation. This legislation is merely a part of the general effort of an important school of business men to get away from the competitive system." (Summarized from pp. 16–9.)

Later, Joseph B. Eastman, as Federal Coordinator of Transportation, stated: "The demand for regulation of the motor-transport industry began with the railroads"; and "The railroads have spent too much time and attention on plans for the restriction of their competitors and too little on the development and improvement of their own service and the readjustment of their own rates." ("Regulation of Transportation Agencies," *Sen. Doc.* No. 152, 73rd Cong., 2nd Sess., 1934, pp. 33 and 35.) Moreover, there can be no doubt that the railroads played an important role in securing the passage of the Federal Motor Carrier Act of 1935.

highways.[1] This state-creation of private monopolies on
the public highways aroused such protest that the legislature,
after an investigation, transferred jurisdiction over motor
trucks to the Department of Public Works and Buildings, and
displaced the public utility type of regulation by police
regulation designed to insure public safety.[2] Recently, the
Association of American Railroads has disseminated a report
in which it is proposed that all highways and waterways be
declared public utilities and that privilege taxes or fees, sufficient to defray all costs, be levied upon those who use them.[3]
This contention seems to have some judicial support, as exem-

---

[1] Statement of Senator Louis J. Menges, as reported in the *Chicago
Tribune*, Dec. 14, 1938.

[2] Illinois Truck Act, Ill. Rev. Stats. 1939, p. 2162.

[3] "Highway Costs," Assn. of Amer. Railroads, Jan. 30, 1939; see especially
c's I and II. The Transportation Association of America, in "A National
Transportation Program," Vols. I and II and Supp. No. 1 (Chicago, 1938),
urges that all forms of transport be brought under uniform regulation
administered by the Interstate Commerce Commission. The National
Highway Users Conference, however, in "Highway Transportation Re-
Makes America" (Washington, 1939) maintains that the highways should be
free. It states at p. 5: "Freedom of the highways is again being threatened
in the United States—not by toll gates erected by men in the attempt to
convert the public highway into a private business, but by drastic restrictions and punitive taxation whose effect is to curb the movement of persons
and goods over the highways. Imposition of heavy burdens upon highway
users is inspired by interests which hope to profit from the resulting curtailment of the use of highways." And again, at p. 10: "to the average person
free access to the highways seems to lie in the same category as free access
to the air and sunlight." On p. 20 an excerpt from the Dillman Report is
quoted to the effect that *highways are not public utilities.* Whereupon the
Association of American Railroads, speaking through its economist, Dr. C.
S. Duncan, issued a counterblast entitled "The Answer to Highway Propaganda" (Washington, 1939) in which, after attempting to expose and discredit the National Highway Users Conference, Dr. Duncan closes with the
dire foreboding that "unless highways are considered as public utilities and
every user of the improved highways is charged fairly for his use of these
facilities, we are headed directly for a socialized industry" (p. 20).

plified in the Brashear case, where a lower federal court, in upholding certain taxes levied on motor carriers, said:

"The highway system owned by the state and its subdivisions is a public utility supplying facilities which constitute an actual monopoly which is subject to inter-government regulation and control. The annual cost of operating such utility should be determined in the same manner as for a privately owned utility."[1]

In the field of electric power, private companies, on numerous occasions, have invoked the public utility concept to prevent or to hinder the development of public organizations for producing and distributing electricity.[2] They have agitated unceasingly to secure inclusion within the public utility category of municipal electric systems so that the latter, despite their institutional dissimilarity, can be forced to conform to the same rules and regulations that govern private operations.[3] They have sought to block municipal competi-

---

[1] *Brashear Freight Lines, Inc. v. Hughes*, in the Dist. Ct. of the U.S. for the So. Dist. of Ill., So. Div., In Equity DC 2273 (1938). See also Edward D. Allen, "Highway Costs and Their Allocation," 15 *Journal of Land & Public Utility Economics* 269–76 (August, 1939) and 404–15 (November, 1939). Professor Allen favors the *public utility* approach and, after outlining the theoretical justification for this view, attempts to derive a practical formula for allocating costs to highway users.

[2] An investigation by the Federal Power Commission reveals that private companies, from 1881 to 1935, filed 278 petitions for injunctions against 195 public authorities to restrain them from constructing electric plants. Of these petitions only 90 were filed during the 50 years from 1881–1930; the remainder, or 188, were filed between 1931 and 1935. ("Restraining Orders and Injunctions Instituted against Public Electric Projects," *Sen. Doc.* No. 182, 74th Cong., 2nd Sess., 1936.)

[3] In 1935, 12 state utility commissions claimed general, and nine others partial, jurisdiction over the rates of municipal electric utilities (Federal Power Commission, *Rate Series* No. 6, 1935, pp. 2–4). For a recent judicial decision, in which a state supreme court explicitly repudiated this contention and held that municipal electric systems are not public utilities, see *Birmingham Elec. Co. v. City of Bessemer*, — Ala. —, 186 So. 569, 28 P.U.R. (N.S.) 151 (1939).

tion by the plea that their franchises and certificates are exclusive.[1] They have even maintained that the Tennessee Valley Authority, an agency of the Federal Government designed to serve economic and social needs entirely outside the public utility concept, should be amenable to the public

---

[1] *Ala. Power Co. v. Ickes*, 302 U.S. 464, 82 L. ed. —, 58 S. Ct. 300, 21 P.U.R. (N.S.) 289 (1938); *Duke Power Co. v. Greenwood County*, 302 U.S. 485, 82 L. ed. —, 58 S. Ct. 306, 21 P.U.R. (N.S.) 298 (1938).

In these two cases a former decision of the Supreme Court rose to plague it. In 1929, in *Frost v. Okla. Corp. Com.*, 278 U.S. 515, 49 S. Ct. 235, P.U.R. 1929 B 634, the Court had held that a license to operate a cotton gin, granted under a state public utility statute, was a property right within the protection of the Fourteenth Amendment and was exclusive as against a farmers' cooperative ginning company. Mr. Justice Brandeis (Holmes and Stone concurring) dissented on the ground that a farmers' cooperative was entirely different from a commercial establishment and, hence, the discriminatory classification of the Oklahoma statute in question was justifiable. Mr. Justice Stone (Holmes and Brandeis concurring) wrote a separate dissenting opinion in which he developed the doctrine of *damnum absque injuria*. When, in 1938, the Alabama and Duke companies relied on the Frost case to substantiate their claim that municipal competition threatened to destroy their property and, hence, contravened the Fourteenth Amendment, Mr. Justice Sutherland, speaking for a unanimous Court, held that the Frost doctrine was inapplicable and that, since the competition complained of was legal, the rule of *damnum absque injuria* applied. Again, in 1939, in *Tenn. Elec. Power Co. v. TVA*, — U.S. —, 83 L. ed. —, 59 S. Ct. 366, 27 P.U.R. (N.S.) 1, the private company relied in part on the Frost doctrine. But, once again, Mr. Justice Roberts speaking for the majority, the Court held that the Frost case was inapplicable and reaffirmed the doctrine of *damnum absque injuria*. Mr. Justice Butler, however, speaking for himself and Mr. Justice McReynolds, dissented on the ground that the Frost case was applicable, and that the competition complained of was illegal and, hence, unconstitutional. It would seem, therefore, that the Frost doctrine, although never expressly repudiated, has been abandoned, for the time being at least, in favor of the rule of *damnum absque injuria*. For a criticism of this latter doctrine, and an exposition of the private utility point of view, see William M. Wherry, "Federal Competition May Be Unconstitutional—but?" 24 *Public Utilities Fortnightly* 3–12 (July 6, 1939) and 24 *Ibid.* 84–91 (July 20, 1939).

utility laws of Tennessee and Alabama.[1] They have harassed
the Authority with continuous propaganda, litigation, and
investigation, much of which has been based on the charge
that its policies with respect to costs, rates, finance, taxes,
promotional expenses, and accounting differ from those followed by private companies.[2] They have attempted to
block the organization of rural electric cooperatives by contending before commissions and courts that the latter should
be classified as public utilities and forced to obtain certificates
of convenience and necessity—which grant the private companies are, of course, prepared to oppose. Although this
attempted perversion of the public utility concept ultimately
failed in most jurisdictions, it has resulted in protracted delays
and considerable expense to the rural cooperatives.[3] Though

---

[1] *Tenn. Elec. Power Co. v. TVA, supra* n. 1, page 290.

[2] These charges culminated in an investigation by a Joint Congressional
Committee, pursuant to Pub. Res. 83, 75th Cong. The majority report
recognizes clearly the inherent differences between TVA and private
utilities. The three minority members, however, refuse to concede such
distinctions and insist that TVA should be subject to regulation in the same
manner as private companies. In their own words: "It should be under the
regulation of local State utility commissions and the Federal Power Commission in substantially the same manner as private utilities are under such
regulation. . . . The TVA should be required to fix reasonable rates that
would cover all costs, including operating expenses, interest on the investment, taxes, and depreciation or amortization. It should pay all Federal,
State, and local taxes in the same way as taxes on similar private property
is [as printed] computed. We recommend that the TVA define its area of
distribution so that present uncertainty may be removed and the private
utilities in adjoining areas feel justified in making much-needed investments
for improvements and expansions." (*Report*, p. 277.)

On April 5, 1939, Rep. Rankin of Mississippi charged in the House that
the minority report had been "ghost written" by private utility propa-
gandists. Rep. Jenkins of Ohio, a minority member of the Committee,
denied this. (See *Congressional Record.*) Drew and Pearson, in their
syndicated column, "Washington Merry-Go-Round," of April 5, 1939,
made the same charge.

[3] *Re West Tenn. Power & Light Co.*, 18 P.U.R. (N.S.) 369 (1937); *Ala.*

generally defeated in this major attack, the private power companies are still able, under existing laws, to continue their program of harassment by securing from some commissions permits for extensions that cut through territory blocked out for unitary development by cooperatives.[1]

The same tendency to invoke the public utility concept in order to forestall the development of new institutions that threaten the security of existing organizations may be observed in other fields. The radio industry, desirous of monopolizing the air but fearful that its temporary licenses may be revoked or that public broadcasting may be established, may ultimately seek refuge in the public utility concept.[2] The real estate interests of Chicago, in an effort to frustrate public housing, recently conducted an active but unsuccessful campaign for the creation of "public service housing corporations."[3] The

---

Power Co. v. Cullman County Elec. Membership Corp., 19 P.U.R. (N.S.) 464, 234 Ala. 396, 174 So. 866 (1937); *Carolina Power & Light Co. v. Johnston County Elec. Membership Corp.*, 20 P.U.R. (N.S.) 208, 211 N.C. 717, 192 S.E. 105 (1937); *Southwestern States Tel. Co. v. Okla. Inter-County Elec. Coop.*, 27 P.U.R. (N.S.) 321 (1938).

The West Virginia Commission is one of the few that have insisted that rural electric cooperatives are public utilities and must show cause in order to obtain a certificate of public convenience and necessity (*Re Harrison Rural Electrification Assn., Inc.*, 24 P.U.R. (N.S.) 7 (1938)).

[1] For a vigorous discussion of the obstructionistic tactics of private power companies against rural cooperatives see *Annual Report*, Rural Electrification Admin., 1938, pp. 5–6, 76–83, and 94–105. For a special form of obstruction—namely, refusal to grant satisfactory wholesale rates to rural cooperatives—see W. Clarence Adams, "Electric Cooperatives Scan Wholesale Power Rates," 22 *Public Utilities Fortnightly* 368–77 (Sept. 15, 1938).

[2] Frank Waldrop and Joseph Borkin, *Television—A Struggle for Power* (New York: William Morrow & Co., 1938), c. 22.

[3] Illinois Sen. Bill 264, introduced March 29, 1939; see *Chicago Tribune*, March 30, 1939. These corporations were to be given a broad power of eminent domain, a relatively free hand in building construction and operation, and their rentals were to be fixed in accordance with the public utility formula. It was charged by the opposition, and never successfully

milk monopolists, unable to suppress competition completely, unable to appease the exploited farmers and consumers, threatened in some areas with municipal and cooperative distribution and under indictment or investigation for restraint of trade, may soon find it expedient to seek admission to the public utility status, provided, of course, that the conditions imposed by government are not too onerous.[1]

The air transport companies have been brought within the public utility category to the extent that they are now being given exclusive certificates of convenience and necessity.[2] The radio broadcasting interests, having built up nation-wide systems under a six months' licensing arrangement, are dissatisfied with their insecurity of tenure and are demanding indeterminate certificates of exclusive character.[3] The

---

refuted, that the real purpose was to block out large slum areas in Chicago so that land could not be secured for public housing. Compare with the strict provisions of the existing Illinois statute governing private *housing corporations*, approved.July 12, 1933 (Ill. Rev. Stats. 1939, p. 922). For propaganda in favor of these "public service housing corporations," see *Chicago Tribune*, beginning Dec. 14, 1938 and continuing through June, 1939.

[1] In 1935 I considered this question on its merits and reached the conclusion that the distribution of milk should not be a public utility. (Horace M. Gray, "Should the Distribution of Milk be a Public Utility?" *Dairy Manufacturers Conference Manual* (Urbana, Univ. of Ill., Jan. 21–25, 1935).) This judgment is not in agreement with the more favorable view expressed a year later by Professor W. P. Mortenson in "Distribution of Milk under Public Utility Regulation," 27 *American Economic Review* 22–40 (March, 1936). At pp. 39–40, Professor Mortenson says that distribution of milk as a public utility can succeed if all the interested parties cooperate to make it succeed. This last condition, however, begs the question, for experience shows that this is the very thing they will not do. After a reexamination of this question in the light of recent experience with public utility control, I am more than ever convinced that it would be a mistake to apply the public utility concept to the distribution of milk.

[2] Oswald Ryan, "The Civil Aeronautics Act of 1938," 23 *Public Utilities Fortnightly* 515–25 (April 27, 1939).

[3] *Chicago Tribune*, April 30, 1939.

chronically chaotic bituminous coal industry has sought and obtained a measure of governmental protection under the Guffey Act; although this form of control does not coincide with public utility regulation, it goes far in the same direction. Likewise, the restriction and proration schemes now in vogue in the oil industry resemble public utility regulation in some respects, although they do not involve fixation of profit margins or prices by government. From the same point of view, the whole NRA experiment may be regarded as an effort by big business to secure legal sanction for its monopolistic practices and to invoke the power of the Federal Government to assist in suppressing competition. Even certain farm groups, finding themselves in desperate economic straits and observing how the mantle of governmental protection has been thrown around public utility monopolists, proclaim that agriculture should be a public utility and should receive the same protection.[1]

Enough perhaps has been said to demonstrate the "institutional decadence" of the public utility concept. It originated as a system of social restraint designed primarily, or at least ostensibly, to protect consumers from the aggressions of monopolists, it has ended as a device to protect the property, i.e., the capitalized expectancy, of these monopolists from the just demands of society, and to obstruct the development of socially superior institutions. This perversion of the public utility concept from its original purpose was perhaps inevitable under capitalism. Here, as in other areas of our economic and social life, the compelling sanctions of private property and private profit, working within a framework of special privilege, determined the direction and outlook of public policy. Just as in the days of the Empire all roads led to Rome so in a capitalistic society all forms of social con-

---

[1] A federal bill of this character, the so-called "cost of production" plan, is reported to have been approved by the Senate Committee on Agriculture (*Chicago Tribune*, March 31, 1939).

trol lead ultimately to state protection of the dominant interest, i.e., property.   The public utility concept has thus merely gone the way of all flesh.[1]

Obsolescence of the Concept

But aside from its perversion to antisocial ends, the public utility concept is obsolete from another point of view.   As previously noted, it was designed to attain limited objectives by negative means.   One may read the early public utility

---

[1] Professor Henry C. Simons in "The Requisites of Free Competition," 26 *American Economic Review* 68–76 (March, 1936) at p. 74 holds that: "Unregulated, extra-legal monopolies are tolerable evils; but private monopolies with the blessing of regulation and the support of law are malignant cancers in the system."   He goes on to affirm that such regulation leads inevitably to fascism; he advocates the stamping out of private monopoly and the public ownership of railroads and utilities.   A similar view is expressed by Professor Clifford T. James in "Commons on Institutional Economics," 27 *American Economic Review* 61–75 (1937).

The Federal Trade Commission has recently deemed it necessary to warn against the application of this doctrine to the steel business: "The classification of industries as necessary [natural] monopolies should be, in the Commission's opinion, kept to as narrow limits as technical considerations permit. . . . The Commission therefore suggests that the steel industry, which it believes to be capable of reasonably efficient operation without monopoly, should be definitely separated in public policy from the 'natural' monopolies, and treated as a free enterprise." ("Investigation of Concentration of Economic Power," *op. cit.*, Pt. 5, p. 2199.)

An English critic describes the fictional character of the public utility concept as follows: "In these cases (natural monopolies) it seemed best to countenance unrighteousness but to limit the plunder.   A pompous and question-begging name—'business affected with a public interest'—was therefore invented by the lawyers to cover such enterprises, and they were placed under special government regulation.

"But the classification soon became a veritable Pandora's box . . . the qualifications necessary for admission to the box have changed so constantly that its present contents form a very ill-assorted miscellany, . . . and the nature of additions thereto is quite unpredictable." (A. S. J. Baster, *The Twilight of American Capitalism* (Westminster: P. S. King & Son, Ltd., 1937), p. 27.)

statutes in vain to discover any express mandate for the positive promotion of public welfare; the whole tenor of these laws is negative and restrictive; they prohibit certain obvious forms of monopolistic misbehavior but fail to impose definite responsibility for socially desirable action. Thus, public utility companies are under no legal compulsion to conserve natural resources, to utilize capital efficiently, to employ the best known techniques and forms of organization, to treat labor fairly, to extend service to non-profitable areas, to improve public health, to strengthen national defense, to promote technical research, to provide service to indigent persons, to institute rate and service policies that will foster cultural and social values, or to develop related benefits such as navigation, flood control, and irrigation. This being the case, private utility monopolists will have regard for these broad social objectives only when by so doing they can increase or maintain their own profit. Experience has shown that they will not voluntarily strive to attain these ends; moreover, it is clear that public utility regulation, as at present constituted, cannot compel them, against their own interest, to do so. Thus, the public utility concept is functionally impotent in the sense that it is incapable of securing the social objectives that are essential in the modern economy. When any institution reaches this advanced state of obsolescence, it tends to be superseded by some new institution that is more positive in character and better adapted to the needs of the time; such a process of gradual supersession seems now to be under way.

Within recent years the "institutional inventiveness" of political leaders and public administrators has produced a number of such new institutional arrangements. Among these are: direct action by departments or bureaus of the Federal Government to supply needed facilities; public corporations chartered under both federal and state authority; multiple-purpose, regional, water-control projects; rural electric cooperatives; federal grants-in-aid; federal-state-municipal cooperation; Public Works loans-and-grants; Reconstruction Finance Corporation loans; and federal subsidy for desirable services.   None of these comes within the traditional public utility concept; they all involve direct, positive action rather than mere negative restraint; they are relatively immune from restrictive, judicial interpretation of the property and due process clauses of the Fifth and Fourteenth Amendments; instead of relying exclusively on the police power of the states and the commerce power of the Federal Constitution, both hitherto narrowly circumscribed by the Supreme Court, they call into play other more positive and less restricted powers of the Federal Government, such as the proprietary, finance, public welfare, and national defense powers.   In every respect, therefore, these new institutional devices appear more capable of serving modern social needs than do private monopolies operating under public utility regulation.[1]

Another related movement that points in the same general direction is the rise of creative economic planning by government.   Under the prevailing system of monopoly capitalism, private enterprise seems to have lost, in large measure, its power to plan constructively for progressive improvement of the economy.   This failure is observable in many areas and, in the utility field, is most apparent in connection with water resources, electric power, natural gas, communication, and transportation.   Now this is a fatal weakness, for when private enterprise falters in the performance of this all-important creative function, government must assume this responsibility, ideologies to the contrary notwithstanding.   No one who has

---

[1] Horace M. Gray, "Recent Changes in the Public Control of Electric Rates," 17 *Journal of Business* (University of Iowa) 7–10 (March, 1937). In this article I analyzed briefly the contributions of certain new institutions to public control of electric rates and came to the conclusion that they are far more effective in this respect than traditional methods under the public utility doctrine.

studied this phase of the problem carefully can fail to be aware
of the serious shortcomings of private enterprise in these areas,
or of the significant progress made within recent years by
governmental planning. No one today believes seriously
that the scientific control and utilization of water resources,
the perfection of socially adequate national systems of electric
power and electric communications, the conservation of
natural gas, and the rationalization of our chaotic transportation system can be accomplished by private enterprise operating within the framework of the traditional public utility
concept. It is generally recognized that the solution of these
problems will require governmental action of a quite different
order than that involved in public utility regulation. This
action must be positive and creative, it must call into play
powers of government not heretofore brought to bear, it must
rest upon a solid basis of economic and social planning, and it
must be free from the creeping paralysis of judicial interference.

Even the Supreme Court, the legal progenitor of the public
utility concept, appears to entertain some doubt concerning
its own handiwork. In a long series of cases, from *Wolff
Packing Co.* v. *Kansas Industrial Commission* in 1922[1] to *New
State Ice Co.* v. *Liebmann* in 1932,[2] the Court used the public
utility concept as a closed legal category with which to
invalidate efforts of the states to regulate certain types of business. This narrow, legalistic interpretation evoked a rising
tide of criticism, both within and outside the Court, which
reached a peak in the classic dissenting opinion of Mr. Justice
Brandeis in the Ice case. Finally, in *Nebbia* v. *New York*
(1934),[3] Mr. Justice Roberts, for the majority practically
abandoned the traditional position. Admitting explicitly
that the milk business was not, and never had been, considered
a public utility, he held, nevertheless, that the state of New

---

[1] 262 U.S. 522.

[2] 285 U.S. 262.

[3] 291 U.S. 502, 78 L. ed. —, 54 S. Ct. 505, 2 P.U.R. (N.S.) 337.

York, if the legislature saw fit to do so, could fix the price of milk without contravening the Fourteenth Amendment.   In short, the question whether or not the milk business was a public utility, or of such nature that it could properly be so classified, was irrelevant to the main issue. The power to regulate was inherent in the state and could be exercised, both with respect to prices and other matters, if the legislature felt that conditions warranted.   A minority of the Court, however, could not stomach such legal heresy.   Mr. Justice McReynolds (Van Devanter, Sutherland and Butler concurring) wrote a dissenting opinion in which he restated and reaffirmed the traditional doctrine that prices could be regulated only when it was clearly shown that the business in question was a public utility or of such nature that it could be so regarded.   The abandonment of this principle would, he asserted, open the door to almost unlimited public regulation of prices.   This prophecy was of course correct but, as Mr. Justice Roberts pointed out, quite irrelevant.

Certain other established features of the public utility concept have likewise been attacked by individual members of the Court. In *McCart* v. *Indianapolis Water Company* (1938),[1] Mr. Justice Black, in a caustic dissenting opinion, condemned the theory of "reproduction value" as productive of interminable delays and hopeless confusion.   After commenting upon the necessity for judicial prophecy to decide valuation cases, he asked: "Can a judge be found who can accurately devine all future prices of commodities to be used for imaginary reproductions of this company's property?" (P.U.R., p. 471.)   He then goes on to describe the chaotic procedure of valuation:

"it is exceedingly difficult to discern the truth through the maze of formulas and the jungle of metaphysical concepts sometimes conceived, and often fostered, by the ingenuity of those who seek inflated valuations to support excessive rates. . . . Completely lost in the confusion of language—too

---

[1] 302 U.S. 419, 82 L. ed. 336, 58 S. Ct. 324, 21 P.U.R. (N.S.) 465.

frequently invented for the purpose of confusing—Commissions and courts passing upon rates for public utilities are driven to listen to conjectures, speculations, estimates, and guesses, all under the name of 'reproduction costs.'"   (P.U.R., p. 472.)

To illustrate the preposterous claims made in the name of "reproduction value," Mr. Justice Black describes, in a delightfully ironic passage, the trials and tribulations of imaginary sailors attempting to navigate the White River and the "devoted" efforts of the company to facilitate their nautical venture, thereby creating a "value" upon which the users of water in Indianapolis are expected to pay a "fair return."

Mr. Justice Frankfurter (Black concurring), in a recent dissenting opinion,[1] not only declares the Smyth v. Ames formula for valuation "moribund" but shows how the states by various devices have sought to escape it.   He is prepared to approve the constitutionality of the new device involved in this particular case—namely, the temporary rate reduction order with future recoupment if necessary.   In his own words:

"the court's opinion appears to give new vitality needlessly to the mischievous formula for fixing utility rates in Smyth v. Ames. The force of reason, confirmed by events, has gradually been rendering that formula moribund by revealing it to be useless as a guide for adjudication. . . . At least one important state has for decades gone on its way unmindful of Smyth v. Ames, and other states have by various proposals sought to escape the fog into which speculations based on Smyth v. Ames have enveloped the practical task of administering systems of utility regulation. . . . The statute under which the present case arose represents an effort to escape Smyth v. Ames at least as to temporary rates. It is the result of a conscientious and informed endeavor to meet difficulties engendered by legal doctrines which have been widely rejected by the great weight of economic opinion, by authoritative legislative investigations, by utility Commissions throughout the country, and by impressive judicial dissents." (P.U.R., pp. 76–7.)

---

[1] *Driscoll v. Edison Light & Power Co.*, — U.S. —, 83 L. ed. —, 59 S. Ct. 715, 28 P.U.R. (N.S.) 65 (1939).

The valuation doctrine has enjoyed a remarkable vitality but it is difficult to see how it can long withstand such criticism from within the Court itself. In the meantime the states, as Mr. Justice Frankfurter points out, are exercising their ingenuity to find practicable avenues of escape.

Conclusion

The conclusion is inescapable that the public utility concept, as we have known it, lacks survival value in the modern economy;[1] its limited objectives, its inherent contradictions,

[1] Commissioner Jerome Frank, of the Securities and Exchange Commission, reaches the same conclusion in "Investigation of Concentration of Economic Power," *op. cit.*, Pt. 5. He suggests at p. 1954 that the traditional kind of "public utility regulation" ought to be severely modified, if not abandoned, and that certainly it ought not to be applied to other industries. He says (pp. 1955–6): "It doesn't seem to me that in facing new and serious problems we need to rely solely upon mechanisms and contrivances heretofore invented, regardless of their proved partial inadequacy. . . . I don't think we are obliged to fall back upon the analyses made yesterday that the only conceivable way of acting is by Government encroachment upon the activities of industry in the particular form we have used heretofore. . . . We oughtn't, so to speak, to operate on the body politic with rusty or antiquated surgical instruments. . . . I think it would help our thinking on the subject of the possible extension of the category of such industries if we could drop the use of the words 'public utility,' for, unfortunately, that phrase has now associated with it a certain kind of so-called 'regulation.' It might help our thinking if we could invent some new word—I don't know what the word would be; for lack of a better one we might call it 'ugwug'— something that has no emotional connotations, no past history attached to it and therefore doesn't call to mind all the apparatus of our present and, I think, largely inadequate method of dealing with those industries which are now in that category."

Again, p. 1959, he insists that we "must use new devices"; that (p. 1960) "we have done too little experimenting; we have closed our minds by fixed categories of what we call regulation' "; and (p. 1975) "no blanket formula [of regulation] should be applied to all."

David Cushman Coyle, in "Social Control of Production," 206 *Annals of the American Academy* 121–5 (Nov., 1939), advocates a general extension of the public utility category to include a wide range of necessary monopolies but he goes on to say (p. 125) that they should be "socially controlled,

its negative character, and its perversion to anti-social purposes render it impotent for the solution of present-day problems. Like other outmoded institutions, it seems destined to decline in relative significance and ultimately to be superseded by new and socially superior institutions. But the "passing of the public utility concept" is not likely to proceed rapidly. It is deeply rooted in our law and social traditions; powerful economic organizations have a vested interest in its preservation as a protective device; and, as a people, our capacity for "institutional inventiveness" is poorly developed. Hence, the rate of change will probably be determined by our ability to originate and perfect new institutions that are better adapted to modern needs.

The fact, however, that the public utility concept is tending to be superseded should serve as a warning to those who propose to extend its application. Why should an obsolete institution, one that is a demonstrated failure, be extended to embrace additional economic activities? What reason is there to suppose that a system of public control which has proved ineffective in the case of transportation, power, and communications will prove successful in the case of oil, coal, milk, housing, and other forms of enterprise? Why, at the very time when it is being superseded in those areas where it has been operative for many years, should it be extended to new fields where the problems are quite different and the complications more numerous? If additional sectors of our economy need to be brought within the orbit of public control, would it not be more realistic to fashion new institutions for this purpose rather than to rely on a model that has outlived its usefulness?

---

excluded from capitalist motivations, detached from all concern with book profits, and ultimately destined for public ownership." It is obvious that Mr. Coyle envisages a type of regulation quite different from traditional public utility regulation, which does not exclude *capitalist motivations and concern with book profits*, or necessarily lead to public ownership.

The view that the public utility concept is tending toward obsolescence and supersession should not, as one critic feels,[1] be construed as pessimistic or as indicating the inevitability of public ownership.   All institutions are subject to the same evolutionary process in a dynamic society.   They arise in response to definite social needs, serve for a time the purposes for which they were created, eventually become impotent or actually detrimental, and are gradually displaced by new institutions designed to meet new needs.   The observation and analysis of this process in the economic field are proper functions of the economist and should be the objects of scientific inquiry devoid of emotional predilections.   One may experience a certain nostalgia for familiar institutions and apprehension concerning new ones, but this is an emotional reaction, not a scientific judgment.   The passing of an obsolete institution, although it may be noted with regret, is on the whole a proper basis for optimism, because it clears the way for the development of new institutions that are better adapted to contemporary needs.   The exact nature of these new institutions is neither predictable nor inevitable.   Their form will be determined by the interplay of numerous forces, many of which cannot be clearly foreseen or evaluated.   Hence, in the present instance, there is no reason to suppose that the public utility concept will be displaced exclusively by public ownership.   If the spirit of "institutional inventiveness" is given a free rein, many new types of control, not heretofore contemplated, may be developed.   These may differ both from public utility regulation and from present forms of public ownership.   The latter is merely one of several possible alternatives and is by no means inevitable.

---

[1] When this paper was presented in rough outline form at the Mid West Economics Association meeting in Des Moines, Iowa, April, 1939, Professor Sidney Miller of the University of Iowa felt that its implications were unduly pessimistic and that it pointed to public ownership as the only available alternative.

10

THE "CONSUMER" AND "PUBLIC" INTERESTS*
UNDER PUBLIC REGULATION

By Ben W. Lewis†

The Nature of the Consumers' Interest

The planning of an economy, even the public regulation of a single industry, requires that the interests to be affected by the plan or the control be carefully stated. Usually there is no great difficulty in identifying and labeling the interests of particular producer-owner groups immediately involved in control schemes; but authoritative thinking and administrative practice have recently developed a pronounced confusion with reference to the interest of the group to whom, in the last analysis and over the economy as a whole, regulation of industry is of the greatest importance—the consumer. In the case of a number of recent ventures in authoritative control (public and semipublic), both in the United States and abroad—notably in the instance of the National Recovery Administration—there has been added, as a kind of conscience-saving appendage to the public agency in charge of administering the particular scheme, a board or committee whose function it is to represent the consumer, to present and even to press upon the "public-at-large administrative board"

---

* *The Journal of Political Economy*, Volume XLVI, Number 1, February 1938, pages 97–107. Reprinted by the courtesy of the University of Chicago Press and the author.

† Oberlin College.

the special interests of the "consuming public."[1] This tendency to accord special representation to the consumer along with that given to other special interests, such as that of "laborers" and "owners," is growing despite a hazy uncertainty as to its basis in strict logic—i.e., despite the feeling that, after all, the interests of consumers are identical with those public interests which the public administrative board itself is established to represent and protect. The problem became really acute, although largely unrecognized (and, hence, not centered for discussion), in the case of the Consumers' Advisory Board of the National Recovery Administra-

[1] The consumer representation movement was given at least ostensible recognition on a wide front in this country during the early days of the New Deal—witness the Consumers' Counsel of the Agricultural Adjustment Administration, the Consumers' Advisory Board of the National Recovery Administration, and the Consumers' Division of the National Emergency Council. More recently, the Bituminous Coal Act of 1937 provides for a Consumers' Counsel to appear in the interest of the consuming public in any proceeding before the Bituminous Coal Commission. The English counterpart of this movement has found expression in the Food Council, set up by the Prime Minister in 1925 to investigate and report to the president of the Board of Trade, in the interests of consumers or traders, on matters relating to the supply or prices of articles of food; the Consumers' Committees established by the Agricultural Marketing Act, 1931, to represent the interests of consumers of products marketed under approved schemes, and to report to the minister of agriculture and fisheries on the effect on consumers of any scheme; and the committees of investigation provided by the Coal Mines Act, 1930, to investigate complaints made with respect to the operation of any of the coal schemes, and to report to the Board of Trade. The international schemes for the control of tin and rubber have each found it necessary during the course of their operation to provide for advisory representation of industrial consumers: in the case of tin two representatives to be named by American and British tin-plate producers were invited to sit as advisory members of the International Tin Committee, and in the case of rubber a panel named by American and European rubber manufacturers offers advice to the International Rubber Regulation Committee. A "consumers' board" with an interesting combination of advisory and plenary powers is the Irish Free State Prices Commission set up by the Control of Prices Act, 1932.

tion.   The following analysis is undertaken with the experience of the Consumers' Board particularly in mind; but such conclusions as may be valid will have substantial implications for any public-control scheme presently or prospectively in operation.   The analysis will not be concerned directly with the organization to be adopted or the practices to be followed by consumers' advisory agencies, nor will it touch upon the desirability or undesirability of public regulation; the issue is simply whether or not in the administration of any scheme of regulation of industry there should be recognized an identifiable "consumer" interest, to be made the subject of representation by a special agency apart from the board set up to represent and to act for the public in general.[1]

It is easy to assume a tripartite division of interests in industrial transactions and affairs—the interest of the owners of the capital, the interest of the laborers, and the interest of the consumers of the industry's products.   These interests appear clearly when attention is paid to the immediate effects of single, given transactions—when, for instance, consumers are required to give more in return for the industry's products or are induced or forced to take products of a lesser quality; or when labor is in a position to demand more (or less) of the amount which consumers pay, and when the relative position of the parties is such that labor's demands are so transmitted through the owners as to fall upon consumers, or the demands of consumers for cheaper goods are passed by owners on to the shoulders of labor in the form of wage reductions.   The National Recovery Administration recognized and felt the force of this tripartite division in a momentary flash almost at the outset of its operation, and the Consumers' Advisory Board (however little it may have prospered at the hands of

---

[1] The argument will proceed along lines followed in an unpublished report which I made to the N.R.A. during the "study period" which succeeded its active life as a regulatory agency.

the Administration in later months) was the immediate result.[1]
But in the days that followed the Administration grew uneasy;
it was never quite certain whether or not it was on sound foot-
ing (theoretically, administratively, or "tactically") in according representation to consumers on ostensibly the same basis
as and co-ordinately with "industry" and "labor." Having
cast the die the Administration did not seriously threaten
thereafter to refuse recognition of a separate consumer interest,
but its conduct in succeeding months suggested an increasing
doubt. For whatever reasons, the Administration was willing
to continue the "extra" protection which it had granted to
consumers through the creation of the Consumers' Advisory
Board, but it could not rid itself of the feeling that "consumers" and "the public" were coterminous groups, and that
the Administration itself in representing the public interest
really afforded to consumers all the protection which they
required and to which they were entitled.

But the Consumers' Board yielded no ground in this direction. Created, full blown, as an agency to represent and
protect a special, identifiable interest apart from that of the
general public, it permitted itself no serious question as to the
existence of this special interest. It maintained an aggressive
and unyielding front against all suggestions that any agency
designed and established to serve the interest of the total

---

[1] "While the Administration itself is directly responsible for safeguarding the
public welfare and effectuating public policy, the actual consumers' interest
is a matter of primary and acute concern. If that is not watched—at all
times and from every angle—the whole plan may be imperilled. To provide against this the Administration itself has chosen a Consumer's Advisory
Board which is responsible for watching every agreement and every hearing
to see that nothing is done to impair the interest of those whose daily living
may be affected by these agreements" (N.R.A. Release No. 11, June 25,
1933). It should be added that the Consumers' Board was at no time in a
position "to see that nothing is done . . . "; its powers were never other
than advisory, and it was several months before it could take even these
powers for granted.

public could effectively (and even appropriately) protect the special interest of the consumer.   None the less, apart from a few sporadic statements by certain of its members acting as individuals and desultory discussion among the staff advisers, no attempt at an analysis of the identifying marks of the special consumer interest was made by the Board.   The Board bent every effort to protection of the consumers' interest, but it cannot be doubted that failure to analyze the exact character and to lay out the specific bounds of that interest resulted in a noticeable scattering of the Board's fire.

A report transmitted by the Secretary of Agriculture to the Senate[1] sets forth the interest of the business man or "owner" as consisting of scarcity, value, and maximum profits, whereas the interest of the consumer lies in goods and satisfactions. The statement goes on to point out that the public consists of producers (owners, industrialists), laborers, and consumers, and that the role of the government, acting impartially in the interest of the entire public, is to stand between the interest groups, each of which is contending for its own selfish objectives. "To place any Government official in the position of having to represent both the public interest and the consumer interest is to make him both judge of all parties and counsel for one of the parties at interest."[2]   Another statement, issued for confidential circulation among members of the Board and its staff, illustrates the difference between the consumer and the public interests by reference to the cases of cotton textiles and bituminous coal, in both of which "consumers got bargains for years at the expense of misery among workers and bankruptcy of owners."   In these cases, "promotion of the public interest required that the consumers' advantage be

---

[1] *Industrial Prices and Their Relative Inflexibility* (Sen. Doc. 13, 74th Cong., 1st sess. [1935]), pp. 28–30, 32–34.   The author of the report, Dr. Gardiner C. Means, was a member of the Consumers' Advisory Board as well as economic adviser on finance to the Secretary of Agriculture.

[2] *Ibid.*, p. 34.

cut down by public authority acting on behalf of workers and owners."

It seems clear that the interest of particular owners lies in such scarcity as will result in a maximization of profits, and the apparent immediate interest of particular consumers in increased production and lower prices, even at the expense of the particular owners. It is clear, as well, that all industrial owners considered as a group might well fix upon "maximum-profit scarcity" as a group objective, although there would inevitably be uneven gains and hence conflict within the group. But, when one turns to the logically co-ordinate group of industrial consumers, a difficulty which was present in a lesser degree in the simpler illustration now arises in a form which cannot be ignored. The simple fact is that there is no such group: consumers of industrial products are, of necessity, consumers as well of agricultural products and personal services. As consumers of all products and services, they can have no group interest in the unrestrained production of certain goods at the expense of shortage of other goods and services. It must be borne in mind that in an economy, productive resources and instruments employed in one direction are, perforce, rendered incapable of being employed for production in any other direction. It may well be true that consumers of cotton textiles and bituminous coal have been advantaged for years at the expense of laborers and owners, but, since this is a world of scarce resources, any such gain has been at the expense also of other consumers, and at the expense even of themselves as consumers of other products. Because of the misdirection of productive resources consumers in general have been forced to pay higher prices for, and been able to enjoy fewer, goods of other kinds. The total consumer interest, no less than the interest of owners and laborers in the coal and textile industries, could best have been served by a better allocation and direction of the resources which (mistakenly, it is assumed) have found their way into the produc-

tion of coal and textiles.[1]   And what else could be demanded
in the interest of the public?   The public interest must consist
in the fullest use of productive factors (consistent with existing
ideals or standards of leisure) employed in the right direction.
It is difficult to discover any divergence between the interests
of the public and those of the total consuming group.[2]

Of course, any single consumer has a special personal
interest as well as his interest as one of the body of consumers
in general in defending his position in given transactions
against overreaching pressure and demands from other special-
interest groups, but any positive special interest of consumers
can at most relate only to an immediate, short-run concern

---

[1] In this discussion it is necessary frequently to refer, explicitly or by implication, to "correct allocation," "proper allocation," or "better allocation."
It is my belief that the points I am interested in making with reference to
the nature of the consumer and public interests do not depend for their
validity upon any choice between allocation under a price mechanism
assuming present ownership of resources and existing distribution of purchasing power, on the one hand, and any other ownership and distribution
situation, or, indeed, any other system of allocation, on the other hand.   A
discussion of the character of and the mechanism for attaining a "correct
allocation" and a "proper balance," while extremely significant, is not
immediately pertinent and would carry this article far afield.

[2] A possible divergence might be worked out on the following lines: since
people prefer in the main to loaf rather than to labor, it is in the interest of
individuals as producers to produce for a minimum number of hours per
day; since people greatly enjoy the consumption of goods and services, it
is in the interest of each individual as a consumer to advocate maximum
production; individuals taken as a group in their *public* capacity must
establish some compromise point between the two extremes.   But the
apparent divergence can be made to disappear by regarding consumers as
having an interest in the consumption of leisure as well as the consumption
of goods and services.   A similar approach can be had to the problem, say,
of "child labor."   It is difficult for me as a consumer to distinguish between
my satisfaction in obtaining goods of desired quality and my satisfaction in
obtaining goods produced under conditions of which I approve.   I doubt
whether the first is to be denominated a "consumer" satisfaction, and the
second, properly, a "public" satisfaction.

of individual consumers of particular goods in particular transactions. This interest is a compelling one in fact because of the importance which the purchase immediately at hand assumes in relation to more distant, "theoretical" consequences; and also because, when one is concerned with the terms governing the immediate disposition of goods already produced or facilities already dedicated irrevocably to certain uses, one is inclined to neglect the bearing of those terms upon the allocation of factors and direction of production in the future. This immediate interest appears in the case of consumers bargaining across the counter with producers; it appears, too, in special cases of public price determination—e.g., where a public-utilities commission, acting for the public, chooses between or compromises the conflicting special interests of producers and special (immediate) interests of particular consumers. So, too, this immediate consumer interest appeared in each of the thousands of cases that came before the National Recovery Administration, particularly if each case be regarded as a unit in itself rather than as an element in a total economic pattern which the Administration was seeking to draw. It is true that N.R.A. problems and decisions related principally to industrial structure and to practices affecting prices only indirectly, but prices, qualities, and quantities were inevitably involved and affected, and the immediate positive interest (as well as the defensive interest) of the consumers of particular products under consideration was correspondingly at stake.

Under the N.R.A., then, the Administration found itself subjected to conflicting pressures from owners, laborers, and consumers. Owners sought restriction and profits, laborers sought restriction and higher wages, and the immediate consumer interest in lower prices was always present, although rarely pressed. But the general, long-run consumer interest, present and pressed in every case, was flatly opposed to all of these special interests—to the hasty, short-run interest of particular consumers as well as to the interests of the other special groups. It was possible (however ill-advised in particular instances) for the Industrial Advisory Board to represent the special interests both of particular industrial owners and of industrial owners as a group; similarly, it was possible for the Labor Advisory Board to press the special interests of laborers in a particular industry and of industrial laborers in general. But it was never possible for the Consumers' Advisory Board to represent at the same time the immediate interest of particular consumers in excessive production and prices lowered without regard to repercussions throughout the rest of the economy, and the interests of consumers as a whole in the proper distribution and balance of society's productive factors and resources. The Consumers' Board could, logically and consistently, defend the interest of particular consumers as part of the general consumer (and public) interest against special claims of industrial owners or laborers; it could not, consistently with its duty to consumers in general, carry its representation of immediate consumer interests positively beyond the point where those interests ran counter not only to the special interests of owners and laborers but to the larger interests of consumers in general. And consumers' interest, in this latter sense, clearly coincides substantively with the interest of the public.

Representation of the Consumers' Interest

Assuming the validity of the foregoing analysis, what place can be deemed to exist for a board or bureau representing the interest of consumers in a regulatory organization already provided with an administration specially charged to protect the interest of the public? Such a board could defend each group of consumers as, in succession, each group came to be considered vis-à-vis its co-ordinate groups of owners and laborers against such demands as the board deemed unwarranted on general public grounds; but if it stopped at this point and failed to urge the special, immediate claims of consumers its activity would be in no way inconsistent with the duties of an agency representing the public in general.[1]   The Consumers' Advisory Board was a representative of consumers in general, and the Recovery Administration which it advised was an appointed guardian of the public interest.   The experience of the Consumers' Board in its relation to the Administration raises sharply the issue as to whether such a board is called for by the demonstrated needs of such a situation as that which faced the Recovery Administration.   The answer of experience is in the affirmative.

The diversity in function between agencies representing consumers n general and those acting for the general public springs, not from any diversity in the substantive, long-run economic interests which they represent, but from a natural diversity in the interests and capacities-to-act of the agencies. An administrative agency is, after all, responsible for action. It must make decisions and those decisions must work.   It has a duty to protect the general public interest—but, by the very nature of its task, it is bound to vest the term "public interest" with a meaning in which far-reaching, economic considerations are modified by considerations of governmental expediency.   It must, in the public interest, and within the highly flexible limits fixed by that interest as influenced by

---

[1] As a special consumers' advocate, the board's immediate objectives would be extremely narrow—special advantages for each consumer group in turn.   Such a board should be staffed by men trained and experienced in the technical details of the industries or trades involved; indeed, industries or trades who were themselves consumers (in process) of the products of other industries and trades might be expected to support a board of this type and to "lend" some of their own employees as staff members.   It might be well for strategic reasons that the staff be trained in broader economic philosophy, but such training would bear little relevance to the avowed objectives of the board, and if, perchance, it came to affect too strongly the board's aims and activities, the "broader" training would be a positive detriment.

political factors, reconcile conflicting contentions and pressures, and merge them into a program of action. And that program, although designed to express and achieve a goal consistent with the interest of the general public, may in any instance be quite different from a program which long-run economic (consumer) considerations alone would have dictated.

Further, by virtue of our centuries-old judicial tradition which conditions the atmosphere and operations even of our administrative tribunals, the public board must be impartial, if not completely "passive," in its approach. In this situation it is imperative that the general consumer interest be pressed with skill, vigorous determination, and courage by an agency specially designated and equipped to perform the task. In the atmosphere of a trial, unrepresented interests of a "general" character are bound to be slighted even by the best-intentioned tribunal. The entire public consumes, and in this capacity it is interested in its own long-run economic welfare; but, as individual producers, members of the public have an active interest which they will urge positively as against general consumer interests in particular goods, and in disregard of the implications of their producer position for their own more remote general interests as consumers.

The conception of a public administrative agency established to serve the general public interest, played upon by special, articulate interests, leaves room for an agency acting in an advisory capacity designed to work out and press for the adoption of an administrative program expressive of the general consumer interest—the unalloyed, nonpolitical, long-run economic interest of the general public.[1] Such an agency is not to be confused with a mere fact-finding bureau. A

---

[1] This is not to suggest that the consumer board may not find it necessary, as part of its own strategy or tactics of persuasion, occasionally to make concessions, to compromise, and to "bargain" with the board or the representatives of other interests.

fact-finding bureau should exist, of course, either as a part of or separate from the consumers' board, but the peculiar function of the consumer agency per se is to advise on matters of policy and not merely to uncover and arrange factual data. In a very real sense, a consumers' board, counterpoised against representatives of narrower group interests, is in a position to serve as a "public conscience" with reference to the presumably impartial public administrative authority,[1] and to counteract group pressures which threaten too marked a deviation of policy from the path pointed by basic, general economic considerations.   It might be added that, where the public administrative agency has a promoting as well as a decision-making function, and where, for whatever reasons, its point of view is almost admittedly "industrial," the necessity for the presence in the organization of a board charged with the task of representing the general consumer interest is even more apparent.

This conception of a general consumer interest coinciding with the interest of the general public, and yet requiring for its effective expression a separate consumers' board to give advice to the governmental agency acting for the general

---

[1] This raises the question, of course, as to whether the public authority which is to be advised on consumer interests is, itself, to appoint the advisers, and from what group. I suggest that the members of any consumer advisory agency be appointed by public authority outside of the particular agency whose "conscience is to be kept"—by the President, in case a federal agency is involved.   They should be drawn from that portion of the general public whose special interests as producers or laborers are not directly involved in matters on which advice is to be given.   Probably the reason why the best consumer representatives in the N.R.A. were to be found in the ranks of the professions and technicians was not because these groups are "purer" than others, but because the N.R.A. held out no possibilities to them as producers.   Consumer representatives might well come from the ranks of voluntary consumer organizations, but only in so far as this suggests an interest on their part and possibly some professional competence, and not because of their "point of view."

public, received a most thoroughgoing operative test during the life of the National Recovery Administration.   There will be few who will argue that the Consumers' Advisory Board did not in fact perform (the quality of the performance is not here in issue) a necessary and worth-while function in the work of the Recovery Administration.   Yet the work of the Consumers' Board had little purpose or meaning save in terms of a general as distinct from a narrow, immediate consumer interest.   The Board was never staffed to represent particular, special interests, and those interests gave it only a minimum of active support.[1]   The Board and its staff had little interest in pressing the claim of special consuming interests beyond the point set by purely defensive considerations—i.e., the point at which they coincided with the interests of consumers in general.   The policies advanced by the Board and the arguments employed in behalf of the policies ran exclusively along lines directed to the establishment and maintenance of a desirable economic system as a whole—a system responsive to the economic demands of the total community.   It urged the preservation—indeed, the creation— of elasticity and flexibility in the country's productive and distributive mechanism; and it fought against the establishment of artificial rigidities calculated to protect existing properties and equities at the expense of the rest of the community.   Almost alone among governmental agencies at the time it was the avowed foe of the hysteria of restrictionism which swept the country as an outgrowth of the depression.

But in all this the Board, although its mode of expression took the form principally of reports on particular codes, made its stand not in the special interest of particular consumers, but in the balanced interest of all consumers.   Every one of its

---

[1] Indeed, in certain instances, the industrial interests of particular parties were so strong that they preferred to sacrifice openly and completely their interests as industrial consumers, and specifically disclaimed any allegiance to the Consumers' Board.

hundreds of individual code reports formed a part of a total consistent pattern. The Board may almost be said to have been unaware of the possibility of urging the advancement of particular consumers at the expense of the general public (consumers in general).

And yet, throughout its life, there always lurked an uncertainty that softened the Board's attack. Consumers' Board code advisers, ostensibly co-ordinate with labor and industrial advisers, were aware, without being able to specify the difference, that they were in reality upon a different plane— doing a different kind of work. Neither the Board nor the Administration halted their feverish activity to make an inquiry whose carefully spelled-out answer, acting imperceptibly, might greatly have increased the Board's effectiveness and saved the Administration many regrets. There was a job to be done and the Board was doing it. But it needed to know explicitly the nature and limits of its task, and why this Board was called upon to perform it.

11

THE CONSERVATION OF OIL*

By Northcutt Ely†

I

Through all the law governing petroleum production there
runs this twofold problem: a very large potential production,
or "presently producible surplus," must be restricted in order
to avoid physical waste of the commodity and the demoraliza-
tion of markets, yet the total known domestic supply is adequate for only a few years' demand, and the continuity of
that supply is dependent upon continuing success in finding
new oil pools. In reaching for the dual objectives of conservation and stabilization, the industry has invoked the aid
of the legislatures and the courts in developing a regulatory
mechanism which is peculiar to this resource, and which
involves an unusual interplay of federal and state powers of
regulation. Before examining this system, however, it may be
helpful to establish certain points in the physical perspective.

The United States currently produces about sixty per cent
of the world's oil.[1] Sixty-four per cent of all oil produced
since the industry's beginning, in 1857, has come out of our
soil. Presently known American reserves are estimated at
about one-fifth the total world reserves, or from thirteen to

---

* *Harvard Law Review*, Volume LI, Number 7, May 1938, pages 1209–
1244. Reprinted by the courtesy of the Harvard Law Review Association, and the author.

† Washington, D.C.

[1] American Petroleum Institute, Petroleum Facts and Figures (1937)
60.

sixteen billion barrels,[1] which is about twelve or thirteen times one year's domestic consumption. But because extraction of that reserve would require a much longer period, it has been estimated that there is a possibility of domestic shortage by 1940, and a strong probability of it by 1945.[2] The essential function of discovery in the operation of this industry differentiates oil from the other minerals.[3] Copper reserves, for instance, likewise amount to the equivalent of about thirteen years' production (excluding secondary or scrap copper), but no major discoveries have been made since 1905.[4] The growth of the country's dependence on petroleum is evidenced by the fact that automobile registrations in 1920 were 9,231,941, whereas in 1937 they totalled 29,613,900.

---

[1] A committee of the American Petroleum Institute, on February 3, 1938, estimated that proven reserves in the United States as of January 1, 1938, after allowing for the production of 1,277,644,000 barrels in 1937, was 15,507,268,000 barrels. The Oil and Gas Journal (issue of Jan. 27, 1938, p. 39) estimated them at 13,489,458,000 as of the same date. For other estimates, within the same range of figures, see Pogue, The Economic Structure of the American Petroleum Industry, THIRD WORLD POWER CONFERENCE (1936) Section II, paper No. 5; Garfias and Whetsel, Proven Oil Reserves (1936) 118 TRANS. AMER. INST. MIN. & MET. ENGINEERS [hereafter abbreviated A. I. M. E.] 211; U. S. Bureau of Mines, Conservation of Petroleum and of Natural Gas, THIRD WORLD POWER CONFERENCE (1936) Section IV, paper No. 12, p. 10.

[2] See Snider and Brooks (Jan. 1936) 20 BULL. AM. ASS'N PETROLEUM GEOLOGISTS 15–50. The question is not necessarily one of how soon the domestic reserves will be exhausted, but rather when the available withdrawals will be controlled by the price factor. See U. S. Bureau of Mines, op. cit. supra note 1 above, at 11.

[3] For discussions of the economic functions and effects of the discovery rate, see a series of papers by Dr. Joseph E. Pogue: The Economic Structure of the American Petroleum Industry, THIRD WORLD POWER CONFERENCE (1936), particularly at 11–14; An Equilibrium Theory of Proration (Feb. 1938) A. I. M. E. TECHNICAL PUBLICATION No. 904; The Economic Aspects of Drilling (Mar. 17, 1938) OIL AND GAS J. 42.

[4] REPORT OF THE MINERAL RESOURCES COMMITTEE TO THE NATIONAL RESOURCES BOARD, 1935.

Domestic production of crude oil in 1920 was 442,929,000 barrels; in 1937 it was 1,277,653,000 barrels. During the same period the production of motor fuel (principally gasoline) rose from 118,022,000 barrels to 570,979,000. Per capita consumption of oil products increased from 4.31 barrels in 1920 to 9.30 in 1937.[1] Whereas 1936 production of bituminous coal was only 83 per cent of the 1923–25 average, that of oil was 149 per cent.[2]

To meet this rate of growth in demand for oil products, the industry has been dependent upon two general classes of effort. The first comprises improved technology, in the phases of exploration, production and refining. These include use of the seismograph, magnetometer, and other devices; improved drilling methods, enabling deeper horizons to be penetrated; greater refinery utilization of crude oil, resulting in an increased yield of gasoline per barrel of oil; and so on. The second comprises legislative restrictions on the drilling and production of oil wells.

As to technologic advances:

The aggregate of new discoveries (including extensions of old fields) has exceeded the aggregate of domestic production during the past decade.[3] Improved drilling methods have increased the maximum depth of wells from 7,319 feet in 1924 to more than 14,400 feet in 1938. Greater refinery efficiencies, achieved through cracking heavy hydrocarbons into lighter ones, and more recently through the reverse process of polymerization, or building up light volatile hydro-

---

[1] Figures from the Bureau of Mines.

[2] AMERICAN PETROLEUM INSTITUTE, PETROLEUM FACTS AND FIGURES (1937) 66.

[3] The term "discoveries" is confusing. The estimates of known reserves have risen in consequence of four factors: (1) the finding of completely new oil areas; (2) lateral and vertical extensions of old fields; (3) increase in the recovery factor applicable to old areas; (4) normal revisions, due to miscellaneous causes. The first element is not necessarily the major one.

carbons into gasoline, have cut in half the quantity of crude that would have been required by the 1937 demands for gasoline if the 1920 technique had been the best available.[1]

In thus developing supplies adequate for a rapidly growing demand, the industry has solved the problem without outside help. By contrast, in controlling the output of the crude supply so successfully created by individual initiative, the industry has invited and received an extraordinary amount of governmental planning and control.

In charting this phase of the petroleum law it is well to remember that although oil is produced in twenty-two states, in 1937 the three states of Texas, California and Oklahoma produced 76 per cent of all the country's output. Add Louisiana and Kansas and this figure rises to nearly 89 per cent. Exclude these five states, and the production of the East Texas field alone exceeds that of the other seventeen states combined. Texas accounts altogether for about 40 per cent.[2] The growing dominance of Texas is the prevailing characteristic of the oil production problem, and hence of the oil legislation. As recently as 1928 Texas' share of the country's production was less than 29 per cent; in 1918 it was only 9.8 per cent.[3] Significant as to the future is Texas' dominance in proven reserves: nearly one-half of the nation's are hers; California is second, with about a quarter; and Oklahoma, third largest current producer, has less than one-thirteenth.[4] The law's foundations were laid in older producing states whose courts now seldom see an oil conservation

---

[1] AMERICAN PETROLEUM INSTITUTE, PETROLEUM FACTS AND FIGURES (1937) 118.

[2] In 1937 the United States produced in round figures 1,277,000,000 barrels, of which Texas contributed 503,000,000, California 239,000,000, Oklahoma 223,000,000, Louisiana 90,000,000, Kansas 69,000,000. East Texas produced about 170,000,000.

[3] 5 REP. FED. OIL CONS. BD. (1932). Chart B.

[4] See sources cited *supra*, note 1, page 319.

case; its growth is at present very largely in the hands of the legislature and courts of Texas, for one decision in that jurisdiction may open or close more production in a single field than a year's accumulation of cases in all the other states together.

Again, it is well to realize that the recent developments of the law are a heritage of an extraordinary period of discovery, between 1926 and 1931, whose economic consequences coincided in point of time with the ensuing depression period. In 1920, the best available data indicated that the "unmined supply" in 1930 would not exceed 3.2 billion barrels.[1] Actually, it was well over 20 billion in that year, according to present data. Between 1926 and 1931 the fields of Seminole, Oklahoma City, Kettleman Hills, and, preeminently, East Texas, were discovered. At least 10 billion barrels were added to the supply during this time, of which 5.5 billion were produced and 4.5 billion were added to reserves, or to the "presently producible surplus." During this period twelve jurisdictions added new conservation legislation to their books.[2] Most of the current conservation and stabiliza-

---

[1] POGUE, ECONOMICS OF PETROLEUM (1921) 20.

[2] The period 1929–32 witnessed enactment of conservation laws by the following jurisdictions: *United States* (unit operation on the public domain), 46 STAT. 1523 (1931), 30 U. S. C. § 226 (1934), supplemented by Interior Dept. Regulations of April 4, 1932 [reprinted in ELY, THE OIL AND GAS CONSERVATION STATUTES, ANNOTATED (1933) 21–23]; *California*, Laws 1929, c. 535 (gas-oil ratio statute); Laws 1931, c. 585 (proration, repealed by referendum); Laws 1931, c. 586 (spacing); Laws 1931, c. 791; *Kansas* (proration), Laws 1931, c. 226; *Louisiana* (miscellaneous), Act 45 of 1930; *Michigan* (general conservation laws), MICH. COMP. LAWS (1929) §§ 5696–5722, 11632–11662; Act 185 of 1931; *Mississippi* (conservation, proration), Laws 1932, c. 117; *New Mexico* (general conservation laws and unit operation), N. M. STAT. ANN. (Courtright, 1929) § 97; *Oklahoma* (revision of the conservation laws), OKLA. STAT. (Harlow, 1931) § 59; *Texas* (proration and market demand), Acts 42d Leg., 1st Called Sess. (1931) c. 26; 42d Leg., 4th Called Sess. (1932) c. 2; *West Virginia* (general conservation), W. VA. CODE ANN. (1932) § 2464 *et seq.; Wyoming* (unit operation), WYO. REV.

tion laws, and the majority of the conservation decisions, are the product of the decade 1926–36. To a great degree, these laws compose a set of economic balances for an industry as a whole, rather than a set of criteria for judging private quarrels. Because of their rapid and continuing development, an appraisal of them is as much a task of prognosis as it is of diagnosis.

II

At the base of the present day production-control structure is the power of the state government to restrict the flow of the individual well; but because of the complexity of that subject, a survey of government's relation to the producing industry, beginning at the top of the pyramid, gives a clearer perspective than the reverse process.

The present mechanism of control follows, with important exceptions, the pattern outlined by the Federal Oil Conservation Board, and particularly by its chairman, Dr. Ray Lyman Wilbur, in a series of reports from 1929 to 1933.[1] It has four phases: First, the determination of the probable demand, and the allocation among areas of the country of the production required to meet certain components of that demand. This is done through a federal fact-finding service, centered in the Bureau of Mines. Second, the cooperation of the producing states through an interstate compact. Third, federal regulation of interstate and foreign commerce in petroleum and its products. Fourth, the enforcement of these interrelated production quotas by the various states, each acting through its own regulatory body. In each phase there is a measure

---

STAT. ANN. (Courtright, 1931) § 91–801. And see also *Alberta*, Act of March 28, 1931; *Ohio*, Laws 1931, p. 603; *South Dakota*, Laws 1929, c. 202.

[1] See 1 and 5 REP. FED. OIL CONS. BD. (1926 and 1931); REP. SEC'Y INT. (1931) 24; statement of Secretary Wilbur to a committee of the American Petroleum Institute, April 12, 1929, quoted in ELY, OIL CONSERVATION THROUGH INTERSTATE AGREEMENT (1933) 18.

of cooperation between state and federal governments and industry.

This composite stabilization machinery did not come into existence spontaneously. It grew out of the flood of over-production in 1930–32, occasioned by the discovery of the East Texas field. In the face of the depression, and of the first decline in the rate of growth of the demand for gasoline, the production in that field mounted from nothing in early 1930 to over 1,000,000 barrels per day in 1931. The price of crude oil dropped from over 90 cents to less than 10 cents per barrel. Attempts of the Texas Railroad Commission to stabilize East Texas' production at approximately 400,000 barrels daily were repeatedly invalidated by a three-judge federal court. The difference between that figure and the field's daily open flow production of better than 1,000,000 barrels was greater than the production of either Oklahoma or California. In 1934 after every proration order from 1931 to 1934 had been struck down by the federal court, and after repeated amendments of the statute and an experiment with marital law, an order fixing production at 400,000 barrels daily was finally sustained.[1]

Paralyzed by the inflow into their market of a wholly new supply greater than the entire production of either of the second and third ranking states, the regulatory bodies of Oklahoma and Kansas, with the encouragement of the Federal Oil Conservation Board, made an agreement in 1931 with the Railroad Commission and Governor of Texas allocating production among those three states.[2] Despite the lack of adequate proration statutes in Texas, and the necessity of resorting

---

[1] Amazon Petroleum Corp. v. Railroad Comm., 5 F. Supp. 633 (E. D. Tex. 1934); cf. note 2, page 335, infra. For a history of attempts to control East Texas' production, see Hardwicke, *Legal History of Proration of Oil Production in Texas* (1937) 56 TEX. BAR ASS'N REPORTS 99.

[2] See REP. SEC'Y INT. (1931) 25. For the text of the agreement see ELY, *op. cit. supra* note 1, page 323, at 21, n.11.

to marital law by the governors of Texas and Oklahoma in the attempt to enforce production quotas, this agreement produced a temporary sort of stability and introduced the states to the cooperative system. But the invalidation of martial law in East Texas[1] resulted in a new rise in production and in a crisis which grew until the enactment of the National Recovery Act.[2] The petroleum Code established under that act corresponded in large degree with the general regulatory machinery which had been recommended by the Federal Oil Conseration Board, introducing, however, a Planning and Coordinating Committee representing the industry, and a Petroleum Administrative Board, representing the Government. The Petroleum Administrative Board was intended to work directly with the state regulatory bodies rather than through the medium of an interstate agreement.[3]

Following the invalidation of the Code, the industry returned with greater seriousness to the study of the interstate compact program.

The four-phase regulatory system, evolved in this manner, functions now as follows:

(1) The fact-finding carried on by the Bureau of Mines is a process for estimating demand for gasoline (based largely on automobile registrations and use), fuel oil, and other products, and equating that composite demand for finished products back to crude production. The process is capable of a high degree of accuracy. Thus, the amount by which stocks of all oils increased between April 1, 1937, and April 1, 1938 (about 45,000,000 barrels), reckoned back into crude-oil

---

[1] Constantin v. Smith, 57 F. (2d) 227 (E. D. Tex. 1932), aff'd, 287 U. S. 378 (1932).

[2] For a dramatic account of the growth of the over-production crisis, see the Government briefs in Panama Refining Co. v. Ryan, 293 U. S. 388 (1935); Hardwicke, op. cit. supra note 1, page 324, at 105.

[3] See WATKINS, OIL: STABILIZATION OR CONSERVATION? (1937) 72. The operation of the petroleum Code terminated in 1935 in consequence of the decision in Schechter Poultry Co. v. United States, 295 U. S. 495 (1935).

equivalents, very closely approximates the quantity by which crude production during that period exceeded the recommendations of the Bureau.[1]

The forecasting service has operated in various forms for eight years. Beginning in 1930, the Federal Oil Conservation Board drew together a volunteer committee; this committee and its successors published eight reports covering the period from April 1, 1930, to June 30, 1933. Notwithstanding the violent fluctuations in price during that period, these forecasts were accurate within a very few per cent.[2] This function, assumed in 1933 by the Bureau of Mines, is one feature of national planning which has operated successfully before, during and after the code period.

(2) On February 16, 1935, the states of Texas, Oklahoma, California, Kansas, New Mexico, Colorado and Illinois entered into an oil conservation compact obligating each state to enact and enforce conservation laws, and to cooperate through an interstate commission which has "power to recommend the coordination of the exercise of the police powers of the several states within their several jurisdictions to promote the maximum ultimate recovery from the petroleum reserves of said states, and to recommend measures for the maximum ultimate recovery of oil and gas."[3] This is a roundabout way of

---

[1] See transcript of proceedings of the Interstate Oil Compact Commission, Jan. 18, 1938, p. 20 *et seq.*, and appendix. The mechanics for determining demand are described in HEARINGS, Part 2, on H. Res. 441, 73d Cong. (1934) 1298.

[2] FEDERAL OIL CONSERVATION BOARD, SURVEY OF NATIONAL PETROLEUM REQUIREMENTS FOR SEASONAL PERIODS OF 1932–1931–1930 (1932). These eight forecasts were never less than 95.5 per cent accurate, although wholly advisory and informal. For a tabulation, see ELY, OIL CONSERVATION THROUGH INTERSTATE AGREEMENT (1933) 238, n.1, 262. For 1937, the Bureau of Mines' estimate on the total gasoline demand was high by six-tenths of one per cent.

[3] For the text of the Compact, see H. R. Doc. No. 306, 75th Cong., 1st Sess. (1937).

saying that the Commission is authorized to bring together the regulatory bodies of the states for discussion of the Bureau of Mines' allocations, and to try to reach an agreement to put them in effect. The Compact was ratified by all but California. The contemplated uniform conservation laws have never been formulated. Such laws, set up by Article 3 of the Compact, have for their objectives the prevention of six kinds of waste: operation at an inefficient gas-oil ratio, destruction of productive formations, escape of gas into the open air, creation of unnecessary fire hazards, drilling operations resulting in loss in the ultimate recovery from the reservoir, and "the inefficient, excessive or improper use of reservoir energy in producing any well." The conservation laws under which the states actually function generally antedate the Compact, and are discussed in later paragraphs.

The Compact is the partial fulfillment of the recommendation in the fifth Report of the Federal Oil Conservation Board (1932) of a compact which would obligate each of the states to enforce production quotas agreed upon by a joint federal and state fact-finding body.[1] However, as now constituted, the fact-finding body is wholly federal, the interstate body is without federal participation, and the states are not committed to enforce quotas. The compacting states were unwilling to admit the Federal Government into participation. In this respect the Compact veers as far in one direction as the Code did in the other. However, in practice, the informal relations of the two groups are very good. A considerable number of states have regulatory bodies described later, which have fact-finding duties comparable to those of the Bureau of Mines. Notwithstanding the absence of any commitment to place the Bureau of Mines' recommendations in effect locally, the compacting states have done so, within reasonable limits.[2] The Compact lacks the adherence of

[1] See ELY, op. cit. supra note 2, page 326, at 216–20, 227–34.

[2] For a detailed tabulation of variations between Bureau of Mines recom-

Louisiana, California, Wyoming, Arkansas and Michigan, of the major producing states, but the sessions of the Compact Commission have been attended by representatives of these states, as well as of Pennsylvania and Indiana. Notwithstanding the limited membership, the Compact has functioned as a reasonably satisfactory clearing house.

(3) In this general stabilization system the Federal Government performs two important collateral functions: the regulation of imports, and the regulation of commerce in oil produced in violation of state production quotas.

Imports, an important factor during the 'twenties, and a controversial one during the growth of proration, had been stabilized under an agreement sponsored by the Federal Oil Conservation Board in 1932.[1] A tariff on oil and gasoline, under the name of an excise tax, was imposed by the Revenue Act of 1932, reenacted in 1935 and again in 1937.[2] Imports now account for less than 5 per cent of the total supply.[3]

The federal "hot oil" statutes appear to be a permanent part of the control measures. Enacted first as Section 9(c) of the National Industrial Recovery Act,[4] and invalidated on the ground of excessive delegation of power by the decision in *Panama Refining Co. v. Ryan*,[5] the policy of the law was embodied in the so-called Connally Act[6] which was reenacted in 1937.

---

mendations and actual performance by the states, 1935–1937 inclusive, see the appendix to the proceedings of the Interstate Oil Compact Commission, January 18, 1938.

[1] See 5 REP. FED. OIL CONS. BD. (1932) i; REP. SEC'Y INT. (1932) 30. An appendix to the former (p. 24) proposed a flexible tariff or quota plan to control imports.

[2] 47 STAT. 259 (1932), 26 U. S. C. 1185 (1934), reenacted by 49 STAT. 431 (1935) and 50 STAT. 358, 26 U. S. C. 362 (Supp. 1937).

[3] In 1937 imports were 57,152,000 barrels, out of a total new supply of over 1,386,141,000 barrels.

[4] 48 STAT. 200 (1933), 16 U. S. C. § 709(c) (1934).

[5] 293 U. S. 388 (1935).

[6] 49 STAT. 30 (1935), reenacted by 50 STAT. 257, 15 U. S. C. § 715 (Supp. 1937).

The Connally Act declared to be "contraband" all oil, and the products of such oil, produced, transported or withdrawn from storage in violation of the laws, regulations and orders of any state, and provided for the forfeiture of such contraband if shipped or transported in interstate commerce. The statute is enforced by the Interior Department through a system of "tenders" or permits to ship.[1]

(4) From this preliminary survey it should appear that the whole regulatory system is now predicated upon the existence of power in the state to restrict production. The following paragraphs deal with the "rule of capture," against which this authority is exerted, and the manner of the exercise of the state's power.

III

Three factors have been primarily responsible for the oil industry's appeal for governmental regulation of production: the "rule of capture"; the differing characteristics of "flush" (flowing) pools and "settled" (pumping) ones; and the interstate character of the petroleum market. At the base and root of all other problems, however, is the first of these.

The natural producing unit is the single oil pool. But access to this common reservoir is controlled by diversified surface ownership, or "leases." Oil was first discovered in Pennsylvania. In disputes between lessor and lessee, it became necessary to state a rule of property as to this fugacious mineral. Pennsylvania, at that time, was a recent convert to the English rule of percolating waters founded on *Acton v.*

---

[1] See statement of Harold L. Ickes, Secretary of the Interior, before the Senate Finance Subcommittee, Feb. 12, 1937; REP. ATT'Y GEN'L (1936). The Connally Act has been sustained in President of the U. S. v. Artex Refinery Sales Corp., 11 F. Supp. 189 (S. D. Tex. 1935); Federal Tender Board No. 1 v. Haynes Oil Corp., 80 F.(2d) 468 (C. C. A. 5th, 1935); Griswold v. President of the U. S., 82 F.(2d) 922 (C. C. A. 5th, 1936); Panama Ref. Co. v. Railroad Comm., 16 F. Supp. 289 (W. D. Texas 1936); Gibson v. Stiles, 90 F.(2d) 998 (C. C. A. 5th, 1937).

Blundell.[1] That rule, it will be recalled, does not recognize correlative rights in an underground reservoir, but accords to each well owner an unlimited right of withdrawal.[2] The Pennsylvania courts applied that rule to oil and gas, although apparently recognizing the power of the legislature to enforce a different one.[3] Unfortunately, no legislature attempted to do so until the principle had been universally accepted as the basic property law.[4] This offspring of *Acton v. Blundell* has been accepted as the common law as to oil even in states which have repudiated the parent doctrine as to percolating waters, such as California.[5] The result, in the absence of legislative restriction, has been to require the development of oil fields in a manner diametrically opposite to that favored by the physical conditions underground.

An oil pool is an engine; it represents an equilibrium of rock pressure, gas pressure and underlying water pressure. Pierced

---

[1] 12 M. & W. 324 (Ex. 1843).

[2] *Cf.* Chasemore v. Richards, 7 H. L. Cas. 349 (1859); Grand Junction Canal Co. v. Shugar, L. R. 6 Ch. App. 481 (1871).

[3] See Brown v. Vandegrift, 80 Pa. 142, 147, 148 (1875); Westmoreland etc. N. Gas Co. v. De Witt, 130 Pa. 235, 18 Atl. 725 (1889); Marshall and Meyers, *Legal Planning of Petroleum Production* (1931) 41 YALE L. J. 33, 42.

[4] The extension of the English rule as to percolating waters into the American law of oil and gas is traced in Jones v. Forest Oil Co., 194 Pa. 379, 44 Atl. 1074 (1900); Williamson v. Jones, 39 W. Va. 231, 19 S. E. 436 (1894); Higgins Oil and Fuel Co. v. Guaranty Oil Co., 145 La. 233, 82 So. 206 (1919); Frazier v. Brown, 12 Ohio St. 294 (1861); SUMMERS, OIL AND GAS (1927) 73, n.13; *id.,* c. 76. For a recent restatement of the rule of capture at common law, see Thompson v. Consolidated Gas Utilities Corp., 300 U. S. 55, 68 (1937). For recent appraisals of the rule's effect, see Oliver, *Can the Rule of Capture be Rationalized?* (1937) 123 TRANS. A. I. M. E. (PETROLEUM DIVISION) 133; Cadman, *Conservation of Petroleum,* THIRD WORLD POWER CONFERENCE (1936); Hardwicke, *The Rule of Capture and its Implications as Applied to Oil and Gas* (1935) 13 TEX. L. REV. 391.

[5] Katz v. Walkinshaw, 141 Cal. 116, 70 Pac. 663 (1902), 74 Pac. 766 (1903). See the distinction attempted to be drawn between oil and percolating waters, at 141 Cal. 134, 74 Pac. 772.

by a well, these forces propel oil or gas or water, or all three, to the surface.[1] The fundamental concept of the early cases was that an oil well produced oil, as a spring might produce water, and was itself, consequently, the subject of a property right. But, from an engineering standpoint, it has been said that the well is nothing but a vertical pipe line which permits the reservoir, as an engine, to transport oil to the surface of the lease,[2] just as a horizontal pipe line is a means permitting a pump to transport oil from the lease to the refinery. Once placed in production, an oil pool is now known to change its underground characteristics. The lessening of the pressure around the well permits the gas which is dissolved in the oil to expand, propelling that oil through the pores of the rock or sand to the well. Concurrently, the underlying water, under a hydrostatic head, pushes upward, driving oil through the rock pores ahead of it. Under ideal conditions, those natural underground forces, i.e., "water drive," gas pressure, and so on, may be so harnessed and controlled as to lift to the surface 90 to 95 per cent of the oil contained in the reservoir, by flowing, over a long period of years.[3] But when oil is produced without restriction, the engine figuratively races itself to pieces: the gas, which has accumulated on top of the oil, is blown off; the underlying water rushes up through the oil-bearing sand to the well, and traps off oil; and the gas dissolved in the oil is permitted to escape so rapidly that the remaining oil is left too thick and viscous to be propelled through the rock by the diminishing pressure.[4] The well

---

[1] Cf. 5 REP. FED. OIL CONS. BD. (1932) appendix 2, at 20; Hardwicke, loc. cit. supra note 4, page 330; Progress Report of the Topical Committee on Allocation of Production, A. P. I. Release, 1934.

[2] Foley, Proration of Allowable Oil Production, A. P. I. Release, June 2, 1937.

[3] Moore, The Effect of Curtailment on Ultimate Recovery, A. P. I. Release, 1934.

[4] A standard reference on the function of natural gas underground is MILLER, FUNCTION OF NATURAL GAS IN THE PRODUCTION OF OIL (1929).

then has to be pumped, producing much smaller quantities at a much higher cost. The result, under the American system of ownership, is that in the older fields which were operated without restriction during their flush periods, from 75 to 90 per cent of the oil has been left underground and capable of production only at a slow rate through pumping, or perhaps ultimately by mining methods.[1] Certain fields in foreign countries, where the concessions were large enough to embrace the entire pool as a single operating unit (in contrast with the American unit of the single lease), have been so drilled and produced as to yield, by flowing, almost the full theoretical recovery.[2]

A corollary of the rule of capture is the dominance of the flush-pool areas over areas of settled production. Because of the haste, necessitated by the rule of capture, in getting oil to the surface before a neighbor drains it away underground, the new pool is rapidly drilled by wells so located as to offset each other, and the reservoir energy is expended at an excessive rate. This period of flush production frequently forces from one-quarter to one-half the pool's entire recoverable production onto the market during a brief period, comprising, perhaps, a tenth or less of the field's total life.[3] During this

---

[1] About one-half of the oil produced to date in the United States was produced before 1926—that is, before the stabilization era and without proration. Many fields discovered before 1926 are still producing, but their flush production was recovered by inefficient methods and over-all efficiencies will be low. Some of them will leave 90 per cent of the oil in the ground. The percentage of oil that will be left unrecovered in fields discovered since 1926 has been estimated to be 55 or 60 per cent. U. S. Bureau of Mines, *Conservation of Petroleum and Natural Gas*, THIRD WORLD POWER CONFERENCE (1936), Section IV, paper No. 12.

[2] See Cadman, *Conservation of Petroleum*, THIRD WORLD POWER CONFERENCE (1936) *passim*, for comparisons of operations in specific American and Iranian (Persian) unit-operated fields.

[3] A study made in 1928, before proration was widely effective, said: "One year after reaching peak production, oil fields show, on an average, a falling

period of incandescent activity, the oil from that pool, produced at low lifting cost by the initial reservoir energy, usurps the markets of all settled pools. Oil once produced will find a market. The rule of capture prevents storage underground, and the hazards of above-ground storage, coupled with the limited space available to the small leaseholder, necessitate selling the oil for whatever price can be obtained. This has necessitated the second phase of proration: proration or allocation of quotas among pools with a view to controlling inter-pool competition.[1]

A third, but less direct result of the rule of capture, is the distortion of interstate competition. It is this effect which has necessitated the superposition, first, of the Code structure, then of the Compact, previously discussed. A state which voluntarily imposes restrictions upon production from its own flush pools has no recourse (in the absence of an interstate agreement) against a neighboring state which permits its flush pools to produce at an excessive rate. Occasionally, the problem is dramatized in a pool which stretches across state lines, such as the Rodessa pool, which extends into Louisiana, Arkansas and Texas. At various times each of the three states has enforced a different rate of production on the wells within

---

off in output amounting to about 60 to 66 per cent. Two years after the peak, the average decline is over 70 per cent and three years after, around 80 per cent. Individual fields show as big a decline after the third year as 94 per cent." AMERICAN PETROLEUM INSTITUTE, PETROLEUM FACTS AND FIGURES (1928) 111.

[1] In the early stages of proration there was controversy as to whether the state commissions were required to first determine each pool's market demand, and integrate those into a state-wide figure, or could ascertain the market demand for the state and break that down by pools. *Cf.* H. F. WILCOX Co. v. Walker *et al.*, 168 Okla. 355, 32 P.(2d) 1044 (1934). In practical operation, a combination of methods is used. The Texas statute directs the Commission to prevent discrimination between pools and to ascertain the demand for each pool. TEX. STAT. (Vernon, 1937) art. 6049(d), § 6.

its boundaries, within that single pool. The resultant loss of market, by the most conservative state to the most reckless one, illustrates in sharper focus the problem presented by more distant pools which are tributary to the same common market.[1]

The local regulatory mechanism which we are about to examine can best be visualized as intended to control the first two of the three factors just discussed: to antidote the rule of capture by the establishment of correlative rights in a common pool and by the conservation of reservoir energy; and to level off the economic impact of flush production as against the production of settled pools.

The problem cannot be conquered in any of its phases unless it be mastered in the initial one: the control of production within the single pool. In this phase the oil industry has devised a form of regulation to which the other mineral industries are as yet strangers.

IV

Oil is produced from over 350,000 individual wells in twenty-two states. Production from most of these wells requires no control; produced at capacity, they give only a small output per day.[2] But in Texas, California, Oklahoma, Louisiana, New Mexico, Kansas, Arkansas, Wyoming and Michigan—particularly the three leaders—there are fields in which wide-open production would cause adverse consequences of two general types: waste, including such tangible elements as escape of gas to the open air and such intangibles as the loss of reservoir energy; and undue drainage along the pressure

---

[1] Following enactment by Louisiana of Act 225 of 1936 [LA. GEN. STAT. ANN. (Dart, Supp. 1937) § 9482], both Louisiana and Texas placed proration in the Rodessa pool on a basis taking acreage into account.

[2] The average production for Pennsylvania's 79,550 wells, for example, is less than two-thirds of a barrel each per day. See (Jan. 27, 1938) OIL AND GAS J. 63.

gradient from the lease which is conservatively drilled and whose flow is restricted to the one which is densely drilled and produced at capacity. Each of these two types of consequences, waste and disproportionate drainage, might conceivably exist independently, but manifestly they are generally interrelated. Consequently, statutes intended to stabilize and conserve a flush field's production, through controls on the spacing of wells and on the production from them, have been sustained on two separate but related bases: the state's power to protect a natural resource against waste, and its power to protect and adjust correlative rights of the owners of a common property, the reservoir. Laws have been sustained on the latter ground even where decisions prior to enactment of the statute had denied that the interests of the landowners in the reservoir were correlative and limited.[1] The limits of both powers remain to be fully tested; it is sufficient to say that no statute has yet been invalidated where the facts bore a fair relation to the accomplishment of either of these two stated purposes.[2] Of the present major flush-pool states, California's

---

[1] See Bandini Petroleum Co. v. Superior Court, 110 Cal. App. 123, 293 Pac. 899 (1930), *aff'd*, 284 U. S. 8 (1931), and People v. Associated Oil Co., 211 Cal. 93, 294 Pac. 717 (1930); *id.*, 211 Cal. 568, 296 Pac. 273 (1931); *id.*, 212 Cal. 76, 297 Pac. 536 (1931) (sustaining the California gas-oil ratio law, Laws 1929, c. 535). Compare with the common-law rule referred to in Katz v. Walkinshaw, 141 Cal. 116, 134, 74 Pac. 766, 772 (1903).

[2] The measures invalidated have related principally to the East Texas oil field and the Panhandle (Texas) gas field. Those relating to the East Texas field include (1) a martial law order of the Governor, invalidated by a decision which specifically left the conservation laws themselves intact [Sterling v. Constantin, 287 U. S. 378 (1932)]; (2) a series of proration orders held to be inconsistent with the statute, without affecting the validity of the act, in several cases, reviewed in Amazon Petroleum Corp. v. Railroad Comm., 5 F. Supp. 633 (E. D. Tex. 1934), which finally sustained a proration order. The invalidated measures relating to the Panhandle field include (1) a "common purchaser" statute (TEX. ANN. REV. CIV. STAT. (Vernon, 1925) art. 6049a) [Texoma Natural Gas Co. v. Railroad Comm., 59 F.(2d) 750 (W. D. Tex. 1932)]; (2) a "shut-down" order [Texoma

decisions lean to the correlative-rights basis,[1] Texas' to the waste basis,[2] and Oklahoma's rest on both.[3] The United States Supreme Court, in decisions on cases coming up from Indiana, New York, Wyoming, California, Oklahoma and Texas, seems clearly to recognize both bases.[4] Texas' statutes now expressly do so,[5] notwithstanding a perplexing distaste for the correlative-rights doctrine shown in some decisions of the federal courts in that state.[6]

Natural Gas Co. v. Terrell, 2 F. Supp. 168 (W. D. Tex. 1932)]; (3) a market-demand order held to be intended to require the plaintiff, which owned a pipe line as well as gas wells, to buy gas from others instead of using its own [Canadian River Gas Co. v. Terrell, 4 F. Supp. 222 (W. D. Tex. 1933)]; (4) proration orders, held to have the same purpose, unrelated to prevention of drainage [Texas Panhandle Gas Co. v. Thompson, 12 F. Supp. 462 (W. D. Tex. 1935); Consolidated Gas Utilities Corp. v. Thompson, 14 F. Supp. 319 (W. D. Tex. 1936), aff'd, 300 U. S. 55 (1937)].

The favorable decisions in the various states are too numerous to cite.

[1] See cases cited note 1, page 335, supra.

[2] Brown v. Humble Oil Co., 126 Tex. 296, 83 S. W.(2d) 935 (1935); Danciger Oil & Ref. Co. v. Railroad Comm. of Tex., 49 S. W.(2d) 837 (Tex. Civ. App. 1932); and see the federal cases cited note 2, page 335, supra.

[3] C. C. Julian Oil & Royalties Co. v. Capshaw, 145 Okla. 237, 292 P. 841 (1930); Champlin Ref. Co. v. Corporation Comm., 286 U. S. 210 (1932); Wilcox Oil & Gas Co. v. Walker, 168 Okla. 355, 32 P.(2d) 1044 (1934); State v. Wilcox Oil & Gas Co., 162 Okla. 237, 19 P.(2d) 572 (1933); Oils, Inc. v. Corporation Comm., 165 Okla. 202, 25 P.(2d) 703 (1933).

[4] Ohio Oil Co. v. Indiana, 177 U. S. 190 (1900); Lindsley v. Natural Carbonic Gas Co., 220 U. S. 61 (1911); Walls v. Midland Carbon Co., 254 U. S. 300 (1920); Bandini Petroleum Co. v. Superior Court, 284 U. S. 8 (1931); Champlin Ref. Co. v. Corporation Comm., 286 U. S. 210 (1932); Constantin v. Sterling, 287 U. S. 378 (1932); Thompson v. Henderson Co., 300 U. S. 258 (1937).

[5] Tex. Ann. Rev. Civ. Stat. (Vernon, 1937) art. 6008, § 10.

[6] See the federal cases cited note 2, page 335, supra, particularly Consolidated Gas Util. Corp. v. Thompson, 14 F. Supp. 319 (W. D. Tex. 1936). Although that decision was affirmed, 300 U. S. 55 (1937), the Supreme Court did not follow the lower court's language with regard to correlative rights, saying (p. 76–77): "We assume, also, that the State may constitutionally prorate production in order to prevent undue drainage of gas from the reserves of well owners lacking pipe line connections."

A third ground, the general power to abate nuisances, exists, and has been relied upon with and without a statutory basis in the prevention of damage to producing formations, and the like.[1] A fourth and distinct basis is perhaps beginning to emerge; the power to restrict production for purposes of economic stabilization, without reference to conservation. California, for instance, which repealed a statute authorizing restriction of petroleum production,[2] has enacted an Agricultural Prorate Act authorizing restriction of agricultural commodities to the market demand for them, and the statute has been sustained.[3]

But, by and large, the laws governing oil production are drawn and sustained as conservation measures, however much the stabilization of markets may have been the dominating factor in causing their enactment. It will be noted that the industry has not sought—indeed has intensely opposed—a public utility status as the basis for these statutes.[4] As examined in the following paragraphs, these laws will be seen to express a relationship between the state and the individual producer as a property owner engaged in a private business, despite the fact that the integrated effect of the impact of these laws upon thousands of wells, regulated in harmony

---

[1] The cases to 1933 are collected in ELY, OIL CONSERVATION THROUGH INTERSTATE AGREEMENT (1933) 28, n.3. The Texas "hot oil" statutes have been sustained on the ground of the state's power to abate commerce in illegal oil as a nuisance. See Hercules Oil Co. v. Thompson, 10 F. Supp. 988 (W. D. Tex. 1935); Melton v. Railroad Comm., 10 F. Supp. 984 (W. D. Tex. 1935); Lacy v. Railroad Comm., 10 F. Supp. 990 (W. D. Tex. 1935).

[2] Laws 1931, c. 585. Repealed by referendum, on petition filed before the effective date of the act.

[3] Laws, 1933, c. 754, § 2; California Agricultural Prorate Commission v. Superior Court, 5 Cal.(2d) 550, 55 P.(2d) 495 (1936).

[4] Williams v. Standard Oil Co. of Louisiana, 278 U. S. 235 (1929), held invalid a Tennessee statute imposing a public utility status on the selling of gasoline. That statute represents one of the very few attempts to bring any phase of the oil business (save transportation) into the public utility fold.

with a common plan, is state-controlled, industry-wide planning of production.

V

The state conservation statutes in general cover three phases of the petroleum business: drilling, production and transportation. Of these, the first two are of primary present interest, although regulation of transportation has become an important auxiliary to production control through federal and state "hot oil" acts, prohibiting the movement of illegally produced oil and its products.

Exploration, refining and marketing scarcely have been touched by the regulatory power. Some state statutes specifically withhold from the regulatory body any control over "wildcatting" (exploratory drilling) and refining.[1] The power of the state has been brought to bear principally on that segment of the industry which begins with the sinking of a well in a proven field and ends with the movement of the oil away from the field.

Because the legislature's power was first exerted in the production phase, and because "proration" is still the backbone of the regulatory system, that phase may be explored first.

Proration

The states of Texas, Oklahoma, Kansas, New Mexico, Louisiana, Mississippi, Michigan and Arkansas have conservation statutes[2] of roughly the same general pattern. These states, together with California and Wyoming, are the ones

---

[1] *E.g.*, Tex. Ann. Rev. Civ. Stat. (Vernon, 1937) art. 6014(a).

[2] Tex. Ann. Rev. Civ. Stat. (Vernon, 1937) arts. 6008, 6014, 6049(c), 6049(d), 6049(e); Okla. Stat. (Harlow, Supp. 1936) § 11574; Kan. Gen. Stat. Ann. (Corrick, 1935) §§ 55-601– 55-609; N. Mex. Laws 1935, c. 72; La. Gen. Stat. Ann. (Dart, 1932) §§ 4784–4789, (Dart, Supp. 1937) §§ 9482.1–9482.16; Miss. Code Ann. (Supp. 1933) Appendix p. 517; Mich. Comp. Laws (1929) §§ 11632–11651, (Mason, Supp. 1935) § 5697; Ark. Dig. Stat. (Pope, Supp. 1937) § 10461 (gas).

in which flush fields have been developed during the past two decades. While this pattern originated in Oklahoma in 1914, when discovery of the Cushing and Healdton pools demoralized the local market, proration did not begin in earnest until the discoveries of 1926–1931.[1]

The proration device involves two essential elements: the determination of what the pool's allowable daily production shall be,[2] and the apportionment of that "allowable." These are sometimes bracketed in the phrase "ratable taking,"[3] *i.e.*, the enforcement of production quotas which result in maximum ultimate recovery from the field as a whole, and in the recovery by each lease of a quantity of oil and gas equivalent to that originally in place under that lease.

The formulas used for the distribution of a field's production quota among its producing properties fall into two general classes: an allotment of a flat quantity per well, and an allotment on a basis recognizing the differing productive capacities of different properties. The first is represented by the "marginal well" acts, and the second by the proration acts, so-called, although both are phases of proration.

The marginal well acts exempt from proration some stated quantity of oil per well.[4] Frequently, the quantity is made

---

[1] See p. 1212, *supra*.

[2] See pp. 1213, 1215–16, 1221, note 2, page 333, *supra*.

[3] For an excellent discussion of "ratable taking" and the factors involved, see *Report of the "Subcommittee on Evils Attending Unnecessary and Unprofitable Drilling in Proven Fields, and the Remedy*," Ind. Pet. Ass'n, Release of Oct. 14, 1937.

[4] For example, in Texas "marginal wells" are defined by art. 6049(b), § 1 [TEX. ANN. REV. CIV. STAT. (Vernon, 1937)], and exempted from curtailment below certain quantities roughly proportional to the depth of the well, ranging from ten barrels minimum for a well not more than 2,000 feet deep to 35 barrels for a well deeper than 8,000 feet. In East Texas by special rules (Rule 19, part I; Rule 21, part I) the proration curtailment orders have been made specifically inapplicable to marginal wells; their quotas are determined by the marginal well law. Such wells are also

proportional to the depth of the well. By these statutes an operator is assured some return, even though a limited one, upon the drilling of a well in a proven area, provided he conforms to the spacing requirements. The economic effect of the marginal well statutes has not been fully recognized. For instance, as of January 1, 1938, the total allowable for the State of Texas was 1,388,575 barrels, of which 1,082,770 barrels were required to be allotted as minimum allowables by the marginal well act, leaving only 305,805 barrels to be prorated. In other words, the marginal well act controlled the allocation of 78 per cent of the allowable production of the state, while the proration laws controlled only 22 per cent.[1] A comparison of these statistics with those of September 1, 1937, shows that the brunt of the recession in market outlet during that period fell on the proratable wells. Between these dates the statewide allowable decreased 90,217 barrels, yet the daily quantity of marginal oil was required to be increased 73,783 barrels because of the 3,474 new wells drilled during that period. The state-wide average of proratable oil per well consequently dropped from 10.56 to 6.68 barrels per day.[2] In East Texas the situation is even more extreme. As of January 1, 1938, the daily allowable was 491,852 barrels, of which 482,385 were absorbed by the marginal allowance, leaving only 9,467 barrels to be prorated among 23,951 proratable wells.[3] The proration laws thus

exempt from curtailment of production under the gas-oil ratio law (art. 6008, § 5).

[1] RAILROAD COMMISSION OF TEXAS, STATUS OF THE ALLOWABLES OF MARGINAL AND PRORATABLE WELLS ON OIL PRORATION SCHEDULES EFFECTIVE JANUARY 1, 1938.

[2] For statistics as of Sept. 1, 1937, see the release of that date corresponding to that cited in note 1 above, *supra*.

[3] Of these, over 16,000 had been drilled under exceptions to the spacing rule, according to figures released by the Railroad Commission in October 1936. Four thousand eight hundred and eighty-four wells were drilled in that field in 1936–37. See RAILROAD COMMISSION OF TEXAS, REVISED

affected less than 2 per cent of the production, and less than one-half barrel per well, in the East Texas field. Although the three-judge federal courts of Texas have insisted that the allowable of proratable oil for a good well must be higher than that for a poor one,[1] the marginal well statute has forced the Railroad Commission to deal with over three-fourths of the state's allowable, and with 98 per cent of the East Texas production, on a basis which ignores any distinction between good wells and bad.

No wholly satisfactory proration formula has been found. In general, three factors have been recognized: per well allowances, potential, and acreage. None is sufficient by itself, and probably an adequate formula must take additional factors into account.[2] In a field of large potential capacity, the per well method is unfair unless both the well-spacing pattern and the reservoir conditions are uniform, since this basis does not take into account the area drained by each well, nor the relative producing ability of different wells. But frequently the other of the primitive methods, that of "potentials," is just as inequitable. Ignoring acreage and spacing, the earlier practice was to measure the potential of the well by permitting it to produce wide open for a limited period, and then to allocate production to it in proportion to the relative potentials of that well and of all the others in the field. It is

---

SUMMARY OF NEW OIL WELL COMPLETIONS BY DISTRICTS AND BY MONTHS FOR THE YEAR 1937 (Jan. 10, 1938).

[1] People's Petroleum Producers, Inc. v. Smith, 1 F. Supp. 301 (E. D. Tex. 1932); same, on final hearing (unreported, Mar. 17, 1933, Nos. 386 and 479 in equity, E. D. Tex., Tyler Div.).

[2] See the following A. P. I. Releases, Nov. 1934: *Progress Report of the Topical Committee on Allocation of Production;* Albertson, *Acreage and Sand Thickness as Factors in Proration;* Kelly, *The Potential or Productivity Factor in Allocation Formulas.* The allocation formulas sustained in Champlin Refining Co. v. Corporation Commission, 51 F.(2d) 823 (W. D. Okla. 1931), 286 U. S. 210 (1932) and C. C. Julian Oil and Royalties Co. v. Capshaw, 145 Okla. 237, 292 Pac. 841 (1930) were straight potential formulas.

a wasteful method of ascertaining the allowable. Further-more, there is now no general agreement that the quantity of recoverable oil is directly proportional to the well potential, or as to what the ratio between the two ought to be. A third method, based on "per acre allowances," that is, disregarding the potential producing ability of the well and allocating the allowable production solely on the basis of the area drained by each well, is equitable only if reservoir conditions are uniform. A fourth method assigns to each well certain values based on each of the three factors of potential, acreage, and per well allowance, and awards a composite allowable arrived at by adding these values together. A fifth method multiplies the acreage factor by the potential factor, instead of adding it; this gives each lease a per acre recovery propor-tional to the well potential, which is an equitable result if the potential happens to be proportional to the recoverable oil under the lease. Engineers are now developing a sixth basis, apparently superior to the others, which involves acreage multiplied by the "index of recoverable oil"; this index in turn takes into account not only potential, but also elements such as permeability, sand thickness, fluidity, the differences between static and flowing bottom hole pressures, and a number of other factors.[1]

---

[1] Foley, *Proration of Allowable Oil Production*, A. P. I. Release, June 2, 1937; Wilde, *An Allocation Formula*, A. P. I. Release, Oct. 1933; Wyckoff, *The Relation of Well Potentials, Sand Permeability, and Well Pressures to Allocation of Production*, A. P. I. Release, Nov. 1934.

Another element, taken into account in some proration formulas, is that of "volumetric displacements." A field generally contains oil, gas and water; wells produce varying quantities of each, depending upon their location on the structure. The volumetric displacement plan is based upon calculating the space underground occupied by a barrel of oil, a barrel of water, and a varying quantity of gas (depending on the pressure), and limiting total withdrawals, whether of gas, water or oil, to an equivalent number of barrels displaced underground. Thus, a well producing princi-pally gas would be limited to a quantity which would have occupied. the

But as experience with proration accumulates, it becomes apparent that the objectives of "ratable taking," *i.e.*, maximum ultimate recovery from the field and equitable apportionment of recovery between properties, can be achieved only by the concurrent control of drilling as well as production.

Drilling

The common law gave to each landowner the right to drill as many wells as he pleased and to produce them at capacity; his neighbor could protect himself by drilling to an equal density and likewise producing at capacity. Proration limited the right of self-help in the second particular alone.[1]

During earlier stages of the industry's development, the producing areas were able to keep pace with the remarkable growth of demand up to 1929 only through what Dr. Pogue has called the "compounding effect" of the rule of capture,[2] which necessitated the drilling of more wells than unified ownership would have required, and hence forced oil onto the market at an accelerating rate. The great discoveries of

---

same space underground as the number of barrels of oil which that well is entitled to produce under whatever proration formula is in force. See Foley, *loc. cit. supra;* Moore, *Application of the Principle of Volumetric Withdrawals to the Allocation of Production,* A. P. I. Release, Oct. 1933; Knowlton, *Effect of Volumetric Withdrawal on Physical Waste in the Oklahoma City Field,* A. P. I. Release, Oct. 1933.

[1] Proration, by definition, is a proportional division or assessment. See discussion of Albertson, *Acreage and Sand Thickness as Factors in Proration,* A. P. I. Release, Nov. 1934. But without control of the drilling density, or without taking into account the area drained by each well, a uniform restriction on production (as under the marginal well acts) automatically results in disproportionate drainage. For examples of proportionate recovery with and without restrictions on drilling and production, see Albertson, *loc. cit. supra;* Hubbard, *Economics and Well Spacing in Texas* (1937) 123 Trans. A. I. M. E. (Petroleum Division) 163; Stephenson, *Acreage and Potential Factors in Allocation, id.,* at 172.

[2] Pogue, *The Economic Structure of the American Petroleum Industry,* Third World Power Conference (1936) 16.

1926–1931 and the improved technology of the industry eliminated the necessity for that acceleration, and proration was invoked as a brake on production. But proration, on a basis of relative potentials or per well allowances, had the effect of multiplying the drilling investment per barrel produced, since it held down the aggregate production of the field to a relatively constant figure and decreased the output per well as each operator increased the number of his wells to get a larger share. Indeed, in such fields as East Texas, it is possible that more wells were drilled under proration than would have been drilled if the field had run wide open.

Defects in the control of drilling constitute the heaviest indictment against the conservation system at its present stage of development. Simple spacing rules preceded proration in most states,[1] but they did not prove effective. And they were least effective in the situation where they were most needed, *i.e.*, in fields composed of small tracts. Thus, in the East Texas field a regulation requires spacing of 660 feet between wells (resulting in one well to 10 acres), yet more than 17,000 of the 24,269 wells drilled in that field prior to January 1, 1938, had been drilled under exceptions which were allowed by the Railroad Commission.[2] These were granted because the size of the tracts, or the density of offset drilling, were supposed to require such exceptions in order to prevent interlease drainage.

---

[1] See Ark. Act 664 of 1923, § 8, and Rule 7; Calif. Laws 1931, c. 791, § 18; Colo. Laws 1921, c. 55, § 3645; ILL. REV. STAT. (1925) c. 93, p. 85; KAN. REV. STAT. (1923) c. 55, §§ 110–11; La. Act 252 of 1924, §§ 2(1) and 6, Act 253 of 1924, § 1(2), Act 123 of 1926, § 1(16); MICH. COMP. LAWS (Mason, Supp. 1935) §§ 5696–5722; MISS. CODE ANN. (Supp. 1933) Appendix p. 517; Mont. Laws 1927, c. 108, § 11 (state lands), Rule 2c; N. Mex. Laws 1935, c. 12, § 12, preceded by Rule 8; OHIO CODE ANN. (Throckmorton, 1936) §§ 898-179, 898-180; OKLA. STAT. (Harlow, Supp. 1936) §§ 11574(b), 11574(d); Tex., Rule 37; Wyo. Reg. 2(c), 2(d) and 4.

[2] Figures based on informal advices from the Railroad Commission. *Cf.* note 3, page 340, *supra*.

The complaint has been that while the law in many states prorates the recovery from a field, it fails to prorate the investment required to win that recovery. Although production is regulated generally by the same commissions which regulate public utilities,[1] it is in the comparative lack of control over the amount of the investment (and the resultant lack of control over the rate of return) that the state distinguishes the oil industry from the utilities. The problem of unnecessary drilling has plagued the industry as severely under proration as it did before, and is currently probably the most agitated question in the oil business.[2]

This complaint, of course, applies not to exploratory drilling, but to drilling in proven fields. The margin of reserves is too small to warrant restrictions on exploratory drilling or wildcatting. Indeed, one writer, in the course of an exhaustive consideration of the statistics, facetiously interjects the suggestion that the figures indicate that the way to find a billion barrels of reserve is to drill five thousand dry holes.[3] The economic burden of drilling holes for purposes of exploration, in order to maintain the margin of working

---

[1] Thus in Oklahoma, the Corporation Commission; Kansas, the Public Utilities Commission; Texas, the Railroad Commission; and so on.

[2] The A. P. I. has appointed a committee on well spacing from members of the Board of Directors. It has gathered considerable data, not yet released. The Independent Petroleum Association's "Committee on Evils Attending Unnecessary Drilling in Proven Fields, and the Remedy" filed reports in December 1936 and 1937. The American Bar Association Mineral Section's subcommittee on oil conservation is conducting a study. The A. I. M. E. has for several years maintained a committee on Stabilization. For excellent recent technical discussions of the economics of the drilling-control problem, see Hubbard, *Economics and Well Spacing in Texas* (1937) 123 TRANS. A. I. M. E. (PETROLEUM DIVISION) 163; Pogue, *The Economic Aspects of Drilling* (Mar. 17, 1938) OIL AND GAS J. 42.

[3] Pogue, *The Economic Structure of the American Petroleum Industry*, THIRD WORLD POWER CONFERENCE (1936) 11. Studies by Frederic H. Lahee indicate that in the gulf coast area about 88 per cent of all wildcat wells drilled in 1937 were dry holes, or about 5.35 feet of dry hole for each foot

reserves, is an unavoidable one, to which the industry is resigned. But the added burden of drilling unnecessary wells in proven fields is one which the industry is becoming impatient to minimize.

Arguments in favor of a high density of drilling generally cite the "Cutler Theory," which is phrased as follows: "recovery of wells of equal size, producing under similar circumstances in the same pool, is proportional to the average distance that the oil moves to get to the well."[1] This conclusion, however, was based on research in unrestricted fields. Later studies by the Bureau of Mines in prorated fields have led to the conclusion that "spacing of wells wider than that in many fields would have given at least equal recovery during the present 'proration period' and would have resulted in more efficient use of reservoir energy and lower cost of production."[2] While opinions may differ as to the effect of intensive drilling where the wells are properly located on the structure and are produced at a minimum rate, there is little dispute as to the adverse result on reservoir pressures where the excessive drilling is at random without respect to reservoir conditions.[3]

---

of productive well. *Wildcat Drilling in 1937* (Mar. 17, 1938) OIL AND GAS J. 41.

[1] Cutler, U. S. BUREAU OF MINES BULL. 228 (1934) 89.

The Railroad Commission of Texas at one time supported the doctrine of "more wells, more oil." See Order of Aug. 26, 1935, cited in dissenting opinion in Magnolia Pet. Co. v. Railroad Comm. of Tex., 105 S. W.(2d) 787, 792 (Tex. Civ. App. 1937), *rev'd*, 109 S. W.(2d) 967 (Tex. 1937). But it has subsequently modified its position. See Orders of Feb. 4, 1936, and March 23, 1936.

[2] Cattell and Fowler, *Fluid-Energy Relations in Production of Petroleum and Natural Gas*, U. S. BUREAU OF MINES YEARBOOK, (1934) 715.

[3] For a discussion of the relation between spacing of wells and ultimate recovery, see Knowlton, *The Future of Well Spacing* (May 17, 1937) OIL WEEKLY 51. The location of the wells, as well as the rate of production, determines the rate and direction of intrusion of water into the sand. See Moore, *The Effect of Curtailment on Ultimate Recovery*, A. P. I. Release, 1934. The belief seems to be growing that the area drained is greater if the well is

Most of the United States reserve overlies a water drive. The location of the wells as well as the rate of production determines the rate and direction of intrusion of water into the sands. Some engineers have suggested that if a field is produced with a minimum number of wells, advantageously located, and at a rate which will exhaust the reservoir in approximately twenty years, perhaps as much as 90 per cent of the recoverable oil can be obtained by flowing, at a cost between one-half and one-third of the cost prevailing under close spacing conditions and the resultant allocation of marginal proration quotas.[1] Curiously, the figure of 400,000 barrels allotted to East Texas, which was originally derided by the federal courts in that state as a "magic figure," but was later accepted by the same courts as reasonable,[2] is about the daily average production which would exhaust an estimated reserve of 3,000,000,000 barrels in 20 years, and that figure is commonly accepted as the remaining East Texas reserve.[3] Of about 490,000 barrels currently produced, 85,000 are water.

Probably between 4,000 and 5,000 unnecessary wells are drilled each year in the United States at a drilling cost between $80,000,000 and $100,000,000,[4] which is a charge upon the industry of about 10 cents per barrel on a billion-barrel production per year. Texas' unnecessary drilling is

---

produced at a slower rate. See Hill, *Essential Engineering Factors in the Allocation of Production*, A. P. I. Release, 1934, at 32.

[1] Moore, *loc. cit. supra* note 3, page 346.

[2] The figure 400,000 barrels per day allotted to East Texas was rejected in People's Petroleum Producers, Inc. v. Smith, 1 F. Supp. 361 (E. D. Tex. 1932), and finally accepted as reasonable in Amazon Petroleum Corp. v. Railroad Comm., 5 F. Supp. 633 (E. D. Tex. 1934).

[3] See discussion by Messrs. John R. Suman and E. O. Thompson of paper by T. V. Moore, *The Effect of Curtailment on Ultimate Recovery* (15th annual meeting A. P. I., Nov. 1934).

[4] The figures on the cost of unnecessary wells used here, unless otherwise credited, are private estimates, made, however, by competent engineers.

estimated to cost more than $50,000,000 per year. In East Texas alone, 13,000 of the 24,000 wells are said to be unnecessary from an eingineering standpoint. They are estimated to have cost $160,000,000, yet over 1,300 wells are being added to that field each year at a cost in excess of $13,000,000.

In New Mexico, by contrast with Texas, one writer has said that during the years 1934, 1935 and 1936, some 317,000,000 barrels of reserves were developed with only 820 wells, while in West Texas 288,000,000 barrels of reserves were developed with 2,346 wells.[1] The reasons are primarily the availability of larger tracts of land, and a different policy in enforcing spacing requirements.

Oklahoma's share of unnecessary drilling has been estimated to cost from $15,000,000 to $20,000,000 annually. Prior to 1937, probably 1,400 unnecessary wells had been drilled at a total cost in excess of $85,000,000.[2] Kettleman Hills, California's greatest potential producer, has suffered severely from unnecessary drilling. The pool is very deep, and had a very high initial gas pressure. The discovery well was located high on the structure, with a high gas-oil ratio. About twenty high-ratio wells drilled in that area of discovery have contributed more to the depletion of reservoir energy than all the other wells in the field. A survey made in 1936, six years after discovery, showed that the average bottom-hole pressure for the entire field had dropped more than one-third. Fifty-five per cent of the field had registered a pressure loss of approximately one-half when oil recovery had amounted to only 122,000,000 barrels. The report showed that reservoir

---

[1] Knowlton, *supra* note 3, page 346.

[2] In the Oklahoma City pool, where 300 wells would have been adequate but where nearly 700 were in fact drilled, the wasted investment has been estimated to be in excess of $31,000,000. See *Report of the "Subcommittee on Evils Attending Unnecessary Drilling in Proven Fields, and the Remedy,"* Ind. Pet. Ass'n Release, Dec. 1, 1936, at 8; HEARINGS, Part 2, on H. Res. 441, 73d Cong. (1934) 1232; Shaw, *Spacing of Wells* (May 10, 1937) OIL WEEKLY 24.

pressure had declined as much as a pound and a half a day. The field has been exploited as a gas field, and produced in a manner to maintain a full supply for the gas utilities which have built pipe lines to it, rather than to promote maximum ultimate oil recovery through the restriction of gas production. The result is that the reservoir pressures are continuing to fall below those necessary to lift oil to the surface from the deep horizons, and expensive pumping must be resorted to.[1]

So long as drilling is not restricted, manifestly the investment per recoverable barrel increases. The attempt to maintain a price that will reward this over-investment requires stabilization of an artificial price level. In many fields, the annual drilling cost probably exceeds the annual income from the field's production, even during the period of cheap flush flow. This has not yet proved critical to the industry as a whole because the new wells in most of the recently discovered fields are capable of paying out their cost in a few years, even under proration. But as the ratio of drilled-up reserves to proven reserves becomes more and more top-heavy, the aggregate return, in barrels of total production per dollar invested, becomes less and less attractive.[2]

VI

Since 1935, there have been no developments of consequence in three of the four strata of regulation: thus, the Bureau of Mines carries on as before, the Interstate Oil Compact was renewed in 1937 in the identical form in which it was executed

---

[1] Collom and Watson, *Review of Developments at Kettleman Hills* (1937) 123 TRANS. A. I. M. E. (PETROLEUM DIVISION) 195.

[2] Statistical studies by Dr. Pogue indicate that on the present trend the daily average allowable per flowing well in Texas, exclusive of the East Texas field, would be 31.8 barrels by 1942; and that if spacing were increased from one well per ten acres (the present rule) to one well per twenty acres, the allowable would be 42.9 barrels, or about 33 per cent greater. Pogue, *The Economic Aspects of Drilling* (Mar. 17, 1938) OIL AND GAS J. 42.

in 1935, and the federal measures (the excise taxes of 1935 and the Connally hot-oil act of 1935) were reenacted in 1937. But in the foundation stratum, the local conservation law, there have been some promising developments, generally toward a more direct relationship between drilling controls and production controls.

In 1935 Oklahoma and New Mexico, and in 1936 Louisiana, enacted statutes[1] of a new pattern. These statutes, which have been the subject of considerable favorable discussion before trade and professional groups,[2] authorize a regulatory body to establish in each pool proration units composing a uniform number of acres, fixed by the area which one well will economically drain and develop. Where the size or shape of an individual tract does not conform to that of the standard proration unit, "pooling" of properties can be required.[3] By "pooling" is meant an arrangement whereby the owners of small tracts club together on the cost of drilling a single well, sharing in the expense and in the recovery in proportion to their acreage. However, these statutes allow the owner of a small tract to drill his well, notwithstanding failure of his lease to equal the size of a proration unit; but in such case he receives only an allowable which is proportional to the ratio between his area and the area of a standard unit.

---

[1] OKLA. STAT. (Harlow, Supp. 1936) § 11574(b); N. Mex. Laws 1935, c. 72, § 12; La. Act 225 of 1936, § 6, LA. GEN. STAT. ANN. (Dart, Supp. 1937) § 9482.

[2] See *Report of the "Subcommittee on Evils Attending Unnecessary and Unprofitable Drilling in Proven Fields, and the Remedy,"* Ind. Pet. Ass'n Releases, Dec. 1936 and Oct. 14, 1937; Ely, *Legal Restraints on Drilling and Production*, Mineral Section, American Bar Association, Sept. 28, 1937.

[3] The New Mexico and Louisiana statutes make "pooling" available to owners who, because of the smallness or shape of their tracts, might be deprived of a fair share of the oil in the proration unit. The Oklahoma statute permits the owners of one or more smaller tracts in the unit to pool with the owner of a majority of the acreage in the unit if the latter drills a well.

These statutes, which have not yet been tested by litigation, have an interesting background. As long ago as 1928, in *Marrs v. City of Oxford*,[1] an ordinance of a Kansas town, which limited the drilling of wells to one per city block, was sustained by the federal courts. The ordinance allocated a one-eighth royalty interest among the landowners of a block in proportion to their acreage, and awarded the right to drill to the operator holding the majority of the acreage in the block under lease. It gave the other landowners the right to contribute to the cost of that well, and to receive in return a share in the working interest, in proportion to acreage. The case, turning on the validity of a city ordinance, did not involve a regulatory statute, although the courts did mention the doctrine of correlative rights in passing. A subsequent decision[2] by a

---

[1] 24 F.(2d) 541 (D. Kan. 1928), *aff'd*, 32 F.(2d) 134 (C. C. A. 8th, 1929), *cert. denied*, 280 U. S. 573, 563 (1929). *Cf.* Ramsey v. City of Oxford, 124 Kan. 713, 261 Pac. 572 (1927).

[2] Tysco Oil Co. v. Railroad Comm., 12 F. Supp. 195 (S. D. Tex. 1935). The court said that the Railroad Commission had power "to, as a conservation measure, establish reasonable drilling districts in oil and gas fields, prescribe the size thereof, space the wells therein, etc." *Id.*, at 201. The city ordinance was sustained in a companion case. Tysco Oil Co. v. Railroad Comm., 12 F. Supp. 202 (S. D. Tex. 1935).

The Texas statute says that "it is not the intent of this Act to require . . . that the separately owned properties in any pool be utilized under one management, control or ownership." TEX. ANN. REV. CIV. STAT. (Vernon, 1937) art. 6014(g). However, several cases which have denied exceptions to the spacing rule and thereby prevented drilling of wells on small tracts have suggested that a fair result could be reached by control of production on the adjoining lands. The power of the Commission to regulate production in relation to spacing was thought favorably settled by the decision in Brown v. Humble Oil Co., 126 Tex. 296, 83 S. W.(2d) 935 (1935), but the opinion on rehearing, 126 Tex. 296, 314, 87 S. W.(2d) 1069 (1935), cast some doubt upon it, and the Commission has indicated that it does not construe the original decision as authorizing it to require pooling. (Statement of Chairman Thompson at hearing, May 17, 1937.) An injunction against production has been denied in some cases until the well owner shall (at some future time) have obtained "the amount of oil he is legally entitled to";

Texas federal court has sustained an order of the Railroad Commission, made in conformity with an ordinance of the City of South Houston, creating drilling districts of 16 acres each, limiting drilling to one well per district, and providing for pooling of expenses and of production among the properties in the district along the same general lines of the ordinance passed upon in *Marrs. v. City of Oxford*.

The drilling district program, involving compulsory localized unitization, is a step in the direction of a plan of field-wide unitization introduced to the industry nearly a decade ago.[1] The legal and engineering bases for requiring and effectuating compulsory unitization of an entire pool seem capable of demonstration,[2] but the political difficulty of enactment and

---

that is, "his fair share of the oil in place under his land." See Stanolind Oil & Gas Co. v. Railroad Comm., 96 S. W.(2d) 664, 665 (Tex. Civ. App. 1936). *Cf.* Humble Oil & Refining Co. v. Railroad Comm., 85 S. W.(2d) 813 (Tex. Civ. App. 1935). In Magnolia Pet. Co. v. Blankenship, 85 F. (2d) 553 (C. C. A. 5th, 1936), *cert. denied*, 299 U. S. 608 (1936), the court refused to enjoin the operation of the offending well, on the ground that the adjoining landowner's remedy was an application to the Railroad Commission "for a rule of proration among all the competing wells," saying (at 557), "We suppose that if the commission denies to any subdivision of such tract its own well that it can make some just apportionment of the oil produced on those subdivisions which are allowed wells; it being implied, if not expressed, in the act of subdivision that owners not allowed a well are not wholly to lose their oil." See also Atlantic Oil Production Co. v. Railroad Comm., 85 S. W.(2d) 655 (Tex. Civ. App. 1935); Sun Oil Co. v. Gillespie, 85 S. W.(2d) 652, 655 (Tex. Civ. App. 1935); Boxrollium Oil Co. v. Smith, 4 F. Supp. 624 (S. D. Tex. 1933).

[1] The unit-operation plan originated with Henry L. Doherty. For discussion of its early history, see HEARINGS, Part 2, on H. Res. 441, 73d Cong. (1934) 1250 *et seq.* See 3 REP. FED. OIL CONS. BD. (1929), containing at p. 26 as Appendix B the *Report of the Committee on Conservation of Mineral Resources of the Section of Mineral Law of the American Bar Association*, to which is annexed (p. 43) a draft of a statute authorizing specific performance of any plan for cooperative development agreed upon by a majority of the operators of a pool, under procedure provided by the proposed act.

[2] German, *Compulsory Unit Operation of Oil Pools* (1932) 17 A. B. A. J. 393

enforcement have kept field-wide compulsory unitization in the blueprint stage.

The drilling district or proration unit contemplated by these statutes is in the nature of an unincorporated association. Perhaps the next step may be to require their incorporation as quasipublic bodies.[1] In somewhat parallel situations, the courts have sustained "mill acts," subjecting landowners along a stream to a compulsory plan for development of a mill site, initiated by one of them. They have also upheld laws authorizing creation of drainage districts, subjecting properties therein, without the consent of their owners, to liens for construction of works benefiting the common area. The mill acts and drainage district acts have been sustained upon the ground that districts of such a character were reasonable devices for the utilization of a common property, without regard to the wider question of general public interest.[2]

The drilling district device, by minimizing the drilling of unnecessary wells, and eliminating the effect of interlease drainage as among the several properties comprising the district, achieves two desirable objectives. But the device does not solve by itself the problem of apportionment as among different districts embracing different parts of the field. That problem is particularly acute as to the area which overlies the "gas cap." Wells drilled on that location, tapping

---

20 CAL. L. REV. 111; *Summary of A. I. M. E. Unit Operation Study* (1930) TRANS. A. I. M. E. (PETROLEUM DIVISION) 11; Oliver and Umpleby, *Principles of Unit Operation, id.*, at 105.

[1] See Oliver, *Can the Rule of Capture be Rationalized?* (1937) 123 TRANS. A. I. M. E. (PETROLEUM DIVISION) 133; ELY, *loc. cit. supra* note 2, page 350.

[2] See Fallbrook Irr. Dist. v. Bradley, 164 U. S. 112, 163 *et seq.* (1896); Head v. Amoskeag Mfg. Co., 113 U. S. 9, 22 (1885); Wurts v. Hoagland, 114 U. S. 606, 611 (1885); Hagar v. Reclamation District No. 108, 111 U. S. 701 (1884); Fiske v. Framingham Mfg. Co., 12 Pick. 67, 70–72 (Mass. 1831). For discussion of the application of these precedents to petroleum engineering problems, see (1931 and 1935) 92 and 114 TRANS. A. I. M. E. (PETROLEUM DIVISION); A. I. M. E. TECHNICAL PUBLICATION No. 778.

the gas pocket or cap overlying the oil, are destructive of reservoir energy, inasmuch as they generally produce at a very high gas-oil ratio. If the field were completely unitized, the gas-cap wells would be shut in and production would be effected first from wells drilled on the outer periphery of the horizon, at the margin between the oil and the underlying water; and as they were successively invaded by water, new wells would be drilled further up the structure, preserving intact the original gas pressure so far as possible. In such fields as Kettleman Hills, failure to restrict production on the gas cap, where the discovery well was apparently located, has irreparably damaged the field. It is important to find a device which will restrict excessive production of gas from that unit or district which lies on top of the structure and excessive production of water from edge properties. Water conditions in the East Texas field illustrate the latter problem. Production of water there, as of January 1, 1938, is reported to have exceeded 85,000 barrels per day,[1] which represents more than nine times the total quantity of proratable oil produced by the field each day, and nearly 20 per cent of the field's daily production. The daily loss of that quantity of water from the reservoir has contributed to rapid acceleration of the rate of decline of reservoir pressure within the past year.

Two remedies have been suggested to restrict the damage done by overproduction of gas and water, in other words to prevent disproportionate production of the reservoir fluids on the gas cap and at edgewater. One is legislative restriction on gas-oil ratios, refusing the right to produce any well at a ratio in excess of that fixed by the regulatory body or by

---

[1] Hearings before the Railroad Commission indicate a daily water production of at least 85,000 barrels; some estimates run as high as 185,000. On the latter estimate, it has been testified that the East Texas field would cease flowing by 1940. See (March 26 and 29, 1938) EAST TEXAS OIL REPORTER. The Railroad Commission scheduled hearings on methods to halt water production, for April 19, 1938.

the courts. California enacted such a statute[1] in 1929, in the expectation that its enforcement would automatically lead to production control. It has failed in that purpose, although it has been sustained[2] by the state courts and by the United States Supreme Court as a conservation measure and has been useful as such. Second is the device or method of computation known as "volumetric displacements." This, as previously indicated,[3] is a method for translating the quota of oil production allowed by the proration formula (whatever that formula may happen to be) into equivalent production of gas, oil, and water—computing the equivalent quantity by estimating the volume it would occupy, or displace, underground. The method has been demonstrated with fair success, but is not yet in uniform application, and probably does not afford a complete remedy. The problem of how to compensate the man on the gas cap for the restriction of gas production which is imposed upon him in the interests of the entire field has not yet been solved satisfactorily. If the drilling district plan takes hold, perhaps the next step may be the enforced shutdown of those districts found to rest above the gas cap, compensating them by contribution of production from all of the other districts in the field on some proportionate basis, in much the same manner that the producing leases within each individual unit or drilling district contribute a share of their production to those leases upon which no wells are permitted to be drilled. The same legal mechanism would provide for the reinjection of water produced by edgewater districts, at the joint expense of all the districts in the field.[4] The drilling district or proration unit is a step toward

[1] Laws 1929, c. 791, p. 923.

[2] Bandini v. Superior Court, 110 Cal. App. 123, 293 Pac. 899 (1930), aff'd, 284 U. S. 8 (1931); People v. Associated Oil Co., 211 Cal. 93, 294 Pac. 717 (1930); id., 212 Cal. 76, 297 Pac. 536 (1931).

[3] See note 1, page 342, supra.

[4] The suggestion has been made in the East Texas field that a sanitary

cooperative development, if not compulsory unit operation, of the entire pool.

Some of the other means which have been suggested for the control of drilling and production include a "chain store tax" on wells and on production per well, graduating upward as the drilling density increases and as the production per well increases;[1] regulation of the form of lease contracts by requiring standard conservation clauses in substitution for the clauses which require immediate development and production;[2] restriction on pipe line extensions to unnecessary wells;[3] and limitation upon the amount moved from such wells into commerce.[4]

VII

The composite set of controls—state, interstate, and federal —has functioned since the invalidation of the Code under conditions which have made success relatively easy. Until the winter of 1937–38, demand was increasing while discoveries were accumulating at an orderly rate. Thus, during the greater part of the Compact period, the industry has been enjoying a breathing spell which has allowed it to turn its attention from emergency production-control measures to the

---

district be formed, to dispose of water produced by oil wells by means of reinjection.

[1] A chain store tax on gasoline service stations was sustained in Fox. v. Standard Oil Co., 294 U. S. 87 (1935).

[2] The drilling requirements in short-term leases are of a character which 'places the burden of a solution of overproduction on control after production is found, not on a drilling moratorium." See Umpleby (1930) TRANS. A. I. M. E. (PETROLEUM DIVISION) 428.

[3] See Stanley, *The Drama of the Oil Industry—Calling for Federal Regulation* (1930) 56 A. B. A. REP. 669. The theory there developed appears applicable to control by the State, as well as by the Federal Government, of extensions to new wells and new fields.

[4] See proposals by Amos L. Beaty, in HEARINGS, Part 1, on H. Res. 441, 73d Cong. (1934) 198; Part 4, 2839.

more fundamental problem of controlling the investment in drilling. However, during more recent months, as the indicated demand has fallen off, the producing states, particularly Texas, have lowered their production quotas in step with each other and with the recommendations of the Bureau of Mines. There has even been agitation for a production control law in California,[1] where production at times has failed to recede in phase with the reductions in the Compact states. While the Compact system has not been tested by a full-length depression, it has at least prompted and enabled the states to trim their sails sooner than they might otherwise have done.

Barring the discovery of another East Texas field in a state without conservation laws, there is reason to believe that the industry has developed a mechanism which, if it chooses to use it, is adequate to steer it away from the Scylla of immediate overproduction.

But there is a Charybdis, more distant yet perhaps more ominous. The efficiency of the state control system has yet to be tested by a down-cycle of supply, when the problem may be how to meet the demand at reasonable prices during a period of diminishing flush flow. That day is certain to come.[2] It is an open question whether the conservation laws will be applied to limit production for conservation's sake alone, when stabilization of overproduction is no longer a factor, and when the market is capable of absorbing all of the diminishing flow at a production rate higher than is warranted by the optimum use of reservoir energy. It is even more questionable whether, if the laws are so applied, the consuming public will be content to pay the higher prices which curtailment would occasion. The complex system now governing petroleum production is essentially producers'

---

[1] Stockman, *Californians Seek Quick Action By Legislature* (Mar. 17, 1938) OIL AND GAS J. 24.

[2] See notes 2 and 3 page 219, *supra*.

legislation. With the exception of the obsolete statutes attempting to restrict the use of gas fields to local consumers,[1] the conservation laws have been enacted upon the insistence of the industry, and the indifference of the consuming public.

Heretofore the legislatures of six or seven producing states have for the most part determined the national petroleum policy; with unimportant exceptions,[2] Congress has acted only to implement their determinations through prohibiting the movement of oil which those states decree shall not be produced, and through restricting imports. The consuming public has never become exercised to the point of transferring the issues to an arena which it might dominate—Congress.

---

[1] See Veasey, *Law of Oil and Gas* (1920) 18 MICH. L. REV. 445, 652, 749; 19 *id.*, 161. *Cf.* Pennsylvania v. West Virginia, 262 U. S. 544 (1923) (invalidating West Virginia statute requiring gas companies to furnish that state's inhabitants before exporting the balance).

[2] Even during the Code period, state regulatory bodies were the designated enforcement agencies, and the federal powers of regulation asserted by the Code were generally kept in reserve insofar as production was concerned. See HEARINGS, Part 2, on H. Res. 441, 73d Cong. (1934) 1296 *et seq.*; WATKINS, OIL: STABILIZATION OR CONSERVATION? (1937) 89 *et seq.* However, the Code did require federal, as distinguished from state, approval of development plans in new pools. Some 353 plans were approved altogether. See PETROLEUM ADMINISTRATIVE BOARD, OPERATION OF THE NEW POOL PLANS (1936). However, the Administrator's regulations were held not authorized by the Recovery Act, and unconstitutional if they were so authorized, in United States v. Eason Oil Co., 8 F. Supp. 365 (W. D. Okla. 1934).

The principal federal "consumers' legislation" is the Hepburn Act [34 STAT. 584 (1906), 49 U. S. C. § 41 (1934)] regulating interstate carriers of oil by pipe line. It was sustained in the Pipe Line Cases, United States v. Ohio Oil Co., 234 U. S. 548 (1914). In practical operation, however, it has had little effect, due to the small volume of oil carried for the account of others by the pipe lines, most of which are integrated with refineries. The Mineral Leasing Act [41 STAT. 441 (1920), 30 U. S. C. § 221 (1934)], while prompted by a fear of oil shortage and enacted to promote development, has necessarily been administered as a conservation measure. See United States v. Wilbur, 283 U. S. 414 (1931).

Yet oil (including its products) moves to market through a pipe line system one-third as long as all the Class I railroads of the country, supplies more than a third of all the energy used in American industry, and constitutes nearly a third of America's ocean freight. Twenty-nine million automobiles, all aircraft, all naval vessels, and indeed over eighty per cent of all the nation's installed horsepower, fixed and automotive, are dependent upon petroleum. A fourth of the nation's population is served by natural gas pipe lines. Like the power business, the petroleum industry serves more than twenty-nine million ultimate consumers, claims an investment of over thirteen billion dollars, has steadily expanded its importance in national life, and has as steadily reduced the cost of its service. Yet of these two energy industries, the industry which delivers energy by the exhaustion of a limited resource is governed only by the laws which it has itself invoked, while the industry which delivers energy largely from falling water and from comparatively limitless supplies of coal is the target of all the regulatory devices which political ingenuity can supply.[1] The differentiation in the consumers' treatment of these two energy industries may be expected to disappear when and if the public is made conscious of the diminishing character of the petroleum supply by a steady rise in prices. Concurrently with a future reaction against the price of gasoline there may be expected a reaction against the control of production by the producing states alone.

The Wagner Labor Act cases[2] have recently overshadowed the Supreme Court's earlier expressions upon the local charac-

---

[1] Perhaps the fact that the pipe line has carried the oil market to the well head, whereas the power line has brought the electrical market to the consumer's back yard, may be significant. See Pogue, *The Economic Structure of the American Petroleum Industry*, THIRD WORLD POWER CONFERENCE (1936) 25; *cf.* Watkins, *Organization of American Oil Industry, Fluctuations in Production, Stabilization Efforts, Price Control*, THIRD WORLD POWER CONFERENCE (1936).

[2] National Labor Relations Board v. Jones and Laughlin Corp., 301 U. S. 1 (1937), and cases decided therewith.

ter of mining and oil production.[1] If it should be demonstrated that the Federal Government may exercise over drilling and production a degree of control equal to that exercisable by the state, the day may be expected, upon a calender yet to be printed, .when the present system will be superseded by a system reflecting the interests of those who consume oil rather than those who produce it.[2]

On these considerations the industry may be thought of as facing two problems: the producers' desire for protection against present overproduction, which is primarily a concern of the producing states; and the national consumers' latent interest in a long-term supply at low cost, notwithstanding the limited size of the known reserves. The proration mechanism is a cushion against the first of these: the second, thus far, has been distant enough to require none. But behind the industry, pushing it into collision with this consumer problem, is a third factor—taxation. Today gasoline taxes nearly equal the refinery price for gasoline.[3] Twenty-seven and one-half cents of the motorist's gasoline dollar went for taxes in 1936, as against 10.3 cents in 1926. Technologic advances

---

[1] *Cf.* Champlin Ref. Co. v. Corporation Comm. of Okla., 286 U. S. 210 (1932); Carter v. Carter Coal Co., 298 U. S. 238 (1936); Kidd v. Pearson, 128 U. S. 1, 21 (1888); Oliver Iron Min. Co. v. Lord, 262 U. S. 172, 178 (1923); Hope Gas Co. v. Hall, 274 U. S. 284, 288 (1927); Lindsley v. Natural Carbonic Gas Co., 220 U. S. 61 (1911).

[2] For discussions of the constitutionality of various federal-control devices, see Stanley, *The Drama of the Oil Industry—Calling for Federal Regulation* (1931) 56 A. B. A. REP. 669; testimony of Amos L. Beaty, HEARINGS, Part I, on H. Res. 441, 73d Cong., (1934) 198 *et seq.*, and Part 4, 2839 *et seq.*, on the "quotas in commerce" theory; Ford, *Controlling Production of Oil* (1932) 30 MICH. L. REV. 1170; Doherty, Federal Oil Conservation Board hearings, May 27, 1926.

[3] The refinery price (weighted average of tank car prices, 12 wholesale markets, for regular grade gasoline) on Mar. 7, 1938, was 5.85 cents. See (Mar. 9, 1938) NATIONAL PETROLEUM NEWS, 45. The average gasoline tax, as of Mar. 1, 1938, was 5.44 cents, including a federal tax of 1 cent. (Figures from the American Petroleum Institute.)

have kept the tax problem at its distance thus far; the remainder of the motorist's dollar bought 5.14 gallons of gasoline in 1936, whereas it bought only 4.27 in 1926.[1] But there is a limit to technologic advances, while apparently there is none to the advance of taxation.

To the eyes of the future consumer, stimulated by the pressure on his pocket nerve exerted by rising taxes and diminishing supplies, the indulgence with which America has allowed an obsolete property law to force the dissipation of one of her natural endowments may well appear to be an incredible indictment. In similar retrospect, the ingenious system of composite state and federal control erected during the past decade may appear primitive. The industry might well have insisted upon the present creation of federal agencies to function as part of the Compact, in order to ensure a gradual and educated development of the federal influence, instead of a sudden and adverse one.[2] It may be impossible for four successors to believe that in the span of less than a century our system of laws allowed the loss of an essential resource and a resort to substitutes; that our people voluntarily submitted

---

[1] AMERICAN PETROLEUM INSTITUTE, PETROLEUM FACTS AND FIGURES (1937) 188.

[2] Congressman William P. Cole, Jr., chairman of a special committee which investigated the oil industry under H. Res. 441, 73d Cong. (1934), introduced a bill (H. Res. 9053, 74th Cong.) which would have created a federal "Petroleum Administrative Board" to act in cooperation with the Interstate Oil Compact Commission. The House Committee on Interstate and Foreign Commerce reported it favorably (REPORT 1801, 74th Cong.), but the bill which actually passed simply ratified the Compact. 49 STAT. 939 (1935). Governor E. W. Marland of Oklahoma had proposed, during negotiation of the Compact, a draft of compact and federal legislation which would have provided for direct federal participation. HEARINGS, Part 4, on H. Res. 441, 73d Cong. (1934) 2864, 2867. Texas declined to accept it. For criticism of the Compact, see H. Doc. 306, 75th Cong., 1st Sess. (1937); REPORT No. 1360 on H. J. Res. 456 by Mr. Cole, from the House Committee on Interstate and Foreign Commerce, 75th Cong., 1st Sess. (1937).

to the process; and that the industry was helpless to avoid it. And one of the unjust consequences may well be that, when the corrective process is appropriated by the consuming public or by those who purport to speak for it, the political penalty for a half-century's subservience to the "rule of capture" will fall upon an industry which already has been penalized financially by it many times over.   Ironically, Great Britain, which bequeathed us the doctrine of *Acton v. Blundell*, very promptly legislated herself out of subservience to the rule of capture when petroleum development was projected for the British Isles.[1]   But we, like the Byzantines of Gibbon's celebrated passage, have preserved the learning of the ancients to the neglect of the potentialities of our own times.

---

[1] The Petroleum (Production) Act of 1934 purports to vest ownership of oil in Great Britain in the Crown.   24 & 25 GEO. V, c. 36.   The Petroleum (Production) Regulations of 1935 provide for prospecting licenses of areas ranging from a minimum of 8 square miles to a maximum of 200, and mining licenses starting at 4 square miles.   In the unlikely event that a structure embraces more than one of these units, unit development may be permitted or required by the Board of Trade.   For a discussion of the system, see *The Organisation of the Production, Refining and Distribution of Petroleum and Petroleum Products* (*Great Britain*), THIRD WORLD POWER CONFERENCE (1936) 2.

12

THE BRITISH MOVEMENT FOR INDUSTRIAL RECONSTRUCTION AND THE CONTROL OF COMPETITIVE ACTIVITY*[1]

By Arthur F. Lucas†

SUMMARY

I. The movement toward the control of competitive activity in Great Britain and its relation to industrial reconstruction.—II. The extent and mechanism of control, 368.—III. Price-fixing, 377.—IV. Control of productive activity, 380.—V. The retirement of redundant and obsolete equipment, 388.—VI. Conclusions, 392.

Great Britain provides us with some highly interesting examples of the concrete application of the policy of controlled competition. In fact, most of the proposals that have been advanced in the United States for "industrial self-government" have their counterparts actually in operation in some section of British industry. It is far from true that Great Britain has been content to let recovery rest upon the unrestrained operation of normal economic forces. The desertion by British industrialists of their traditional policy of individualistic competition would be significant if undertaken for any reason. It has an added interest because its primary objective is not so much the extortion of monopoly profits as it is the establishment of a sound basis upon which industry

---

* *Quarterly Journal of Economics*, Volume XLIX, Number 2, February 1935, pages 206–235. Reprinted by the courtesy of the Harvard University Press and the author.

† Clark University.

[1] The author wishes to acknowledge the financial assistance of the Social Science Research Council in securing the data for this study.

may regain its former prosperity. The following exposition is concerned primarily with two aspects of this movement, first, its general nature including its underlying objectives and the type of machinery employed; and second, the procedure followed in meeting the chief issues that have arisen with an estimate of the success that has been attained.

I

The stage was set by the morass of economic difficulties that has afflicted Great Britain since the War and the rôles were taken by those industrialists and public officials who perceived the necessity for creating a new and improved organization in the productive mechanism of British industry.[1] It is not necessary to catalog the economic misfortunes in which British industry has been plunged since the War nor to emphasize the fact that the restoration of prosperity to many sections has required their complete reorganization. Neither are we able to discuss the manifold directions along which the reconstruction process has proceeded. The point that does need to be stressed is that centralized control has emerged as an essential feature of this process. A brief consideration of the objectives and the mechanism of reorganization will indicate its intimate relation to the control of competitive activity.

In the first place, the successful execution of many of the proposed measures of reform has seemed to be quite beyond the scope of individual effort. The bitter experience of the past decade has given rise to a strong conviction that permanent reconstruction demands the welding of an industry into a single administrative unit. While an industry "can do well

---

[1] It is true, of course, that even prior to the War successful assaults had been made on the competitive system in some sections of British industry. This pre-war development has been described by numerous authors and needs no comment here beyond the statement that it was not designed primarily as a measure of industrial reconstruction.

enough in ordinary times as an unintegrated mass of independent atoms," as a manifesto of the Liberal Party stated, "a prolonged period of severe adversity brings the same need for closer organization, for common purpose, for discipline, and above all for deliberate policy."[1]   As certain members of the Balfour Committee pointed out, "it is in proportion as the principle of co-operative action and control is accepted that we find economic success achieved, both at home and abroad."[2]   The numerous governmental and private investigating bodies that have dissected British industry so minutely in recent years have repeatedly stressed the fact that little progress toward permanent reorganization could be made until the traditional individualism of the British producer was replaced by vigorous coöperation.[3]

Centralized control is to promote the work of reconstruction in various ways.   First and foremost is the elimination of undesirable forms of competition.   There has been a widespread acceptance in Great Britain of the philosophy current in this country that the suppression of extreme forms of competition is a useful measure of recovery.   It is generally agreed that many of the technical features of reconstruction will never be adopted unless producers are released from the fear of incurring some competitive disadvantage.[4]   The London Times reflects a widely prevalent point of view when it states that competition has "proved extraordinarily wasteful in a

---

[1] Liberal Industrial Inquiry, Britain's Industrial Future, p. 135.   This report also states, "In modern conditions a tendency towards some degree of monopoly in an increasing number of industries is, in our opinion, inevitable and even, quite often, desirable in the interests of efficiency." Ibid., pp. 93–94.

[2] Committee on Industry and Trade, Final Report, p. 304.

[3] For examples see The Royal Commission on the Coal Industry Report, vol. I, pp. 233–234; Economic Advisory Council, Committee on, the Cotton Industry, Report, pp. 22–26; and The National Committee of the Iron and Steel Industry, Iron and Steel Reorganization Scheme, pp. 5–8.

[4] See Meakin, W., The New Industrial Revolution, p. 19.

period of contracting trade" and that "the abandonment of the old régime of free competition is necessary . . . because under modern industrial conditions, unless it is restricted, it no longer fulfills its economic function."[1] We find numerous industries adopting the point of view of the steel industry, that "the orderly progress of the industry can only be secured by the regulation of production in relation to demand both by international agreements and also, . . . by applying some degree of control to the individual producers. . . . "[2]

The control of competitive activity has another major objective in the reduction of the volume of productive facilities. Reorganization involves not merely the limitation of production, but also of the very capacity to produce. A large proportion of the productive equipment of the basic industries of Great Britain is either redundant or obsolete and the elimination of this "dead wood," to use the words of the Balfour Committee, "may be essential for the speedy restoration of prosperity and the resumption of growth from the more vigorous branches."[3] The strong statement of a representative group of cotton manufacturers, that the elimination of surplus capacity "is one of the most urgent problems before the industry and is an essential condition of any return to a sound basis for the trade as a whole," could have been said with nearly equal validity of most sections of

---

[1] The Times (London), May 17, 1930, p. 13.

[2] National Committee of the Iron and Steel Industry, op. cit., p. 5.

The suppression of competition has been so important a feature of most proposals for reorganization that Professor Gregory is reported to have characterized rationalization as "the new-fangled phrase to describe the old-fashioned device of eliminating competition." Quoted in Meakin, op. cit. p. 13. See also the statement of Professor MacGregor, League of Nations, Economic and Financial Section, International Cartels, p. 3; Haslam, A. P., The Law Relating to Trade Combinations, p. 190; and Rees, J. M., Trusts in British Industry, pp. 250–251.

[3] Committee on Industry and Trade, Final Report, p. 179.

British industry.[1] The impressive feature of this campaign is that its successful prosecution rests upon the mobilization of the entire industry behind a unified program of action. Competition has shown itself to be nearly impotent to reduce the congestion of redundant and obsolete units. The Balfour Committee summed up the situation when, in reference to the elimination of these firms, it stated that "the operation of free competition is a very slow and costly method for the purpose of securing such elimination" and suggested that the goal could be achieved "more speedily and 'rationally' and with less suffering through the mechanism of consolidation or agreement than by the unaided play of competition."[2]

Still another link between reorganization and the suppression of competition exists through the extension of the combination movement. It is generally agreed that in some cases nothing short of outright financial control will suffice to produce the needed reforms. The dictum of the Balfour Committee, that "generally speaking, the greater the completeness and permanence of the fusion of interests, the greater is the opportunity of substantial economy,"[3] reflects a widespread opinion among British industrialists. The result has been the formation of a large number of noteworthy mergers in recent years with far-reaching effects on the vigor of competitive activity.[4]

The suppression of competition has also been encouraged by numerous other developments in British industry, even tho some of these have only a remote connection with the program of reorganization. The efforts to reduce marketing

---

[1] Joint Committee of Cotton Trade Organizations, Proposals for Concentrating Production.

[2] Committee on Industry and Trade, Final Report, p. 179.

[3] Committee on Industry and Trade, Factors in Industrial and Commercial Efficiency, p. 9.

[4] For additional facts on recent combinations in British industry, see Fitzgerald, Patrick, Industrial Combination in England, and Allen, G. C., British Industries and Their Organization, Chap. xi.

costs have produced far-reaching changes in the mechanism of distribution whereby producers have embraced coöperative selling, the pooling of output, and similar arrangements merely as devices for efficient marketing. Technical and commercial research has been undertaken more and more on a coöperative basis. The steady growth of monopoly in foreign countries, particularly the rapid increase in the number of international cartels, has induced similar organizations in British industry either for purposes of participation or as a means of equalizing bargaining strength. The rapid growth of many new industries has brought into existence numerous groups of producers who are relatively free from the individualism of the basic industries. The progressive improvement in the means of transport has served to bring producers into closer proximity to one another and thus has facilitated coöperative action. Meanwhile, the adoption of the protective tariff has given monopoly an unprecedented opportunity.

Brief as the foregoing account of recent developments in British social philosophy and industrial structure necessarily has been, it will suffice to indicate the intimate relation between the process of rehabilitating industry and the movement toward centralized control. The recovery of British industry from its prolonged depression is considered to be a remote possibility so long as producers cling to their individualistic traditions. Even if competition is not charged with the entire responsibility for flooded markets, depressed prices, perpetuation of many uneconomic units, and the other disorders that have afflicted British industry since the War, it still is felt that only through control can these evils be eradicated. A glance at the concrete results of this movement will indicate that it already has served as the basis for a definite and comprehensive program of action.

II

The mere fact of the rapid development of centralized control in British industry needs no extended exposition here as the movement has been almost continuously under the scrutiny of governmental investigating bodies since the War. There was, for instance, the Committee on Trusts, which not long after the War was so impressed by the "increasing tendency to the formation of Trade Associations and Combinations, having for their purpose the restriction of competition and the control of prices," that it warned that these organizations "may within no distant period exercise a paramount control over all important branches of the British trade."[1] Again, in 1929, we find the Committee on Industry and Trade referring to the "tendency for separate productive undertakings to associate themselves with other similar enterprises with a view to regulating output, prices, marketing, or other matters."[2] Still later, in 1931, the Board of Trade felt it necessary to appoint a special committee to investigate certain practices in restraint of trade and a similar conclusion was drawn.[3]

Our primary interest lies in those comprehensive projects of control that have recently been devised for all of the basic industries and for some less important ones. Unquestionably the most significant of these is to be found in coal mining. As the author has described this experiment on a previous occasion, the briefest outline will suffice.[4] The industry was subjected to control by Parliamentary action in 1930 altho a voluntary system of restriction was already in operation in some sections. The Coal Mines Act of that year set up

---

[1] Ministry of Reconstruction, Committee on Trusts, Report, pp. 2 and 11.

[2] Committee on Industry and Trade, Final Report, p. 176.

[3] Board of Trade, Restraint of Trade, pp. 6–7. See also, Fitzgerald, Patrick, op. cit.; Gordon, A. P. L., Problem of Trust and Monopoly Control, 1928; Levy, H., Monopolies, Cartels and Trusts in British Industry, 1927; Marquand, H. A., The Dynamics of Industrial Combination, 1931; and Rees, J. M., Trusts in British Industry, 1922.

[4] Lucas, Arthur F., A British Experiment in the Control of Competition, in this Journal, May, 1934, pp. 418–441.

a Central Council and seventeen regional boards.[1] The former is charged with the duties of determining the total output of the industry and the allocation of this output to the several districts, while the regional boards determine the quotas for individual collieries and fix minimum prices. The Act also created a Coal Mines Reorganization Commission, which is attempting to rehabilitate the industry largely through the encouragement of combination.

The Government also has taken the initiative in the drafting by the iron and steel industry of an equally comprehensive program of reorganization and control. Altho many price-fixing arrangements[2] and even more rigid unions have been formed of late years in this industry, the inroads of foreign competition have been so serious that further control has appeared desirable to suppress disastrous price-cutting and to achieve the thoro reorganization necessary for a permanent recovery. In 1932, when the Government gave the industry a protective tariff, the Import Duties Advisory Board warned that the continuance of protection would be contingent upon the adoption of strong measures of reconstruction. The industry finally formulated a scheme, which it adopted in principle early in 1934, and is now engaged in putting into operation, altho it must be said with a marked lack of enthusiasm. The proposal calls for the organization of the entire industry into not more than twelve divisions, organized on a sectional rather than a regional basis.[3] These sections are to be placed under the immediate control of autonomous associations, which in turn are to be supervised in matters of general policy by a national federation. With the assistance of the federation, the associations are to control

---

[1] Coal Mines Act, 1930, 20 and 21, Geo. 5, Ch. 34.

[2] A so-called National Committee of the industry stated recently that there are about 50 price-fixing associations in the industry. National Committee of the Iron and Steel Industry, op. cit., p. 8.

[3] Ibid.

prices and output and are to promote combination, the reduction of excess capacity, and other measures of reconstruction.[1]

The other member of the big three of British industries, cotton textiles, has been considerably more faithful to its competitive traditions than its sister industries, altho it also is permeated with price rings.   In fact, some of the specialized sections such as finishing, cotton thread, and fine yarns can show groups as restrictive as any to be found in British industry.[2]   Strenuous efforts to bring the basic sections under control have, however, been made as the decline in cotton exports left such a wide margin between consumption and potential production that price-cutting and flooded markets have seemed to preclude all possibility of profitable operation for most mills.   As early as 1924 the Federation of Master Cotton Spinners' Associations attempted to enforce plans for concerted short-time working and the fixing of minimum prices.   The weakness of these agreements has led to efforts to form more rigid unions such as that of the American Cotton Yarn Association, Ltd., in 1927.   These, as well as several other similar expedients, have met a common fate in their failure to command adequate support.[3]

Progress toward the permanent rehabilitation of this vital industry was so slow that in 1930 the Economic Advisory Council turned its attention to the problem and appointed a committee to lay down the general lines along which reorganization should proceed.   This committee emphatically

[1] Chief progress in the adoption of this scheme has been made in the re-rolling section of the industry where strong measures of price control have been instituted.   The Economist, January 13, 1934, pp. 55–56.

[2] See Committee on Industry and Trade, Survey of Textile Industries, pp. 27–28.

[3] An attack along another sector has been made through the formation of several large combinations, chief of which is the Lancashire Cotton Corporation, Ltd.   But while possessing undoubted merits from a technical standpoint, combination has placed too great a financial burden on the constituent units to be generally successful.

declared that the industry could not hope to solve its troubles unless it could agree on a unified program of action.[1] The general association in the industry thereupon made a determined effort to eliminate what appeared to be the most serious evil by securing the consent of the industry to the imposition of a levy to purchase and scrap redundant and obsolete equipment.[2] In spite of the prominence of its supporters, the scheme aroused little favorable response. Following an unsuccessful poll in 1932 the scheme was virtually abandoned. The latest proposal, now being advanced by the Federation of Master Cotton Spinners' Associations, is an ambitious effort to eliminate redundant plants to encourage combination under the aegis of a voluntary association, which will also have power to fix prices and to limit output by a quota system.[3] The mill-owners, somewhat chastened by their troubles of the past few years, seem to be more responsive to this latest scheme.

In shipbuilding and flour milling we find two of the most significant examples in England of the centralization of authority to eliminate undesirable competition. These industries have been suffering from the same disorder and have adopted similar measures of relief—measures which stand out in sharp contrast to those adopted by the coal and steel industries. The malady is ruinous competition arising from surplus productive facilities and the remedy is a levy to finance the retirement of the redundant firms. In the shipbuilding industry a company, reassuringly called The National Shipbuilders' Security, Ltd., was formed early in 1930 to "purchase with a view to closing . . . any business or proper-

---

[1] Economic Advisory Council, Committee on the Cotton Industry, Report, pp. 24–26.

[2] The provisions of this scheme have been published by the so-called Joint Committee of Cotton Trade Organizations in a document with the title, Proposals for Concentrating Production.

[3] The Economist, July 21, 1934, pp. 106–107.

ties which may seem or be deemed likely to injure by competition or otherwise any business which the company is authorized to carry on," to quote its Memorandum of Association.[1] It is owned by shipbuilders possessing over 90 per cent of the capacity of the industry. Funds to purchase moribund yards have been secured from a £1,000,000 bond issue, the service charges of which are met by a one per cent levy on contracts. The Company itself does not directly control prices or output. It is believed, however, that there is a substantial unanimity of policy in the industry on these matters.

In milling, competition had become disastrously severe because of the profusion of small and inefficient mills that had sprung up during the War. In spite of sporadic efforts at reorganization, little of moment was accomplished until 1929 when a number of the most influential millers united in the Millers' Mutual Association for the purpose of imposing a rigid program of restriction on the industry. This association is reputed to have almost entirely suppressed competition between its members and to be a potent check upon the independent millers. To produce the necessary curtailment of capacity the Association has created an offspring, a limited company with the ambiguous title of The Purchase Finance Company, Ltd., which is aggressively purchasing and dismantling the undesired mills. Funds are secured from a levy on the industry, altho it is impossible to ascertain its amount or the basis upon which it is made. That it has brought in very substantial sums is common knowledge.

In the chemical, distilling, and match industries we find notable examples of the suppression of competition through complete financial control. The process of unifying the important sections of the chemical industry reached a culmination in 1926 in the formation of The Imperial Chemical Industries, Ltd., as the result of the merger of the four most

---

[1] The Companies' Search Office, Somerset House, London.

important chemical producing companies in England.[1] Many other firms have since been acquired so that the manufacture of chemicals is today probably the most thoroly centralized industry in the United Kingdom. The evolution of the distilling and match industries has been similar. Since 1925 and 1927, respectively, these industries have been organized into rigid combines which now have nearly exclusive control over the British production of these two commodities.

In addition to these elaborate schemes for controlling competition, British industry is replete with examples of the simpler types. Many associations have been formed since the War in an effort to bring order out of the chaos that has existed in the markets of most commodities.[2] A few selling organizations have also been formed such as the Associated China Clays, Ltd., and its successor, China Clay Producers, Ltd. The true cartel, however, has never been a favorite form of organization in Great Britain.

The program of control that is being imposed on agriculture should not be overlooked. The passage by Parliament of the Agricultural Marketing Act of 1931 meant the total desertion of the doctrine of free competition so far as it applies to this field.[3] This legislation aims to facilitate the marketing of agricultural products by the establishment of centralized control over all sales. It authorizes "schemes"

---

[1] These firms were Brunner Mond, Ltd., The British Dyestuffs Corporation, Ltd., The United Alkali Company, Ltd., and The Nobel Industries, Ltd. As these firms already possessed monopolistic powers in many lines, their merger in 1926 did not by itself create a monopoly.

[2] Some of the more outstanding associations formed since the War are: The National Sulphuric Acid Association, The National Benzol Federation, The Electric Lamp Manufacturers' Association of Great Britain, the famous BEAMA (The British Electrical and Allied Manufacturers' Association), The Cement Makers' Federation, The British Lead Manufacturers Association, The Federation of Calico Printers, and The Associated Brass and Copper Manufacturers of Great Britain.

[3] 21 and 22 Geo. 5, Ch. 42.

for all primary agricultural products as well as for many derived commodities such as bacon, cheese, and canned goods. Each scheme is to set up a central board, which may be a trading body, merely a regulatory agency, or both. If a trading organization, a board will in most cases have exclusive control of the distribution of the commodity concerned and may even engage in manufacturing. If a regulatory agency, a board will have the authority to specify grades and standards, to stipulate terms of sale, and to fix prices and quantities to be sold. Boards have already been set up for hops, potatoes, pigs, and milk and schemes are being drafted for several other important commodities. The Minister of Agriculture expects eventually to bring nearly all of the important agricultural commodities produced in the Kingdom under the control of these boards.

The foregoing list is not exhaustive but suffices to indicate the scope and vigor of the movement and to direct our attention to certain significant characteristics. It shows, for instance, the vigorous rôle played by the Government in the adoption of these schemes. In the coal industry and in agriculture, control was instituted by definite Parliamentary action. In iron and steel the Import Duties Advisory Board has been actively supported by governmental officials in its efforts to force reorganization. The cotton project was encouraged by the Economic Advisory Council. The shipbuilders were greatly assisted in financing their scheme by the Bank of England acting through The Bankers' Industrial Development Company, Ltd. The Imperial Chemical Industries, Ltd., was formed under the supervision of the Board of Trade, which at one time had representation on its directorate. Altho the Government has actually forced the suspension of competition in only a few cases, it has nearly always been ready to lend its active encouragement.

On the other hand, the Government has deliberately refrained from taking an active part in administration.

External interference has been limited to the general supervision exercised by the Board of Trade, the Mines Department, or other appropriate governmental office and to the surveillance of certain public boards such as the committees of investigation which have been authorized in the coal industry. No attempt has been made to dictate either in matters of general policy or in details of administration. Even the task of enforcement has generally been left to industry itself.

It should also be noted that by and large the attitude of industry itself toward control cannot be characterized as universally favorable. Certainly in the basic industries British producers cannot be said to be wholehearted disciples of the philosophy of control. The Coal Mines Act of 1930 was necessary because of the weakness of the voluntary schemes. The cotton industry has steadfastly refused even to adopt a scheme. The delay in putting the iron and steel project into operation is due to the open hostility of many steel producers. Complete acquiescence has been forthcoming only in relatively small and compact industries such as chemicals, shipbuilding, and flour milling. The lack of more enthusiastic support coupled with the policy of self-government obviously will have a considerable influence on the final results of these measures.

A further point to be noticed is that except where outright financial ownership has been instituted, as in chemicals, matches, and distilling, the effective instrument of control has been merely a loose association or its equivalent. Individual financial interests have generally been preserved intact. Not only does this add to the difficulty of enforcement, but it raises the serious problem of distributing the benefit and the burden of control equitably among individual producers. These underlying characteristics of the British projects should be borne in mind when considering the chief issues which have been encountered.

III

In discussing the issues presented by these projects of control, I shall confine attention to their three basic functions: the fixing of prices, the control of output, and the disposition of the moribund firms.   In regard to the first of these, the matter of price regulation, we should at the outset distinguish between control for the purpose of suppressing price-cutting and control to produce a generally higher level of prices.   The latter aspect is essentially a question of the limitation of output and will be discussed in that connection.   For the moment we are interested in control merely as a remedy for extreme price competition.

As to the mere fact of the suppression of price competition, little need be said.   Provided adequate support is received, the cessation of price-cutting may be expected to follow as a matter of course.   Innumerable examples could be cited to show that the elimination of price-cutting has been successfully achieved.   Among British industries mention might be made of electric cables, textile finishing, most chemicals, many sections of the iron and steel industry, cement, flour milling, and many others.   Numerous restrictive groups have been either complimented or condemned because of their success along these lines.   Sometimes the whole problem of price-cutting is entirely removed by the very nature of the machinery employed.   Financial control as in chemicals, pooling of sales as in china clay, or common marketing as in agriculture automatically render the continuance of competition an impossibility.

When the mechanism of control itself does not remove the very opportunity for price-cutting, the goal is generally attained by the adoption of some purely arbitrary rule that will insure the desired uniformity.   Thus the producers of re-rolled steel products are forbidden to quote prices below a given differential over the price of steel billets.   In the coal industry a procedure followed at one time by some ten districts was to accept the prices each mine actually was receiving prior to the initiation of control as the "basic" prices for that colliery. Future prices were to be determined by uniformly increasing or decreasing these basic prices.   If no such mechanical procedure is available, prices will generally be determined by "agreement among our leading members after a careful consideration of the state of the market," as one official described to the author the practice in his association. But even this uncertain procedure will result presumably in a uniform policy.

Altho the methods of fixing prices may be effective in stamping out price-cutting, they are open to serious objection on the grounds that they make little attempt to arrive at fundamentally sound answers to the innumerable questions that arise concerning specific prices.   Not only are these problems so complex as to be nearly incapable of satisfactory solution by even the most effective of methods; they frequently involve also such a direct clash of interests that acceptable solutions are obtainable at all only by the most empirical of compromises.   A detailed study of these problems would lead us far afield into the realm of practical price determination.   The mere mention of a few will indicate the folly of trying to settle them by rule-of-thumb methods.   A controversy that has threatened to cause the collapse of the whole program of price control in the coal industry arose over the question whether or not coal for export should be given the same price as coal for inland sales.   Exporters have insisted that in their overseas trade they should be permitted to quote prices below those set for the domestic market. Until recently, however, they have been successfully opposed by those producers who are confined to the domestic market and who fear that some of the low-priced coal supposedly intended for export would find its way into their markets.

A settlement was finally secured only by the threat of further Parliamentary action.[1] The coal industry has also been sharply divided over the question whether prices should reflect the utilization of their product. At present the law does not permit this. Many producers feel, however, that this restriction has caused a serious loss because some markets, as, for instance, the bunker trade, cannot bear as high a price as others.[2] The familiar delivered price controversy has also arisen—whether prices should be uniform at the point of production or at the point of consumption. Many districts of the coal industry have asked for some form of zoning system, but have been bitterly opposed by the smaller sections. Or what about quantity discounts? Frequently the large firms find it to their interest to quote more liberal discounts than the small firms can offer. Whether or not this constitutes price-cutting has been a sore point for years in cotton finishing. A few years ago an abrupt increase in the production of sulphuric acid by zinc smelters threatened to disrupt the market for the primary producers. Being only a by-product to the former, it was dumped on the market for what it would bring. Was this price-cutting and if so, how could prices be so adjusted as to meet the needs of both groups? Even apart from their human setting these questions are sufficiently perverse, while the personal interests involved are so directly antagonistic that a sound solution from an economic and social standpoint is a remote possibility.

This brings up another point, which in spite of its importance will be merely mentioned here, being as it is not a strictly economic issue. This is the matter of enforcement. Unsatisfactory compliance has been undoubtedly the greatest single difficulty faced in the control of prices in Great Britain.

---

[1] The Central Council has recently been authorized to fix separate quotas for inland and foreign sales and to name distinct prices for each.

[2] Mines Department, Coal Mines Act, 1930, Report . . . on the Working of Schemes . . . during the year 1932, p. 10.

More projects have foundered on this obstacle than on any other. For examples we have only to look at the early schemes in cotton textiles, at the many defunct associations in iron and steel, and at coal mining where the prevalence of evasion has been a potent reason for the lack of greater achievements.[1] The difficulty becomes particularly acute when, as has been the case in many industries, control has been adopted under pressure from the Government. No project of control, other than those which have eliminated individual initiative in the matter of sales entirely, has escaped the danger of overt non-compliance. This means that no procedure can be adopted that fails to secure nearly universal support. Herein lies not only the necessity for a uniform standard for fixing prices but also its weakness. For only by some arbitrary rule that will insure uniformity can support be retained at all. But this same standard falls so far short of harmonizing the diverse and sharply conflicting interests that any solution of the underlying questions of specific prices is possible only by a continuous succession of compromises.

IV

Our second major issue has to do with the control of output or, as it is commonly expressed, with the proper "coördination" of output to demand. Our concept of control will be somewhat simplified, however, if we dismiss the "coördination" of output as such entirely from consideration. After all, control aims not only at a common price but also at a higher price, and the only means whereby this can be accomplished is through the limitation of output. Whether one volume of output is better "coördinated" than a larger or smaller amount obviously depends upon the resulting movement of prices. To an industry suffering from a severe con-

---

[1] For the situation in the coal industry see my article already cited, pp. 433–434.

traction of its markets, therefore, coördination means nothing more than such a limitation of output that prices will be prevented from falling to a disastrously low level.

The evidence of the extent to which this has been done in British industry is rather meagre. It is true that coal prices have been maintained not far from their 1930 level in spite of the fact that the market has grown continually weaker. During the first quarter of 1930, for instance, the average proceeds per ton were 14s. 5.4d., while for the corresponding period in 1934 they were 13s. 7.6d., a decline of less than 10d.[1] It is generally agreed that this relative stability of prices is to be attributed largely to the program of control. There is certainly a marked contrast between coal mining and those sections of the textile industry where severe competition still exists. Again, the program of amputating the redundant and obsolete firms in shipbuilding had resulted by the beginning of 1934 in the elimination of berths possessing a capacity of more than 700,000 tons, nearly one-fourth the tonnage of the industry.[2] The dismantling of these yards apparently has materially aided the maintenance of prices. Nearly as much has been accomplished in flour milling.[3] It is also a fact that the newly created marketing board for hops secured prices for the 1933–34 crop nearly double those of the preceding year.[4] Other noteworthy illustrations could be found in certain chemical products, some sections of the steel industry, and in those industries which have long been under the control of powerful monopolies such as electric lamps, soap, and salt.

---

[1] Mines Department, Coal Mining Industry, Statistical Summary, by Quarters, 1930 and 1934.

[2] The Iron and Coal Trades Review, January 26, 1934, p. 163.

[3] The Miller, the leading trade journal of this industry, stated in 1933 that of the 600 mills in existence at the close of the War, 103 had been closed down. The Miller, March 7, 1933, p. 235.

[4] The Economist, August 4, 1934, p. 210.

On the other hand, these results cannot be attributed entirely to a deliberate policy of curtailment, if for no other reason than for the simple fact that such a policy has seldom been put in force.   In the coal industry, for instance, the fact that the Central Council has made little attempt to engineer a substantial curtailment of production, is indicated by the degree to which its allotments have been in excess of the tonnage the industry found advisable to raise anyway.   In some periods allotments have exceeded the actual tonnage raised by as much as 15 per cent.[1]   Furthermore, these restrictions have done little to rescue the coal industry from its threatened insolvency, inasmuch as the net proceeds fell from £3,782,000 in 1930 to £2,810,000 in 1931 and to £1,493,000 in 1932.[2]   In 1933 some improvement set in, but even at £2,178,000 earnings were considerably below their 1930 volume.

Likewise, in neither shipbuilding nor flour milling have there been serious efforts to curtail the volume of output, while in regard to the operations of the Hops Board, it is only necessary to note that the limitation of acreage is not one of its functions at all.   A surprisingly large number of associations, some of them among the strongest groups in British industry, make no attempt to curtail output directly, but—as for example, those in electric cables and tin-plate— simply designate the relative position of each producer by giving him a percentage of the total output, whatever it may prove to be.   Numerous industries such as shipbuilding and textile finishing are almost necessarily precluded from evolving a definite program of planned production, anyway, because they operate almost entirely upon individual orders.

---

[1] Mines Department, Coal Mines Act, 1930, Reports . . . on the Working of Schemes, 1931–34, passim.

[2] Mines Department, Coal Mining Industry, Statistical Summary, by Quarters, 1930 to 1932.

The whole experience of British industry with the control of output raises considerable skepticism as to the ability of centralized control even to assist materially in restoring profitable operations to a depressed industry. Of the many serious obstacles encountered, three should be given careful consideration. The first has to do with the practical difficulties of making accurate predictions of future market conditions. It goes without saying that success is in direct proportion to the accuracy with which future trends in the market are anticipated. But the demand has been so capricious during the past decade, not only because of the ravages of the depression but also because of the unpredictable impact of foreign conditions on the British market, that a long-run program is nearly worthless. The only available method of approach is that of trial and error and the margin of error is inevitably large. A good illustration of these difficulties is afforded in the coal industry at the time England abandoned the gold standard. The Central Council expected an increase in the demand and for the first quarter of 1932 permitted an output about 15 per cent larger than that for the same period in 1931.[1] As it happened, however, actual sales were even less than in the preceding year. Beneficial results through curtailment have been possible at all only because the market has been so demoralized that there has been no doubt that some degree of limitation has been clearly justified.

Serious as are the practical difficulties of reviving a prostrated industry through the limitation of productive activity, the task may become quite impossible because of the effects of restriction on the volume of sales and unit costs. A depressed industry is afflicted not only with a weak market, but frequently also with decreasing costs. To produce an appreciable rise in prices under these conditions frequently

---

[1] Mines Department, Coal Mines Act, 1930, Report . . . on the Working of Schemes . . . during the Year 1932, pp. 4–5.

will require such an extreme reduction in output that the resulting increase in unit costs coupled with the diminished gross return nullifies the potential profit from the increase in prices. That this is not mere speculation is shown by the situation in the coal industry. We have already noted that prices have been slowly but continuously receding since 1930 and it might seem that further support could well have been given by a more vigorous policy of curtailment. As a matter of fact, while output was reduced rather sharply at first, since 1932 it has been permitted to expand. From the first quarter of 1930 to the corresponding period in 1932 output declined about 17 per cent, while from 1932 to 1934 it increased about eight per cent.[1] Let us see what happened to costs and profits. From 1930 to 1932 costs actually increased notwithstanding falling prices generally and the introduction of almost desperate measures of economy. This increase in cost coupled with the decline in prices just about halved the net profit per ton, reducing it from *1s*. 1.4*d*. to 6.5*d*. Furthermore, the volume of sales upon which the net profit was earned also declined so that the total net revenue fell off about 60 per cent. These figures should now be compared with those for the period since 1932. Costs, which had stayed up all during 1931 and 1932, immediately began to fall. For the first quarter of 1934, despite the continued drop

---

[1] The following table shows the output, unit costs, and proceeds of the British coal industry for the first quarters of the years 1930, 1932, and 1934.

	1930	1932	1934
Output (In thousands of tons)*	59,958	49,637	53,121
Gross proceeds per ton	14*s*. 5.4*d*.	14*s*. 0.7*d*.	13*s*. 7.6*d*.
Net cost per ton	13*s*. 4.1*d*.	13*s*. 6.3*d*.	12*s*. 7.3*d*.
Net profit per ton	1*s*. 1.4*d*.	6.5*d*.	1*s*. 0.3*d*.
Total net return (In thousands)	£3,342	£1,337	£2,726

    * Tonnage of commercial sales.

Source: Mines Department, Coal Mining Industry, Statistical Summary, by quarters, 1930, 1932, 1934.

in prices, the unit net profit exceeded one shilling. With the larger volume of sales, the total return amounted to £2,726,-000, more than double its amount two years earlier.

Whatever the underlying factors may have been that produced this situation, its existence is undeniable and its implications must not be overlooked. Restriction of output was virtually powerless to produce any substantial improvement in the financial position of the coal industry during this time. It gave some support to prices, yes; but with little benefit to the industry in view of the increase in unit costs and the drop in total sales. The industry might have been better off financially if even the mild restrictions imposed in 1931 and 1932 had been held in abeyance in order to take advantage of a lower unit cost and a larger gross return. While this dilemma does not necessarily face all projects of control, it does suggest a serious limitation upon their effectiveness.

Pursuing our analysis in a somewhat different direction, we find a third serious obstacle to the effective control of output in its varying effects upon individual producers. A fundamental prerequisite for the successful functioning of control would seem to be not only an effective basis for applying restraints upon individual firms, but also an equitable one. The restrictions upon output as upon prices should take cognizance of the special needs of each producer as far as these needs are consistent with the general interests of the industry. As a matter of practical necessity, however, most large industries have adopted as arbitrary a basis for determining quotas as they have in fixing prices. This assures uniformity of treatment, to be sure, but by virtue of this very fact, also works serious injury on many individual firms.

Individual quotas have generally been based simply on past output. Thus in the coal industry the so-called "standard tonnages" upon which actual quotas are based are, for the most part, nothing but a reflection of output during some period in the past. Other factors are considered, to be sure,

but they have admittedly had little influence. In the manufacture of electric cables quotas are usually based on production figures for the three years prior to the time of determination. The Hop Marketing Board allots quotas on the basis
of the average annual production for the years 1928–32.
Manufacturers of electric lamps are permitted to increase
their output by not more than a given percentage in any one
year. Many schemes in cotton textiles have contemplated
merely a uniform reduction in working hours. Some such
procedure has been followed by nearly all projects. These
arbitrary standards are doubtless inevitable, for no touchstone has been found by which it is possible to single out the
less competent producers for special restraints and by which
those most worthy to survive may be released. Nevertheless
their employment is far from being a desirable course of procedure. One of the causes for the collapse of the schemes for
short-time working in cotton textiles was the refusal of firms
which needed continuous operation because of their large
investment in up-to-date equipment, to submit to the same
treatment that was given to the most antiquated plants in
the industry. In this industry also many firms still maintain
very close relations with their customers and saw a serious
threat to their markets by the program of control. Again,
the output of many plants which are closely integrated with
producing units in other industries depends entirely upon
external conditions and has little relation to their past operations. Or consider the many collieries which have opened up
new seams in recent years and are able to expand on a low
cost basis. Past output is obviously no criterion by which
to measure their future output. It is also said that the most
bitter opposition to the iron and steel project comes from
efficient producers who fear its effects on their operations.[1]
These illustrations could be multiplied almost indefinitely.

---

[1] Iron and Coal Trades Review, March 9, 1934, p. 419.

An inescapable handicap to the effective control of output is the injury that results from the application of a uniform basis of restriction.

This leads us to mention an inevitable but nevertheless anomalous feature of most projects of control. The difficulties of applying a uniform rule have been so great that most programs of restriction have necessarily stipulated certain conditions under which an individual firm might find relief. Thus, it is nearly always possible for a producer to exceed his quota upon payment of a fine. There may even be a provision, as in most sections of the coal industry, for the nearly unlimited transfer of quota from one firm to another either free of charge or at a nominal price. Many of the strong associations rely almost entirely upon voluntary limitation induced by systems of bonuses and penalties. The very fact that these expedients have been necessary is a confession of the inability to determine proper quotas. Furthermore, in removing one difficulty they but create another. For the cost to a producer of exceeding his official quota must be kept relatively low; otherwise permission to do so is meaningless. But this simply means that the official limits themselves become meaningless.[1] The whole program of restriction becomes little more than an instrument for compelling the ambitious producers, who may also be the most efficient ones, to contribute to the support of their erstwhile competitors.

---

[1] Consider, for example, the procedure followed in electric cables. The association does not set an arbitrary limit to the output of the industry as a whole, but merely fixes the relative position of each producer by designating his percentage of the total output of the industry. At the end of a given period the producer who has exceeded his official ratio pays a fine while the one who has failed to attain his ratio receives a bonus. These fines and bonuses are not excessive as they are adjusted as closely as possible to the average rate of profit in the industry. The Director himself stated to the author that this arrangement does not limit output at all, but simply discourages competition in securing orders.

V

Our third major issue has to do with the proper disposition of the moribund firms. It cannot be too strongly emphasized that no régime of control could be adopted as a permanent policy that did not make adequate provision for the elimination of these units. Cut-throat competition is, after all, merely symptomatic of a more basic difficulty, that of excess capacity. Price-cutting and other weapons of cut-throat competition can be used to lower the cost of production only when the producer possesses facilities which otherwise he cannot fully utilize.[1] The mere fact that control seems to be necessary to prevent extreme price-cutting is usually prima facie evidence that a surplus of productive facilities exists. This is true at any rate in Great Britain where the major programs of control have been evolved without exception for industries suffering from a deep-rooted maladjustment between productive facilities and market requirements.

What then is the effect of control on these surplus facilities? In the first place, it is evident that the control of prices and output will not by itself force the redundant and obsolete units into retirement. To anaesthetize the patient against the secondary results of a serious disease may make him more comfortable but hardly suffices to effect a permanent cure. The suppression of competition may curtail production but it does not affect the capacity to produce and thus leaves intact the burden of fixed charges and other costs arising from unused facilities. As an instrument for indus-

---

[1] That imaginary phenomenon, an enterprise operating at the point of optimum efficiency, would obviously have no incentive for cutting prices below its normal costs in an effort to increase its sales. Even if it succeeded in attracting custom from its competitors, its income account would suffer not only because of its lower prices, but also because of its higher costs. This is not asserting, however, that a producer who is well adjusted to the market has no incentive to acquire a monopoly. The lure of monopoly as an instrument of exploitation exists in any case.

trial reconstruction, therefore, the mere suppression of competition is futile. This fact would seem to be too obvious to need elaboration.

A far more serious indictment of the systematic control of competition, but also one that must be made with greater caution, is that control actually tends to retard the process of industrial rehabilitation by insulating the individual producer from the pressure of economic necessity. The thoro reorganization necessary to administer a lasting cure for the basic ills of industry inevitably affects many of the existing equities adversely and will in most cases be accomplished only under the rowell of stern necessity. When competition is eliminated this stimulant is lost. The British record supplies numerous illustrations of this fact. The first attempts at control in the cotton industry, for instance, contemplated merely a uniform curtailment of operations with the fixing of minimum prices and made no provision for the retirement of the many uneconomic mills. As the Managing Director of the Lancashire Cotton Corporation has stated, the idea of "a very great number" of producers "was to raise prices so that those prices would give them satisfactory returns, and that they could fold their hands and do nothing."[1] But, he adds, "we very early discovered that that particular policy would lead to disaster, as, in fact, it did." Or consider the situation in the coal industry. Official efforts to reorganize this industry have been made since 1926 when Parliament gave some encouragement to combination by granting relief from the onerous stamp duties. Numerous important mergers did actually result. But after competition was suspended by the Act of 1930, the combination movement came nearly to a standstill. The basing of quotas largely on past output has led inevitably to the preservation of many

---

[1] Ryan, J., The Economic Journal, September 1930, p. 358; at a meeting of the Royal Economic Society.

mines which undeniably should have been closed.[1]   This situation led The Economist to remark in 1932 that "there has been little advance during recent years towards greater aggregate efficiency in the industry. . . . The unification movement . . . has not been accelerated, despite the efforts of the Commission set up to promote amalgamations; there is some evidence, indeed, that it has been retarded."[2]

Again, the proposed program of restriction in the iron and steel industry has been strongly criticized on the score that it places altogether too much emphasis on the suppression of competition and too little on permanent reorganization.   One of the most prominent steel men in Great Britain has condemned ,the project on the grounds that it would aggravate the existing unsatisfactory conditions by prolonging the life of the inefficient firms and by delaying the erection of modern plants, the centralization of operations, and the adoption of other devices to increase efficiency.[3]   Many price-fixing groups have also called forth repeated complaints on the same score.   The grievances of Lancashire against the price rings in cotton textiles are due apparently not merely to the fact that prices are exorbitant, but also to the latters' policy in permitting full profits to every firm regardless of its efficiency. The sub committee of the Committee on Trusts investigating

---

[1] For examples see my article previously cited, pp. 433–434.

[2] The Economist, July 30, 1932, p. 213.   This journal also referred to the actual case of a contemplated merger which failed of completion because apparently "some concerns, assured at least of a precarious existence by the quota, were holding out, as the price of absorption, for better financial terms than their true value as part of a larger organization would warrant."   On another occasion The Economist expressed its belief that the general effect of a quota system "must ultimately, if it is left unsupplemented by a thoro reorganization, be to maintain precisely that dispersion of output which it is the main object of rationalization to correct.   As a permanent feature of an unrationalized industry a quota system is obviously most undesirable." Ibid., November 26, 1932, p. 978.

[3] Iron and Coal Trades Review, February 23, 1934, p. 356.

the salt industry also stated that the Salt Association "aimed at and achieved" a standard of prices "such as has enabled the manufacturing company, responsible for 60 per cent of the total output of this country and whose costs of production are highest (viz., The Salt Union) to make, instead of a loss on salt, a profit."[1]

As we have already noted, various expedients have been devised to replace the influence of competition in forcing the obsolete and redundant units out of existence. Thus in the coal industry there is the program of compulsory combination under the supervision of a governmental commission. In shipbuilding and flour milling the goal is being achieved through a tax on current output to provide funds for the dismantling of obsolete equipment. A similar arrangement has been tentatively tried in one section of the coal industry and has been suggested for cotton textiles and for iron and steel. In the chemical industry the complete fusion of interests has permitted the ready closure of any plant that has once outlived its usefulness.[2] Several associations have attempted to concentrate production by their systems of rewards and penalties in conjunction with their restrictions on output.[3]

---

[1] Committee on Trusts, Findings and Decisions of a Sub-Committee Appointed to Enquire into the Existence and Effect of a Ring in the Salt Trade, p. 11.

[2] The procedure in chemicals has been described by the Chairman of the Imperial Chemical Industries as follows: "We have thus steadily aimed at concentrating manufacturers, not only by the transfer of business from one group to another, but by the fresh capital expenditure at the most appropriate point. The other side of the picture is the closing down of plants judged on the facts to be redundant. Some factories have been sold, some have been demolished, others are still held for fresh developments." Imperial Chemical Industries, Ltd., Proceedings at the Fifth Annual Meeting, 1932, p. 7.

[3] In the Cable Makers' Association, for instance, the bonuses and fines are adjusted as closely as possible to the average rate of profits in the industry. The high-cost producer, therefore, presumably finds it to his interest

A detailed analysis of the operation of these devices is beyond the provision of this paper. It is enough for our purpose to note that they do not solve the underlying difficulty of disposing of the moribund firms on satisfactory terms. With the removal of economic pressure the retirement of these firms can be accomplished only upon conditions acceptable to them. The various expedients that have been devised are essentially merely methods of distributing the burden, not of reducing it. Those devices have been most successful, therefore, which have embodied ways and means of securing the necessary funds such as the levy in shipbuilding and outright ownership in chemicals. Even here, the enervating influence of suppressing competition is not removed even tho it may be counteracted. It might also be noted in passing that the reduction of capacity could probably be achieved just as effectively without the suppression of competition and certainly more economically.[1]

VI

In assessing this movement toward industrial government, what can be said of the legitimate province of control in our industrial organization? In particular, has it been possible to devise artificial agencies to perform the traditional functions of competition? While conclusions based merely on these experiments in British industry must be drawn with caution at the present time, there are certain inferences that

---

to produce even less than his allotted amount as his profit from his bonus is greater than that from actual operation. On the other hand, the low cost producer finds it equally advantageous to exceed his official quota as his profits from operation more than compensate him for the fines he is compelled to pay. The Director of this Association is very positive that this arrangement is concentrating production in the efficient firms.

[1] For further discussion of the problem of eliminating surplus capacity, see two articles by the author, British Experiments in the Reduction of Excess Industrial Capacity, The Harvard Business Review, July 1934, pp. 389–397 and The Bankers' Industrial Development Company, The Harvard Business Review, April 1933, pp. 270–279.

would seem to possess a sound basis in fact. There is little question, for instance, that control over competitive activity is useful in restoring some semblance of order to an industry demoralized by the ravages of a serious depression. No one could doubt this fact who has observed conditions in coal mining, shipbuilding, chemicals, flour milling, or in numerous industries governed by strong associations. Control has produced a greater stability in prices and has discouraged some individual producers from indulging in excessive production. As a prohibitory measure designed to eradicate undesirable competitive practices, control unquestionably has some utility.

On the other hand, it is equally clear that except under unusually favorable circumstances the attainable benefits of control are limited to this purely negative function of proscribing objectionable practices. The severe restrictions necessary to achieve anything like the commonly accepted objectives of control are, for the most part, both impracticable and socially undesirable. If British experience teaches us nothing more, it has at least demonstrated the inherent difficulties of minutely regulating prices, of imposing rigid restraints upon the productive activity of individual enterprises, of manipulating total output to meet fluctuations in the demand, and of concentrating output in the most efficient firms—all of which are essential functions of a strong, inclusory, and permanent program of control.

The effectiveness of control is obviously impaired by the slight possibility of arriving at sound solutions to the innumerable technical questions involving the determination of prices, the fixing of quotas, and the anticipation of market requirements. British experience does not speak well of human abilities to administer even a mild program of control successfully and it is obvious that the greater the degree of control the more complex and controversial do these problems become. Furthermore, the sharply conflicting interests that exist within all large and diversified industries and the

inability to give adequate recognition to the special needs of
individual firms tend to preclude any very coercive restrictions. Most projects of control in Great Britain have of
necessity adopted a policy of moderation to avoid the aliena-
tion of large groups of producers. The utility of control is
further limited by the fact that it must function for the most
part through arbitrary and inflexible standards. Likewise,
no means have been discovered for imposing severe restraints
upon the less competent members of an industry without
injury to the more proficient enterprises. Either the efficient
producers must submit to the same restraints as the inefficient, or they must contribute financially to the support of
the latter through some form of penalty and bonus system,
or else buy them out altogether. Still again, there is the fact
that the manipulation of output may be more of a detriment
than a help in rescuing a depressed industry from its financial
distress because of the weakness of the market and the existence
of large fixed costs.

It further cannot be denied that strong control has a
decided tendency to cushion the weak and inefficient producers against normal economic pressure. This fact has been
clearly demonstrated in regard to permanent rehabilitation.
While the suspension of competition may have some use as a
sweet coating to the less attractive medicine of reorganization,
it is itself a deterrent rather than a help because of its protection of the indigent enterprise. The suspension of competition is to be tolerated only in conjunction with stronger
measures of reorganization and even here its effect is to make
the task of reform more costly and less likely to be successfully
accomplished.

So long as control attempts to function through a form of
organization patterned after the association, there would
seem to be no escape from its basic defects except possibly
in small and compact industries. The retention of financially
independent units inevitably leads to the imposition of harsh
restraints upon competent producers, to undue considera-

tion for moribund enterprises, to internal dissension, and to the constant threat of overt non-compliance. If control is to become a permanent feature of our industrial organization, complete financial unification would thus seem to be necessary. It was with the weakness of the association in mind that a prominent member of the British Government expressed to the author his opinion that thoro control of the coal industry will not be possible until it is fused into a single entity after the example of the chemical industry.

In any case, a highly restrictive policy of control will inevitably compel the government to take an active part in administration. No one could watch the operation of these projects of control in British industry without considerable apprehension of their effects upon the public welfare. At best, self-government has been utilized to advance the interests of a majority of producers in an industry while in certain cases it has led to control by a small minority. It is hardly necessary to give illustrations of the nearly complete disregard for the public welfare that will result when the policy of control is determined under these conditions. It is inconceivable that a strongly restrictive program would be tolerated in this country without close government supervision.

If competition is no longer able to perform a useful social service, it should presumably be abandoned, but certainly not until alternative agencies have been devised that are competent to take its place. This clearly has not been done in Great Britain. The broader objectives of control are not only nearly unattainable but to some extent, also, clearly undesirable. Their realization will probably necessitate a profound recasting of our industrial structure by extending centralization to the point of complete financial unification. It will also vastly increase the participation by the government in industry. It is extremely doubtful if the evils of competition are sufficiently serious to require such drastic treatment.

13

THE ORGANIZATION OF INDUSTRY
AND THE THEORY OF PRICES*

By Arthur Robert Burns†

I. The Need for Better Information about the Operation of the Industrial System

The sad state of our knowledge concerning the operation of the industrial system is beyond dispute. The system is widely criticized, but largely in terms of its failure to retain forever the gay vitality of youth. It has outgrown the nineteenth-century theory based upon the existence of competitive individualism. Half a century ago legislatures perceived tendencies in this direction but their response was to pass laws prohibiting it from growing up. Opportunities for the small man were to be preserved together with freedom for enterprise in the reduction of costs and the attraction of increased business as a reward. With the inherent contradictions in this policy the courts were left to wrestle. They decided that, where choice was necessary, the opportunities for enterprise should be preserved; "mere size is no offense," although it may fundamentally change the market. More recently the economies of large-scale production have been

* *The Journal of Political Economy*, Volume XLV, Number 5, October 1937, Pages 662–680. Reprinted by the courtesy of the University of Chicago Press and the author.

A paper presented to a round-table meeting of the American Economic Association of Chicago, Illinois, in December, 1936.

† Columbia University.

most actively sought in the distribution of consumers' goods where the inefficiency of many middlemen had been criticized.   Here again the reaction of the legislature has been to seek to protect the small man.   Discriminatory taxes have been levied on chain stores and the Robinson-Patman Act has been passed, also in response to pressure to prevent the growth of large units in the field of distribution.   But basically the law rests upon ideas derived from that very competitive individualism that has brought about the elimination of the small man.   In general terms the price advantages to large buyers must, under the Act, be no more than are justified by differences in the cost of such business.   Proposals for dealing with basing-point systems have similarly been derived from theories born out of the conditions of a previous age.   These governmental policies hamper in unpredictable ways those operating larger businesses and incur their resentment.   The smaller business man and the broader public is disillusioned. None but the legal profession has cause for satisfaction.   The lack of an adequate basis of theory upon which to base control was demonstrated upon the grand scale by the career of the National Recovery Administration.

Competitive individualism was as short-lived in America as in Germany.   Evidences of the emergence of monopoly capitalism began to appear in the seventies of the last century. But the evidence accumulated for half a century before economists were moved to reformulate the theory of prices more in harmony with existing conditions.   Theories of imperfect competition resting ultimately upon the theory of monopoly (of which pure competition is a limiting case) have, however, emerged during the past decade and are one of the most notable developments in economic theory.   These developments of theory, equally with urgent problems of public policy, call for more adequate analysis of the operation of the industrial system.   But theory cannot make great advances without far more adequate data than are now available. Studies of the operation of individual industries are, therefore, seriously needed.

This regeneration of interest in the analysis of production requires a reconsideration of the orientation of industry studies. Industrial studies during the last thirty or forty years have, in general, been very inadequate. For this inadequacy there is a variety of reasons. The segregation of the study of industry under the despairing title, "Trust and Corporation Problems," has insulated it from contact with theory, while theorists have, perhaps, not been free from a lofty disdain of practical industrial problems. The state of theory and the objectives of social policy impelled discussion into an attempt to separate the black sheep from the white, the monopolistic from the competitive businesses. Even this separation was often made by implication, because of the scarcity of data apart from that derived from litigation. Social policy itself, of course, was largely responsible for this scarcity. Out of fear of the antitrust laws business men took refuge in secrecy where possible, and otherwise in a language of ambiguity. The predominance of records of prosecutions of trusts among the sources of data also diverted energy into a sterile analysis of judicial rationalizations of decisions.

In this setting studies of particular industries assumed a conventional pattern. They discussed mainly the technique of production and the organization of the industry. The technical processes of production were described. The organization of the industry was discussed in terms of the size and location of plants, the scope of ownership control (the size and extent of integration of firms), the organization of marketing, labor conditions, and the history of mergers in the industry. The purpose of these studies was never explicit or clear: they seem to have sought justification implicitly in a belief in "art for art's sake." The discussion of wages and possibly profits implied an interest in the functioning of the industry, but the aspect of its functioning most vital to theorists and purchasers, namely its price policy, received scant attention.

II. The Desirable Type of Industrial Study

A change of orientation is clearly necessary. The desirable direction of analysis can be stated briefly in terms of two interdependent requirements. The central objective of such studies should be the analysis of the behavior of prices. The methods of analysis should be aimed at facilitating the improvement of general price theory. Analysis of the behavior of prices means a generalized explanation of the reasons why prices behave as they do. This explanation must, of course, run in terms of conditions of supply and demand.

If analysis begins from prices, these prices may be described at the outset by reference to characteristics such as the frequency and amplitude of fluctuations (or its obverse—the degree of their stability), their geographical pattern (more especially with reference to the existence of basing-point or zone systems of pricing), the differences in the prices of similar products sold to different types of buyers, and the behavior of the margins between the prices of vertically related products. They may also be examined to discover the incidence of changes in the cost of raw materials or labor, of taxation, and of improvements in methods of production, organization, and selling. All these approaches must, however, be regarded as achieving no more than the posing of important questions worth investigation. Implicitly these approaches rest upon theories of prices arising out of competitive individualism. Stable prices, for instance, attract attention because of their improbability in the conditions to which nineteenth-century price theory relates. This type of beginning is useful in shaking faith in these price theories, provided it stimulates efforts to substitute a better theory.

The primary necessity, therefore, is some broad framework within which price behavior can be analyzed in various indus-

tries.   It must explain the relationship between the organization of production and distribution and the behavior of
buyers and of prices.   The theory of competitive individualism provided for this interrelationship by the use of the
categories of the entrepreneur, the competitive market, and
the rational individual buyer.   The unsuitability of these
categories is now evident.   But the logical foundations of the
interlocked concepts of the entrepreneur and the market
suggest the broad basis of a more realistic approach.   The
significance of the entrepreneur concept lay in its emphasis
upon the concentration under a single hat of the functions of
risking capital and making price and production policy.   It
assumed the exercise of these powers in a social setting which
stimulated attempts to maximize income and provided for its
enjoyment by the individual.   The concept of the competitive
market assumed restrictions upon the field of influence of the
entrepreneur sufficient to prevent attempts to maximize his
income by the exercise of control of the market price.   It
implied also the absence of any inducement to seek the
enhancement of his income by influencing demand.   The
seller did not incur expenditure directed to influencing
the appraisals made by buyers of the satisfactions from various
ways of disbursing their income.   The categories of the entrepreneur and the market rest, therefore, upon analysis in terms
of the distribution of various functions.   While the particular
distribution implicit in the categories may be rejected, analysis
in terms of the present distribution of these same functions
provides a basis for theoretical advance.

A. THE DISINTEGRATION OF THE ENTREPRENEUR

This approach, in terms of the distribution of functions, is
implicit in recent analysis of the functioning of the corporation
as an economic enterprise unit.   But while the separation
of ownership and control has been emphasized, there are
many more steps to go.   If the entrepreneur has been thus

disintegrated, where are now located the various functions grouped under the word "control"? What forces playing upon those exercising these functions will determine the nature of production and price policy? Shall we continue to assume that controllers seek to maximize their individual incomes? If so will they, in so doing, be likely to bring about the most effective adjustment of the means of production to effective demand? Or must we make fresh assumptions concerning the motivation of directors and business executives? If so, what are these assumptions and what do they imply concerning the utilization of the means of production? These may appear to be questions of so broad a nature as to lie outside the scope of studies of particular industries. Yet they are fundamental to the understanding of policy in most industries, and only by synthesizing the answers suggested by one industry after another can we discover whether there is any approach to realism in the contemporary practice of regarding the corporation as a not too seriously modified kind of entrepreneur.

Contemporaneously with the disintegration of the entrepreneur, and largely influenced by it, other relocations of function have occurred. These relocations have been of three major types. First, there has been an enlargement of the area within a given industry in which the decisions of an entreprise unit as to prices and production are effective. In other words, the scale of production has increased. Second, the variety of activities within the scope of an enterprise unit has changed. The disintegration of productive activities characteristic of the earlier stages of industrialization, when the major emphasis was upon the pursuit of the economies of specialization, has been replaced in considerable measure by a reverse movement of reintegration. Third, the function of appraising anticipated utilities has been in part transferred from buyer to seller. The analysis of prices must be made in the light of the present pattern of arrangement of these functions.

B. THE SCALE OF PRODUCTION

The growth of the size of firms in relation to the markets in which they operate has been one of the major stimulants to the revision of general price theory. Attempts have been made to determine the level of prices where there are few or only two firms. These theories depend upon the seller's estimate of the effect upon costs of slight increases in output, and upon revenue of slight increases of sales. Estimates of marginal costs depend upon estimates of the points at which slightly greater output would involve the operation of various units of the factors of production at more than the rate that is most efficient from the technological point of view. So long as every unit of every factor is capable of greater utilization and the price of raw materials would not have been raised if the demand for them had been greater, marginal costs fall. Unless marginal revenue would have fallen faster, increased output would be profitable. But, in fact, additional units of some factors, especially labor, would usually be necessary if output were greater. Frequently additional units of equipment are also necessary. Estimates of the additional costs of additions to output depend upon the way in which producers calculate them. Timeless curves consisting of a series of alternative "might have been" situations cannot, moreover, be used in practice. Time marches in. Although the major equipment may not need extension if added output is planned, minor equipment may. This minor equipment may be durable. Within very short periods, and limits which vary from plant to plant, added output might be attempted by "overworking" parts of the plant or labor force. Within longer periods such a policy may not be possible.

The size of firms in relation to the market is even more important in relation to calculations of marginal revenue. Here also the time period of calculation is important. It is sometimes said that business men take account of the possibility that increases in price will stimulate the investigation of substitute materials. The fewness of firms in a market also makes it impossible for firms to ignore the effects of changes in their production policy upon their revenues by way of the effect of such changes upon market prices. If open changes in prices are likely to be met immediately by rivals, sellers must choose between secret price-cutting and attempts to calculate the effect upon revenues of changes in price as well as output. This latter policy necessitates calculation of the elasticity of demand for the product generally. How are these estimates of elasticity made? Is there any reason to believe that they are biased in the direction of underestimating elasticity? How far is elasticity affected by the price policies of enterprisers engaged in processes nearer to the buyer? How far is it affected by the price policies of enterprisers producing commodities demanded jointly with that under consideration? How do sellers estimate the elasticity of demand for their own product, i.e., their probable share of the probable future total market? How do conflicting estimates of these various matters work out in the market? Changes in price may affect the demand for their output by hastening the departure of firms from the industry. In what manner and under what conditions have firms departed from the industry?

Finally, in the longer run, prices are influenced by the expansion of capacity by new or old firms. It is often said that business men now take account of the likelihood that prices above a certain amount will attract new investment. Such investment tends to reduce the rate at which plants can be operated. Thus sellers may calculate marginal revenue over periods long enough to permit the expansion of the industry. Their estimates of the point at which such additional investment will occur are an important influence upon price policy, and the manner in which they are made may partly explain prices. But even where managers pursue the most profitable

policy in the shorter run, that policy is influenced by the
actions of those who introduce new investment. Theoretically
investment is attracted when anticipated prices over the life
of the firm or plant exceed anticipated average costs. But
plants frequently have no determinate life; they are often in
a state of continuous partial renewal. Firms, still less, are
regarded as having any particular expectation of life. Over
what future period are prices and costs estimated? In calculating average costs over long periods for the purpose of
determining the profitability of new investment some average
rate of utilization of plant must be assumed. How is this rate
determined? How important an element in total costs are
overhead costs? Upon what basis is obsolescence calculated?
In other words, no full explanation of prices can be obtained
without information concerning the rules by which business
men are guided in calculations of average cost and, therefore,
profit or loss. Strictly speaking these are questions that arise
wherever overhead costs are important, and are incurred in
anticipation of continued production over long periods of time,
irrespective of the number of firms in the market. They
assume significant proportions, however, generally with
increases in the size of firms. They are an application of the
general principle that increases in the scale of production and
the durability of the means of production, both physical and
organizational, blur calculations of unit cost. The manner
in which business men meet this difficulty is an important
influence upon prices and an important subject for investigation.

Analysis of the number of firms in a market raises two types
of difficulty. On the one hand it is necessary to define the
market in the geographical dimension, and, on the other, in
the commodity dimension. Where the high cost of transportation and the wide distribution of markets and the means of
production induce the decentralization of production, but the
economies of large-scale production lead to a measure of local
concentration, there may be a number of plants, although in

any local market there may be relatively few sellers.   There are, for instance, many cement plants in the United States, but there are large areas in which the number of sellers in competition is few.   These markets are somewhat interconnected upon a "chain" principle because there is a wide measure of overlapping in the market territories of the various producers.   These conditions are likely to lead to basing-point systems, the fuller investigation of which would throw much light upon conditions of price-making in industries of this type.

Definition of markets in the commodity dimension has also attracted the attention of theorists interested in imperfect competition.   If physical homogeneity of products is made the basis of the definition of the market there is no more than one seller in each of a number of markets in which each make of automobile is sold.   If assumed identity of utilities offered is the basis of definition each brand of a "product" is sold in a separate market.   Calculations of marginal revenue depend upon the assumed preferences of buyers for one brand or model over another.   What is the basis of calculation of these preferences?

Concentration of the power to make price and production policy in a market, combined with the possibility of subdividing demand into classes with different elasticities of demand, suggests the profitability of discriminatory prices for identical products.   Discriminatory prices can be maintained, of course, only if the sales in the low-priced market can be prevented from seeping into the higher-priced market.   Such discriminatory prices have existed in the aluminum, glass, and milk markets, as well as in the market for public utility services.   The analysis of the causes and consequences of such policies is a prerequisite to the understanding of prices in industries where they occur.

The foregoing discussion of the concentration of functions within markets implies that the concentration rests upon a basis of ownership (such as the development of large corporations). But concentration may occur, although more tenuously, without such a basis. The managers of corporations who are, from the legal point of view, able to make independent decisions concerning prices and output, may find it undesirable to exercise this power. They may accept the leadership of some other firm in the matter of prices. Allegations of price leadership, however, require careful scrutiny. Within what limits can the leader make policy and remain a leader? Does he lead only in making changes in open prices although actual prices are often secret and different from open prices? Over what periods in the past has the same firm initiated changes that have been generally followed by rivals? A mere speedy acceptance by others of price changes initiated first by one and then by another firm is not evidence of leadership. Discussions of statistics of production and prices by trade associations or their managers, or by trade journals, may involve a partial concentration of some of the functions of making price and production policy. In these various ways a partial concentration of price-making powers may occur without a similar concentration of powers to decide upon methods of production. Analysis of the effects of this distribution of functions will help to explain the behavior of some prices.

C. THE INTEGRATION OF INDUSTRIAL ACTIVITIES

The second aspect of the distribution of functions to which attention has already been directed concerns the variety of productive activities falling within the scope of a single planning policy. This planning replaces the market as the means of effecting the larger co-ordination of economic activity. The discussion of integration has suffered especially from a crudity of approach indicated by the use of such terms as "vertical," "horizontal," "collateral," and "circular." The principles of specialization and integration are everywhere in conflict. The unintegrated enterprise unit would be difficult to define and more difficult to discover. The prevalence of integration, the forms in which it expresses itself, and its consequences must be analyzed in every industry as an integral part of the explanation of prices.

Vertical integration is a pattern of control covering activities related to each other in that the raw material of one is the finished product of another. Every enterprise controls more than one process defined in narrow terms. Vertical integration, of course, rarely results in control of a series of activities which can be visualized as lying along a single line. Developments back toward raw materials or forward toward the final buyer usually result in a fan-shaped pattern of development. First there is need of information concerning the actual shape of the field of influence of a single planning policy and especially of the differences from one enterprise unit to another. Then causes and consequences must be sought. Physical economies in the saving of energy in the form of heat, transportation, etc., may explain some degree of integration, but at what point are such considerations outweighed by others and what are these other considerations? Vertical integration may derive from attempts to escape monopoly prices for raw materials or to share in their profits. It may limit such monopoly policies. It may curb price competition in types of activity nearer to the ultimate buyer. At least it tends to eliminate the market as a check upon the efficiency of production at frequent stages on the way to the ultimate purchaser. Costs at each stage of production can be calculated only after arbitrary allocations have been made of the cost of functions carried on for more than one branch of activity, within which class at least some of the functions of management must fall. Where equally integrated firms compete, even though their costs may be similar, some may be more efficient in some stages and others in other stages. None may attain the lowest costs in every stage. On the other hand, however, vertical integration by enlarging the field of conscious rational planning may co-ordinate various types of economic activity more effectively than the kind of market that would otherwise be available.

The types of integration other than vertical have hitherto received scant attention, as is indicated by the crudity of the terminology applied to them. Investigation of the underlying forces impelling integration is essential and may even supply a better basis for classifying and describing integration. Integration can often be traced to efforts to utilize to the full the resources applied to some one branch of activity, which may be that of sales promotion or management. Here also there are difficulties of definition. Is retail distribution a single function or is the retail distribution of tooth paste a function? In the latter event retailing is a widely integrated activity.

One of the major consequences of integration lies in its tendency further to blur the concept of cost. It has been suggested that mass production blurs unit costs partly because of the number of units produced simultaneously and partly because the production of units at different times is bound together, owing to the fact that some costs cover production over long periods. Integration blurs even the costs of different classes of goods. Few enterprise units have an output completely homogeneous. They produce different sizes, grades, and patterns of commodity, if not products differing still more widely. The calculation of both marginal and average costs now rests also upon the allocation of costs between products. It has already been remarked that vertical integration presents this problem with regard at least to the cost of management. Where integration follows other patterns there is frequently a wider range of costs requiring allocation.

Where machinery is transferable from the production of one product or style of product to another the quantities of the various products produced depend upon estimated costs of transfer and adaptation and upon detailed allocations of the total costs of machinery to particular products. In some branches of the engineering and textile industries the relative production and prices of a variety of products may be influenced by the basis of this calculation. Far more information is needed, therefore, concerning the policies of business managers with regard to such allocations of cost.

The transfer of productive facilities from the production of one type of product to another may be regarded as integration in the time dimension. It is not, however, limited to transfers from the production of one established commodity to that of another. In most industries there have been changes in the physical nature of the product over long periods of time. Such changes are one of the ways in which sellers compete for the favor of the buyer. They may take the form of attempts to meet the buyer's need more adequately, or to meet them less adequately (at a saving of cost), without his realizing until too late the error of his appraisal of anticipated utilities. Thus, on the one hand, there is need for analysis of the manner in which the costs or savings resulting from changes in the nature of the output are calculated. On the other hand, there is need for analysis of the effects of these changes upon buyers. It is necessary to check the statement that while prices have remained stable or risen in some industries where there is reason to believe that the cost of producing an unchanged product has fallen, the purchaser has gained because he is "getting more for his money." Is he getting more? If so, is it as much more as he should get in view of the improving techniques of production? Has he had an opportunity to purchase the constant commodity at the declining price as well as the allegedly improved commodity at a higher price than the unchanging one? If not, why not?

The integration of varying patterns of productive activity under a single planning policy, like the concentration of functions within a single market, is most simply conceived of on a basis of property control, e.g., of the organization of corporations controlling a variety of activities. But integration of some of the functions still conventionally associated with entrepreneurship is also secured without any property basis. We are too apt to accept one of the implied assumptions of the entrepreneur and market concepts, that entrepreneurs sell their goods on the market at the prevailing price and that ownership passes immediately and possession soon after. There are few industries in which goods are thus sold. Contracts of sale have been rapidly elaborated. The urge to modification has often been strong enough to induce the discovery of ways of surmounting legal obstacles placed in the way of elaboration. Distributors have been transformed into agents of the manufacturer, rather than buyers for resale on their own account. Provisions in sale and agency contracts for resale price maintenance, tying clauses, and conditional rebates in fact transfer some of the functions of the entrepreneur in a later stage of production or distribution into the hands of managers in earlier stages. The analysis of price behavior can be approached in terms of the new location of functions and the interests of those now exercising them. The substitution of leasing for selling goods, and especially producers' goods, shifts the incidence of overhead costs and changes the pressures toward economical utilization, the basis of payment being a vital element affecting these reactions. Long-term contracts and guaranties against price decline can be analyzed in similar terms. In short, apart from the disintegration of the entrepreneur within the structure of the corporation, major functions affecting industrial policy can be and are transferred by such devices from enterprises in one line of activity to those in another. The scope of managerial power varies from enterprise to enterprise. The extent of the functions of enterprise units, more particularly with regard to price and production policy, must be studied partly in the types of contract by which his output is disposed of and the means of production secured. Furthermore, there must be sought some explanation of the forces making for these relocations of function. They may lie in monopoly elements on the other side of the market. These may be due to the fewness of sellers. But they may be due to vaguer types of concentration already referred to, such as trade-association activities aimed at standardizing contracts of sale. These transfers of powers to determine price policy and the range of activities are not accompanied by transfer of control over the technique of producing the goods or providing the services. In this respect they differ from integration based on property control and necessitate separate analysis.

D. SALES PROMOTION AND SIMILAR ACTIVITIES

The third aspect of the relocation of functions referred to above is the partial transfer to the seller of the function of appraising the utilities of products to buyers. In other words, in many industries, and especially in those selling consumers' goods, sellers find it profitable to apply economic resources to efforts to influence the attitudes of buyers. They do not adjust to an assumed demand but they seek to change that demand. They endeavor to promote sales, and any tendency toward normal profits works out, at least partly, through the raising of costs rather than the decline of prices. Expenditure on sales promotion causes a different allocation of the means of production from that likely under competitive individualism. The explanation of prices in such industries necessitates, therefore, an analysis of the causes influencing the cost of sales promotion and of the reasons for any expenditure on such activities.

The costs of sales promotion are, however, difficult to segregate. The nature of a product may be changed in order to provide a peg upon which to hang advertising claims of superiority over rival products. The superiority may be real.

Quality competition is reinforced by sales promotion. But the change may be merely a "talking point" for salesmen. What seem to be manufacturing costs are in reality partly selling costs. Style competition is equally difficult to segregate from quality competition on the one hand and sales promotion on the other. It is difficult to draw a sharp line between changes which improve the quality of the product and those which merely accelerate the obsolescence of stocks of goods already in the hands of consumers.

The cost of style competition needs more penetrating analysis than it has yet received. Because from the point of view of manufacturing it involves time integration similar to that involved in quality competition, it involves calculations of cost which are similar. It may involve also greater fluctuations in business in industries affected by style, and also in industries from which they obtain supplies.

But both sales promotion and style competition may also tend toward cost reduction. Where buyers like change, style sometimes limits the range of choice at any given time by prescribing limits on the subvarieties of products sold at any given time. Sales promotion may, by standardizing demand, increase the economies of large-scale production. These are all possibilities calling for verification, and no doubt conditions vary from industry to industry.

From the point of view of the buyer, both sales promotion and style competition may involve diminutions of satisfactions, both because of the price-raising tendencies of these policies and because of their tendency to obstruct the rational spending of incomes. Where style and quality changes are frequent, the appraisal of utilities becomes extremely difficult and burdensome. But at least style competition may make way for changes that in fact turn out to be improvements in quality. Changes in the aesthetic aspects of commodities may, moreover, yield a direct satisfaction. There is no justification for the argument that satisfactions of this kind should not be provided by the industrial system. It may, of course, be contended that opportunity to enjoy them is ill distributed owing to the general pattern of income distribution and that a different distribution might place less emphasis upon them. It is sometimes said that consumers obtain style at the expense of quality and especially durability. But satisfaction derived from changes in the aesthetic aspects of commodities suggests the rationality of reducing the durability of products. The measurement of the satisfactions obtained from style changes is of course extremely difficult.

The relation between these types of rivalry and rivalry in prices also needs analysis. Sales promotion and style competition may arise out of the relative unimportance of price competition. Price competition may fall into decline because of fears of its consequences among sellers with large overhead and unemployed capacity. But it seems also to decline because of a lack of interest on the part of buyers. Conventional "price lines" have been established, for instance, in a number of branches of the clothing industries. Rivalry remains, however, in sales promotion and also in matters of quality and style. But adjustments in the constitution of the garment are often necessitated, or made possible, by changes in costs. A rise in the price of cotton tends to bring about changes in the nature and quantity of the fabric used and the trimmings of the product sold at a stable price.

III. THE NEED FOR PRICE DATA

The study of industry beginning from the study of prices presupposes the existence of data concerning prices. At the present time economists using published series are often the jest of industrial specialists. The commodities for which price series are available are sometimes of decreasing importance in the industries of whose price policies they seem at first sight to be an index. If the commodity continues to be important it may be defined in terms that permit wide changes in the attractiveness of the product to buyers or in the cost of production to sellers. The prices may be list prices which are subject to large and fluctuating discounts with the result that the series is no guide to actual prices. The prices may be collected from a few large firms and for that reason be unrepresentative of the actual prices.

The improvement of information concerning prices is not a matter merely of widening the scope of administrative action or of more intensive statistical effort, although both are needed. The problem of constructing price series that allow for changes in quality and style is one in the solution of which the economic theorist must co-operate. Individual research workers can undoubtedly contribute in designing series, but co-operation on a considerable scale is necessary to supply adequate data, and there is urgent need for a large and expensive extension of the activities of the United States Bureau of Labor Statistics in reporting wholesale prices. In some fields there appear to be great difficulties in the way of adequate reporting. The calculation of a price for an "industry" or "market" in which the products of different sellers vary presents a problem requiring the exercise of considerable ingenuity.

IV. THE PROBLEM OF ORGANIZING RESEARCH

These observations present questions concerning the organization of research along the line suggested. If the field of primary study is marked off in terms of "industries" there are obvious problems of demarcation. It has already been suggested that very rigid definitions of the market may narrowly restrict fields of study to individual firms. The integration of production, on the other hand, results in single enterprise units being concerned with a number of markets. The wider the scope of the definition of a "market" or an "industry" for the purposes of study the greater is the task of analysis. Fairly wide definition is desirable but the task of investigation is usually so large as to be beyond the reach of an individual worker. Special organization and financing is necessary. But there is an alternative method of approach. A particular aspect of price behavior may be studied comparatively in a number of industries or markets. Industries with basing-point systems may be selected for study in terms of the apparent causes of the adoption of such a method of marketing and its more immediate consequences. Even such studies tend to broaden out into studies of these industries as a whole, but they can be arbitrarily limited. Such devices differ in their operation in different industries, but a knowledge of the nature of these differences and their causes can throw much light upon the working of the industrial system. Open price systems, resale price maintenance, seasonal prices, and various types of relationship between manufacturers and distributors all suggest aspects of market operation that could be approached in this manner. Although many of these studies also require large-scale research activities, useful studies can be made upon the basis of carefully selected samples.

V. CONCLUSION

Our knowledge of the operation of the organization for the production and distribution of industrial goods is woefully inadequate. General price theory must, of course, remain general in the sense that it must be protected from developing into an unwieldy collection of information concerning particular industries. But it must also truthfully reflect the broader outlines of the outside world. At present, in spite of the efforts of theorists to modify general theory to take account of fundamental changes in the organization of industry, general theory remains open to criticism in terms both of its doubtful general validity and its weakness as a basis for social policy. The remedy for this situation is not, however, to cast all theory aside on the ground that it is too early to establish any general theory in relation to the operation of the present industrial system. Industrial studies based upon no theory are, of course, impossible. But industrial studies have been made upon the basis of assumptions never made explicit and which would appear naïve if they were.

Studies of industry should be oriented by reference to the best theories that can be established in the present state of knowledge. A basic uniformity of approach is necessary in order to facilitate the attainment of the ultimate objective of a generalized description of the functioning of industry.

The theory upon which the general approach is based must not, of course, be regarded as a framework into which the facts must be crammed even at the expense of their distortion. It is a set of tentative and interrelated assumptions to be tested.

The desirable point of major emphasis in future studies is the explanation of prices. Prices seem to be the best starting-point for investigation because they offer a basis for the appraisal of the efficiency of the system. They are, of course, no more than the point of emphasis. The basic ideas out of which concepts of the entrepreneur and the market developed suggest a theoretical framework for industry studies in terms of the new distributions of function that are evolving. The location of the major functions concerning the making of price and production policy should be sought out behind their legal façade. Information must then be sought concerning the influences affecting the way in which powers so located are exercised.

Effective research depends upon the availability of data and upon large-scale research activities. Means must be sought for reducing the secrecy with which data are now surrounded, and funds must be made available for its assembly and the improvement of methods of summarization.

There should be constant mutual interaction between industry studies and the general theories by reference to which they have been organized. It is sometimes suggested that the integration of the results of the studies of different industries can be too speedy and that it should be postponed until some later date when more information shall be available. The principle of unripe time does not appear to be valid here. The time is always ripe for the integration of separate industry studies in the sense of an attempt to embody their results in broad descriptions of the industrial system, just as it is always ripe for the rechecking of the new theory in particular industries. There should also always be kept in view the obvious fact that the subject of analysis—the industrial system —is in process of constant change. The description of conditions as they are should always be a prelude to an attempt to discover how they came to be so, as well as the consequences of past changes.

Competition has in the past been defined, if at all, in terms of a particular organization of industry. That organization has now so far diverged from the type essential to competition as formerly conceived that a better description of the organization of industry and of its functioning has long been needed. The suggested reformulation of the general theory of prices is proposed as a way of discovering how the system at present operates. If the concept of competition continues to be found useful in some modified form the nature of the modifications will be best described in terms of a statement of past changes in the structure and functioning of the industrial system. Thus will the nature of contemporary competition emerge.

14

"FULL UTILIZATION," EQUILIBRIUM, AND THE EXPANSION OF PRODUCTION[*][1]

By A. B. Wolfe[†]

Summary

I. The problem, 419.—II. The utilization of productive resources in a static equilibrium economy: (1) The formal theory of prices and price-margins in an equilibrium economy, 422, (2) Static equilibrium and continuity, 425; (3) The meaning of "full utilization" in a static equilibrium economy, 428.—III. The determinants of margins in a static equilibrium economy: (1) The limiting power of the strategic factor, 432; (2) Real costs as determinant of margins of utilization, 434; (3) Institutional limitations on the utilization of resources, 437; (4) The monetary supply as the limiting factor, 439.—IV. The expansion of production without increase of the supply of money: (1) Through saving of monetary income, 441; (2) Through technological improvement, 444.—V. Expansion of production with increase in the monetary supply, 445.—Overcoming inflated price-resistances, 446.—Effect of reduction in the interest rate, 449.—Conclusion, 450

---

[*] *The Quarterly Journal of Economics*, Volume LIV, Number 4, August 1940, Part 1, Pages 539–565. Reprinted by the courtesy of the Harvard University Press and the author.

[†] Ohio State University.

[1] While he has not adopted them in every case, the writer desires to acknowledge valuable criticisms and suggestions from his colleagues, Messrs. H. J. Bittermann, Benjamin Caplan, and Michael Sapir.

Professor W. H. Hutt's recent book, The Theory of Idle Resources (London, 1939), came to hand after the completion of the present article. While Professor Hutt deals with certain conditions making for non-utilization or under-utilization not touched on in the present paper, his treatment is preponderantly taxonomic, and it does not give consideration to the importance of institutional limitations such as are emphasized here.

I. The Problem

The assumption of "full utilization" of productive resources has crucial significance both in the theory of the business cycle and in that of capital formation and expansion of production. It has been basic to all equilibrium theory, at least prior to Keynes,[1] because the presence of unused resources has been deemed incompatible with full equilibrium. It is crucial in the theory of capital accumulation, because whether resources are fully employed or not makes a vast difference in the conditions under which production can be increased. If resources are already fully utilized, it is commonly argued, and if they are distributed among the various industries in the economical and efficient way required by the theory of ideal equilibrium, no amount of increase in the monetary investment fund can increase production. According to this view, and taking full utilization in a physical or technological sense, the only possible way to arrive at a net increase in aggregate production is through technological improvement, which makes possible the more efficient use of resources already employed.

While the physical or technological concept of "full utilization" is probably not the usual one, it is a possible and for certain purposes a logical meaning. But there are at least two other possible interpretations: (1) that in which the limit of full utilization is taken as fixed by the price margins and productivity margins of the objective system of prices in the assumed equilibrium economy; (2) that in which the limit is not thus found in the pure relativities of the price structure, but in (a) the subjective valuations and rationalizations of the owners of resources, and (b) the institutional restrictions which prevent the use of factors which would otherwise be economically available. It is impossible to tell what exact meaning most writers attach to the term, because they have apparently assumed that it is *per se* clear, exact, and determinate. Proba-

---

[1] The General Theory of Employment, Interest and Money, 1936.

bly most writers mean by it simply that all the resources which can be used at the prevailing prices are used. So far as the present writer knows, the only economists who suggest that the term "full utilization" is vague and slippery are Haberler and Hutt. Haberler issues the caution: "The term 'unused capacity' must be interpreted with great care. There is always some inferior capacity which can handle an increase of demand."[1]

Since, as will be shown, the objective price-margin concept of full utilization is purely formal, since it tells little as to what the actual limitations on the use of any factor are, and since the possible alternative meanings of the term have thus far not received adequate consideration, the present discussion has the following objectives: (1) to discover whether a definite and understandable meaning can be attached to the concept, "full utilization"; (2) to examine the relation between full utilization (however defined) and total equilibrium; (3) to show that even in an economy in complete equilibrium, full utilization can be taken in a physical or absolute sense only for the limiting or strategic factor; (4) to emphasize the fact that "full utilization," and the concept of equilibrium itself, are at best only relative, and that they are indeterminate except in reference to (a) margins (both physical and price) of utilization, (b) the price-resistances and real costs of the owners of factors of production, and (c) the limitations set by institutional patterns on the available supplies of resources. It will be shown (5) that in any actual economy there is rarely, if ever, full utilization, even of the strategic factor or factors, in other than the limits set, not by potential physical supply, but, more or less elastically, by custom, by the differential economic power of property rights, and by owners' real costs, genuine or rationalized. And finally (6) it will be argued that the chief obstacle to expanding production is not

[1] Prosperity and Depression, 1937, p. 91, note. Cf. also p. 185, note.

the "full utilization" of the physical factors of production but the lack of an additional monetary investment fund available at a rate of interest low enough to counterbalance the use of inferior (and hitherto submarginal) resources.[1]

Were the meaning of "full utilization" merely a verbal question, it would not be worth discussion. It is far more than verbal, however, because the whole theory of capital accumulation, and of the terms on which production can be expanded, in the absence of technological improvement, pivots on the "availability" of an additional supply of the factors of production, especially an additional supply of the limiting or strategic factor or factors.[2] The usual argument that if all the factors of production are already fully utilized, additional investment funds can find outlet only in bidding up the price of factors and taking part of the supply of them away from entrepreneurs who are already employing them depends for its validity on the meaning to be attached to "full utilization." If "full utilization" be taken in the purely formal sense, in relation to the price-margins of the other factors within the equilibrium, full utilization is itself a purely relative term. It

---

[1] Explicit justification of the assumption of "full utilization" is made by Hayek, who assumes that in full equilibrium there are no "available" unused productive resources. "It is not true," he says, "that the existence of unused resources is a *necessary* condition for an increase of output, nor are we entitled to take such a situation as a starting point for theoretical analysis. . . . The existence of such unused resources is itself a fact which needs explanation. It is not explained by static analysis and, accordingly, we are not entitled to take it for granted. . . . On the contrary, it is my conviction that if we want to explain economic phenomena at all, we have no means available but to build on the foundations given by the tendency toward an equilibrium. . . . If we are to proceed systematically, therefore, we must start with a situation which is already sufficiently explained by the general body of economic theory. And the only situation which satisfies this criterion is the situation in which all available resources are employed." *Prices and Production*, 1931, pp. 31, 32.

[2] The nature and influence of strategic factors are discussed below, pp. 432.

amounts to little more than a formal distinction between infra-marginal and submarginal resources. It does not tell us why the margins are where they are. No reason is at once apparent why full utilization in this purely formal and relative sense should bar the expansion of production, given some increase in the monetary investment fund and some slight change in the price structure. If, on the other hand, "full utilization" be defined in terms of price-resistances, which are, to be sure, relative to one another, but which are fundamentally conditioned and determined by the matrix of institutional custom, convention, sentiments, differentials in economic power, and emulative rationalizations of "real costs," it is quite possible to conceive of conditions in which production cannot be expanded.

II. The Utilization of Productive Resources in a Static Equilibrium Economy

1. The Formal Theory of Price and Price-margins in an Equilibrium Economy

Formalistically, the demands, supplies, and prices of all economic goods in an equilibrium economy are mutually interdependent, and consequently the only "solution" which objective price analysis can offer as to the configuration of price-relativities is a set of hypothetical Walrasian simultaneous equations. Such a solution is, of course, purely conceptual. It contributes to an understanding of the theoretical unity of the price system, but it cannot evaluate the real forces which make any single price what it is. The same observation holds true of the "margins" on which all equilibrium price analysis is based. Any one margin—of utility or vendibility, or of productivity—is a function of all other margins. Mathematical price analysis, without recourse to institutional determinants, has no choice but to regard these mutual functions and relativities as a self-determined system. In pure price analysis they have no frame of reference in any even relatively independent variables, such as real costs or institutional restrictions.

Within its own limits, the pure logic of these mutual relativities is unassailable. All prices, all quantities demanded and supplied, and all margins of utilization fall automatically into their prearranged places. But only a logical ideal is described. Pure price analysis, however elegant mathematically or however sound logically, is inherently superficial. Nothing substantive, either as to a static equilibrium situation or as to passage from one equilibrium to another, can be contributed without reference to the subjective valuations, and their resultant price-resistances, of the owners of productive resources and consumption goods. These price-resistances are doubtless relative to one another and to the established price structure, but back of the price-resistances—the prices held out for, the prices regarded as the "going prices," the prices regarded as in some sense "fair"—lies a whole system of institutional configurations: the established habits and customs as to rights and duties, the rules of property and contract, the customary use of economic power, and the accepted standards of just price, going wage, reasonable profit, and individual and class status. All these institutional and sociopsychological influences are powerful agencies in the maintenance of the subjective valuations, emerging in price-demands and price-resistances, upon which all objective prices and price-margins rest.

Full utilization can be defined, of course, only with reference to some margin. Theoretically this is a margin of productivity, first of physical, but in the last analysis value, productivity. Whether a given unit of a resource is economically infra- or submarginal depends on its quality or grade and upon the price which the owner demands for it. If there should happen to be a relatively large potential supply of factoral units only slightly inferior in quality to units utilized in the equilibrium, a relatively small decline in owners' price-resistances would occasion a relatively large increase in actual supply by making submarginal units inframarginal and available for utilization in expanding production.[1]

Prior to Keynes, as above noted, it was commonly assumed that equilibrium and full utilization are correlative, and that the presence of unused resources is evidence of disequilibrium. It is desirable, however, to ascertain whether the presence or absence of unused factors is a proper criterion of distinction between equilibrium and disequilibrium. The issue may be, in part, one of definition, not only of full utilization but of equilibrium. If full utilization be taken in purely price-margin terms, equilibrium must be understood in the same sense. A dollar invested in any factor yields the same value return as a dollar invested in any other factor. The boundary line between employable and unemployable resources is fixed

---

[1] The price-resistances which make a factor submarginal produce what Keynes calls *voluntary* unemployment—"unemployment due to the refusal or inability of a unit of labor, as a result of legislation or social practices or of combination for collective bargaining or of slow response to change or of mere human obstinacy, to accept a reward corresponding to the value of the product attributable to its marginal productivity." (The General Theory of Employment, Interest and Money, p. 6.)

Keynes' concept of involuntary unemployment obscures the definition of margin of utilization. For if men are willing to accept a lower real wage (provided the money wage be not reduced), and could earn the lower real wage if employed, they are, in terms of real productivity and the real (disutility) costs of their services, inframarginal, though unemployed. Keynes appears to argue that workers ordinarily get a real wage in excess of what would be necessary to counterbalance their real costs, and that, so long as reduction of real wages is "put over" on them by a rise in the monetary cost of living (the price of wage-goods), they will not demand higher monetary wages until the rise in the price of wage-goods brings about an equality between real wages and real costs of labor.

It must be remembered, however, that objective price equilibrium analysis refuses to go back of sheer price margins to these "real" margins—and it is one of the arguments of this paper that that is a critical shortcoming of the "objective" approach.

by the marginal productivities, in monetary terms, of the respective factors. In pure price analysis these margins are, of course, determined by the mutual price relativities, pressures, and competitions within the closed economy, or more narrowly within the mutual competitions of the factors actually employed. So long as there are no technological, institutional, or psychological changes which alter the price-resistances of owners of factoral units, both inframarginal and submarginal, the equilibrium will remain stable. But the moment any such changes occur, the equilibrium is upset and the process of establishing a new equilibrium is begun. When such institutional influences as change in the monetary supply or such psychological influences as changes in the propensity to consume or in liquidity preference are introduced, as they are by Keynes, the hitherto stable equilibrium becomes unstable, for any slight change in psychology or in institutional controls shifts the margins and may change unemployable into employable resources, or *vice versa*. So long as we think of equality of marginal value-productivities, arrived at solely through the relativity of pressures within an autonomous price structure, it would seem to make no difference whether the unutilized factoral units (which are presumably but not necessarily of inferior grade) are voluntarily or involuntarily unemployed. Keynes' equilibrium is essentially an unstable equilibrium, and it is difficult to see how we can conceive of a stable equilibrium, in any other than the superficial price-relativity sense, without positing some basic datum line, or parameter, either in the limited physical supply of some strategic factor, or in certain stable institutional restrictions, or in some basic real cost which must be remunerated if employment is to be accepted.

2. *Static Equilibrium and Continuity*

A complete list of all the assumptions necessary to the theory of the "static state" would be very long. It would have to include not only logically necessary assumptions, such as those noted by Marshall and J. B. Clark, but also an impressive list of institutional assumptions which never overtly appear in the analysis of pure price theorists. Among the logically necessary assumptions are: a given and unchanging state of the arts, a population stationary both in size and in demographic composition, unchanging efficiency of management and organization,[1] and a fixed potential supply of all the respective factors of production and of their respective grades.

The assumption of fixed potential supplies is not only contrary to fact but also to possibility, if we are to assume that the equilibrium is to be a continuous economy lasting through any considerable period of time. In a given state of the arts, the available reserves of certain basic raw materials—those commonly known as "wasting" or more accurately as exhaustible —must be continuously decreasing, and the real cost of their extraction continuously increasing. This is equivalent to saying that the price structure will have to undergo continuous change and that, in consequence, the concept of a continuous static equilibrium is one which can never have a counterpart in the real world. The only escape from this difficulty is to assume that any "stable" equilibrium is an affair of a moment only. In any case, it is necessary to ignore the diminishing supplies of raw materials, since we wish to keep conditions constant while we introduce some one variable—

---

[1] Professor Hayek, while excluding technological change from the total equilibrium which he assumes, allows improvement in management and organization, in the form of change to more "roundabout" and more time-consuming productive processes. While nominally excluding technological change, he therefore practically admits it. He starts with total equilibrium, but immediately departs from it by introducing a dynamic disturbance. This however, is really all that can be done with complete equilibrium. For in a total and stable equilibrium nothing ever happens except repetition of routine processes. To make anything happen, one must introduce a "disturbance."

an added supply of liquid investment capital—and observe the effect.

If our economy be in static and continuous equilibrium, there will be continuously utilized, per unit of time, a certain quantity of each factor, and within certain marginal limits, a certain quantity of each grade of each factor. There will also, of course, be a certain physical output, per unit of time, of each kind of product, a certain aggregate physical output, and a certain total output of services. Each factor of production, or its owners, will receive a fixed share in the total output-flow of consumption goods and services, in ratio to the respective scarcities, whether natural or institutional, and the respective marginal productivities or technological efficiencies of the respective factors and grades of factors. Within this fixed system of functions and rewards, each utilized unit of a factor will receive a value-return according to its productivity, or efficiency, relative to the productivity, or efficiency, of other units (of different grades) of the same factor.[1]

It is important to note that in a continuous economy such as we are here assuming, production, and indeed the whole economic process, is essentially timeless. Viewed as an organic whole, as distinguished from the efforts of individuals or groups to buy (through monetary savings) places of permanent advantage (annuities) for themselves on the stream of

---

[1] This will be true, however, only on the assumption that each unit is paid according to its productivity. This means, in effect, payment at piece rates. If time rates are not accurately adjusted to what would be the equilibrium—the economic—piece rates, the assumption of pay according to productivity will not hold, or will hold only institutionally, in that the owners of certain factors, through the device of rigid time-rates, are able to maintain economic pressure (threat of withdrawal of supply) and thus to an extent define their own "productivity." Were it not that even under perfect competition institutional habits of sentiment as to fair price, going wages, etc. are always present, we could say that all such pressures are connected with the price rigidities of monopolistic attitudes and practices. (Cf. Hutt, op. cit., chs. 10, 11.)

income—the productive process turns out at constant rate of flow, a continuous stream of consumption goods and services.[1] This is the continuous national dividend or net social income. In this sense, not only may capital be regarded as an abstract immortal continuum, as J. B. Clark conceived it; every other factor may also be so regarded. It is not capital only which synchronizes production and consumption; it is the entire continuous production-marketing-consumption process.

The continuous static economy may be regarded essentially as a huge going concern. Between its various parts and functions there are contractual and accounting relations (as there must be in any form of economic organization, whether capitalism or communism). These inner relations, social, legal, customary, determine the distribution of income, and they may either promote or hamper its production; but in a broad view—that of "social" or "engineering" economics— they are incidental to the main process, which is that of the technological production of goods and services—the real national dividend. The national dividend is always a present dividend. As long as the economy remains in full and stable equilibrium, it produces this stream of goods and services at unchanging unit cost. The total monetary cost, per unit of time, is of course also the total monetary income.

3. *The Meaning of "Full Utilization" in a Static Equilibrium Economy*

Obviously, when a theorist assumes without definition of terms that "all available productive resources are fully utilized," he must regard the meanings of "available," "productive resources," and "full utilization" as self-evident. But there are puzzling ambiguities in each of these terms. Is the criterion of availability physical or economic? If it is

---

[1] Cf. A. B. Wolfe, "The significance of the concept of continuity in organismic economic theory," in Explorations in Economics, Notes and Essays contributed in honor of F. W. Taussig, 1936, pp. 391–402.

physical, does supply mean the amount that can be produced by the existing productive process in a given unit of time, or, if we have in mind natural resources of raw materials, does it mean the total known reserves of these materials? Are workers who are older than the customary age of retirement "resources" and part of the labor supply? Is coal producible at no greater cost than that currently being mined, but in excess of current mining equipment, a "resource"? Is a factory site held by its owner at an exorbitant price, and thus caused to remain a weedy lot, part of the "available" supply of factory sites?

It is evident that those who speak of full utilization cannot be thinking in terms of physical potential supply, even of the better grades of factoral units, because some of these physically utilizable units are kept off the market by the high prices demanded by their owners, and also because there are inferior units which are not utilized. Certainly, those who assume full utilization cannot mean that *all* units of every factor are utilized. They must mean by "available" those units which are of such grade as to be above a certain level of physical quality or productive efficiency. There are always grades of factors which are submarginal in this physical sense, in any given state of the arts. We cannot assume that all the units of a given factor are homogeneous as to quality, unless, with Walras, we are willing to increase the number of "factors" to infinity by regarding each separate grade, or even each unit, as a distinct factor. There is a technological margin of factoral efficiency, or availability, regardless of price, below which margin inferiority of grade precludes utilization, from sheer technological considerations. But within these physical or technological margins there is another margin, the price margin, set by the price-resistances of the owners of resources. Given a static economy, in a static institutional matrix, the margins between the utilized and the non-utilized resources are fixed margins—but fixed by, or in relation to, what?

It is necessary here to give some consideration to what we may call potential supply, although it may be objected that such a concept has no place in the theory of equilibrium. The potential physical supply of a factor consists of three parts: the economically inframarginal units, which are used to their appropriate intensities; the marginal units, which are economically (under the existing price structure) just worth using; and the submarginal units, which are unutilized either because of their inferior physical quality or because of the high price-resistances of their owners. The difference between the actual (i.e., the utilized) supply and the potential supply is constituted by the submarginal units of the factor. The "availability" of a resource must be defined either in terms of the potential physical supply, including units technologically usable but not used, because of owners' high price demands, or in terms of these price-resistances themselves. It is these price-resistances which, in conjunction with technological considerations, and in an "acquisitive" economy, fix the economic margin of utilization.

If we attempt to define full utilization in physical terms, we get into difficulties, since we are referring to the potential physical supply of technologically usable units, some of which, however are economically submarginal (and therefore unutilized), because the owners will not permit their use at a price corresponding to their value productivity. This submarginal part of potential supply can become part of actual supply only on relaxation of owners' price-resistances. But if, on the other hand, we conceive full utilization in terms of the equilibrium price-margins—marginal productivity in price terms—then full utilization applies only to the economically inframarginal units. These are the only units which are economically available (as long as there is no change in owners' psychology) in the established system of relative prices and margins. But if we define full utilization in this way, about all that we say is that resources which are utilized are utilized.

Given the assumption of a rigid equilibrium price structure, it is clear that units which are submarginal for any reason are not economically available for utilization. It must be remembered, however, that the purpose of assuming equilibrium to start with is to introduce later some influence which will produce a change in the price structure and enable us to note the results. It is then a specific question whether we can introduce a change, producing a temporary disequilibrium, which will transform some submarginal units into inframarginal units.[1]

It is possible that monetary theorists have taken over, somewhat uncritically, the idea of "full utilization" from the theory to an individual establishment (Betriebswirtschaft) and applied it analogically to a total economy. When the full utilization or full capacity of an individual plant is spoken of, what is usually meant is the amount of output the plant was designed to produce, not on a spurt, but at continuous "normal" operation. If the plant was properly designed, it was built for a certain optimum proportion in the use of the various factors of production, given their respective prices. At full capacity or full utilization in this sense, output is produced at least unit-cost, because at full capacity there is no "unused overhead."[2] So long as there is no change in the price of the product or in the relative prices of the factors, and no change in the aggregate demand for the plant's output, the plant can run at ideal efficiency and its least-cost point.

---

[1] It is to be noted that as soon as consideration is shifted from strict equilibrium to the conditions of business depression, most writers do not hesitate to speak of unemployed resources—idle laborers, idle instrumental capital, idle land—as if they were a part of the actual supply, although these unemployed resources are economically no more "available," under depression conditions, than are the submarginal resources in a strict equilibrium economy.

[2] Cf. A. B. Wolfe, "Arten und Erscheinungsformen von Kosten und Erträgen," Weltwirtschaftliches Archiv, September, 1934, Vol. 40, pp. 241–245.

If, however, the relative prices of the factors change, the point of least unit-cost will be shifted, because the plant will have to use a different proportioning of factors than that for which it was designed. Occasionally a change in the price of one factor may be precisely offset by contrary change in the price of another, but this is not likely to be a common occurrence.

Whether the plant is running at its ideal capacity, defined by its original design, or at the degree of capacity permitted by the current prices of factors, the important fact is that these factoral prices are fixed by the general market for factors. For the individual firm (unless it be monopsonoid in respect to the buying of factors), unlike the whole equilibrium economy, the prices of factors are *externally* determined. They are not fixed by the firm itself nor by its internal relativities. They are constants—fixed market facts which the firm has to accept. The margins of utilization in a closed economy, on the other hand, are fixed by the price configuration which is *internal* to the economy. They are not relative to any external market situation. The analogy between an individual firm and a total economy therefore breaks down.

III. The Determinants of Margins in a Static Equilibrium Economy

1. *The Limiting Power of the Strategic Factor*

Within the total equilibrium the price margins are like Marshall's[1] marbles in a bowl—or better, they are like toy balloons of different sizes and different elasticities, confined to a room and then all blown up to uniform pressure. Each marble or balloon is where it is because the others are where they are. But this is not especially illuminating. It does not, for example, tell us why the bowl or the room is not bigger or of different shape, or why the margins of utilization have not been pushed down to utilize some of the submarginal factoral

---

[1] *Principles*, 8th edition, 1929, p. 323.

units. The answer to this question is to be found in (1) the limited physical supply of some strategic factor or factors, (2) monopoly power to withhold supply, (3) owners' calculations or rationalizations of real costs, (4) institutional limitations on supply.

Broadly speaking, the strategic, or limiting, factor is the one which is scarcest, supplies of other factors taken into consideration.[1] A factor may be strategic from one or all of the causes just mentioned, but it is clear that we should distinguish between natural scarcity (limitation of physical supply, regardless of price) and the institutional scarcity which rests on private property and the power of owners to charge what the traffic will bear. If we assume a strategic factor utilized to the limit of its physical supply, we have a physical determinant of the volume of output of which the economy is capable, and of the amount and marginal grades of the other factors utilized. This may seem equivalent merely to saying that the volume of production is limited by the state of the arts, but in this case the state of the arts limits only the use of the strategic factor. Were there a larger supply of it, the state of the arts would permit a larger use of all factors.[2]

The institutional restrictions which make a factor scarce enough to be strategic may be due to law or custom, or, more generally, simply to the fact that the right to own property is the right to withhold its use from other persons. Without this right of withholdal, private property would be meaning-

---

[1] Cf. John R. Commons, Institutional Economics, 1934, pp. 58, 628, 629. Commons defines the limiting factor as "the one whose control, in the right form, at the right time and place, will set the complementary factors at work and bring about the results intended." In a dynamic economy first one then another factor will be strategic. In a static equilibrium the same factor remains the limiting factor as long as the equilibrium lasts. Cf. also Keynes, General Theory of Employment, p. 300.

[2] It is assumed, of course, that no substitution of other factors for the limiting factor is possible. All such substitutions have already been made in the establishment of the equilibrium.

less.   Under the private ownership of the means of production, the basic principle of business is to charge what the traffic will bear.   The owner of any productive resource gets as much for it as he can, by bringing pressure—economic power—on the owners of other resources to surrender to him as large a share of the joint product as they can be induced or compelled to give up.   There are, of course, limits of law, custom, and expediency, to this gouging.   It is also to a degree mutual; for if the strategic factor is indispensable to the employment of the others, some part of their supply is also necessary to the employment of the strategic factor.   Nevertheless, the owners of limiting factors, whether their scarcity be natural or artificial, hold the whip hand.

Only in the case of a strategic factor whose supply is *naturally* so restricted that it has to be used to the limit of its technological availability, have we a non-relative and definite meaning for the term "full utilization."   The use of a factor to this extreme extent would definitely fix the boundaries and the magnitude of the equilibrium economy.   Under such circumstances, in the absence of technological change, the economy could not be expanded, no matter how much additional money for investment might be provided.

The relativity of full utilization can be brought out in another way.   Suppose that no factor is used to the limit of its physical supply.   Suppose further that all inframarginal factors are now suddenly destroyed, leaving only the inferior grades of factoral units, which have hitherto not been utilized. Would production cease?   Or would the remaining inferior managerial capacity make such use as it could of the remaining inferior land, capital instruments, and labor?   It is safe to say that production would continue, however inefficiently.

2. *Real Costs as Determinant of Margins of Utilization*

It must be admitted that the cautious theorist will appeal to real costs somewhat warily.   Caution in the use of any "real" or "psychic" concept need not be confined to those who prefer the behavioristic approach, nor need these concepts be avoided simply because they cannot be made objectively quantitative. More valid ground for caution lies in the consideration that real cost is itself, to no slight degree, relative—relative to the institutional patterns to which the economy conforms. Real costs are in large measure in the nature of conditioned reflexes, habituations. They are in part rationalizations of opportunity, of the sheer economic motive of getting something for nothing, of charging what the traffic will bear. They are resultant upon social suggestion, imitation, emulation, jealousy, class consciousness, and conventional standards of justice or propriety in remuneration. As habit patterns, real costs are responsible for much price rigidity.

Nevertheless, whatever their institutional background or their psychological character, real costs lie back of the prices of factors and limit the economic supply. The price margins which set the utilization margins are derived from the price-resistances of owners of factors. These price-resistances are in turn based on physiological states, feelings, sentiments, rationalizations, and inertias, which we lump together with the term "real cost." The main trouble of real costs as a datum line from which to measure the relativities of the market is that real costs are in part conditioned, reflexively, by the established prices.

According to the theory of imputed productivity, each factor, and each factoral unit, is paid just the value it produces. If this is so, why are there ever any submarginal, or unutilized resources? Unless the physical supply of the (completely utilized) strategic factor is so limited that it sets margins for the other factors, so that residues of unutilized units of them are left, why is there any limit—as there is—to the use of progressively more inferior units?

The main answer lies in the high price-resistances of the owners of the inferior factoral units, which because of their

inferior productivity are unable to earn the established market
rate of remuneration.   But in addition to these there are
others who could earn the going *piece* rates but are unable to
earn the going *time* rates of remuneration.   We here encounter
an unexpected significance in the distinction between piece
rates and time rates.   Workers probably tend to figure the
real costs of employment less on the intensity of the work than
on the length of time they have to be on the job.   Workers,
however, are not the only ones who may hold out for more
than the product imputable to their services.   The owner of
inferior land is frequently unwilling to accept its low economic
rent.   In general, most persons are inclined to overvalue their
own abilities and the services of their property.   The lower
the actual values the more likely they are to be overestimated.[1]

Even, however, where there are no such viscosity and inflation of owners' valuations, calculations or feelings of real cost
set a margin of utilization.   Where factoral prices are strictly
in accord with productivity, measured directly or indirectly
in piece rates, there still are inferior factoral units which in
the existing state of the arts cannot earn enough to counterbalance real costs.   Some laborers, for example, cannot earn
the value of their own subsistence, if employed at a wage
measured by what they can produce.   In such cases it is
clear that inferiority, rather than cost, real or imagined, fixes
the margin of labor utilization.   Such cases are at the extreme.
Closer, in quality, to the actual price-margins of utilization
are workers who, if employed, could earn their own subsistence, but who refuse employment because of their lively
sensitiveness to the irksomeness of toil, and their unwillingness
to work unless they are paid as much as superior workers.

Appeal to such psychological and institutional influences
robs the theory of utilization of the exactitude of mathematical

---

[1] "The overweening conceit which the greater part of men have of their
own ability is an ancient evil remarked by the philosophers and moralists
of all ages."—Adam Smith, Wealth of Nations, Bk. I, Ch. X, Pt. 1.

analysis, but that is in no way proof that subjective feelings as to real cost and real income are not the fundamental and ultimate determinants of margins of utilization. If these margins are fixed, even in part, by the excessive price-resistances of the owners of submarginal factoral units, it is evident that the economy could be expanded if these hypertrophied rationalizations of real cost could somehow be broken down. It is also evident, however, that even were this done, uninflated price-resistances, based on legitimate feelings and sacrifices, would still remain, and that they would set a limit to the extension of utilization beyond some point in the downward scale of the quality of factoral units.

3. Institutional Limitations on the Utilization of Resources

Neither objective price analysis nor behavioristic psychology can really be cut off from the institutional matrix, the social patterns which provide the grooves in which behavior, whether of prices or persons, runs. Even an abstract theory of total equilibrium, constructed in an armchair, must necessarily involve a number of inescapable institutional assumptions. These assumptions should be made explicit, in order that their bearing and significance may be seen. It is necessary to make certain assumptions concerning (1) the customary length of the working day, (2) the customary ages at which workers begin and end their working career, (3) the conventions which exclude certain castes or classes of persons, and a large part of one sex, from the labor market, and (4) the normal intensity of labor.

These conventional limitations all apply to labor, but they also effectively, if indirectly, limit the use of land, raw materials, and instrumental capital, and thus the total productivity of the economy. Rational economy of operation, both from the technological and from the financial point of view, would require the operation of all plants wherever technologically possible, 365 days a year and twenty-four hours a day, with, of course, time out for repairs and replacements. In no

Western country, probably, is the normal number of working days in the year over 300. There is no scientific warrant for one day's rest in seven rather than one in five or ten. The six-day working week is traditional and institutional, and the numerous holidays are based on sentiment. Attempt to run plant twenty-four hours a day, with a number of shifts, would probably encounter some practical difficulties. Theoretically it should be possible to determine the physiologically optimum length of working day for each type of labor, but as the optimum would differ in different employments, even scientific management would have to make a pragmatic compromise on a uniform day for all classes of labor. It could make this compromise to better effect, however, were it not hampered by the ruling institutional patterns and sentiments.

These patterns prescribe that certain types of work shall be done only by a certain class or a certain sex. Here the most wasteful restriction on the utilization of potential productive resources is the limitation on the gainful employment of women. Whatever may be the social considerations which argue for or against women working for pay, it is indisputable that economically speaking in every Western country outside Russia and perhaps present-day Germany there is in the unemployed women an enormous reserve of unutilized labor power.

We may either take these institutional customs and sentiments as given data, without inquiry into their historical origins or *raisons d'être*, or we may seek their origin and causation in subjective attitudes toward real costs and real income. If we choose the latter alternative, we encounter the complication that these subjective attitudes are conversely conditioned by the traditions, customs, and current patterns, the cause of which we are seeking. But whether we attempt to "explain" our assumptions, on psychological or sociological ground or otherwise, we must, in assuming equilibrium, assume also a fixed cultural complex, else our equilibrium economy is left hanging in the air, with no connection with human experience.

4. *The Monetary Supply as the Limiting Factor*

The only exception to the sheer relativity of price-margins of utilization which we have found is the possibility that some superlatively scarce factor is utilized to the limit of its technologically available supply. Thus far we have spoken in terms of price margins, but the thought would apply as well to a barter as to a pecuniary economy. We have now definitely to assume that we are dealing with a monetary economy, and to canvas in outline the bearing of the supply of money on the utilization of productive resources.

In a static continuous equilibrium not only the general price level but the prices of all specific commodities and services are constant. The economy is equipped with a certain amount of money, circulating at a certain rate, which rate is fundamentally conditioned by the institutional patterns of the equilibrium society and is appropriate to those patterns. Ignoring seasonal changes, which have no significant bearing on our problem, we logically assume that no part of the monetary supply is unused. We ignore hoarding, because in equilibrium, hoarding either has no place or is assumed to be constant. For the same reason, liquidity preference can also be ignored. All money, whatever its nature or origin, is in continuous circulation against a continuous flow of goods and services. We assume, therefore, the full technological utilization of a constant monetary supply at a fixed intensity of utilization (transactions velocity), or in other words a constant efficiency of the monetary function. What the supply and the rate of circulation (supposing the latter to be capable of measurement) are makes no difference, so long as both are constant or so long as variations in the one are offset by converse variations in the other. Nor does it make any difference what the money is, so long as it is confidently accepted as money, and so long as the cost of its upkeep does not vary. It may be metallic currency, government paper, bank notes, or sheer money of account—bank deposits and bookkeeping.[1] The logically necessary desideratum is that the monetary function shall be of constant efficiency and maintain a constant price level.

In a developed economy, production is impossible without exchange, and exchange is impossible without money. Money is therefore essentially a factor of production.[2] Furthermore, under equilibrium conditions, which assume a stable price level, a fixed configuration of prices, and a fixed structure of the economy, money is the one factor which must be assumed to be fully utilized. There is, however, an obvious difference between full utilization of the monetary supply and full utilization of the technologically strategic factor discussed above. The latter was assumed to be utilized to the limit of its technologically usable supply. Full utilization in this precise sense is hardly applicable to the monetary function, since any quantity of money can effect any volume of transactions, the volume depending on the price level. Moreover, it is difficult to say just how the concept "quantity of money" is to be understood when a large proportion of business transactions is affected by the simple bookkeeping device of offsetting debits and credits.

Under certain conditions, the monetary supply, or function, is *the* strategic factor. An increase in the monetary supply is not always a prerequisite to the expansion of pro-

---

[1] Cf. Philip P. Schaffner, "Intra-account clearing and the supply of money," Journal of Business, April, 1938, pp. 115–124; Charles A. Dice and Philip P. Schaffner, "A neglected component of the monetary supply," American Economic Review, September, 1939, Vol. XXIX, pp. 514–520.

[2] Von Mises (The Theory of Money and Credit, 1935, pp. 79–86) argues that money is not a production good, because production is possible without money, and because money, unlike production goods, does not derive its value from product. "No increase in the welfare of the members of society can result from the availability of an additional quantity of money." This is also Wicksell's idea. In fact it is implicit in all classical economics back even to Hume—a phase of the reaction to Mercantilism.

duction, but, provided the financial structure of the productive process remains unchanged, an increase in the monetary supply is imperative, if the price level is to remain constant, as soon as aggregate output is increased. In this *ex post* sense the monetary supply is strategic with regard to the maintenance of a stable price level. But an increase in the supply of money is only under certain circumstances necessary *before* production can be expanded. Production can be increased (1) through monetary savings out of current income,[1] (2) through the lowering of costs by technological improvement, (3) through increase in the monetary supply, and thereby the investment fund, in the absence of either monetary saving or of technological improvement. In the first case the strategically necessary increase in the investment fund is provided without increase in the aggregate money supply. In the second case production can be increased without either monetary saving or increase in the aggregate monetary supply. But in the third case, in which the funds necessary for the financing of additional production are derived neither from saving nor from the lowering of monetary costs, the additional investment fund is available only through increase in the aggregate monetary supply, which accordingly becomes the strategic factor. It is strategic in this case, not in the sense that to increase its supply is more difficult than in the case of the other factors—for the opposite is true—but in the sense that the supply must be increased before additional production can be undertaken, if the price level is to remain constant.

IV. The Expansion of Production without Increase in the Supply of Money

1. *Through Saving from Current Consumer Monetary Income*

For convenience we shall refer to the established flow of production in the equilibrium as the "old production," and

---

[1] Corporate savings are included, because they are income withheld from stockholders.

to the additional production now to be instituted as the "new production." We shall also speak of the "old producers" and the "new producers," meaning in each case not only laborers and managers but anyone who has claim to a share in the aggregate output (=income) of the economy. We shall also think of the productive process as inclusive of all physical stages from extraction of raw materials to the final retail marketing of consumption goods. The new production must start with the extractive stage and be developed through the successive stages until, like the old production, it reaches the point of continuous output of consumption goods.

Assume now that the old producers save part of their current income and invest in new (i.e., additional) production. It is commonly held that the saved money, paid out in the process of investment to new producers, is forthwith spent by them for that part of the "old" output of consumption goods which the old producers, by reason of their saving, no longer buy, and that consequently saving and investment do not occasion any deficiency in aggregate demand for consumption goods. It must be observed, however, that the idea that all invested money returns promptly to the stream of consumer purchases is erroneous, not only because saving and reinvestment, seriatim, of part of the monetary returns from investment, but also because of the impossibility of investment of a fixed amount of savings, period by period, in new production which has to start from the extraction stage, where the amount of investment required is small relatively to the requirements in the succeeding stages and periods. For in the succeeding periods, if production is to arrive at continuity of output of consumption goods, not only do the successive stages of physical production have to be financed, but also the extractive stage, and all successive stages, have repeatedly to be started anew and kept going. Only by such overlapping of "cycles" or "batches" of production, in which, at the end of the developmental phase and continuously thereafter, all stages of the productive process are operative simultaneously, can we have continuity of output.

If the saving be either a constant amount or a constant percentage of income, period by period, it can be shown that during the time it takes to bring the new production to continuity not all the current savings of the earlier periods can possibly be invested.[1] Some interim hoarding, some temporary unemployment of old producers, and some temporary surplus of old output of consumption goods are inevitable. If, on the contrary, saving and investment are accurately adjusted, period by period, to the increasing investment needs of the developing new production, it can be shown that no hoarding, no temporary unemployment, and no surplus of consumption goods will result, and that the price level will remain constant. It is only on the assumption that saving is adjusted to the varying—and progressively increasing—investment requirements of the developing new production that saving and investment are always equal to each other. If saving and investment could be thus accurately adjusted to the financial requirements of the developing new production, production could be expanded without disturbance to the price level and to the equilibrium of aggregate demand and supply. It must again be noted, however, that the moment the new production reaches full development and continuity, thus resulting in a permanent increase in the aggregate supply of consumption goods, the price level will inevitably fall unless there is an equivalent increase in the monetary supply or in the efficiency of the monetary function.

In the absence of technological improvement, no amount of saving can increase aggregate production, if only the inframarginal resources hitherto utilized can be employed, or if

---

[1] In the present analysis the cost of unsold inventories of consumption goods, or of unfinished goods which are not finished for lack of demand, is not regarded as investment. Saving and investment may therefore be unequal.

some strategic factor is already utilized to the physical or technological limit. Production can be increased only if hitherto unused resources can in some way be made available. Otherwise, investment in "new" production will result only in a shifting of production, not an increase in it.[1] If the price margins of utilization in the equilibrium are fundamentally determined by subjective estimates of real costs and by institutional restrictions on employment, expansion of production can take place only if some of these estimates or restrictions can be modified. This holds true of expansion through monetary saving as well as through the provision for new investment by increase in the monetary supply.

2. *Expansion of Production with Technological Improvement*

Here we assume, as in the case of saving, that there is no increase in the supply of money, but that additional funds for new production are provided by the lowering of the physical, and hence the monetary, unit-cost of the old production. This lowering of unit-costs comes not from any reduction in the rate of remuneration of the factors employed, but from reduction in the number of factoral units required for the production of a given aggregate output. There is no need in this case for a downward modification of estimates of real costs, withholdal prices, or institutional restrictions. The

---

[1] It might be argued that even where the strategic factor is technologically fully employed, aggregate production could be expanded by shifting productive resources from consumer-goods to capital-goods industries. This would mean a short-run fall in the output of consumption goods during the process of shifting. But unless the factors shifted to the capital-goods industries are there more productive than they were in the consumption-goods industries, there will not be, even in the long-run, any increase in aggregate output of consumption goods. On the contrary, there will be an oversupply of unfinished goods, for the completion of which the later stages of production will lack the necessary productive resources. Only in case of technological change is there a chance to increase aggregate output by this sort of shift.

availability of resources for additional production comes solely from technological reduction of input (productive units used) per unit of output. At the same time that the technological change reduces unit costs, it also frees (disemploys) a certain amount of resources, which are now available for the development of additional production.

There will be no increase in the income of the factors employed until the additional production is fully developed, and at no time, even after full development, will the number of productive units employed exceed the number employed in the old equilibrium. When the new production has reached continuity, the amount of employment will be the same as at the start, but the aggregate output of consumption goods will be larger. There will be some unemployment, however, during the developmental phase of the new production, for the same reasons as those we found in the case of financing expanding production by means of money saving. Only in case the technological improvements came gradually, starting first in the extractive stage, and then progressing, perfectly timed, to the succeeding stages, could some temporary unemployment of hitherto utilized resources be avoided.

However skillfully technological change may be taken advantage of in increasing aggregate output of consumption goods, it cannot, *per se*, result in any increase in employment, since to effect this requires bringing into utilization factoral units which have hitherto not been used. But if increase of employment is not a desideratum, technological improvement offers the best basis for the expansion of output without undue disturbance to equilibrium.

V. EXPANSION OF PRODUCTION WITH INCREASE IN THE MONETARY SUPPLY

We now assume that production is to be expanded without monetary saving, and without technological change. Purchase or hire of the additional productive resources required is to be financed either through expansion of bank loans or through the issue of government paper. An increase in the gold supply, while more costly, would do as well.

We have assumed in the discussion so far that only inferior productive units of submarginal quality are unutilized in the equilibrium. It would be just as logical, and nearer to reality, to assume that factoral units, especially labor units, which are *per se* just as good as some of the inframarginal units, are kept from employment by institutional controls—law, custom, convention, and prejudices. In order, however, to deal with the problem under the more difficult condition, we will assume that no factoral unit equal or superior to the equilibrium marginal units has been left unutilized, and hence that the new monetary investment fund can be invested only in factoral units which have hitherto been of submarginal quality. There are still two possible alternate cases, according to the presence or absence of excessive price-resistances on the part of the owners of these inferior resources.

If there is no tendency to ask more for these units than they can earn if employed, at piece rates, then they can be made available for utilization in expanding production only by the modification of some of the institutional restrictions.[1]

---

[1] Equally well, of course, units of quality equal to those already employed could be made available by such relaxations. A still unwritten but important chapter in Economics would deal with the deleterious effect of these restrictions, especially those based on race and sex prejudices, local loyalties, and protective monopolistic impulses. Many of these bars to employment, some of which attain the status of legal enactment, are due to desire to protect the "ins" from the competition of the "outs," or to the feeling that jobs should be allotted on some system of priority other than ability. In 1939, for example, bills were introduced in half the state legislatures of this country prohibiting the employment of married women in state jobs. In general, the bearing of anti-Negro, anti-Jew, and anti-alien sentiment on the "full utilization" of potential labor supply is obvious.

Abstracting from these institutional restrictions, we now proceed to the problem of breaking down excessive or inflated[1] price-resistances on the part of the hitherto unemployed and inferior factoral units, in order that the necessary quota of such units may be made available for the development of expanded production. If none of these excessive price-resistances can be broken down, additional investment and production will not be possible. If they can all be broken down, additional production is feasible. Furthermore, barring the previous use of some strategic factor to its technological margin, reduction in the price-resistances of any *one* of the hitherto submarginal factors to a price below the imputed value-product of the previously utilized units will make additional production possible; for in this case the other higherto submarginal factors can be paid more than they are "worth." Theoretically, a change in law or custom, or a change in owners' rationalizations of real cost, could result in lessening price-resistance of any factor. We could, for example, compel unemployed laborers to accept a wage commensurate with their low productivity by simply letting them starve if they would not accept such a wage. We might by negotiation get a reasonable price on unused instrumental capital, but as such equipment is either obsolete or worn out, it would be cheaper to construct new equipment. Conceivably, inducements or compulsions might be brought to bear on the owners of submarginal raw materials and land to reduce their inflated ideas of the value of the properties.

This line of thought may perhaps be regarded as a generalized extension of the Keynesian theory of the function of a decline in the interest rate. The difference, theoretical but highly important, between breaking down the price-resistances of laborers or landlords and the price-resistances of the owners of the productive factor, monetary capital, lies mainly in the

---

[1] It need hardly be pointed out that the term "inflated price-resistances" is not meant to connote anything in the nature of currency inflation.

fact that control of the monetary supply affords a far more powerful leverage for the reduction of the interest rate (rent of the use of monetary capital) than can be brought to bear on rates of remuneration of the other factors of production. On the whole, the possibility of additional production rests on the loan-price—interest—of monetary investment funds.

Money is *the* strategic factor in the expansion of production, under the conditions we are now considering. Increase of the money supply means, directly or indirectly, increase of the investment flow. But under the assumption of inflated price-resistances, potential investment will become actual investment only if the interest rate (barring breakdown of price-resistance somewhere else) is low enough to make possible the use of inferior resources at prices above their marginal productivity.[1] If the added monetary supply goes into circulation through the purchase of consumption goods, the price level will rise, thus making possible (barring immediate rise in the prices of factors) a lowering of the margin of utilization. If the added money goes into circulation directly through investment in new production, it will do so only because its owners accept a rate of interest on it lower than the hitherto prevailing equilibrium rate. There is nothing startling in the inference that they probably will be willing to do so, for the existence of an unemployed investment fund makes for a buyers' rather than a sellers' market for monetary funds.[2]

---

[1] As measured under the previous equilibrium interest rate.

[2] This inference ignores the possible effect of uncertainty on the strength of liquidity preference. However, it is not liquidity preference, *per se*, which is significant, but changes in it. A constant liquidity preference would mean simply that a certain amount of money is kept out of circulation permanently. This hoarded money is analogous to till money or reserve or monetary working capital. It may be thought of as a sort of psychological working capital. Only *change* in liquidity preference will affect the price level, or the amount of money in circulation, or the efficiency of the monetary function.

There may be a minimum "necessary" rate of profit, though what it is no one knows. There is no discernible necessary minimum rate of interest. Instrumental capital is produced, not saved, and from the point of view of the economy as a whole the same may be true of monetary capital or investment fund. In fact, the additional investment fund necessary for additional production is the strategic factor in more than one sense. If the interest rate demanded by the holders of uninvested money is so high that entrepreneurs cannot pay the prices held out for by the owners of the other factors of production, additional production cannot be developed without an *ad hoc* increase in the available investment fund through an increase in the aggregate supply of money. And in the second place, an additional monetary supply can be created at very low cost. Moreover, it can be created, by the government or the banking system, without curtailment of aggregate current consumption.[1] Theoretically and ideally, looking at the economy as a whole and as a productive organism (that is abstracting from the many proprietary, institutional, political, and acquisitive aspects), a people could well afford to *give* the necessary additional investment fund outright to responsible entrepreneurs, who would put it into circulation in the purchase or hire of productive resources not hitherto utilized. Once so paid out the money would remain permanently in circulation against an equivalent flow of goods, as long as the economy remained a continuous going concern. In fact, since the additional money (*not* provided by gold mining) is so comparatively costless, an outright gift would be preferable to a loan, for a loan imposes a debt, and the debt can be paid off only at the expense of reduction of the price

---

[1] This is not saying that the additional production can be developed without some incidental real ("forced") saving—curtailment of current consumption—on the part of the old producers.

level and employment, or only nominally, as another loan must immediately be incurred if production is to go on.[1]

Envisioning the productive process as a whole, rather than restricting attention to the contractual relations between the owners and users of productive resources, the present view is (1) that continuous production does not "take time," and (2) that additional production can be started and brought to the stage of continuous output of consumption goods without monetary saving, though not without some incidental and temporary real saving. Even in an expanding economy, where there is a time-interval between the starting of additional production and its full development to continuous output, the provision of the monetary funds, *as needed*, to finance this developmental period involves no monetary saving. The volume of the "old" production's output of consumption goods continues unabated, and there is no decline whatever in aggregate demand and consumption.

If the additional production is financed by increase of the money supply and without more than incidental and temporary disturbance in the price level, so that even for the individual firm the time element, insofar as its influence depends on interest, loses its significance, there is no theoretical reason why a well managed economy should not eliminate the drag of the interest charge which is the chief obstacle to the expansion of production, by furnishing the monetary purchasing power essential to that expansion free of any net or "pure" interest.

Assuming that the inferior factoral units brought into utilization in expanding production are paid their imputed product, it is clear that their time-rate of remuneration will be less than that of the hitherto inframarginal factors. This means, to repeat, that production can be expanded if some factors can be persuaded to accept a lower remuneration, per

---

[1] Cf. Frederick Soddy, Wealth, Virtual Wealth and Debt, 1926.

unit of their real costs, than the superior units receive. It seems clear, also, that as Keynes has argued, the easiest way of bringing money costs down so as to permit a fall in the marginal productivity of (real) capital is to reduce the interest rate, since this can be done by judicious increase of the money supply.

The extent to which production can be expanded, even with free subsidy of monetary investment fund, will depend on how far inferior laborers and owners of other inferior factors can be induced to supply their services at less and less real income. Beyond this, there is the probability that secular diminishing returns due to exhaustion of the better grades of material resources will set a limit of expansion. Ultimately it is possible that diminishing utility of consumption goods would set a definite limit to expansion, but this depends on whether aggregate demand for consumption goods is subject to the law of diminishing utility. On this there may be valid difference of opinion. These matters, however, lie beyond the scope of the present analysis.

15

TOWARD A CONCEPT OF WORKABLE COMPETITION* ·

By J. M. Clark †

The paper of which this is an enlarged and revised version was read at a joint Round Table of the American Economic Association and the Econometric Society, during the meetings at Philadelphia, December, 1939.

Where one of the conditions of perfect competition is absent, the presence of others may lead to greater rather than less imperfection. Long-run curves of individual demand and cost are flatter than commonly represented, and the imperfections of competition correspondingly less. Industry subject to fluctuating demand requires prices in excess of short-run marginal cost. Favorable conditions appear to include a sloping individual demand curve, and some uncertainty whether a reduction of price will be promptly met.

With standardized products, a chaotic market tends toward ruinous competition. Pure oligopoly is seldom found; the important case being that of openly-quoted prices with varying amounts of deviations on actual sales. Standard products with sloping individual demand curves are also possible.

While extreme quality differentials approach monopoly, more moderate ones may be workably competitive, especially with further growth of closer substitutes and better knowledge of qualities on the part of buyers.

I. *Introduction*

Theories of imperfect and "monopolistic" competition have for some time been current, in an unformulated state, in the field of economic policy; and important beginnings have been made at formulation by economic theorists. As a necessary

---

* *The American Economic Review*, Volume XXX, Number 2, Part 1, June 1940, pages 241–256. Reprinted by the courtesy of the American Economic Association and the author.

† Columbia University.

step in this last development, the conception of "perfect competition" has itself for the first time received really specific definition and elaboration. With this has come the realization that "perfect competition" does not and cannot exist and has presumably never existed, for reasons quite apart from any inescapable tendency toward collusion, such as Adam Smith noted in his familiar remark on the gettings-together of members of a trade. What we have left is an unreal or ideal standard which may serve as a starting point of analysis and a norm with which to compare actual competitive conditions. It has also served as a standard by which to judge them.

I am not quarreling with proper use of this standard as an ideal. However, it has seemed at times to lead to undesirable results, in that it does not afford reliable guidance to the factors which are favorable to the closest available working approximation to that ideal, under actual conditions. With this problem the present paper is concerned.

The theory of the subject has defined for us the results of various forms of imperfect competition—some of the results being still debatable. It has defined these results in abstract terms which might be quantitative if the controlling functions could be measured, but which in the absence of such measurement remain qualitative, indicating to most minds chiefly the *direction* of departure from the standard of "perfect competition." There has been some speculation as to the amount and seriousness of these departures, but no very definite conclusions. And there has been speculation as to ways of reducing the imperfections, chiefly in specific cases.

It seems that a contribution might be made to this process, of an orienting sort, by attempting to formulate concepts of the most desirable forms of competition, selected from those that are practically possible, within the limits set by conditions we cannot escape. This would at least be an antidote to mere "historic homesickness"; but might render a more positive service. For some of the features listed as "imperfections" in our present theoretical scheme may turn out to have some positive use in actual situations. It would be a truism to say that the most effective forms of competition we have, or can have, are imperfect forms, since there are no others. But it will mean something if we can find, after due examination, that some of these forms do their jobs well enough to be an adequate working reliance—more serviceable, on the whole, than those substitutes which involve abandoning reliance on competition. And it will be useful if we can learn something about the kinds and degrees of "imperfection" which are positively serviceable under particular conditions.

One central point may be put abstractly. If there are, for example, five conditions, all of which are essential to perfect competition, and the first is lacking in a given case, then it no longer follows that we are necessarily better off for the presence of any one of the other four. In the absence of the first, it is *a priori* quite possible that the second and third may become positive detriments; and a workably satisfactory result may depend on achieving some degree of "imperfection" in these other two factors.

Suppose the first requisite is perfect two-way mobility of the factors of production, with no specialized and irrecoverable fixed capital. Granted this, an industry can stand the most rigorous conditions in all other respects. It may have a multitude of small producers, who produce a supply and then place it on a market for what it will bring instead of quoting a price and seeing how much they can sell at that price; and it may produce a standardized commodity, so that individual demand curves are infinitely elastic: but efficient producers will still cover their total costs of production. Take away the saving grace of perfect two-way mobility and leave the other conditions; let demand decline, and competition becomes too strong: you have a "sick industry" on your hands. Reduce the number of producers and let them sell on quoted prices and anticipate one another's reactions and you have a form of "oligopoly."   Change one more condition, substituting a chaotically imperfect market in which irregular, temporarily secret and discriminatory pricing is the rule rather than the exception and you have (whenever demand decreases or fails to grow as anticipated) a situation tending strongly to degenerate into a cut-throat price war, driving prices below an efficient producer's total cost of production, though, if producers are few and large, this condition is not likely to be permanent.[1]

These examples are merely illustrative.   They point toward a thesis, which finds reflection in the apparent confusion of our present policies (trying to raise some prices and lower others)—namely, that imperfect competition may be too strong as well as too weak; and that workable competition needs to avoid both extremes.

II. *Competition and Its Forms*

By way of a generic definition of competition in price between business units in their capacity as sellers, we might consider the following.

> Competition is rivalry in selling goods, in which each selling unit normally seeks maximum net revenue, under conditions such that the price or prices each seller can charge are effectively limited by the free option of the buyer to buy from a rival seller or sellers of what we think of as "the same" product, necessitating an effort by each seller to equal or exceed the attractiveness of the others' offerings to a sufficient number of buyers to accomplish the end in view.

This is not a complete definition, but brings out certain features crucial to the following argument.   Specifically, it is not limited (as are some current implied definitions) to cases in which one seller succeeds in excelling the offerings of others; and it focuses attention on a crucial point which is

---

[1] These conditions are sufficiently familiar to permit the reader to fill in the gaps in the above shorthand statement of the conditions necessary to these various results.

sometimes neglected—namely the nature of the option actually open to the buyer.

The specific character of competition in any given case depends on a surprisingly large number of conditions—so many, in fact, that the number of mathematically possible combinations runs into the hundreds or thousands—and suggests the possibility that every industry may be in some significant respect different from every other, or from itself at some other stage of development. At least ten conditioning factors appear worth noting, within each of which there are a number of variants or gradations.

1. *The standardized or unstandardized character of the product.* Standardization may be so complete that an open market tolerates no price-differential between different sellers at any one point of purchase, or it may tolerate moderate quality-differentials which are in effect subject to competitive forces, or the differentials may be large and subject to little or no competitive check. The commodity may be standardized while services rendered in connection with it permit some price differential, or it may be standardized by segregation of "seconds."

2. *The number and size-distribution of producers.* There may be many, all small, or few, all large, or a few large and numerous small, in which case the large producers may or may not be the "dominant" factor in the market.

3. *The general method of price-making.* The producer may create a supply and then sell it at whatever the market will bring ("supply-governed price"); or he may quote a price and sell what he can at that price until he sees fit to change it ("quoted price"). In the latter case, he may produce to stock or to order. Or he may sell on sealed bids.

4. *The general method of selling.* Sale may be by brokers in a produce-market, by exclusive agents, through general dealers or direct *via* traveling salesmen or by mail.

5. *The character and means of market information.*

6. *The geographical distribution of production and consumption.* This is important where transportation cost is a material factor.

7. *The degree of current control of output.* Production may be seasonal, or non-seasonal with a significant lag between the initiation of a change in the rate of production and the resulting change in supply available for sale, or inventory-changes may be sufficient to cushion the effect of this lag and so minimize its importance.

8. *Variation of cost with varying size of plant or enterprise.*

9. *Variation of cost with short-run fluctuations of output.*

10. *Flexibility of productive capacity.* Increase may be easy and rapid, or difficult and slow; while rapid decrease may be virtually impossible, owing to fixed capital investment.

The following outline, which is tentative and admittedly incomplete, attempts to take account of some of the more important conditioning factors, selecting as the basis for the main heads those which appear to have more effect on price behavior. The distinction between "quoted" and "supply-governed" prices has already been defined, and appears to deserve an important place. The term "quoted" is used instead of "administered" because the latter term carries implications of some degree of discretionary control, which may not always accompany the mere quoting of a price. For "supply-governed" the phrase "market-made" might be used to indicate that the making of the price quotations is literally *done by* the market machinery (as on a produce exchange) instead of being merely conditioned or controlled by it; but it seemed desirable to avoid any possible implication that the only real markets are those of the produce-exchange type, and to use terms consistent with a more inclusive concept of a market. A producer who does not sell his goods on a produce exchange or the equivalent might be surprised to be told that he had no market for them at all. The outline is herewith presented, with apologies for the amount of familiar material it contains. Its indebtedness to Professor Chamberlin is obvious.

I. *Pure (rigorous, unmitigated) competition.* Requisites: standard product, known price, many sellers available at any locality, free entry. Price may be quoted or supply-governed. Price tends to equal marginal cost.

    A. *Perfect competition.* Probably the outstanding requisite, in addition to the above, is perfect two-way mobility of the factors of production; also assumptions as to cost-behavior and relationships consistent with the continued presence of many sellers. Current control of output is probably implied.   Price covers average cost, which equals marginal cost.

   B. *Imperfect pure competition.*   Lacking perfect mobility, marginal cost is less than average cost when demand at average-cost prices falls below capacity.

     1. Output currently controlled by each producer.

       a. Capacity such that price exceeds average cost at peaks of demand, and covers cost on average of fluctuations.

       b. Conditions such that average price is less than this.   ("Sick industry" problem; ex., bituminous coal-mining.)

     2. Output not currently controllable (ex., agriculture).   This includes the problems giving rise to the "cobweb theorem," and related problems.   Sub-heads a and b as above.   (Under b, "sick industries"; ex., unregulated agriculture.)

II. *Modified, intermediate or hybrid competition.*   ("Monopolistic competition" in the broader sense.)

   A. Standard products, few producers.   The most important cases involve formally free entry, but no exit without loss.

     1. Quoted prices, horizontal individual demand schedules if others' prices unchanged, and variants.

       a. Open price, perfectly conformed to (rarely found): *first species of oligopoly.*

       b. Imperfectly-known price and chaotic discrimination.

         (1) Enduring ignorance: local near-monopolies.

         (2) Temporary ignorance: tendency to "cut-throat competition."

       c. Open price with limited departures, all or part of the time: secrecy temporary.   Probably the most important case.

     2. Supply-governed prices (implies an open market).   Individual demand schedules sloping, but more elastic than general demand schedule: *second main species of oligopoly.*

     3. Quoted prices, sloping individual demand schedules.

       a. Demand schedules definite and calculable (spatially separated producers with uniform mill prices).   May result in a third species of oligopoly.

       b. Demand schedules indefinite (ex., above condition with limited freight absorption).

   B. Unstandardized or quality products: *"monopolistic competition."*   Individual demand schedules sloping, but more elastic than general demand schedule.[1]   Importance of competitive element hinges

---

[1] For this purpose the "general demand schedule" would presumably

largely on extent to which quality differences are open to free imitiation. Schedule of response to selling outlay a complicating factor.

1. Quoted prices; single producer's product usually standardized or graded, with separate disposal of "seconds."
2. Supply-governed prices; price-differentials for quality made directly in market. For agricultural products number of suppliers usually nullifies any monopoly element.

Certain competitive categories cross the divisions of this outline. For example, "imperfect competition" covers headings, I, B, and II. What may be called "atomistic competition" covers heading I, and an undivided share of the cases under II, B, though it may be noted that the outline suggests some reservation as to whether atomistic competition in the sale of quality products deserves the designation "monopolistic competition."

Among the omissions from the outline are the effects of durability *versus* perishability of products; and most of the complications of cost-behavior, including the problem of joint *versus* separable costs. And it may be that a separate set of headings should have been devoted to retail selling, which presents special problems. For instance, even physically identical commodities need not sell at identical prices in neighboring stores. This fact could be forced into the headings of the outline, but might better be separately dealt with. Most important, perhaps, the outline makes no note of differences between long-run and short-run adjustments. This is vital, since it seems probable that one of the criteria of workable competition is that there shall not be too gross discrepancies between the action of short-run pressures and long-run tendencies.

---

have to be defined in terms of the response of sales to simultaneous and proportionate changes in the prices of all the grades or sub-species of "the commodity" in question.

III. *Long-run Considerations*

At the risk of being convicted of an optimistic bias, I should like to point to certain ways in which long-run forces serve to mitigate the seriousness of the effects of imperfect competition. These considerations center largely in the proposition that long-run curves, both of cost and of demand, are much flatter than short-run curves, and much flatter than the curves which are commonly used in the diagrams of theorists. In fact, it may appear that much of the apparent seriousness of Professor Chamberlin's results derives from what I believe to be the exaggerated steepness of the curves he uses to illustrate them. This, of course, is a matter of degree only; but in the field of imperfect competition, and especially in the search for workable adjustments, these matters of degree are of the essence of the problem.

In the first place, the more attention centers on the imperfections of active competition, the more important become the forces of potential competition and substitution (both of which find a place in Chamberlin's system). Neither is a perfect check; but both together may come near it under favorable conditions.

As to potential competition, it is this, or the materializing of it, on which Chamberlin relies for the tendency to wipe out monopoly profits in the production of quality goods, and to bring individual demand curves and cost curves into tangency. But there seems to be a tendency to regard the business-man as having too little foresight to anticipate the materializing of potential competition, and as following an unduly grasping policy in regard to price, and an unduly restrictive policy as to output, until potential competition becomes actual, and the industry is burdened with too many producers, whose individual output is restricted short of the optimum. This undoubtedly has some truth. It would be expecting a great deal of business-men that they should generally have perfect foresight of the emergence of potential competition, and on that account should avoid unduly restrictive policies. Nevertheless, there is apparently a tendency of somewhat similar effect on the part of some or many businesses, even if not guided by such impossibly perfect foresight. There is a tendency to strive to maintain and increase output, as if this were an end in itself, aside from the resulting net earnings and perhaps at a short-run sacrifice of net earnings which a more grasping policy might secure. In such cases, business, whether putting its reasoning in this form or not, acts as if it were governed by anticipations of potential competition, and by the desire to forestall its materializing.

As to substitution, it is a commonplace that the triumphs of modern industrial chemistry have vastly increased its range and flexibility; and it is increasingly spoken of as one form of competition. Indeed, it seems that the differences between substitute products, in cost of production and service value, are nowadays often no more serious than similar differences between different varieties of what we think of as the "same" product. This fact is so much in the business-man's consciousness that there is no need to emphasize it. Both potential competition and substitution have the effect of flattening the slopes of individual demand curves.

To develop the full importance of this it is necessary to take account of the time dimension of these curves. The abstraction of a timeless demand-schedule has tended toward the neglect of this factor. Yet in actual elasticities of demand a crucial element is the time required for a given change of price to bring about a given effect on volume of sales. In some instances the full effect may be felt in a matter of hours, while in others it may require a generation. In the latter case, of course, the effect of the price factor will be inextricably tangled with that of a complex of other changes.

One feature of this relationship might be expressed by a skewed surface or contour-map in which the vertical dimension measures price—or possibly price minus optimum selling expenses, if such a quantity could be given a usable definition.[1] The price should be that of one producer's grade of the product, those of others' grades being held constant. What we may call the west-east dimension would represent the length of time during which a given price-relationship remains in effect; and the north-south dimension would represent physical volume of sales of this producer's grade of the product. The intersection of the surface with any vertical north-south plane would be a demand-schedule representing the sales under various price-differentials, each being assumed to remain in effect a length of time represented by the distance of the plane from the west end of the diagram, where time equals zero. These curves would grow less steep from west to east. The horizontal contour-lines would be growth-curves (positive or negative) each representing the increasing effect, with time, of a given price-differential on volume of sales.

Such a surface would, however, represent only a beginning of analysis. Action by one producer would provoke responses by others which, if the original action had gone some distance, would act on a modified set of growth-curves. Changes in quality are, of course, not represented. Actual demand-curves may depend, not only on the price-factor represented, but also on the relation between the price-range of the various grades of this commodity and those of various substitutes; and on the profits made by this producer and by others in the industry, as an incentive to the materializing of potential competition. Even this affords an unduly simplified picture, and the whole functional relationship is probably so complex as to defy mathematical plotting.

The chief proposition remains—namely, that the long-run effects of a high-price policy on the part of any one producer would tend to a much larger falling-off in sales than would occur in the short run. The long-run schedule might in

---

[1] It would presumably vary with price, and also be complicated by the time-factor.

numerous cases approach the horizontal so closely that the slope would not be a matter of material moment, in the light of all the uncertainties involved. And this fact may be roughly represented by the attitude of some businesses, that it is "good business" to maintain and expand their sales volume, even at some sacrifice of immediate profits.

Long-run cost curves also tend toward the horizontal. There are two quite distinct types of cost-curve for a given productive unit in relation to volume of output. One has to do with changes in output within the physical capacity of an existing plant, and the other with changes in the amount of plant capacity without change in the percentage which is utilized. Long-run cost curves are apparently dominated by the second factor; and I shall take it for present purposes as representing the long-run function. Evidence of its character is difficult to secure, some of the best indications being derived from simultaneous comparisons of costs in considerable numbers of plants of different size, with the effect of percentage utilization eliminated where possible. Such evidence of this sort as I have analyzed points to the conclusion that it is likely to be only the very small plants which show materially higher costs causally traceable to their small size, while most plants are in a range of size which shows little or no downward or upward trend with increased size, while other factors account for much greater differences in cost between plant than those due to size itself.

The indicated conclusion is that there is typically no definite "optimum size," but rather a wide optimum range of size, within which most plants fall; and that economies due to size are far from being such a vitally important factor as is suggested by the type of theoretical cost curve now in general use. A further conclusion is that imperfections in competition arising from the slopes of the long-run curves of cost or demand may, so far as these curves affect actual policy, be relatively unimportant. So far as immediate price policies are governed by long-run demand curves, or behave as if they were so governed, they are likely not to differ materially from those of perfect competition (this would have little application to the problem of unduly expanded selling costs). And even if the long-run scale of production is somewhat restricted, cost of production, as distinct from selling, is not likely to be thereby materially increased.

IV. *Short-run Conditions*

The most serious problems of imperfect competition seem, as already noted, to center in the fact that the immediate short-run pressures are out of harmony with the conditions of long-run equilibrium. And the starting-point of a search for the conditions of workable competition seems to be the search for ways and means of reducing these discrepancies, under the conditions actually encountered. One approach to this question is by way of some of the paradoxes or conflicts in prevalent ideas as to the symptoms of a satisfactory competitive condition.

Perfect competition requires a market with such full knowledge that a standard commodity cannot sell at two prices at the same time at the same point of purchase and delivery. Actually, at least in large-scale industry, such a condition of "identical prices" is frequently taken as an indication of a monopolistic condition (Outline, II, A, 1, a.). And a state of less perfect market knowledge, permitting differences in price, is sometimes spoken of as causing active price competition to arise, where presumably there had been none previously (Outline, II, A, 1, b, (2)). This attitude implies a theory that one kind of imperfection requires another to take part of the curse off it. And there would be no paradox about it if the same persons did not at other points maintain the attitude that any departure from any of the conditions of pure or perfect competition is evidence of a monopolistic tendency.

The above implied theory suggests that the standard character of the product is not in itself favorable to workable competition between few and large producers, and that in such cases effective competition requires some uncertainty whether a reduction in price will be met or not. This in turn points toward a search for the least undesirable form of remedial "imperfection" (uncertainty).

Among the apparent inconsistencies of prevailing attitudes is the position that discrimination is a non-competitive symptom, coupled with the view that, when buyers invite sealed bids, unless they get a price lower than the general market affords, this result proves monopoly. In part, this seems to be a manifestation of the fairly general psychology of buyers, who do not object to discrimination so long as they get the benefit. So far as there is a real economic theory involved, it seems to imply the abandonment of the idea that competition and discrimination are mutually inconsistent. There is *prima facie* ground for the hypothesis that some forms and degrees of discrimination have a place in a scheme of workable, as distinct from perfect, competition. And as part of this problem, the theory of sealed-bid competition stands out as an unworked field for economists.

Perfect competition requires operation at full capacity, which is sometimes defined as the point of minimum cost, or as the point where marginal and average cost are equal. Actual competition has to make terms with the fact that, when demand fluctuates, industry must inevitably be operating short of full capacity much of the time. Workable competition must be workable under these conditions. Some of the requirements of such a result may be briefly indicated.

A price which at all times covers only short-run marginal cost would lead to large operating deficits whenever demand is short of capacity, and would bankrupt most industries, no matter how shock-proof their capital structures. And since the horizontal individual demand curve of pure competition leads to a price that covers only marginal cost, it is not one of the conditions of workable competition. Instead, the requirement is an individual demand curve with sufficient slope to bring price, on the average, far enough above marginal cost so that average cost may be covered, over the run of good times and bad. Along with this should go, presumably, enough price flexibility to afford a stimulus to demand in dull times, and the reverse in boom times. These are not easy requirements, but at least they mean that workable competition has some positive use for the sloping individual demand curve.

This will be disputed by some on the ground that competition can be trusted automatically to limit capacity at such a point that even under pure competition profits in good times will compensate for losses in bad times; and that this is the desirable adjustment.[1] A realistic view of this objection seems to involve the whole theory and practice of maintaining stand-by units (usually of inferior quality) to handle peak demands. Without going into this matter at length, it may be sufficient to indicate that, in the ordinary course of modernization and replacement, the stand-by units (the best units which are just not good enough to justify keeping them at continuous or nearly-continuous operation) are not likely to be sufficiently obsolete and inefficient to bring their marginal costs of operation up to a point that would yield large profits for the plant as a whole: large enough to offset operating deficits incurred most of the time, and to make the average represent an attractive return on investment. Hence the indicated result is extremely unlikely to follow.

Cost curves for varying output with a fixed plant probably fall into two main groups or types. In one, physical capacity has fairly rigid limits, and marginal cost appears to remain approximately uniform, nearly or quite up to the limit of

---

[1] *Cf.* Outline, I, B, 1, a. In the discussion at the Round Table where a shorter form of this paper was read, this objection was raised by Professor George Stigler.

physical capacity. This type may provisionally be taken as characteristic of continuous-process industries, dependent on heat or chemical action, which cannot be substantially speeded up behind the ordinarily economical rates. The other type would include processes which can be speeded up or worked overtime. Here it may be possible to produce considerable amounts beyond the point of lowest average cost, with marginal cost above average operating expenses, though possibly not far enough above so that a price equal to marginal cost would yield a fair return on the fixed investment.

The use of stand-by units might bring the first type a little nearer the second. But in the instances of steel and cement, this factor does not appear to modify the pattern of costs materially —possibly for the reasons already briefly indicated.   In either case, it seems fair to conclude that the industry could not survive under prices which were always limited to marginal costs of the short-run variety, unless it deliberately destroyed its superseded units instead of leaving them to serve as stand-by capacity, and thus created an artificial bottle-neck on industrial expansion.   And that may be dismissed as a possibility, for reasons hardly necessary to state.   Under these circumstances, certain types of competitive situations may be distinguished and briefly analyzed.

First we may consider the standardized product, sold in a chaotic market in which discrimination is possible; any sale may be a subject for special bargaining, and special prices will permit the producer making them to gain a volume of business of material size, relative to his total sales, before these special prices are discovered and met by his competitors.   This condition has been represented in the outline (II, A, 1, b) by a time-lag in the spread of market knowledge, which may be longer or shorter; but this is not the only controlling factor. A few hours during which the price-cutter can make fast one very large future order may be as good as a much longer period in an industry where there are no very large buyers or where firm long-term contracts cannot be secured. The size of the price-cutter relative to that of his rivals also has a bearing on the outcome. Variants are possible; but the general conclusion of a tendency to drive prices below cost seems justified.[1]

The reason for this may be suggested by an abstract limiting case, which does not, however, accurately express the operation of actual cases. If a particular bit of business can be secured by a special reduced price, applicable to it exclusively, and will be lost if this special price is not made, and if this transaction is expected to have no effect at all on other business, then it is a source of increased net revenue at any price above marginal cost. Actually, such reductions would not have the general effect indicated above unless they did spread to other business; and if this is their usual result, rational business-men would naturally come to expect it. But the deterrent effect of this expectation may be partially counteracted in a number of ways. Most important, perhaps, is the likelihood that someone will hope to "get away with it this once," coupled with the suspicion that others will start the process, or have already done so, and that the first seller will not succeed in protecting the price structure by refraining, but will merely lose business. Then there are the sellers who are so hard-pressed for cash that they may disregard all but immediate effects on net income. The result is a nibbling process which can almost always go a little farther than it has gone. This may be mitigated by intermittent attempts to introduce more open and uniform prices.

At the other extreme comes the standardized product, with prices completely open and uniform for each purchasing locality (Outline II, A, 1, a). Here a reduction is sure to be

---

[1] This might be modified by adopting schemes of cost-accounting with heavy allocations of capital-overhead to peak output. Such allocations represent a mixture of short-run and long-run considerations, and may fairly be disregarded here.

met almost instantaneously, so long as price is above marginal cost; and the producer initiating it may, in the extreme case, hope to gain only his *pro rata* share of the general increase in sales of all producers resulting from the reduction in price. His sales would then be expected to increase in the same proportion as if he had a complete monopoly; and if this were the whole story, the incentive to reduce prices might be expected to stop at the same point as if a monopoly existed.   However, the incentive to raise prices, if they get below this point, is a different matter, since an increase will not be automatically met; and thus the conclusion that this situation yields results identical with complete monopoly, is not warranted.

Among numerous modifying circumstances, there is still the possibility of securing a few large forward contracts, or at least some valuable goodwill, by taking the initiative in a general price reduction.   In the second place, the market is governed by whichever among the several producers has the lowest price-policy. If one of them is keenly alive to the desirability of forestalling potential competition, he may fix a price close to the long-run normal, and the others will have to follow.   There is much room in such a situation for the personal equations of different producers to modify the result. Or an increase of wages or prices of materials may, without changing the selling-price of the product, bring it nearer the competitive norm; and if for this or any of the other reasons mentioned, it gets below the monopoly level, there is no force tending to bring it back up, and it may remain there for a considerable period. The generally indicated result is, not so much a monopoly price as a decidedly sticky price, somewhere between the levels of pure competition and monopoly.

All this is on the assumption that the open prices are perfectly adhered to; and this is probably an extremely rare case. In fact it would not be very rash to assume that in most cases some degree of irregular pricing is chronic, and that there are hardly any in which occasional fits of it do not occur.   The pure case may prove to be almost entirely limited to instances of open-price systems with waiting periods and otherwise implemented; and it is probable that even these should not be expected regularly to result in 100 per cent uniformity.

Thus it seems that the really important problem is not so much the case of pure "oligopoly," but the case in which the existence of openly-quoted prices exercises some degree of restraint on more or less chronic "chiselling" which is irregular, temporarily secret, and usually more or less discriminatory. Such a situation contains no guarantee of ideal prices; but it is something intermediate between pure oligopoly and the ruinously low prices likely to result from unlimited market chaos: more strongly competitive than the first, and more workable than the second. And something intermediate appears to be well-nigh a necessity. Incidentally, such limited "chiselling" seems likely in a general way to become more active in times of slack demand, and thus to tend to some degree in the direction of price flexibility.

Economic theory has not attacked the special problem of this form of pricing; and perhaps it cannot shed much light on it. But it appears to be one of the most important forms of imperfectly-competitive pricing, and might under favorable conditions prove to be fairly "workable." These conditions may be rather subtle and intangible matters; and the facts bearing on them are certainly not easy to secure. Nevertheless, it seems rather important to know more about them than we do.

As an approach to such analysis, a few tentative propositions may be considered. First, the actions of business-men in such a situation may be interpreted in the light of a complex of motives and considerations, among which the following might be mentioned. (1) The immediate effect on net earnings. (2) The effect with some account taken of the probable early reactions of others. (3) Long-run effects, chiefly reflected in effects on volume of sales. (4) Intangibles, including effects on good-will and on the satisfaction or dissatisfaction of customers, bearing largely on the expediency of setting limits to discriminations and discrepancies between actual and openly-quoted prices. This may lead to a desire to make openly-quoted prices "fairly representative" of prices actually received, which may mean "equal to the prices actually paid by those customers who have no exceptional bargaining leverages," or may have somewhat different shades of meaning. There are obvious reasons for not wishing one's openly-quoted prices to give one the reputation of charging more than one is actually charging.

Reductions in openly-quoted prices may be classified according to the proportion of actual sales that the reduction is expected to affect. The intention and expected effect may be to reduce the whole scale of prices actually charged. Or the openly-quoted prices may apply to a considerable part of the business, and the intent may be to bring these prices down without reducing the lower ones, and thus reduce the spread. Or the reductions may occur at a time when the openly-quoted prices have come to apply to little or no business; and the intent may be simply to make them more "representative." Increases would presumably be intended to bring about an increase in the general scale, and would occur naturally at a time when demand was strong and competitive pressures toward irregular departures were therefore relatively weak. Or they might occur after a period of ruinous price-cutting had made producers ready to follow an upward lead—preferably one substantial enough to afford real relief, but not so large as to make the industry too invitingly prosperous. The preceding price-war would need to have driven home the bad effects of irregular pricing sufficiently to keep it temporarily in abeyance, or within narrow limits.

Special departures from openly-quoted prices are made for obvious reasons; and the large customer has an obvious advantage in securing such special prices. Such prices are not likely,

however, to go close to the theoretical limit of marginal cost
unless the whole price-scale has become demoralized to an
extent that would bring it into the class of the chaotic market,
already discussed. In typical large-scale industries, if the
whole price-scale is such as to yield anything approaching a
normal return on investment, special prices could not go close
to short-run marginal cost without creating such discrepancies
as a market of the sort we are now considering is not likely to
tolerate.   Special prices are, however, likely to be made without full recognition of their ultimate effects in dragging the
whole price-structure downward, and to be lower than they
would be if these ultimate effects were acurately forecast and
fully taken into account.

Particular cases may be influenced by a number of specific
pricing practices, including probably the looser forms of open-
price arrangement, which, as already indicated, are not likely
to bring about complete elimination of irregular pricing.
Advance announcements of price changes may facilitate
increases by enabling the initiator to learn whether others
are following suit, without losing too much business in the
interval. The practice appears likely to have less effect on
price reductions. Protection of customers against price
declines subsequent to the giving of orders is a practice of
some significance, largely neglected by students.   It seems to
have little applicability except in cases of quoted prices in
industries with a limited number of sellers and a fairly well
organized price-structure. Its effects would be different
according as it was applied in an industry in which orders are
given at a particular time of year for the coming season (for
example, retail sale of oil for household heating) or an industry in which there are always some outstanding orders which
would be affected by a price reduction. These are only a
few instances of special practices which a more complete study
would need to take into account.

A standard product is consistent with a sloping individual demand curve, chiefly in the case of few sellers and a supply-governed price (Outline II, A, 2). The slope of the curve is a function of the output of the producer in question, relative to the total output; and the resulting excess of price above marginal cost, while worth study, may not be a real "imperfection," from the standpoint of workable competition. Price flexibility with fluctuating demand would theoretically depend on the nature of the fluctuation as affecting elasticity near the existing price-range. But these problems need not detain us here.

Another special case is that of a standardized product, with sloping individual demand-curves which are definite and knowable—the case of spatially separated producers selling at uniform mill prices (Outline II, A, 3, a). As a first approach, we may assume the marginal costs of the various producers to be equal, and known. Here there would be a point, above marginal cost, below which price would not go. If the slopes of the individual demand curves were just the right ones, this point might be the long-run normal price, but it seems more likely that it would be below it. These slopes would depend on the spatial distribution of demand; and one difficulty is that, with large consuming centers, the curves would be discontinuous. Another difficulty is that, if prices were above this stopping-point, there would be no incentive to lower them, since a reduction would be sure to be met. If the marginal costs of the producers were different and uncertain, there might be a range instead of a point, within which active price competition might prevail. But there would still be a higher range within which there would be no reliable force tending to reduce prices. Thus the conditions of a tendency toward equilibrium would not be present. "Chiselling" would, by definition, be eliminated and the conditions leading to it (incentive plus opportunity to do it undetected) would be limited to the boundary-points between different producers' selling areas.

A variant permitting limited freight absorption would make the individual demand curves steeper and more indefinite and uncertain, leading to uncertainty whether a price reduction would be met. It might also leave substantial room for "chiselling." In both this and the preceding case, the outcome would vary with the geographical facts of each particular industry. Neither can safely be regarded as a universally workable, *a priori* formula.

Finally, we may turn to quality products, where there are sloping individual demand curves and considerable uncertainty whether, or to what extent, a given reduction of price will be met. Here it is worth while distinguishing degrees of quality differential. There is the extreme degree, in which the individual producer's product has a rather steep demand curve and will stand a very considerable price differential for a long time. This approximates the condition of monopoly. In some cases, where the customer is a poor judge of quality, this kind of situation can apparently be built up by sheer advertising.

But there is also the case of more moderate quality differentials, or those of which the consumer is better informed. Here the individual demand curve is flatter, especially if a moderate time is allowed for the consumer to find out what quality is being offered in return for any given price differential. It seems that some of the healthiest cases of workable competition in large-scale industry are of this type. Automobile production is generally regarded as a fairly workable example. And in the case of tires, price competition appears to be even stronger, though tires are a quality product, and therefore come under the head of "monopolistic competition."

As to directions in which to look for possible improvement in the future, it may be worth considering the possibility that technical progress may bring about still closer and more general substitution; and also that the increased use of specifications, and more widespread knowledge of them, may help to bring more of these substitutes, or price-insensitive quality differentials, within the range of moderate and price-sensitive differentials.   This would increase the number of industries which, despite large-scale production, have the characteristics of fairly healthy and workable imperfect competition, rather than those of slightly-qualified monopoly.   In such cases, one may hope that government need not assume the burden of doing something about every departure from the model of perfect competition.

BIBLIOGRAPHY OF ARTICLES
ON THE SOCIAL CONTROL OF INDUSTRY

Compiled by

HORACE G. WHITE, JR.

Index of Authors, pages 491–497

1900–1919

BERNHARDT, J., Government Control of Sugar During the War, Quarterly Journal of Economics, XXXIII (1919).

BULLOCK, C. J., Trust Literature: A Survey and a Criticism, Quarterly Journal of Economics, XV (1901) 167–217.

DURAND, E. D., The Trust Problem, Quarterly Journal of Economics, XXVIII (1914) 381–416, 664–700.

JENKS, J. W., The Trusts: Facts Established and Problems Unsolved, Quarterly Journal of Economics, XV (1901) 46–74.

LIEFMANN, R., Monopoly or Competition as the Basis of a Government Trust Policy, Quarterly Journal of Economics, XXIX (1915) 309–25.

ROGERS, E. S., Unfair Competition, Michigan Law Review, XVII (1919).

TOSDAL, H. R., Price Maintenance, American Economic Review, VIII (1918) 28–47, 283–305.

TOSDAL, H. R., The German Steel Syndicate, Quarterly Journal of Economics, XXXI (1917) 259–306.

TOSDAL, H. R., The Kartell Movement in the German Potash Industry, Quarterly Journal of Economics, XXVIII (1913) 140–90.

YOUNG, A. A., The Sherman Act and the New Antitrust Legislation, Journal of Political Economy, XXIII (1915) 201–20, 305–26, 417–36.

1920

BERNHARDT, J., The Transition of Government Control of Sugar to Competitive Conditions, Quarterly Journal of Economics, XXXIV (1920) 720–36.

JONES, E., Is Competition in Industry Ruinous? Quarterly Journal of Economics, XXXIV (1920) 473–519.

MERCHANT, E. O., The Government and the News-print Paper Manufacturers, Quarterly Journal of Economics, XXXII (1918) 238–56; XXXIV (1920) 313–28.

TAWNEY, R. H., The British Coal Industry and the Question of Nationalization, Quarterly Journal of Economics, XXXV (1920) 61–107.

VIRTUE, G. O., The Meat Packing Investigation, Quarterly Journal of Economics, XXXIV (1920) 626–85.

1921

GREGG, E. S., The Failure of the Merchant Marine Act of 1920, American Economic Review, XI (1921) 601–615.

TUGWELL, R. G., The Economic Basis for Business Regulation, American Economic Review, XI (1921) 643–58.

1922

WATKINS, M. W., The Change in Trust Policy," Harvard Law Review, XXXV (1922) 815–37, 926–49.

1923

CLARK, J. M., Overhead Costs in Modern Industry, Journal of Political Economy, XXXI (1923) 47–64, 209–242.

DUNN, C. W., Resale Price Maintenance, Yale Law Journal, XXXII (1923) 676–705.

NELSON, M. N., Effect of Open Price Association Activities, American Economic Review, XIII (1923) 258–273.

Price, L. L., Industrial Policy, Economic Journal, XXXIII (1923) 352–61.

1924

BERGLUND, A., The United States Steel Corporation and Industrial Stabilization, Quarterly Journal of Economics, XXXVIII (1924) 607–30.

BOWIE, J. A., The British Coal Agreement, Journal of Political Economy, XXXII (1924) 236–49, 393–415.

COMMONS, J. R., Delivered-Price Practice in the Steel Market, American Economic Review, XIV (1924) 505–19.

DRESCHER, W. F., Unfair Competition Under Federal Law, St. Louis Law Review, IX (1924) 294–307.

HAMMOND, M. B., The Coal Commission Reports and the Coal Situation, Quarterly Journal of Economics, XXXVIII (1924) 541–81.

HANKIN, G., Judicial Review of the Federal Trade Commission's Orders, Illinois Law Quarterly, VI (1924) 264–95.

MAY, R. A., The Trade Association and its Place in the Business Fabric, Harvard Business Review, II (1923–24) 84–97.

NOTZ, W., Recent Developments in Foreign Antitrust Legislation, Yale Law Journal, XXXIV (1924) 159–74.

ROSS, E. A., The Case for Industrial Dualism, Quarterly Journal of Economics, XXXVIII (1924) 384–96.

1925

FRANK, L. K., The Significance of Industrial Integration, Journal of Political Economy, XXXIII (1925) 179–95.

HANKIN, G., Conclusiveness of the Federal Trade Commission's Findings as to Facts, Michigan Law Review, XXIII (1925).

LIEFMANN, W. R., German Industrial Organization Since the World War, Quarterly Journal of Economics, XL (1925) 82–110.

ORCHARD, J. E., A Proposal for Regulation of the Coal Industry, Quarterly Journal of Economics, XXXIX (1925) 196–240.

STEVENS, W. H. S., What Has The Federal Trade Commission Accomplished? American Economic Review, XV (1925) 625–51.

1926

HENDERSON, G. C., Statistical Activities of Trade Associations, American Economic Review, XVI (1926, Suppl.) 219–226.

HEWES, A., The Task of the English Coal Commission, Journal of Political Economy, XXXIV (1926) 1–12.

JONES, F. D., Historical Development of the Law of Business Competition, Yale Law Journal, XXXV (1926) 905–38.

JONES, J. H., The Report of the Coal Commission, Economic Journal, XXXVI (1926) 282–97.

LAY, G. C., The Federal Trade Commission—Its Origin, Operation and Effect, American Law Review, LX (1926) 338–61.

MORGAN, A., The Coal Problem, As Seen by a Colliery Official, Economic Journal, XXXVI (1926) 563–76.

OLIPHANT, H., Trade Associations and the Law, Columbia Law Review, XXVI (1926) 381–95.

PROBST, N., Jr., The Failure of the Sherman Antitrust Law, University of Pennsylvania Law Review, LXXV (1926) 122–38.

ROTTSCHAEFFER, H., The Field of Governmental Price Control, Yale Law Journal, XXXV (1926) 438–60.

SHARFMAN, I. L., The Trade Association Movement, American Economic Association, XVI (1926, Suppl.) 203–218.

WATKINS, M. W., The Federal Trade Commission: A Critical Survey, Quarterly Journal of Economics, XL (1926) 561–85.

1927

DANIELS, G. W. and JENKES, J., The Crisis in the Lancashire Cotton Industry, Economic Journal, XXXVII (1927) 33–46.

JONES, F. D., Historical Development of the Law of Business Competition, Yale Law Journal, XXXVI (1927) 351–83.

LAMB, H. R., Relation of Patent Law to Federal Antitrust Laws, Cornell Law Quarterly, XII (1927) 261–85.

LEVY, F. H., The Sherman Law Is Outworn: It Should Be Amended, Virginia Law Review, XIII (1927) 597–610.

MACGREGOR, D. H., The Rationalization of Industry, Economic Journal, XXXVII (1927) 521–50.

MacGregor, D. H., Recent Papers on Cartels, Economic Journal, XXXVII (1927) 247–54.

Montague, G. H., Price Fixing, Lawful and Unlawful, Wisconsin State Bar Association Reports, (1927) 57–79.

Montague, G. H., The Antitrust Laws and the Federal Trade Commission, Columbia Law Review, XXVII (1927) 650–78.

Montague, G. H., Present Tendencies in the Antitrust Laws, New York State Bar Association Reports, (1927) 311–37.

Podell, D. L. and Kirsh, B. S., Problem of Trade Association Law, St. John's Law Review, II (1927) 1–21.

1928

Clay, H., The Liberal Industrial Report, Economic Journal, XXXVIII (1928) 193–203.

Dietrich, E. B., The Plight of the Lancashire Cotton Industry, American Economic Review, XVIII (1928) 468–76.

Klaus, S., Sale, Agency and Price Maintenance, Columbia Law Review, XXVIII (1928) 312–333, 441–64.

Schmidt, E. P., The Changing Attitude of the Supreme Court Toward Monopoly, Marquette Law Review, XII (1928) 125–37.

Tugwell, R. G., Experimental Control in Russian Industry, Political Science Quarterly, XLIV (1928) 161–87.

Washburn, C. G., History of a Statute: Sherman Antitrust Act of July 2, 1890, Boston University Law Review, VIII (1928) 95–116.

Court Decisions on Price Maintenance and Commentaries, Harvard Business Reports, III (1927) 470–582; V (1928) 415–26.

1929

Naujoks, H. H., Monopoly and Restraint of Trade Under the Sherman Act, Wisconsin Law Review, IV (1928) 387–423, 451–62; V (1929) 1–30, 65–91, 129–141.

Notz, W., Ten Years' Operation of the Webb Law, American Economic Review, XIX (1929) 9–19.

Watkins, M. W., The Sherman Act: Its Design and Its Effects, Quarterly Journal of Economics, XLII (1929) 1–43.

1930

Homan, P. T., Industrial Combination as Surveyed in Recent Literature, Quarterly Journal of Economics, XLIV (1930) 345–75.

Koch, F. E., Methods of Regulating Unfair Competition in Germany, England and the United States, University of Pennsylvania Law Review, LXXVIII (1930) 693–712, 854–79.

1931

Means, G. C., The Large Corporation in American Economic Life, American Economic Review, XXI (1931) 10–42.

WATKINS, M. W., Trustification and Economic Theory, American Economic Review, XXI (1931, Suppl.) 54–76.

1932

BEER, H. W., The Federal Trade Commission and Its Due Process of Law, Notre Dame Lawyer, VII (1932) 170–84.

COPELAND, M. T., Revising the Antitrust Laws, Harvard Business Review, X (1931–32), 292–301.

CORWIN, E. S., The Antitrust Acts and the Constitution, Virginia Law Review, XVIII (1932) 355–78.

DAVIES, D. S., Further Light on the Case of Monopolies, Law Quarterly Review, XLVIII (1932) 394–414.

DONOVAN, W. J. and McALLISTER, B. P., Consent Decrees and the Enforcement of Federal Antitrust Laws, Harvard Law Review, XLVI (1932) 885–932.

ELY, R. S., The Work of the Federal Trade Commission, Wisconsin Law Review, VII (1932) 195–212.

FETTER, F. A., The Economists' Committee on Antitrust Law Policy, note, American Economic Review, XXII (1932) 465–67.

FOURNIER, L. T., The Webb-Pomerene Law, American Economic Review, XXII (1932) 18–33.

HAMILTON, W. H., The Problem of Antitrust Reform, Columbia Law Review, XXXII (1932) 173–78.

HANDLER, M., Industrial Mergers and the Antitrust Laws, Columbia Law Review, XXXII (1932) 179–271.

JAFFE, L. L. and Tobriner, M. O., Revision of the Antitrust Laws, California Law Review, XX (1932) 585–606.

JAFFE, L. L. and Tobriner, M. O., Legality of Price-Fixing Agreements, Harvard Law Review, XLV (1932) 1164–95.

McALLISTER, B. P., Sales Policies and Price Discrimination under the Clayton Act, Yale Law Journal, XLI (1932) 518–38.

MEANS, G. C., The Separation of Ownership and Control in American Industry, Quarterly Journal of Economics, XLVI (1932) 68–97.

WATKINS, M. W., An Appraisal of the Work of the Federal Trade Commission, Columbia Law Review, XXXII (1932) 272–89.

1933

BURNS, A. R., The Process of Industrial Concentration, Quarterly Journal of Economics, XLVII (1933) 277–311.

DEMUTH, F., German Trade Associations, Journal of Business of the University of Chicago, V (1932) 307–20; VI (1933) 55–61.

GULICK, C. A., JR., Some Economic Aspects of the NIRA, Columbia Law Review, XXXIII (1933) 1103–46.

HARDY, R., Loose and Consolidated Combinations under the Antitrust Laws, Georgetown Law Journal, XXI (1933) 123–46.

MURCHISON, C. T., Requisites of Stabilization of the Cotton Textile Industry, American Economic Review, XXIII (1933, Suppl.) 71–80.

RYAN, G. S., Industrial Recovery and the Antitrust Laws, Boston University Law Review, XIII (1933) 577–635.

STOCKING, G. W., Stabilization of the Oil Industry: Its Economic and Legal Aspects, American Economic Review, XXIII (1933, Suppl.) 54–70.

WAHRENBROCK, H. E., Federal Antitrust Law and the National Industrial Recovery Act, Michigan Law Review, XXXI (1933) 1009–65.

1934

BURNS, A. R., First Phase of the National Industrial Recovery Act, Political Science Quarterly, XLIX (1934) 161–94.

GRETHER, E. T., Retail Price Maintenance in Great Britain, Quarterly Journal of Economics, XLVIII (1934) 620–44.

HALE, R. L., The Constitution and the Price System: Some Reflections on Nebbia v. New York, Columbia Law Review, XXXIV (1934) 401–25.

HORACH, F. E., JR. and COHEN, J., After the Nebbia Case: the Administration of Price Legislation, University of Cincinnati Law Review, VIII (1934) 219–49.

ISAACS, N. and TAEUSCH, C. F., The N.I.R.A. in the Book and in Business, Harvard Law Review, XLVII (1934) 458–78.

KESSLER, W. C., The New German Cartel Legislation, American Economic Review, XXIV (1934) 477–82.

KREIDER, J. S., A Brief History of the Growth of Antitrust Legislation in the United States, Southern California Law Review, VII (1934) 144–82.

LEVIN, J., Status of the Antitrust Laws under the N.I.R.A., Federal Bar Association Journal, II (1934) 75–86, 112–13.

LUCAS, A. F., A British Experiment in the Control of Competition: the Coal Mines Act of 1930, Quarterly Journal of Economics, XLVIII (1934) 418–41.

WATKINS, M. W., Business and the Law, Journal of Political Economy, XLII (1934) 178–201.

1935

BURKE, S. P., Price Fixing in the Bituminous Coal Industry—a Legal Economic Problem, Virginia Law Quarterly, XLI (1935) 225–48.

DORSEY, W. C., Price Fixing under N.I.R.A. Codes, Notre Dame Lawyer, X (1935) 120–32.

HERRING, E. P., Politics, Personalities and the Federal Trade Commission, American Political Science Review, XXVIII (1934) 1016–29; XXIX (1935) 21–35.

HOLBROOK, J. K., JR., Price Reporting as a Trade Association Activity, 1925 to 1935, Columbia Law Review, XXXV (1935) 1053–70.

LEWIS, B. W., Berle and Means on the Modern Corporation, Journal of Political Economy, XLIII (1935) 548–54.

LUCAS, A. F., The British Movement for Industrial Reconstruction and the Control of Competitive Activity, Quarterly Journal of Economics, XLIX (1935) 206–35.

MASINCUPP, W. E. and Sherbondy, D. J., Price and Marketing Practices under the Petroleum Code, George Washington Law Review, III (1935) 309–55.

MASON, E. S., The National Recovery Administration, review, Quarterly Journal of Economics, XLIX (1935) 668–79.

McCONNELL, D., The Chilean Nitrate Industry, Journal of Political Economy, XLIII (1935) 506–29.

NATHAN, O., N.I.R.A. and Stabilization, American Economic Review, XXV (1935) 44–58.

PRIBRAM, K., Controlled Competition and the Organization of American Industry, Quarterly Journal of Economics, XLIX (1935) 371–93.

SHARP, M. P., Monopolies and Monopolistic Practices, University of Chicago Law Review, II (1935) 301–16.

WOLFF, J., Business Monopolies: Three European Systems in their Bearing on American Law, Tulane Law Review, IX (1935) 326–77.

1936

COOKE, C. A., Legal Rule and Restraint of Trade, Economic Journal, XLVI (1936) 21–43.

CORWIN, E. S., The Schechter Case—Landmark or What? New York University Law Quarterly Review, XIII (1936) 151–90.

DALTON, J. E., Sugar, A Case Study of the Relationship of Government and Business, Harvard Business Review, XIV (1935–36) 172–85.

DEÁK, F., Contracts and Combinations in Restraint of Trade in French Law, a Comparative Study, Iowa Law Review, XXI (1936) 397–454.

DONOVAN, W. J., Effect of the Decision in the Sugar Institute Case upon Trade Association Activities, University of Pennsylvania Law Review, LXXXIV (1936) 929–42.

ELIOTT, S. D. and CUPP, J. W., A Symposium: Fair Trade and Unfair Practices: Fair Trade and Resale Price Maintenance, The Unfair Practices Act, Southern California Law Review, X (1936) 1–28.

EVANS, C. D., Anti-Price Discrimination Act of 1936, Virginia Law Review, XXIII (1936) 140–77.

FELDMAN, G. J., Legal Aspects of Federal and State Price Control, Boston University Law Review, XVI (1936) 570–94.

FLY, J. L., The Sugar Institute Decisions and the Antitrust Laws, Yale Law Journal, XLVI (1936) 228–54.

FLY, J. L., Observations on the Antitrust Laws, Economic Theory, and the Sugar Institute Decisions, Yale Law Journal, XLV (1936) 1339–72.

FUCHS, R. F., Alternatives in Governmental Control of Economic Enterprise, Iowa Law Review, XXI (1936) 325–54.

GOLDSMITH, B. and Winks, G. W., Price Fixing: from Nebbia to Guffey, Illinois Law Review, XXXI (1936) 179–201.

GRETHER, E. T., Experience in California with Fair Trade Legislation Restricting Price Cutting, California Law Review, XXIV (1936) 640–700.

Handler, M., The Sugar Institute Case and the Present Status of the Antitrust Laws, Columbia Law Review, XXXVI (1936) 1–26.

HANDLER, M., Unfair Competition, Iowa Law Review, XXI (1936) 175–262.

KESSLER, W. C., German Cartel Regulation under the Decree of 1923, Quarterly Journal of Economics, L (1936) 680–93.

KOLB, I. S. and JAFFE, W., Equity and the Restraint of Unfair Competition, John Marshall Law Quarterly, I (1936) 292–327, II (1936) 30–51.

MARTIN, W. H., The Fair Trade Act, Fordham Law Review, V (1936) 50–62.

McALLISTER, B. P., Government and Some Problems of the Market Place, Iowa Law Review, XXI (1936) 305–24.

McLAUGHLIN, J. A., Legal Control of Competitive Methods, Iowa Law Review, XXI (1936) 274–304.

MERMIN, S., Sugar: A Rugged Collectivist, Illinois Law Review, XXXI (1936) 320–49.

PREST, W., The British Coal Mines Act of 1930, Another Interpretation, Quarterly Journal of Economics, L (1936) 313–32.

RICHBERG, D. R., Suggestion for Revision of the Antitrust Laws, University of Pennsylvania Law Review, LXXXV (1936) 1–14.

VOLD, L., The N.R.A. and AAA Experiments in Government, Economics and Law, Nebraska Law Bulletin, XIV (1936) 417–57.

WALLACE, D. H., Monopolistic Competition and Public Policy, American Economic Review, XXVI (1936, Suppl.) 77–87.

WATKINS, M. W., Economic Implications of Unfair Competition, Iowa Law Review, XXI (1936) 263–73.

WOLFF, R., Social Control Through the Device of Defining Unfair Trade Practices—The German Experience, Iowa Law Review, XXI (1936) 355–96.

1937

ARENS, O. R., Fair Trade Acts, the Latest Attack on the Loss-Leader Problem, Washington University Law Quarterly, XXII (1937) 549–58.

BEEHLER, V. D., A Patent is a Monopoly—or is it Monopolies? John Marshall Law Quarterly, II (1937) 600–620.

BROWN, E. M., Scope of Federal Power over Price Discriminations, University of Cincinnati Law Review, X (1936) 430–53; XI (1937) 1–23.

BURNS, A. R., The Anti-Trust Laws and the Regulation of Price Competition, Law and Contemporary Problems, IV (1937) 301–320.

BURNS, A. R., The Organization of Industry and the Theory of Prices, Journal of Political Economy, XLV (1937) 662–81.

COPELAND, M. T., The Problem of Administering the Robinson-Patman Act, Harvard Business Review, XV (1936–37) 156–73.

FETTER, F. A., The New Plea for Basing Point Monopoly, Journal of Political Economy, XLV (1937) 577–605.

FETTER, F. A., Planning for Totalitarian Monopoly, Journal of Political Economy, XLV (1937) 95–110.

GALLAGHER, M. F., The Robinson-Patman Act, John Marshall Law Quarterly, II (1937) 464–77.

GEORGE, E. B., Business and the Robinson-Patman Act: The First Year, Law and Contemporary Problems, IV (1937) 392–409.

GRETHER, E. T., Solidarity in the Distributive Trades in Relation to the Control of Price Competition, Law and Contemporary Problems, IV (1937) 375–91.

HAMILTON, M. F. and LOEVINGER, L., Second Attack on Price Discrimination: the Robinson-Patman Act, Washington University Law Quarterly, XXII (1937) 153–86.

HAMILTON, W. H., Cost as a Standard for Price, Law and Contemporary Problems, IV (1937) 321–333.

JACKSON, R. H., The Struggle Against Monopoly, Georgia Bar Association Reports, (1937) 203–14.

LEARNED, E. P. and Isaacs, N., The Robinson-Patman Law: Some Assumptions and Expectations, Harvard Business Review, XV (1936–37) 137–55.

LUM, R. E. and BIUNNO, J. J., Unfair Competition: A Reconsideration of Basic Concepts, University of Newark Law Review, II (1937) 1–24.

MASON, E. S., Monopoly in Law and Economics, Yale Law Journal, XLVII (1937) 34–49.

McALLISTER, B. P., Price Control by Law in the United States: A Survey, Law and Contemporary Problems, IV (1937) 273–300.

McLAUGHLIN, J. A., The Courts and the Robinson-Patman Act: Possibilities of Strict Construction, Law and Contemporary Problems, IV (1937) 410–420.

McNAIR, M. P., Marketing Functions and Costs and the Robinson-Patman Act. Law and Contemporary Problems, IV (1937) 334–55.

PHILLIPS, C. F., The Robinson-Patman Anti-Price Discrimination Law and the Chain Store, Harvard Business Review, XV (1936–37) 62–75.

PREST, W., The Problem of the Lancashire Coal Industry, Economic Journal, XLVII (1937) 287–96.

SARGENT-FLORENCE, P., Economic Research and Industrial Policy, Economic Journal, XLVII (1937) 621–41.

SAUNDERS, C., Recent Trends in the Lancashire Cotton Industry, Economic Journal, XLVII (1937) 70–76.

SCHECHTER, F. I., Trade Morals and Regulation: The American Scene, Fordham Law Review, VI (1937) 190–211.

SHARFMAN, I. L., The Interstate Commerce Commission: An Appraisal, Yale Law Journal, XLVI (1937) 915–54.

SMITH, B., The Patman Act in Practice, Michigan Law Review, XXXV (1937) 705–31.

STRICKLAND, P., Comparative Study of the Antitrust Laws of the British Dominions and of Their Administration, Journal of the Society of Comparative Legislation, 32d Ser., XVIII (1936) 240–56; XIX (1937) 52–76.

VEENSTRA, T. A. and FRITZ, W. G., Major Economic Tendencies in the Bituminous Coal Industry, Quarterly Journal of Economics, LI (1937) 106–30.

WALLACE, D. H., Monopolistic Competition At Work: Review of A. R. Burns' *The Decline of Competition*, Quarterly Journal of Economics, LI (1937) 374–87.

WITHROW, J. R., JR., Basing-Point and Freight Zone Price Systems under the Antitrust Laws, University of Pennsylvania Law Review, LXXXV (1937) 690–715.

WYLIE, F. M., Regulation of Trade Practices by Codes, Wisconsin Law Review, XII (1937) 265–79.

1938

ARNOLD, T., Fair and Effective Use of Present Antitrust Procedure, Yale Law Journal, XLVII (1938) 1294–1303.

BOBER, M. M., The Economics of the Iron and Steel Industry, review, Quarterly Journal of Economics, LII (1938) 179–85.

COHEN, J., The Antitrust Acts and "Monopolistic Competition," Cornell Law Quarterly, XXIV (1938) 80–101.

COHEN, M., Canadian Antitrust Laws, Doctrinal and Legislative Beginnings, Canadian Bar Review, XVI (1938) 439–65.

COLTON, H. E., Federal Antitrust Law, Tennessee Law Review, XV (1938) 300–10.

DECHAZEAU, M. G., Public Policy and Discriminatory Prices of Steel: A Reply to Professor Fetter, Journal of Political Economy, XLVI (1938) 537–66.

ELY, N., The Conservation of Oil, Harvard Law Review, LI (1938) 1209–44.

FETTER, F. A., Rejoinder to Professor DeChazeau's Reply, Journal of Political Economy, XLVI (1938) 567–70.

FEUER, M., The Patent Monopoly and the Antitrust Laws, Columbia Law Review, XXXVIII (1938) 1145–78.

HAMILTON, W. H., Price—By Way of Litigation, Columbia Law Review, XXXVIII (1938) 1008–36.

HARBESON, R. W., The Public Interest Concept in Law and Economics, Michigan Law Review, XXXVII (1938) 181–208.

JACKSON, R. H. and DUMBAULD, E., Monopolies and the Courts, University of Pennsylvania Law Review, LXXXVI (1938) 231–57.

KIRSH, B. S., Patent Pools and Cross Licensing Agreements, Journal of the Patent Office Society, XX (1938) 733–67.

KIRSH, B. S. and SHAPIRO, H. R., Trade Association Reporting under the Antitrust Laws, United States Law Review, LXXII (1938) 444–67.

LEWIS, B. W., The Consumer and "Public" Interests Under Public Regulation, Journal of Political Economy, XLVI (1938) 97–107.

LINDAHL, M. W., The Federal Trade Commission Act as Amended in 1938, Journal of Political Economy, XLVII (1939) 497–525.

MCLAUGHLIN, J. A., The Fair Trade Acts, University of Pennsylvania Law Review, LXXXVI (1938) 803–22.

NEUMEYER, F., Restraint of Trade by Patent Licenses, Journal of the Patent Office Society, XX (1938) 571–92.

SHARP, M. P., Discrimination and the Robinson-Patman Act, University of Chicago Law Review, V (1938) 383–97.

WATKINS, M. W., The Monopoly Investigation, Yale Review, XXVIII (1938) 323–39.

WHEELER, J. E., Comments on the Robinson-Patman Act, Connecticut Bar Journal, XII (1938) 171–96.

WHITE, E. W., Competition and the Law, Journal of the Society of Comparative Legislation, 3rd ser., XIX (1937) 38–51; XX (1938) 29–44.

WYNNE, M. R., Price-Fixing and the Fair Trade Acts, St. John's Law Review, XII (1938) 304–17.

1939

ARNOLD, T., The Policy of the Government Toward Big Business, Proceedings of the Academy of Political Science, XVIII (1939) 180–87.

ARNOLD, T. W., Antitrust Activities of the Department of Justice, Oregon Law Review, XIX (1939) 22–31.

BIRNBAUM, H. F., Auto-Finance Consent Decree: A New Technique in Enforcing the Sherman Act, Washington University Law Quarterly, XXIV (1939) 525–60.

BROWN, J. L., Exporting Through Webb-Law Associations, Comparative Law Series, II (1939) 257–85.

BURLING, E., JR. and SHELDON, W. D., Price Competition as Affected by the Robinson-Patman Act, Washington and Lee Law Review, I (1939) 31–62.

CASSODY, R. R., The Maintenance of Resale Prices by Manufacturers, Quarterly Journal of Economics, LIII (1939) 454–64.

COHEN, R., Milk Policy and Milk Prices, Economic Journal, XLIX (1939) 79–90.

DENNISON, S. R., Vertical Integration and the Iron and Steel Industry, Economic Journal, XLIX (1939) 244–58.

EDWARDS, C. D., Antitrust Action and American Housing, Journal of Land and Public Utility Economics, XV (1939) 456–63.

EVANS, C. D., An Inquiry into the Legality of the Basing Point System in the Steel Industry, Virginia Law Review, XXV (1939) 890–945.

M. S. J. and K. J. L., Monopolistic Competition and the Fair Trade Acts, Temple University Law Quarterly, XIV (1939) 95–111.

MASON, E. S., Methods of Developing a Proper Control of Big Business, Proceedings of the Academy of Political Science, XVIII (1939) 162–71.

PHELPS, D. M., Petroleum Regulation in South America, American Economic Review, XXIX (1939) 48–59.

PRESTON, J. J. D., Regulation of the Natural Gas Industry, West Virginia Law Quarterly, XLV (1939) 250–65.

RANSOM, W. L., The Sherman Antitrust Act and the Newer Problems of Trade Restraint and Competition, Proceedings of the Academy of Political Science, XVIII (1939) 211–25.

REUSCHLEIN, H. G., Aluminum and Monopoly; A Phase of an Unsolved Problem, University of Pennsylvania Law Review, LXXXVII (1939) 509–45.

RICHBERG, D. R., The Monopoly Issue, University of Pennsylvania Law Review, LXXXVII (1939) 375–89.

SMITH, F. G., The Attempted Stabilization of the Bituminous Coal Industry, Harvard Business Review, XVII (1938–39) 177–88.

1940

ARNOLD, T., Antitrust Law Enforcement, Past and Future, Law and Contemporary Problems, VII (1940) 5–23.

BERGE, W., Some Problems in the Enforcement of the Antitrust Laws, Michigan Law Review, XXXVIII (1940) 462–78.

CALLMAN, R., Patent License Agreements between Competitors and the Monopoly Issue, Georgetown Law Journal, XXVIII (1940) 871–907.

CARP, R. E., Resale Price Control under State Fair Trade Acts, California Law Review, XXVIII (1940) 477–92.

CHAFFEE, Z., JR., Unfair Competition, Harvard Law Review, LIII (1940) 1289–1321.

CLARK, J. M., Toward a Concept of Workable Competition, American Economic Review, XXX (1940) 241–56.

COMER, G. P., Price Leadership, Law and Contemporary Problems, VII (1940) 61–73.

EDWARDS, C. D., Can the Antitrust Laws Preserve Competition? American Economic Review, XXX (1940, Suppl.) 164–79.

FOLK, G. E., Scope and Limitations of the Patent Monopoly, Journal of the Patent Office Society, XXII (1940) 135–54.

GALLAGHER, M. F., Federal Price Fixing Laws and Decisions on the Regulation of Business, John Marshall Law Quarterly, III (1940) 230–40.

GRAY, H. M., The Passing of the Public Utility Concept, Journal of Land and Public Utility Economics, XVI (1940) 8–20.

GRETHER, E. T., Price Control under "Fair-Trade" Legislation, American Economic Review, XXX (1940, Suppl.) 112–17.

HALE, G. E., Trust Dissolution: "Atomizing" Business Units of Monopolistic Size, Columbia Law Review, XL (1940) 615–32.

HAMILTON, W., Common Right, Due Process and Antitrust, Law and Contemporary Problems, VII (1940) 24–41.

HAMILTON, W. and TILL, I., Antitrust—The Reach After New Weapons, Washington University Law Quarterly, XXVI (1940) 1–26.

HANDLER, M., Unfair Competition and the Federal Trade Commission, George Washington Law Review, VIII (1940) 399–426.

HARBESON, R. W., The Present Status of the Sherman Act, Michigan Law Review, XXXIX (1940) 189–212.

HOMAN, P. T., In What Areas Should Antitrust Policy be Replaced? American Economic Review, XXX (1940, Suppl.) 180–93.

HOMAN, P. T., Notes on the Antitrust Law Policy, Quarterly Journal of Economics, LIV (1940) 73–102.

ISENBERGH, M. S. and Rubin, S. J., Antitrust Enforcement Through Consent Decrees, Harvard Law Review, LIII (1940) 386–414.

KATZ, M., Consent Decree in Antitrust Administration, Harvard Law Review, LIII (1940) 415–47.

KESTER, R. B., The War Industries Board, 1917–18; A Study in Industrial Mobilization, American Political Science Review, XXXIV (1940) 655–84.

MONTAGUE, G. H., The Federal Trade Commission's Jurisdiction over Practices in Restraint of Trade, George Washington Law Review, VIII (1940) 365–98.

PABST, W. R., JR., Monopolistic Expectations and Shifting Control in the Anthracite Industry, Review of Economic Statistics, XXII (1940) 45–52.

PEGRUM, D. F., The Public Corporation as a Regulatory Device, Journal of Land and Public Utility Economics, XVI (1940) 335–43.

PEPPIN, J. C., Price Fixing Agreements under the Sherman Antitrust Law, California Law Review, XXVIII (1940) 297–351, 667–732.

PITIGLIANI, F. R., The Development of Italian Cartels Under Fascism, Journal of Political Economy, XLVIII (1940) 375–400.

PROLIKOFF, H., Commodity Price Fixing and the Supreme Court, University of Pennsylvania Law Review, LXXXVIII (1940) 934–56.

REYNOLDS, L. G., Cutthroat Competition, American Economic Review, XXX (1940) 736–47.

ROGERS, E. S., New Directions in the Law of Unfair Competition, New York Law Review, LXXIV (1940) 317–41.

ROSE, M. E., Federal Trade Commission Enforcement of Section 3 of the Clayton Act, George Washington Law Review, VIII (1940) 639–70.

SADTLER, R. F., Unfair Competition—Past and Present Trends, Tennessee Law Review, XVI (1940) 400–14.

WALLACE, D. H., Kinds of Public Control to Replace or Supplement Antitrust Law, American Economic Review, XXX (1940, Suppl.) 194–212.

WESTON, C. H., Application of the Sherman Act to "Integrated" and "Loose" Industrial Combinations, Law and Contemporary Problems, VII (1940) 42–60.

WOLFE, A. B., Full Utilization, Equilibrium and the Expansion of Production, Quarterly Journal of Economics, LIV (1940) 539–65.

The Federal Trade Commission: A Symposium, George Washington Law Review, VIII (1940) 249–748.

1941–42

BACKMAN, J. and FISHMAN, L., British Wartime Control of Aluminum, Quarterly Journal of Economics, LVI (1942) 18–48.

BACKMAN, J. and FISHMAN, L., British War Time Control of Copper, Lead and Zinc, Quarterly Journal of Economics, LV (1941) 210–38.

BAYLY, C. B., Four Years under the Robinson-Patman Act, Minnesota Law Review, XXV (1941) 131–88.

BRADY, R. A., Policies of National Manufacturing Spitzenverbände, Political Science Quarterly, LVI (1941) 199–225, 379–91, 515–44.

DONOVAN, J. M. F., JR., Trade Association Administration and Protection under the Antitrust and Other Laws, Georgetown Law Journal, XXX (1941) 17–52.

EVINS, J. L., The Federal Trade Commission, Tennessee Law Review, XVI (1941) 772–79.

HEXNER, E., American Participation in the International Steel Cartel, Southern Economic Journal VIII (1941) 54–79.

LAKE, I. B., Development of Legal Restraints on Discrimination in Prices, Louisiana Law Review, III (1941) 559–604.

MELONE, N. G., Controlled Competition: Three Years of the Civil Aeronautics Act, Journal of Air Law, XII (1941) 318–58.

ORRICK, W. H., JR., Price Leadership as a Violation of the Sherman Act, California Law Review, XXIX (1941) 507–14.

YNTEMA, T. O., The Future Rôle of Large-Scale Enterprise, Journal of Political Economy, XLIX (1941) 833–48.

INDEX OF AUTHORS
CITED IN THE BIBLIOGRAPHY

The articles in the bibliography are listed alphabetically in groups by year of publication. The numbers in the index refer to the year of publication.